Charities Act 2006

Related titles by Law Society Publishing:

Companies Act 2006: A Guide to the New Law
Gary Scanlan, Andrew Harvey, Terence Prime and Tunde Ogowewo

Inheritance Act Claims
Tracey Angus, Anna Clarke, Paul Hewitt and Penelope Reed

Practical Education Law
Angela Jackman, Deborah Hay and Pat Wilkins

Trust Practitioner's Handbook
Gill Steel (with contributions by Robert Mowbray and Charles Christian)

Titles from Law Society Publishing can be ordered from all good legal bookshops or direct from our distributor on 0870 850 1422 or email **lawsociety@prolog.uk.com**. For further information or a catalogue, email our editorial and marketing office at **publishing@lawsociety.org.uk**.

CHARITIES ACT 2006

A Guide to the New Law

Michael King and Ann Phillips
Stone King LLP

The Law Society

© Michael King and Ann Phillips 2007

ISBN-13: 978–1–85328–913–2

Published in 2007 by the Law Society
113 Chancery Lane, London WC2A 1PL

Typeset by J&L Composition, Filey, North Yorkshire
Printed by Antony Rowe Ltd, Chippenham, Wilts

CONTENTS

15.   Miscellaneous amendments   128

APPENDICES

PREFACE

The Charities Act 2006 had a lengthy gestation, from its origins in the work of the Cabinet Office's Strategy Unit in 2001, to Royal Assent on 8 November 2006. The law is stated as at that point, although we were pleased to see at the time of going to press that the first commencement order had just been made, effective 27 February 2007. Reference should be made to the *Charities Act 2006: Implementation Plan*, reproduced in Appendix 5. A plethora of supporting regulations and Charity Commission guidance has also yet to appear. Meanwhile, the charity sector is rapidly assessing and assimilating the changes flowing from the Act, and there is a sense that it has already become simply part of the landscape.

Our aim was to provide a ready guide to the new legislation. We hope it will be helpful to charities and lawyers alike, especially perhaps those lawyers who deal with charities as part of a wider, varied practice, rather than as charity specialists.

Every member of Stone King's Charity and Education Team has been involved in the preparation of this book and our thanks go to them all. Particular thanks are due to Tamsin Wilkinson, Avia Johnson and Margie Ramsey.

We have also had invaluable assistance from Richard Corden and his successor, Ben Harrison, of the Cabinet Office and we thank Richard Bowman, former Chancery Master, and Andrew Pitt, formerly of KPMG, for their helpful comments on our text.

We are also most grateful to the Law Society for taking on the unenviable task of producing the amended legislation, which appears in Appendices 1–4.

Last but not least, thanks are due to our families for equal measures of support and sympathy during the writing of this book as well as to our respective selves for putting up with each other's amendments.

Michael King
Ann Phillips
Stone King, 28 Ely Place, London EC1
February 2007

TABLE OF CASES

TABLE OF STATUTES

TABLE OF STATUTORY INSTRUMENTS

International conventions and treaties

ABBREVIATIONS

1601 Act	Statute of Charitable Uses 1601 (the Statute of Elizabeth)
1916 Act	Police, Factories, Etc. (Miscellaneous Provisions) Act 1916
1939 Act	House to House Collections Act 1939
1958 Act	Recreational Charities Act 1958
1960 Act	Charities Act 1960
1985 Act	Charities Act 1985
1992 Act	Charities Act 1992
1993 Act	Charities Act 1993
2006 Act	Charities Act 2006
CIC	community interest company
CA 1992	Charities Act 1992 (Appendix 2)
CA 1993	Charities Act 1993 (Appendix 3)
CIO	charitable incorporated organisation
HMRC	HM Revenue and Customs
SORP	Accounting and Reporting by Charities Statement of Recommended Practice
TII	trustee indemnity insurance

1 OVERVIEW

1.1 REGULATION OF THE CHARITY SECTOR

Everyone knows from their own experience what a home is but defining 'a home' is not that easy – one would have to think of the home's location, size and construction, the family or group which lives in the home or visits it, its resale or rental value, the legal interest of the occupiers, the use to which the home is put and so on. Definition of 'a charity' is equally difficult, even though everyone has their own idea as to what is or is not charitable. The charity sector in the UK is both large and diverse; it stretches from very small local charities, like village halls or family grant-making trusts, to very large charities whose brand-names and logos are as well known as those of the largest supermarkets. The sector is engaged in a huge variety of issues, activities and interests.

In England and Wales the majority of charities must be registered with the Charity Commission. At the time of writing, there are approximately 190,000 registered charities of which about 168,000 are main, rather than subsidiary, charities. Registration confirms their charitable status, it does not make them charities. In addition there may be up to 100,000 exempt charities and 10,000 excepted charities[1] which have not previously been required to register with the Commission.

While the total income of registered charities now exceeds £40 billion, all but £2 billion of that is received by the top 14 per cent of charities whose annual income exceeds £100,000; indeed at the very top of the tree are just over 600 charities which receive nearly half that sum each year, £19.2 billion.[2]

While not ignoring the overwhelming majority of registered charities whose aggregate income represents a mere five per cent of the annual income of registered charities, there is little doubt that the Charity Commission is concentrating its efforts on the top 14 per cent and that philosophy of targeting resources efficiently and effectively lies behind much of the new Charities Act 2006 (2006 Act).

The charity sector is an important part of the economy of the country, employing very many people and providing services for millions more; it is not surprising that successive governments have been keen to ensure that charities work efficiently and that public confidence in this sector is retained. Even during its passage through Parliament the government switched the sponsorship of the Bill from the Home Office to the Cabinet Office, created an 'Office of the Third Sector' and appointed a Director General of that Office.

The regulation of the sector has been by a series of seminal Acts of Parliament, in the last half century the Recreational Charities Act 1958 (1958 Act), the Charities Act 1960 (1960 Act), 1992 (1992 Act), 1993 (1993 Act) and now the 2006 Act, but in centuries past Commissioners (appointed by the Sovereign and later the courts) were very much involved in ensuring that charitable institutions did what they were set up to do and did not use their assets to benefit the already-favoured, particularly the trustees.

1   *Charity Commission Simplification Plan*, December 2006, available at **www.charity-commission.gov.uk/**.
2   Charity Commission Facts and Figures for 2006, available at **www.charitycommission. gov.uk/registeredcharities/factfigures.asp**.

1.2   400 YEARS OF CHARITY LAW

Development of the legal concept of charity has largely been in the hands of the courts which over several centuries have held that to be charitable an organisation must both have exclusively charitable purposes and be established for the benefit of the public.

The root of this definition of charity is a list in the preamble to the Statute of Charitable Uses 1601 (often called the Statute of Elizabeth) (1601 Act). The 1601 Act was itself repealed in 1888[1] but the 400-year-old preamble is worth recording here for posterity (albeit rephrased in modern English):

> The relief of aged, impotent and poor people; the maintenance of sick and maimed soldiers and mariners, schools of learning, free schools and scholars in universities; the repair of bridges, ports, havens, causeways, churches, sea-banks and highways; the education and preferment of orphans; the relief, stock or maintenance of houses of correction; the marriages of poor maids, the supportation, aid and help of young tradesmen, handicraftsmen and persons decayed; the relief or redemption of prisoners or captives; and the aid or ease of any poor inhabitants concerning payment of fifteens, setting out of soldiers and other taxes.

Over the ensuing 400 years the courts (and since the 1992 Act also the Charity Commission) have developed this list by analogy to the charitable purposes set out in 1601. In 1891 Lord Macnaghten[2] classified charitable purposes into four heads or categories of charity:

1. The relief of poverty.
2. The advancement of religion.
3. The advancement of education.
4. Other purposes beneficial to the community and within the spirit and intendment of the preamble to the 1601 Act.

Successive court decisions gave rise to the presumption that the first three heads were for the benefit of the public, and that public benefit need not be established in individual cases unless there was some doubt or ambiguity. For that increasingly large group of charities whose purposes came under the fourth head, public benefit needed to be proved in each case. Of course the presumption of public benefit for the first three heads could always be rebutted – see for example *Re Pinion*,[3] where expert witnesses agreed that the contents of a somewhat ordinary house which a testator wanted to endow as a museum were of low quality and of no educational value, the judge describing them as 'mere tat'.

However, there has been growing clamour for all charities to have to prove that they are established, and continue to work, for public benefit, culminating in the proposal made in the Cabinet Office's Strategy Unit Report *Private Action, Public Benefit*[4] which proposed in September 2002 that:

> all charities will have to demonstrate public benefit. There [will] not therefore be a presumption that certain categories are for public benefit.

The government stuck to that principle throughout the parliamentary process and in proposing the Third Reading of the Bill in the House of Commons in 2006 the Minister for the Cabinet Office, Hilary Armstrong told the House that:

> As well as putting public benefit at its heart, the Bill gives the Charity Commission a new objective of promoting public awareness of, and understanding of, the public benefit requirement.[5]

---

1   Mortmain and Charitable Uses Act 1888, s.13.
2   *Special Commissioners of Income Tax* v. *Pemsel* [1891] AC 531.
3   *Re Pinion; Westminster Bank Ltd* v. *Pinion* [1964] 1 All ER 890.
4   In July 2001, the Prime Minister established a review of the law and regulation of the charity and not for profit sectors by the Strategy Unit which reported in September 2002 as *Private Action, Public Benefit*.
5   *Hansard*, 25 October 2006, col.1617.

1.3   SCRUTINY AND DEBATE

The 2006 Act has been one of the most carefully scrutinised examples of primary legislation in recent years. Following widespread consultation in 2001–2 the Cabinet Office's Strategy Unit produced the report already mentioned, analysing the strengths and weaknesses of existing charity regulation, following which the Home Office also consulted publicly and produced its own report in July 2003, *Charities and Not-for-Profits: A Modern Legal Framework* and the promise of primary legislation.

A draft Bill was published in May 2004 and was then examined by a parliamentary Scrutiny Committee[1] which took evidence over the summer and produced its report on 30 September 2004. The 'real' Bill was then introduced in the House of Lords in December 2004 but was unfortunately lost in the pre-election 'wash up' when Parliament was dissolved on 11 April 2005, although assurances were given by the relevant political parties that the Bill would return as soon as possible to Parliament.

The Bill therefore was reintroduced in the House of Lords in May 2005, immediately following the 2005 General Election, where it completed its Third Reading in November 2005. It was then sent to the House of Commons for the first debate by elected members, but it did not receive its Second Reading there until June 2006.

Announcing the Bill on 21 December 2004, the Home Office Minister responsible for charities, Fiona Mactaggart said:

> Charities can make a real difference to countless people's lives. Thousands of people benefit from charitable action. Many others donate money, volunteer their time and talents or work as a trustee. Charities are held in high regard.
>
> The Charities Bill builds on this foundation of confidence in the work of the sector, reforming charity law and regulation with an emphasis on public benefit and the significant regulatory role of the Charity Commission.

While announcing the Second Reading Hilary Armstrong, as Minister for the Cabinet Office, said:

> We have three clear aims for the Bill. First, we wish to provide a legal and regulatory environment that enables all charities, however they work, to realise their potential. Secondly, we wish to encourage a vibrant and diverse sector, independent of Government, and thirdly, we wish to sustain high levels of public confidence in charities through effective regulation.[2]

Considering the lengthy consultation and scrutiny which the Bill in its various forms received, it is not surprising that the 2006 Act has been widely welcomed across the charity sector. However, there remain concerns for some charities, while the sector's many umbrella and interest groups will be carefully watching the implementation of the 2006 Act and in particular the passing of relevant secondary legislation.

---

1 The House of Lords and House of Commons Joint Committee on the Draft Charities Bill which scrutinised the Bill, took written and oral evidence and reported on 20 September 2004.

2 *Hansard*, 26 June 2006, col.21.

1.4   CHARITABLE PURPOSES AND PUBLIC BENEFIT

The 2006 Act now lists 13 charitable purposes or categories of which the first three are broadly unchanged from Lord Macnaghten's 1891 list and the thirteenth, although restated, ensures the survival of 'other charitable purposes within the spirit and intendment of the Preamble to the 1601 Statute' but preserves too the possibility of development of charitable purpose. This concept of development by analogy has served the sector well enough over the last 400 years and it is to be hoped that the Charity Commission will continue to assist in the development of charitable purpose in an imaginative and constructive way where there is a clear charitable intent.

As already mentioned, the old presumption of public benefit has been removed from the first three heads, so existing charities whose purposes are within those first three heads will now be tested to check that they are operating for the benefit of the public. In effect, there is now a level playing field for all charitable purposes because public benefit will have to be shown in all cases.

There was considerable debate during evidence to the Scrutiny Committee and later during the passage of the two Bills through Parliament, about the criteria for testing public benefit. Despite concerns that independent schools and private hospitals, in particular, were not run for the benefit of the public at large, rather only for people who could afford 'high fees', the government consistently supported the concept of leaving the testing of public benefit to the Charity Commission and the result is that the Commission will indeed be responsible for issuing guidance on and monitoring public benefit.

1.5   THE CHARITABLE INCORPORATED ORGANISATION – A NEW VEHICLE FOR CHARITIES

The 2006 Act creates a new legal vehicle specifically for charities, the charitable incorporated organisation (CIO), designed to allow charities to take on corporate status with limited liability. This will avoid the need for charities that want corporate status and the protection of their members from liability for contractual and tortious claims to register as companies and thus have to report to two regulators, the Charity Commission and the Registrar of Companies.

1.6   A NEW CHARITY COMMISSION

1.6.1   A makeover after one-and-a-half centuries

The Charity Commissioners for England and Wales have been in existence since 1853[1] when they were established in the wake of certain scandals immortalised by Anthony Trollope in his *Barsetshire Chronicles*. Although they were given considerable teeth in the 1992 and 1993 Acts, there was a concern that their powers should be updated and certain anomalies removed.

In addition it was considered that the Commissioners should be reconstituted as a statutory corporation and given a list of general functions as both adviser and regulator, as well as certain clear objectives, functions and duties. One of the most hotly debated issues was the extent to which the Commission should in its actions be required to be proportionate in the way in which it targeted its functions. The 2006 Act now enshrines the need for proportionality, consistency and transparency in the Commission's decision-making and regulatory activities – a very important concept given the diverse nature and size of the charities which the Commission regulates. In any event, even during the passage of the Bill the Commission has undergone an extensive makeover in its public image and accountability, way beyond the new 'T-shirt' logo which the Commission unveiled in 2005.

1.6.2   Charity Commission checks on public benefit

The 2006 Act requires the Commission to issue guidance on the public benefit issue, having first consulted publicly.

The Charity Commission will be looking at groups of charities which charge 'high fees' and has indicated it is likely to start with independent schools and move on to healthcare and possibly arts charities. The Commission has already issued some publications[2] and will undoubtedly produce more. It appears that the Commission will try to establish generally accepted standards and encourage such charities to ensure that they reach out beyond those members of the public who benefit because they can afford the fees of such charities.

1.6.3   Charity Commission's objectives

The Charity Commission's objectives have been restated in the 2006 Act and perhaps the most important point to make is that the Commission remains a source of advice as well as a regulator. The Commission's roles continue to include increasing compliance and accountability as well as public trust and confidence in charities, but now also include the requirement to promote awareness and understanding of public benefit. However, the requirement in the May 2004 consultative draft Bill that the Commission should ensure that charities should 'maximise their social and economic impact' smacked too much of central control by the government and has now become simply a requirement to promote the effective use of charitable resources.

As will be seen in **Chapter 5**, in addition to these new regulatory objectives, the 2006 Act sets out six general functions and six general duties for the Commission to follow in the performance of those functions.

New powers given to the Commission to enhance its compliance role have been balanced by objectives and duties which should, where charities and their trustees have erred through administrative or constitutional failings rather than conspiracy to defraud, ensure that such charities return quickly to good governance.

1.6.4   Independence of the Commission from government

There is ever a concern that governments of any hue might wish to influence and set policies for the charity sector to ensure that politically desirable targets are attained without any increase in taxation. The Charity Commission has in the past been a champion of the independence of charities and their trustees.

Although charities and their advisers will wish from time to time to criticise the Commission for a particular decision, or even the lack of one, we believe that this regulator remains an important defence against political control of charities by government.

---

1   Charitable Trusts Act 1853.
2   *Public Benefit – the Charity Commission's Approach*; *Public Benefit – the Charity Commission's position on how public benefit is treated in the Charities Bill*; *The Charity Commission's approach to public benefit, appendix to Parliamentary briefing*; and *Indicative Programme: Taking forward public benefit*. All available at **www.charity-commission. gov.uk/**.

1.7   CHARITY TRIBUNAL

While being warmly welcomed within the charity sector, the Charity Tribunal's jurisdiction in the draft Bill was severely limited in that several important decisions, or non-decisions, of the Commission would not have been covered. The Tribunal's remit has now been widened to include upholding, quashing, varying or substituting many more decisions of the Commission.

It remains to be seen how the Tribunal will work in practice and whether legal advice or advocacy will be essential for charities appearing before the Tribunal. Questions of importance may be referred to the Tribunal by the Attorney-General but there is, despite requests during the passage of the Bill, no 'suitors fund' or legal aid to cover the cost of legal fees before the Tribunal. Furthermore, the Tribunal will have power to award costs in cases where parties have acted vexatiously or unreasonably, which may deter some potential claimants.

The principal benefit of the establishment of the Tribunal may well be the clarity with which the Commission will have to make and present its decisions in future lest these decisions be examined by the Tribunal.

1.8   REGISTRATION

In an endeavour to be proportionate, not burdening very small charities with regulations whilst ensuring that larger charities will in future be regulated, even if they do not currently have to register with the Commission, the 2006 Act:

- raises the income threshold at which registration is compulsory from £1,000 to £5,000 p.a. (although charities below that level will eventually be able to register voluntarily);
- phases out the concept of charities being excepted by the Commission from registration;
- introduces the concept of a principal regulator for exempt charities (for example, universities);
- removes exempt status from those charities which have no principal regulator.

1.9   TRUSTEES

The concept of the unpaid, volunteer trustee remains at the heart of the charity sector but in addition to creating the new CIO vehicle which will give trustees the protection of limited liability, the 2006 Act does attempt to ease the personal burden of regulation, including allowing the remuneration of a minority of trustees for particular services, with appropriate safeguards.

1.10   CY-PRÈS

The 2006 Act introduces significant changes to this long-established legal rule under which a charity's objects have passed their 'sell-by' date and would need to be altered by the court or the Charity Commission if the charity's property or funds are to continue to be used for suitable charitable purposes.

The Commission will now have to take into account when considering whether a scheme should be made to alter a charity's purposes, not only the spirit of the gift by the original donor(s) but also the social and economic circumstances prevailing at the time of the proposed alteration of those original purposes. In effect, the Commission will have to second guess what purposes the donor(s) would approve if confronted with the needs of contemporary society.

1.11   SPENDING OF CAPITAL

Whilst the 2006 Act has not gone as far as many charity lawyers would have wished in redefining permanent endowment[1] there are welcome powers for smaller charities to spend capital, while larger charities will also be able to spend capital if the Charity Commission concurs. After considerable pressure from the Charity Law Association surrounding the restriction on the spending of the sale proceeds of endowed land, the government did concede that the power to spend capital could include endowed land.

---

1   1993 Act, s.96(3).

1.12   MERGERS

The 2006 Act contains several measures to facilitate mergers and reorganisations as charities seek to evolve to meet the needs of their beneficiaries and the communities they serve. Most importantly, future legacies and other gifts to the original charity can now carried through to the new or merged charity if the merger has been registered with the Commission.

1.13 FUNDRAISING

To the relief of many involved in the organisation of charity fundraising, the original proposal simply to amend Part III of the 1992 Act has been discarded during the parliamentary process and the 2006 Act entirely replaces Part III which, in any event, was never brought into force.

As will be seen later, the 2006 Act brings in a new unified system to regulate public charitable collections, including a new regime for the licensing of charities as being appropriately managed to carry out and control such public collections. Importantly, benevolent and philanthropic organisations which are not necessarily charities will also be covered by these rules. Inevitably, this will require a great deal of preparation within the Commission and production of guidance, and the suggested start date of 2009 appears optimistic.

The 2006 Act also requires much clearer statements to be made by professional fundraisers and commercial participators when complying with Part II of the 1992 Act which, until consolidation takes place, will remain in force.

The Secretary of State has under the 2006 Act a reserve power to control fundraising if the current framework[1] for self-regulation and good practice is not successful. However, the government has learnt from the failure to bring into force Part III of the 1992 Act that trying to regulate fundraising by statute is always going to be difficult and that self-regulation is the way forward.

---

1 Largely promoted by the Institute of Fundraising.

1.14 CHARITY ACCOUNTING

The government has responded to criticism about the standard of charity accounting information and the 2006 Act has strengthened the reporting and accounting framework by:

- drawing closer together the rules for company and non-company accounts, including the requirement for group accounts where there is a non-company parent charity, and paving the way for further harmonisation;
- simplifying thresholds for accounting compliance and external scrutiny; and
- introducing changes to encourage 'whistle-blowing' to the Commission or to the principal regulator of exempt charities.

New thresholds have been set for annual reports and returns and, although not a requirement of the 2006 Act, larger charities already have to produce annually a Summary Information Return, as recommended by the Strategy Unit Report, *Private Action, Public Benefit*.

1.15   CONSOLIDATION OF THE CHARITIES ACTS?

The 2006 Act is difficult to read, given that many of its provisions make substantial changes to the 1958, 1992 and 1993 Acts and given that Part III of the 1992 Act (now repealed by the 2006 Act) was never brought into force. In the Second Reading debate in the House of Lords[1] Lord Bassam of Brighton on behalf of the government expressed sympathy with the view that charity legislation should be consolidated but that the matter was for the Law Commission which was giving the question fair consideration.

As 'fair consideration' by the Law Commission may take a little time, the 1958, 1992 and 1993 Acts are therefore reprinted in the Appendices as amended and the 2006 Act itself is reproduced to the extent that its provisions stand alone.

As is often now the case within primary legislation, the Secretary of State (currently the Minister for the Third Sector in the Cabinet Office) must review the operation of the 2006 Act within five years of its passing. However, the government has pledged to review within three years the operation of the public benefit requirement.[2]

1   Charities Bill Second Reading, House of Lords, 20 January 2005.
2   Minister for the Third Sector at Charities Bill Third Reading, House of Commons, 25 October 2006.

1.16   IMPLEMENTATION

The 2006 Act will be brought into force over two years or more. The current proposal is set out in the Implementation Plan for the Act produced by the Office of the Third Sector (see Appendix 5). Within each chapter of this book we have indicated the likely implementation dates of the 2006 Act but the reader should refer to the Office of the Third Sector website[1] for updates.

1   See www.cabinetoffice.gov.uk/third-sector.

2 CHARITABLE PURPOSE AND THE PUBLIC BENEFIT TEST

2.1 BEFORE THE ACT

It has often been said that there is no statutory definition of 'charity' or 'charitable purposes'. Strictly speaking that is not the case because s.96(1) of the 1993 Act defined a charity as: 'any institution, corporate or not, which is established for charitable purposes and is subject to the control of the High Court in exercise of the Court's jurisdiction with respect to charities'; while s.97(1) of that Act defined charitable purposes as: 'purposes which are exclusively charitable according to the laws of England and Wales'. However, these were somewhat circular definitions and in truth it has been necessary (leaving aside the case of certain recreational charities as defined by the 1958 Act) to look to case law for the meanings of these important words.

We have already mentioned in our overview of the 2006 Act the historical importance of the preamble to the 1601 Act[1] which contained a list of charitable purposes. The 1601 Act was repealed in the nineteenth century and the preamble itself did not in any event form part of that Act so this list could not be said to have statutory force. Nevertheless it came to have profound importance in being the firm foundation on which the courts developed the modern definition of charitable purposes, above all in the judgment of Lord Macnaghten in *Pemsel's* case.[2] In his judgment, Lord Macnaghten remarked somewhat opaquely that the word charity 'unmistakably has a technical meaning in the strictest sense of the term, that is, a meaning clear and distinct, peculiar to the law as understood and administered in this country. . .'. However, he redeemed himself in the eyes of later generations of lawyers by reclassifying charitable purposes under the following four well-known heads of charity:

1. The relief of poverty.
2. The advancement of religion.
3. The advancement of education.
4. Other purposes beneficial to the community and within the spirit and intendment of the preamble to the 1601 Act.

By including in the fourth head of charity a reference to the spirit of the 1601 Act preamble, Lord Macnaghten not only acknowledged the development of charity law which had taken place in England in the previous 300 years but paved the way for the huge evolution of charity law which took place in the twentieth century.

Initially, the courts developed the fourth head simply by direct analogy to the 1601 Act preamble but gradually the analogy was to charitable purposes within the fourth head; the concept of purposes which are analogous to such analogous purposes is, as we will see later, retained in the 2006 Act.

---

1   Statute of Charitable Uses 1601 (see **Chapter 1**).
2   *Special Commissioners of Income Tax* v. *Pemsel* [1891] AC 531.

2.2   AFTER THE ACT

So, why change a definition which has helped the understanding of what is a charitable purpose to evolve in line with demographic trends and other changes in society? There were two principal reasons:

1.   The number of charities falling under the fourth head of *Pemsel's* case had increased markedly in comparison to those under the first three heads.
2.   There was growing disquiet that, while judges had permitted there to be a presumption, albeit rebuttable, that charities falling under the first three heads existed for the benefit of the public, there was no such presumption for fourth head charities. It might therefore seem to the less well-informed that there were two classes of charity, those which had to prove they were charitable and those which did not. Indeed, some commentators in the media considered that fourth head charities provided more benefit to the public than those which fell under the other heads. Government and the Charity Commission saw a need to increase public understanding of charities and to correct this misconception.

In an Opinion, prepared on behalf of the Charity Law Association in relation to public benefit and the advancement of religion, Francesca Quint of counsel commented generally on the proposal to remove the presumption of public benefit:[1]

> It should be noted that it is the *purpose* (i.e. of the particular charity) not the general *description* of the purpose as set out in s.2(2) of the Act that is referred to. Therefore, when the question of charitable status arises before the court or the Charity Commission, it will not be enough that there is nothing to show that the religion in question is morally harmful; a more positive demonstration of public benefit will be required in order to obtain recognition as a charity.

Mrs Quint went on to refer in a footnote to the religious writings of Joanna Southcott examined in *Thornton* v. *Howe*[2] where the court held those writings to be 'foolish but not likely to corrupt the morals of [the charity's] adherents' and she considered that publication of Joanna Southcott's writings was unlikely to be considered charitable following the 2006 Act, given the new public benefit requirement.

Throughout the debates which both preceded and succeeded the report of the Strategy Unit,[3] there has been an important minority arguing for a statutory definition of charity and charitable purposes. In the event, the Strategy Unit opted for the concept of continued evolution by the courts, which effectively means 'by the Charity Commission' which has concurrent jurisdiction with the High Court. This option was accepted by the Home Office and, as we shall see, the debate in the Scrutiny Committee[4] and later in the parliamentary process, centred chiefly on the question of how 'public benefit' should be defined rather than on the definitions of 'charity' and 'charitable purposes'.

So, the 2006 Act confirms in s.1 that for England and Wales a charity is an institution which is established exclusively for charitable purposes and is subject to the jurisdiction of the High Court – not at first sight very different from the old definition of charity in s.96(1) of the 1993 Act. The current rule, that an organisation or a trust which has both charitable and non-charitable purposes is not a charity, is thus preserved. If a different definition of 'charity' is contained in another Act, such definition is, however, unaffected.

1   See 2006 Act, s.3(2).
2   *Thornton v. Howe* (1862) 26 JP 774.
3   Cabinet Office's Strategy Unit's Report *Private Action, Public Benefit*, September 2002.
4   Joint Committee on the Draft Charities Bill, see Introduction, n.3.

2.3   DEFINITION OF CHARITABLE PURPOSE

However, the real change appears in s.2 of the 2006 Act which for the first time defines a 'charitable purpose'. In s.2(1) there are two tests:

- that the purpose falls within one of the 13 new heads or descriptions; and
- that the purpose is for the public benefit.

The 13 heads as they appear in s.2(2) of the 2006 Act are set out as follows in bold:

1.   **The prevention or relief of poverty.**
2.   **The advancement of education.**
3.   **The advancement of religion** (which by s.2(3)(a) includes a religion which involves belief in more than one god and a religion which does not involve belief in a god).
4.   **The advancement of health or the saving of lives** (by s.2(3)(b) 'the advancement of health' includes the prevention or relief of sickness disease or human suffering).
5.   **The advancement of citizenship or community development** (which by s.2(3)(c) includes rural or urban regeneration and the promotion of civic responsibility, volunteering, the voluntary sector or the effectiveness or efficiency of charities).
6.   **The advancement of the arts, culture, heritage or science.**

7. **The advancement of amateur sport** (which is defined in s.2(3)(d) as 'sports or games which promote health by involving physical or mental skill or exertion').
8. **The advancement of human rights, conflict resolution or reconciliation or the promotion of religious or racial harmony or equality and diversity.**
9. **The advancement of environmental protection or improvement.**
10. **The relief of those in need by reason of youth, age, ill health, disability, financial hardship or other disadvantage** (which by s.2(3)(e) includes relief given by the provision of accommodation or care to such people).
11. **The advancement of animal welfare.**
12. **The promotion of the efficiency of the armed forces of the Crown, or of the efficiency of the police, fire and rescue services or ambulance services.**
13. **Any other purposes within subsection (4)** (which includes purposes recognised as charitable within the existing law or analogous to or within the spirit of such purposes or analogous to those analogous purposes – see 2.4).

This list of 13 heads covers everything which is now within the definition of a charitable purpose. These heads are descriptions of charitable purposes rather than a comprehensive list of all the purposes which might now or in future be recognised as charitable. Such a list would take up very many pages and many months to produce. The government's intention clearly is to continue to allow charitable purposes to develop as society, its needs and its methods of tackling problems develop, rather than produce a fixed and inflexible definition of all charitable purposes.

Certain of the new purposes or definitions have caused surprise when measured against the original intention of the government to clarify the existing law as to what is charitable (as well as to ensure that all charities existed for the benefit of the public), rather than to create new charitable purposes:

1. **Advancement of religion** – the concept of a religion without a god or two might well have been unknown to the judges who over the last 400 years have pronounced on the charitability or otherwise of religious bodies, but the provision in s.2(3)(a) of the 2006 Act, that religion includes one that 'involves belief in more than one god' or 'does not involve belief in a god' was designed to ensure the continuing status as religious charities of non-theistic religions such as the Buddhists.
2. **Advancement of arts, culture, heritage and science** – previously such charities had generally been presented as advancing education and sometimes it was difficult to get acceptance by the Charity Commission of arts and culture as charitable purposes if the activities were not classical or mainstream.
3. **Advancement of amateur sport** – the concept of 'mere sport' was looked at askance by the Chancery Court in *Re Nottage*[1] but recently the government gave a modicum of tax relief to community amateur sports clubs which did not have charitable status, so the door was open for amateur sport to be charitable. The original definition in the Bill of amateur sport had to involve both physical skill and exertion which led to concerns at to whether darts, snooker or chess would be regarded as charitable if amateur. The new definition,

allowing sports and games promoting health by physical or mental skill or exertion would appear to open up sport to include almost any competitive, health-giving pastime, so long as public benefit can be proved – bingo for the elderly or computer games for their grandchildren perhaps?

4. **Animal welfare** – originally charitable on the grounds that caring for animals made human beings better people, now it is a charitable purpose in its own right, which is probably more honest.

5. **Efficiency of the armed forces** – not in the original draft Bill, but always charitable on the grounds that defending the realm was in the interests of the public, and included on the insistence of members of the House of Lords; the several rescue services were included during the Bill's passage through the House of Commons but in truth they would already be charitable under several of the new charitable heads.

It is important to emphasise that the 12 descriptive heads are just that – they are descriptive rather than prescriptive. In effect, they give flexible definitions to those charitable purposes into which the vast majority of established charities would already fall.

---

1 *Re Nottage (No.1); Jones v. Palmer* [1895] 2 Ch 649.

2.4   ANALOGY – THE THIRTEENTH HEAD

Section 2(4) continues the evolutionary development of charitable purposes by making clear that the purposes within s.2(2)(m) (the thirteenth head) include:

- any charitable purposes which are already recognised by the law (including s.1 of the 1958 Act) as charitable, even if not set out in the first 12 categories;
- any charitable purposes which are reasonably analogous to the above purposes; and
- any purposes which are analogous to the analogous purposes already mentioned.

In other words, the old fourth head ('other purposes beneficial to the community within the spirit and intendment of the 1601 Preamble') survives as the thirteenth head to ensure the continued evolution of charities by analogy. Like it or not, the link with 400 years of legal history is retained.

2.5   PRESUMPTION OF PUBLIC BENEFIT ENDS

The law prior to the 2006 Act assumed that the relief of poverty, the advancement of religion and the advancement of education were in themselves charitable, unless there was clear evidence either that the organisation pursuing those purposes was doing so for an insufficiently wide section of the public or that the activity involved did not provide any real benefit to the public. This presumption has now gone and charities under the first three heads will have to show not only that they are established for a recognised charitable purpose but also that they benefit the public.

So how will the presence or absence of public benefit be tested?

2.6   THE PUBLIC BENEFIT TEST

The 2006 Act provides in s.3 that the presumption of public benefit, which historically has been available to those charities falling within the first three heads, no longer exists and that public benefit is 'as that term is understood for the purposes of the law relating to charities in England and Wales'. Therefore, it will be necessary to look at existing case law in addition to statute to determine whether a given charitable purpose does provide public benefit.

Given the understandable reluctance of newly formed charities and their lawyers to spend large sums in arguing public benefit issues in court, testing of public benefit will largely be in the hands of the Charity Commission and in doing so the Commission must have in mind its new public benefit objective.[1] Under s.4 of the 2006 Act the Commission is required to issue guidance in pursuance of that objective and it will undoubtedly be looking at all existing charities falling under the first three heads, starting with those charities which charge significant fees to their beneficiaries. We have little doubt that the Commission's testing of public benefit will before long be examined by the new Charity Tribunal established under the 2006 Act, possibly at the instance of such charities.

Charities which, after the coming into force of the 2006 Act, apply for registration will be subject to scrutiny by the Charity Commission to decide whether they meet the public benefit requirement, having regard to the relevant charitable purposes and activities of the organisation and the context within which they operate. These checks are of course already made in relation to those charities falling under the fourth head, so it is to be assumed that the Commission will follow the same methodology in considering for registration organisations falling within the first three heads.

Partly because of the cost of taking such cases to the High Court and partly because the Charity Commission has shown increasing willingness to develop the law in relation to what is or is not charitable, there have been few High Court decisions on the subject in recent times. However, Russell L.J. suggested in the *Council of Law Reporting* case[2] that one had to look at what the legislators in 1601 might have contemplated if they had been faced with the circumstances of later centuries. Lord Justice Russell went on to say that:

> [where] the object cannot be thought otherwise than beneficial to the community . . ., I believe the proper question to ask is whether there are any grounds for holding it to be outside the equity of the Statute [of 1601].

The Charity Commission has for several years endeavoured to spell out its approach to purposes which seemed to be somewhat remote from the 1601 Act preamble or from a purpose which has previously been accepted as charitable. As long ago as its 1988 Annual Report, the Commission undertook to take 'a constructive approach in adapting the concept of charity to meet the constantly evolving needs of society' and promised to act 'constructively and imaginatively' when considering whether a particular organisation had a clear charitable intent within the spirit of the 1601 Act preamble.[3]

In the leading *Oppenheim* case[4] the House of Lords considered that, even though the potential beneficiaries were themselves numerous (namely the children of some 110,000 employees of particular companies), there was not in that case a sufficient section of the community being benefited.

Suppose, for example, a small town was dominated by a single company which employed the majority of its citizens and a trust was established to educate the children of its employees – would that trust be charitable assuming always that the education offered was of an acceptable standard?

It is not enough for a charitable purpose simply to confer a benefit; it must benefit the whole community or a sufficient section of it. So, any *private* benefit must be ancillary to the carrying out of the charity's objects; it is not just a question of numbers of people that might benefit but whether the section of the community benefiting is representative of the public at large, or even of a particular place, as opposed to being defined by a relationship with a particular person or organisation.

Following the *Oppenheim* ruling, the answer would be:

- *No*, if the potential beneficiaries were defined as the offspring of that company's employees.
- *Yes*, if the potential beneficiaries were defined as the offspring of the inhabitants of that town.

1 See 1993 Act, s.1B(2) added by 2006 Act, s.7.
2 *Incorporated Council of Law Reporting for England and Wales v. Attorney General* [1972] Ch 73.
3 Charity Commission Report, 1988, paras.50–55.
4 *Oppenheim v. Tobacco Securities Trust Co.* [1951] AC 297.

2.7 EFFECT ON EXISTING CHARITIES OF THE PRESUMPTION ENDING

The removal of the presumption will affect all existing charities falling within the first three heads but those that the Charity Commission has stated it will consider first will be those who charge what the Strategy Unit called, somewhat pejoratively, 'high fees'. Independent schools and private hospitals and some performing arts charities were clearly indicated as being in need of re-examination as to whether and how they benefited the public or a sufficient section of the public.

Some organs of the media have suggested that organisations charging fees were simply not charities and were just as much businesses as any other provider of services to the public. Other commentators – and it would seem a majority of those who gave evidence on the subject to the Scrutiny Committee – were of the opinion that the charging of fees was not inimical to charitable status; had that been so, very many service-providing charities would have been in danger of being regarded as non-charitable. The general tenor of evidence before the Scrutiny Committee was that charities of this ilk should, however, be tested for public benefit, not least on the grounds that the charging of significant fees would, on the face of it, exclude large sections of the public.

The fact is that charitable independent schools, private hospitals and arts organisations which charge fees are already charities and cannot, short of legislation to the contrary, become non-charitable; therefore, such charities must operate for the benefit of the public and prove that they do. Furthermore any such legislation would have had to address the vexed question of what should happen to the property and assets of charities which ceased to be charitable.

There appears no will on the part of the government, still less on the part of the Charity Commission, to remove charitable status from these organisations. If, after being given the opportunity to address a perceived lack of attention to public benefit, an organisation were to find itself unable to make the changes recommended, enforced changes to the organisation's constitution, or even removal of its trustees, would be a far more likely result than de-registration as a charity.

2.8   CHARITY COMMISSION CONSULTATION AND GUIDANCE

The Commission is required under s.4 of the 2006 Act to issue (and revise) guidance in pursuance of its public benefit objective and to publish and update such guidance. The Commission has already been considering what tests might be put in place to check whether a given charity is for the public benefit.[1] Indeed, the Commission had prior to the passing of the 2006 Act begun informal consultations with representatives of religious and educational charities, as the result of which the Commission has produced early draft guidance on public benefit issues.

The Commission has stated that the basis of its test for public benefit will be the Australian appeal Re Resch[2] decided in 1969 by the Judicial Committee of the Privy Council. The Judicial Committee made it clear that:

- A private hospital open to the public, but in fact mainly benefiting its patients who paid fees (whether directly or through medical insurance), nevertheless benefits a sufficient section of the public.
- A private hospital, even if it charges fees, is a charity unless it has been established for the private profit of individuals.

- Possibly a charity which charged fees so high that the poor would effectively be excluded might not be charitable, but Lord Wilberforce, delivering judgment in this case, said: 'The service is needed by all, not only by the well-to-do. So far as its nature permits it is open to all; the charges are not low, but the evidence shows that it cannot be said that the poor are excluded'.[3]

An indication of what the Charity Commission will propose in terms of guidance on the public benefit issue can be found in *Public Benefit – the Charity Commission's Approach* which can be found on the Commission's website **www.charitycommission.gov.uk**. However, it should be stressed as we go to press that this guidance is not likely to be set in tablets of stone; of its nature, it is very likely to be reviewed regularly.

The Charity Commission is required by s.4(4) to carry out consultations before issuing the public benefit guidance. We anticipate that it will consult widely, particularly amongst the sectors which charge significant fees, in developing criteria for its assessment of whether a charity is pursuing its objects or purposes for the benefit of the public.

As already mentioned the Charity Tribunal will in due course have an influence on the evolution of the *Re Resch* principles, because the 2006 Act does not in itself contain any guidance on the meaning of public benefit, nor does it make the Commission's guidance or advice on this subject legally binding on charities, new or old. That said, charity trustees do have to take into account the Commission's guidance when exercising their powers and duties (s.4(6)), so ignoring the guidance entirely would not be sensible.

While not in the nature of a *Pepper* v. *Hart*[4] statement, it is worth recording the comments of the Parliamentary Secretary at the Cabinet Office Edward Miliband[5] when discussing the question of public benefit and the removal of the presumption:

> [the Charity Commission] has promised to look specifically at the fee-charging sector, and it will consult the public about their attitudes . . . There has not been a directly relevant case for 40 years so the Commission is right to develop its approach by consulting the public, taking account of the passage of time since *Re Resch*. The Bill seeks to establish confidence in the charity brand.

1   See 1993 Act, s.1B, introduced by 2006 Act, s.7.
2   *Re Resch's Will Trusts; Le Cras* v. *Perpetual Trustee Co. Ltd* [1969] 1 AC 514.
3   *Re Resch's Will Trusts*, 544.
4   *Pepper (Inspector of Taxes)* v. *Hart* [1993] AC 593.
5   *Hansard*, 25 October 2006, col.1610.

2.9   RECREATIONAL CHARITIES

The 1958 Act was introduced to ensure that certain organisations providing facilities for social welfare, recreation and leisure activities, such as the Women's Institutes and miners' welfare organisations were established for charitable purposes. In order to ensure compatibility with the European Convention on Human Rights,[1] s.5 of the 2006 Act amends the 1958 Act by providing that such organisations offering facilities to men only are no less charitable than those which make such provision for women or, indeed, for men and women in mixed clubs.

References in the 1958 Act to miners' welfare organisations are now removed so such organisations have to prove their charitable status in the same way as all other charities. The 2006 Act does not address the question of whether miners' welfare organisations ceasing to be charitable would be able to retain their assets, which until the Royal Assent were charitable assets. However, a clue can be found in the Charity Commissioners' decision in 1993 that gun clubs were no longer charitable.[2] To the surprise of many, the gun clubs have been able to retain their assets.

1 European Convention for the Protection of Human Rights and Fundamental Freedoms 1950.
2 *Statement of Reasons for the Commissioners' decision to disallow applications for charity registration from the City of London Rifle and Pistol Club and the Burnley Rifle Club,* Charity Commission 1993.

2.10 SPORTS CLUBS

Those sports clubs which are registered with HM Revenue and Customs (HMRC) as community amateur sports clubs[1] and are entitled, as such, to some fiscal reliefs, are deemed by virtue of s.5(4) of the 2006 Act not to be charitable. If such a club wanted to be a charity (given the fact that advancement of amateur sports is now a charitable purpose under s.2(2)(g) of the 2006 Act) it would have to de-register as a community amateur sports club before being entered in the register of charities.

1 Finance Act 2002, Sched.18.

2.11 INDEPENDENT SCHOOLS

The reaction to the Bill and to the 2006 Act by the independent schools sector has on the whole been positive. The sector has not seen the 2006 Act as an attack on its existence, rather as providing 'a mechanism to ensure that schools actually do provide public benefit'.[1]

At the time of going to press the Charity Commission is already well on the way with discussions with the independent schools sector to audit the way in which they provide public benefit. During the debates on the Bill independent schools were encouraged by the government to share their knowledge and their facilities with the maintained sector of education, recognising in the words of Edward Miliband that:

a rural private school miles from a neighbouring state school has a different ability to co-operate with the state sector than an urban private school, for example.[2]

1   Jonathan Shepherd, General Secretary, Independent Schools Council, in oral evidence to the Scrutiny Committee, June 2004.
2   *Hansard*, 25 October 2006, cols.1610–1611.

2.12   COMMENCEMENT

This part of the 2006 Act is not likely to come into force until early 2008, to give the Commission time to carry out its consultation on how the public benefit requirement will be assessed.[1] The Implementation Plan for the 2006 Act indicates that the new definition for charity and the public benefit test will not be brought into effect 'until there is an accessible appeal right through the Charity Tribunal'.[2]

1   See the Charity Commission's publication *Indicative Programme: Taking Public Benefit Forward*, available at **www.charitycommission.gov.uk/library/spr/pdfs/timetable.pdf**.
2   Cabinet Office, *Charities Act 2006: Implementation Plan*, 5 December 2006, reproduced at **Appendix 5**.

3 REQUIREMENT TO REGISTER

3.1 BEFORE THE ACT

Since the 1960 Act charities established or operating in England and Wales have been required to register with the Charity Commissioners, unless exempted or excepted by statute from registration or excepted by order of the Commission. Entry on the Commission's register of charities has never of itself given an organisation charitable status but, importantly, has confirmed to benefactors and to HMRC, as well as to central and local government, that the organisation was a charity.

Exempt charities, while enjoying the fiscal and status benefits accorded to charities and being required to comply with charity law, were not required to register with the Commission on the grounds (often theoretical) that they were already supervised and regulated as charities in other ways by government or public authorities. Exempt charities included most universities and their colleges, voluntary aided schools, the Church Commissioners, industrial and provident societies, certain national museums and galleries (mainly London-based) and even two independent schools, Eton and Winchester.[1] On the whole, charities were exempted because they had been exempted under the Charitable Trusts Act 1853, often because they were regulated by other arms of government. One has the impression of a degree of special pleading by individual members of the legislature in the distant past that their favoured charities were already regulated by themselves and so required no interference by the charity regulator.

Many excepted charities were small charities excused by successive Acts from the need to register with the Commission because they had neither permanent endowment nor the use or occupation of land and their annual income was below a somewhat arbitrary threshold (£15 under the 1960 Act and £1,000 under the 1993 Act). Also excepted were registered places of worship, if registered under the Places of Worship Registration Act 1855.[2]

Other charities, some sizeable, were excepted by order of the Commission or by regulations; these were largely charities which had umbrella organisations with a regulatory role, such as scouts and guides groups, some armed forces charities, some religious charities and universities which were not exempt by virtue of being included in Sched.2 to the 1993 Act. Excepted charities did not have an ongoing relationship with the Commission and so did not have to present annual reports and accounts to the public via the Commission. However, unlike exempt charities, they were still subject to the Commission's supervisory jurisdiction, including their investigatory and monitoring powers.

1   1993 Act, s.3 and Sched.2.
2   1993 Act, s.3(14).

3.2   RATIONALE FOR THE CHANGES

Both exempt and excepted charities have historically enjoyed the status and fiscal benefits accorded to registered charities and were required to comply with the key principles of charity law. However, because they did not have to account in the same way to the Commission, such charities, as well as their own regulators or umbrella groups, were often unaware of the requirements of charity law regarding governance, benefits to trustees and the safeguarding of funds. The Strategy Unit considered that allowing exempt and excepted charities to avoid regulation as charities created anomalies which it felt 'was both confusing to the public and threatened the integrity and status of charities'.[1] By ensuring that information regarding excepted charities was readily available to the general public, it felt that public confidence in charities in general could be increased.

The 2006 Act therefore provides for the removal of exempt or excepted status from many charities or groups of charities and for the removal of excepted status entirely in the long term. Accountability is also tightened up for those retaining exempt status and for charities which will, for the time being, continue to be excepted.

To ease the transition of smaller charities from exempt and excepted status to registered status, the 2006 Act sets a threshold of £100,000 p.a. income, below which charities previously exempt by statute or excepted by Charity Commission order will not for the time being be required to register. That interim threshold is likely to be adjusted downwards when the 2006 Act falls for review five years after Royal Assent.

The regime for exempt and excepted charities is dealt with in greater detail in **Chapter 4**.

1   Cabinet Office Strategy Unit Report, *Public Action, Private Benefit*, September 2002.

3.3   CHARITIES WHICH NOW HAVE TO REGISTER

All charities will have to register, save those which fall below the £5,000 annual income threshold or which remain exempt or excepted. A flowchart is set out in **Figure 3.1** indicating broadly which charities are registrable, exempt or excepted.

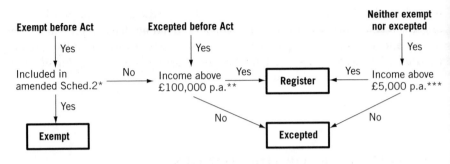

*   Further changes are expected to be made to Sched.2 by the Secretary of State
**   Threshold to be reviewed after 5 years (possibly in 2011)
*** Voluntary registration will eventually be allowed (possibly 2008)

Figure 3.1   New requirements to register with the Charity Commission

Aside from the question of what makes an organisation charitable, which is dealt with in **Chapter 2**, it is not the purpose of this book to consider the process of registration which has increased in complexity in recent years, but the Charity Commission's website **www.charitycommission.gov.uk** is a helpful resource.

3.3.1   Below income threshold

Registration of small charities will not be required if their gross income is below £5,000 p.a. Under the new s.3A of the 1993 Act (introduced by s.9 of the 2006 Act) there is no longer a requirement for charities under the income threshold to register if they possess permanent endowment or use or occupy land. The combined effect of these changes is likely to release several thousand very small charities from the duty to register.

However, there has always been uncertainty as to whether a charity under the income or property thresholds set in the 1993 Act was nevertheless able to register if it wished. A small charity's trustees might wish to do so if grant-making trusts or other potential grant-makers had a policy to make grants only to registered charities. Alternatively, they might believe that, if their charity were not registered, their supporters would, albeit wrongly, consider it 'not a proper charity'. The new s.3A(6) of the 1993 Act makes it clear that any charity which is no longer required to register may nevertheless register, if its trustees so wish. Unfortunately, this provision is unlikely to be brought into force until the Commission has registered the bulk of those charities which have fallen out of exempt or excepted status; until then, a charity with an income under £5,000 p.a. will have to persuade the Commission to exercise its discretion to register, for example because it is about to embark on a fundraising campaign.

3.3.2   Exempt charities

Schedule 2 to the 1993 Act which listed exempt charities is amended by s.11 of the 2006 Act and ss.12 and 13 of the 2006 Act introduce provisions to ensure that the only charities which will remain exempt will be those with an identified principal regulator which has agreed to take responsibility for ensuring that the trustees of the charities which it regulates comply with their obligations under charity law.

Charities which are no longer exempt under Sched.2 to the 1993 Act include:

- The Church Commissioners.
- Student unions.
- Eton and Winchester Colleges.
- Voluntary aided schools (mostly 'faith schools' which represent about 30 per cent of the schools in the maintained sector of education) and foundation schools but these may become excepted charities (see **3.3.3** below). For the regime to be followed, see **Chapter 4** below.
- Industrial and provident societies which are charitable. It should, however, be mentioned that those industrial and provident societies which are charitable housing associations and are registered with the Housing Corporation as registered social landlords will remain exempt from registration and, of course, the Housing Corporation will be the principal regulator of such charitable registered social landlords for the purpose of ss.12 and 13.

In addition, the Minister may under s.11(11) make orders removing particular institutions from, or adding others to, Sched.2 to the 1993 Act, respectively removing exemption from registration or granting such exemption. Before making any such order, the Minister must reach the conclusion that to bring a charity into or out of exemption will ensure the charity will be properly regulated and that its trustees will comply with their legal obligations under charity law. One such group of exempt organisations which are intended to be removed from Sched.2 and therefore from exempt status are the halls and colleges of the Universities of Oxford, Cambridge and Durham (see **3.5** below).

3.3.3   Excepted charities

Charities previously excepted by order of the Charity Commission included some religious charities, scout and guide charities and some regimental or service charities. These orders will remain effective for the time being but excepted charities will nevertheless be required to register if their gross income exceeds £100,000 p.a. This £100,000 threshold is likely to be temporary as the intention of the government is to allow the registration of all currently excepted charities to be phased in gradually.

As already mentioned, if a charity has previously been excepted from registration by order of the Commission, that order remains in force. However, s.3A(3)(b) provides that the Commission may not after the appointed date create any new exceptions to registration. The same applies in s.3A(4) to the Minister's power to except charities, apart from being permitted for the time being to except from registration any of those formerly excepted charities which do not have an annual income in excess of £100,000.

As is the case with charities falling below the £5,000 p.a. income threshold, any charity which is excepted from registration, whether by order of the Commission or by order of the Minister, may nevertheless register voluntarily when this part of the 2006 Act is in force. In the meantime, such charities will have to persuade the Commission to exercise its discretion to register, for example because they are about to embark on a fundraising campaign which will almost certainly result in the £100,000 threshold being reached.

Voluntary aided and foundation schools may well be in a curious position under the new regime. Although moved from exempt status to the excepted charity category, each such school might be thought to have an annual income well in excess of £100,000 and thus be required to register as a charity. However, it is evident that there are ongoing consultations between the Department for Education and Skills and the Commission about the receipts that will be included in calculating the school's annual income. It may be that the following receipts will not, in the event, be regarded as income of the school:

- capital grant, if made subject to a condition that it is not part of the charity's income; and
- income provided by the local education authority under a delegated budget to pay revenue expenses.

If so, it is quite possible that such schools will have a charitable income below the £100,000 threshold and thus be excepted from registration for the time being.

3.4   REGISTRATION OF CHARITIES WHICH ARE NO LONGER EXEMPT OR EXCEPTED

At the time of writing, the Cabinet Office's Implementation Plan for the 2006 Act indicates that the provisions relating to the registration of those charities which are no longer exempt or excepted will not be in force before 2008. This is to 'enable those charities, the proposed principal regulators of exempt charities, and the Charity Commission, time to prepare for the changes'.[1] As mentioned in 3.3.1 above, until this process is completed the provisions allowing voluntary registration for charities with income under £5,000 p.a. are unlikely to come into force.

The Commission has estimated that between 4,000 and 5,000 excepted charities with a gross income in excess of £100,000 p.a. will be required to register and that the figure for charities which fall out of exemption is around 7,700. However, the figure for previously exempt charities includes about 7,200 foundation and voluntary aided schools and it remains to be seen whether their income will be treated in such a way as to remain below the £100,000 threshold (see **3.3.3** above).

---

1 Cabinet Office, *Charities Act 2006: Implementation Plan*, 5 December 2006; see Appendix 5.

3.5 COLLEGES OF OXFORD, CAMBRIDGE AND OTHER UNIVERSITIES

In Sched.2, para.(c) to the 1993 Act the colleges and halls in the Universities of Oxford, Cambridge, Durham, Newcastle and Queen Mary and Westfield College, University of London are stated to be exempt from registration, so far as they are indeed charities. Although it had been previously announced by the government that these colleges and halls (as distinct from their universities) would lose their exempt status, the opportunity to amend Sched.2 in this respect was not taken, apparently because of the perceived danger of making the Bill hybrid[1] which the government was keen to avoid, given the potential parliamentary delays which could have resulted.

The Minister has the power under s.11(11) of the 2006 Act to make an order removing these colleges and halls from Sched.2 and we are told by the Cabinet Office that the Minister currently intends to exercise that power in relation to the colleges and halls of Oxford, Cambridge and Durham, when this part of the 2006 Act comes into force in early 2008. Queen Mary and Westfield College will remain exempt under its principal regulator, the Higher Education Funding Council for England. Notwithstanding the terms of Sched.2, there are, according to the Cabinet Office, no such colleges at Newcastle University.

---

1 A hybrid Bill is a public Bill which significantly affects particular private interests and special parliamentary procedures are required, including public notices about the Bill and the establishment of a select committee to take evidence from individuals and organisations affected, see **www.parliament.uk/factsheets**.

3.6 COMMENCEMENT

As has already been mentioned, the government is giving both principal regulators and the Commission time to prepare for the changes to excepted and exempt charities and the bulk of the new provisions will not come into force until 2008.[1]

---

1 See **Appendix 5**.

4 REGIME FOR EXEMPT AND EXCEPTED CHARITIES

4.1 EXEMPT CHARITIES – INCREASED REGULATION BY THE CHARITY COMMISSION

Exempt charities have always been subject to the key principles of charity law, although it must be said their inclusion in Sched.2 to the 1993 Act, listing charities exempt from registration, did not of itself deem them to be charities. Being exempt, however, meant they were not accountable to the public via the Commission. While they always could take advantage of most of the Commission's enabling powers, for example to make constitutional amendments to their governing documents, exempt charities tended to think of themselves more as public bodies than as charities.

A charity which has retained its exempt status is nevertheless under Sched.5 to the 2006 Act[1] subject to increased regulation by the Commission and may now be:

- required to change its name under s.6 of the 1993 Act, for example if it is misleading or too like that of another charity;
- investigated under s.8 of the 1993 Act, provided that the Commission has been asked to do so by the charity's principal regulator;
- required to produce documents or have its records searched under s.9 of the 1993 Act;
- stopped from promoting a parliamentary Bill without the Commission's consent;
- required to obey the Commission's directions about dormant bank accounts;
- required to obtain consent under s.33 of the 1993 Act to take charity proceedings;
- required to obey orders directing a trustee who has been disqualified to repay sums he has received from a charity.

The Commission's powers under s.18 of the 1993 Act to act for the protection of a charity (for example, to freeze bank accounts, suspend or remove trustees, suspend contractual operations or appoint an interim manager) now apply equally to exempt charities. However, it should be borne in mind that most such powers arise in the context of a s.8 inquiry being opened into the charity and, in the case of an exempt charity, that needs a prior request from the charity's principal regulator.

---

1 For commencement, see Appendix 5.

4.2   EXEMPT CHARITIES – THE PRINCIPAL REGULATOR

The principal regulator of an exempt charity may be a Minister of the Crown, a non-ministerial government department or some umbrella group or non-governmental organisation. The Minister now has power to make regulations for a particular body or Minister of State to become the principal regulator of an exempt charity. As a principal regulator, that body or minister has a duty under s.13 of the 2006 Act to do all he reasonably can to ensure compliance by the charity trustees of the exempt charity with their obligations in exercising control and management of the administration of the charity.

The Minister is also given the power to amend the existing statutory powers of a principal regulator in order to ensure that the regulator meets the compliance objectives in relation to the exempt charities for which it is responsible.[1]

Under s.86A of the 1993 Act (inserted by s.14 of the 2006 Act) the Commission is required to consult the principal regulator before exercising its powers under the Act in relation to an exempt charity. As already mentioned, the principal regulator could ask the Commission to investigate one or more of the charities within its purview.

The 1993 Act does not require exempt charities to audit their accounts or produce an annual report, but for those which do, the new whistle-blowing obligations on auditors and independent examiners in s.44A of the 1993 Act (see **Chapter 12**) have been extended to exempt charities which are not companies, although the report of any material issue should be made to the principal regulator rather than the Commission.

---

1   2006 Act, s.13.

4.3   EXCEPTED CHARITIES – REGULATION BY THE CHARITY COMMISSION

As with exempt charities, exception from registration does not allow excepted charities to consider themselves outside the remit of charity law, nor indeed are they out of reach of the Commission.

Excepted charities will remain subject to charity law generally, although they will not need to produce annual reports and accounts to the Commission unless so required. They continue to be subject to the Commission's monitoring and investigation powers but, given that the Commission is required by the 2006 Act (see **Chapter 5**) to be 'efficient, effective and economic in the use of its resources', it is open to doubt whether it will devote much time to the deficiencies of a small, excepted charity unless there is a clamour in the media for action.

5 THE CHARITY COMMISSION

5.1 A NEW INDEPENDENT COMMISSION

Although it had been known for many years as 'the Charity Commission' the charities' regulator was strictly speaking a Chief Charity Commissioner acting with up to four additional commissioners, known collectively as the Charity Commissioners for England and Wales.

The 2006 Act substitutes a new s.1A for s.1 of the 1993 Act which establishes in place of the Commissioners a corporate body known as the Charity Commission for England and Wales and references in earlier enactments to the Commissioners are now to the Commission. In Welsh the Commission is to be known as *Comisiwn Elusennau Cymru a Lloegr* and one of the Commissioners must represent Wales.

In the 1993 Act the Commissioners were appointed by the relevant Secretary of State and were required to present an annual report to Parliament via the Secretary of State. In practice, the Commissioners were treated as a non-ministerial government department, albeit with a sponsoring Minister, in the past usually the Home Secretary but currently the Minister for the Third Sector, based in the Cabinet Office.

The constitution and procedures of the Commission are set out in a new s.1A of and Sched.1A to the 1993 Act. During the scrutiny of the two Bills, there was much debate in the House of Lords about the need for both charities and their regulator to be independent of government. In consequence, s.1A(4) now makes it clear that the Commission is not, save for provisions in any other Act or expenditure controls by HM Treasury, subject to control by government. Under para.11(2) of Sched.1A to the 1993 Act the new requirement is that the Commission must report to Parliament direct.

The new Charity Commission will have a chairman and between four and eight members, all appointed by the Minister who can also remove them on the grounds of incapacity or misbehaviour. Members of the Commission are appointed for terms of up to three years but cannot serve for more than 10 years in aggregate. Two members must be suitably qualified lawyers and one has to be appointed following consultation with the Welsh National Assembly. In addition, the Minister has in making these appointments to reflect experience in charity law, accountancy and finance and the operation and regulation of the charities of all sorts. From early transitional appointments it seems that there will be greater input from those with personal experience of charities rather than from the Civil Service.

The role of the former Chief Charity Commissioner is split between the Chairman and the Chief Executive, the latter being an appointment of the Commission rather than of the Minister, although terms and conditions of service are set by government, as is the case with all the Commission's staff who continue to be civil servants.

As already mentioned the Commission must lay a copy of its annual report (to the end of March) before Parliament and this must now deal with:

- the discharge of its functions;
- the extent to which its newly stated objectives have been met;
- the performance of its general duties; and
- the management of its affairs.

The report must be followed within three months by a public meeting to include a general discussion on the report and an opportunity to put questions to the Commission on the discharge of its functions. Accountability of the Commission is to be towards the charity sector as well as to Parliament.

Schedule 2 to the 2006 Act makes supplementary provision for the establishment of the Commission, in particular attempting a seamless transition between the former Commissioners and the new Commission in relation, for example, to previous terms of office, decisions and litigation or other proceedings by or in relation to the Commissioners.

5.2 CHARITY COMMISSION'S OBJECTIVES, FUNCTIONS AND DUTIES

5.2.1 Objectives

Although the 1993 Act as originally enacted set out the general functions and purpose of the Commissioners, the new s.1B of the 1993 Act (inserted by s.7 of the 2006 Act) is much clearer about the objectives, functions and duties of the Commission as regulator and the objectives are worth summarising here:

1. To increase public trust and confidence in charities.
2. To promote awareness and understanding of the operation of the public benefit requirement.
3. To promote compliance by trustees with their legal obligations in managing their charities.
4. To promote the effective use of charitable resources.
5. To enhance the accountability of charities to donors, beneficiaries and the public.

5.2.2   General functions

Under the umbrella of these five objectives the Charity Commission has been given by virtue of the new s.1C of the 1993 Act six general functions:

1. Determining whether institutions are, or are not, charities.
2. Encouraging and facilitating the better administration of charities.
3. Identifying and investigating apparent misconduct or mismanagement in the administration of charities and taking appropriate remedial or protective action.
4. Determining whether public collections certificates should be issued and remain in force (see **Chapter 14**).
5. Obtaining, evaluating and disseminating information in relation to the performance of any of the Commission's functions or regulatory objectives.
6. Giving information or advice, or making proposals, to the government on matters relating to any of the Commission's functions or meeting any of its regulatory objectives.

The Commission is required under the new s.1C(3) of the 1993 Act (pursuant to its fifth general function) to keep the register of charities up to date and accurate. This will undoubtedly give the Commission further reason to insist on the timely production by registered charities of annual returns, report and accounts and the Commission's recently appointed Chairman has indicated that on her watch compliance will be more rigorously enforced.

In the debates in the House of Lords great concern was expressed that the sixth general function was another unnecessary example of an ever-watchful Big Brother. Charities value their independence from government and do not wish the sector to become the proverbial political football, allowing charities to be used by the government to further its own policies. The worry was that this could happen even if the Commission remained a non-ministerial government department. In the Second Reading Debate[3] in relation to the first Bill, the Minister of State at the Home Office, Lady Scotland, declared:

> The Government believe that the Commission's independence [as an independent regulator, completely free of ministerial direction or control] is of paramount importance for the proper regulation of charities and for the public's confidence in charities.

5.2.3   General duties

The new s.1D of the 1993 Act sets out six general duties which, subject to the usual provisions that this is insofar as it is reasonable, relevant or appropriate, the Commission must follow in performing its functions. In summary, these duties are:

1. To act in a way which is both compatible with and appropriate to the Commission's new objectives.

2.   To act in a way which is compatible with the encouragement of all forms of charitable giving and voluntary participation in charity work.
3.   To have regard to the need to use its resources in the most efficient, effective and economic way.
4.   To have regard to the principles of best regulatory management, namely to be proportionate, accountable, consistent, transparent and to target only cases where action is needed.
5.   To have regard to the desirability of facilitating innovation by charities.
6.   To have regard to the principles of good corporate governance.

These new duties were much debated in the House of Lords during the passage of legislation and many in the charity sector were particularly pleased that the government did eventually allow the inclusion of the proportionality requirement in the fourth general duty.[1] It had been considered by some commentators that the Commission had a tendency to pursue small charities in a disproportionate way in relation to minor compliance infringements, whilst allowing off the hook larger charities or those where there were political sensitivities. The Commission's duties to be proportionate, accountable, consistent and transparent in performing its functions will doubtless be considered before too long by the Charity Tribunal.

The second general duty is to act so far as reasonably practical in a way which is compatible with the encouragement of charitable giving in its several forms and voluntary participation in charity work. In other words, the Commission does need to consider at all times how its functions encourage the involvement of more people in giving their time and money to the charity sector. There is a necessary balance to be struck between ensuring compliance and accountability on the part of charity trustees (in default of which the public's perception of and confidence in the charity sector could be diminished) and being heavy-handed with trustees in relation to minor matters (in which event it might become yet more difficult to find new charity trustees for existing as well as future charities).

The Commission is required in the third general duty to use its resources 'in the most efficient effective and economic way'.[2] Whilst it is right, speaking as tax-payers, that we should not encourage the Commission to be spendthrift and to waste money on minor issues, we do, as practitioners, come across situations where the Commission could, without spending extensive time or resources, encourage a charity itself to be more efficient but will not do so, possibly because of a broad policy decision already made. For instance, we find that the Commission is, in practice, unwilling to become involved in what it considers to be internal disputes between trustees of charities even in terms of mediation; whilst that is understandable where the dispute is about personalities, there are often instances where disputes arise on matters of principle and mediation might in fact be both efficient and economic. Proportionality works both ways.

5.2.4   Incidental powers

The Commission has a general power under the new s.1E(1) of the 1993 Act to do anything which will facilitate its functions or duties; however, the new s.1E(2) does restate the important rule, formerly in s.1(4) of that Act, that the Commission may neither act as a charity trustee nor become directly involved in the administration of a charity. It has to be noted that the new s.19A (giving the Commission power after a s.8 inquiry has been opened to direct action to be taken on behalf of the charity)[4] and the new s.19B (power to direct application of a charity's property)[5] of the 1993 Act are important exceptions to this rule. Our expectation is that the Commission will be careful to exercise these new powers in accordance with its fourth general duty (s.1D(2), para.4 of the 1993 Act), namely following principles of best regulatory practice, including being proportionate, accountable, consistent, transparent and targeting only cases in which action is needed.

---

1   2006 Act, s.7, inserting s.1D(2)4 into 1993 Act.
2   1993 Act, s.1D(2)3.
3   Baroness Scotland of Asthol, House of Lords Second Reading, Charities Bill, 20 January 2005, *Hansard*, col.886.
4   Inserted by 2006 Act, s.20.
5   2006 Act, s.21.

5.3   RE-EXAMINATION OF POLICIES

5.3.1   Campaigning by charities

Not all recommendations contained in the Cabinet Office's Strategy Unit Report required legislation; some simply encouraged the Commission to re-examine its policies. One such policy was campaigning by charities where the Commission's previous guidelines were considered by the Strategy Unit to be too cautionary, providing insufficient emphasis on those non-party-political campaigning activities which charities were permitted to undertake as ancillary to their charitable purposes. Following discussions in the charity sector the Commission has reissued guidance on *Campaigning and Political Activities by Charities* (CC 9) and has done the same with the linked issue of *The Promotion of Human Rights* (RR 12).

5.3.2   Open board meetings

Similarly, the Commission has reacted positively to the Strategy Unit's suggestion of making its board meetings open to the public, including publishing the agenda and minutes on the website (**www.charitycommission.gov.uk**). The first open board meeting took place in September 2004. Time will tell, but probably salacious matters of interest to certain organs of the media will be marked 'reserved business' and discussed in private. Currently, attendance by the public is in the region of 10–15 people.

5.3.3   Guidance

In the consultations leading up to the 2006 Act there was a suggestion that the Commission should cease to provide help and guidance for the sector and concentrate on its role as regulator, but there were few voices raised in support of the 'regulator only' role. Indeed, it would be difficult for the Commission to comply with some of its new objectives and general duties if it was solely in regulator mode. The Commission's guidance notes have improved considerably, even during the passage of the Charities Bills through Parliament, and its website **www.charitycommission.gov.uk** is a very useful resource for both charities and professional advisers.

5.4   COMMENCEMENT

The provisions for the new style Commission will be amongst those in the first commencement order for the 2006 Act, due in early 2007.[1] In some matters (for example, the appointment of a chairman and chief executive of the Commission) the government has long since anticipated the legislation.

---

1   See **Appendix 5**.

6 THE CHARITY TRIBUNAL

6.1 WHY IS A CHARITY TRIBUNAL NEEDED?

The volume and range of decisions taken by the Charity Commission is immense. In its role as 'gatekeeper' of registered charity status, the Commission makes hundreds of decisions each year, entering and sometimes removing organisations on the register. As regulator, the Commission's decisions, such as whether to open inquiries and take protective measures under ss.8 and 18 of the 1993 Act, often have far reaching implications for charities and charity trustees. There are also literally thousands of decisions taken every year in connection with more routine aspects of charity administration, covering matters such as dealings with charity property, altering trusts cy-près and authorising charity proceedings, to name but a few.

The 2006 Act confers further and more extensive powers on the Commission. In addition, the Commission's ongoing Review of the Register and now the planned systematic review of public benefit, may lead to some controversial decisions being made as to the removal of organisations or classes of organisations from the register.

As the range and scope of the Commission's powers have been enhanced, there has rightly been a call for an accessible and low-cost means of challenging Commission rulings. Prior to the 2006 Act, a review of the Commission's decisions, on matters of law rather than administration, could be pursued up to Charity Commissioner level but, if this was unsuccessful, the next stage was an appeal to the High Court. Not surprisingly, given the costs and delays that High Court proceedings inevitably entail, appeals had been few. The Strategy Unit[1] concluded that the Commission was 'virtually unchallengeable in practice'. The creation of a new independent tribunal to hear appeals against Commission decisions was therefore a key recommendation of the Strategy Unit and is one that has been warmly endorsed across the charity sector. It remains to be seen whether, in the absence of legal aid or a suitors' fund, charities, trustees or others affected by decisions of the Commission will take cases to the Tribunal in any number.

1 Strategy Unit Report, *Private Action, Public Benefit*, September 2002, see pp.83–5.

6.2   KEY FEATURES OF THE NEW TRIBUNAL

The Charity Tribunal is established under s.8 of the 2006 Act, which introduced new ss.2A–2D as Part 1A of the 1993 Act. New Scheds.1B–1D to the 1993 Act deal with the Tribunal's composition, jurisdiction and procedures. The relevant provisions are scheduled to be included in the third commencement order under the 2006 Act, due in early 2008.

The Tribunal will act as 'court of first instance', hearing appeals or reviewing a range of decisions made by the Commission. It will also be able to consider questions regarding the operation of charity law referred to it by the Attorney-General or (with the Attorney-General's consent) by the Charity Commission.

The Tribunal will be concerned with matters of law, not administration. The Charity Tribunal will not therefore displace the current mechanism for complaints in relation to the conduct or service of the Commission. These will continue to be dealt with under the internal complaints review procedure,[1] with onward reference to the independent complaints reviewer,[2] failing that to the parliamentary Ombudsman.[3]

Neither will the Tribunal be able to hear complaints about the conduct of individual charities by aggrieved members of the public, beneficiaries, users or employees – these remain an issue for charities' own complaints procedures to deal with, a topic on which the Charity Commission published the findings of its research in June 2006.[4]

1   *Complaints about Commission Standards of Service* (OG 93), June 2006.
2   See **www.icrev.demon.co.uk**.
3   See **www.ombudsman.org.uk** – although note that this service is one of last resort (only three cases have ever been referred) and complaints can only be forwarded to the Ombudsman via an MP.
4   *Cause for Complaint? How charities manage complaints about their services*, available at **www.charitycommission.gov.uk/publications/rs11.asp**.

6.3   MATTERS THAT CAN BE REFERRED TO THE TRIBUNAL

6.3.1   Appeals

The new Sched.1C to the 1993 Act, inserted by Sched.4 to the 2006 Act, sets out (in table format) a list in column 1 of all decisions, directions or orders made by the Commission which may be referred to the Tribunal. These represent the majority of decisions which the Commission makes as part of its functions, and in most cases, the Commission's decisions are subject to full appeal, although there are some decisions which are subject to review only (see **6.3.2** below). Matters which can be appealed include, for example, decisions as to whether or not to enter an organisation on the register and decisions to take action for protection of a charity under s.18 of the 1993 Act (including the removal of a charity trustee) as well as decisions on a range of more routine matters. In addition, although not listed in the Table in Sched.1C, the Commission's decisions in relation to public collection certificates will be capable of being appealed to the Tribunal as set out in s.57 of the 2006 Act. The Minister may amend, add or remove entries in the Table, but only by a positive resolution of both Houses of Parliament.

In most cases the Tribunal must consider the matter afresh and may take into account new evidence not previously available to the Commission. The exceptions are reviewable matters (see 6.3.2 below) and appeals against an order under s.9 of the 1993 Act requiring a person to supply information or documents, usually used in connection with inquiries. In the latter case the Tribunal's role is limited to determining whether the information or documents relate to a charity and are relevant to the Commission's functions or those of the official custodian. The restrictions reflect concerns that, if the Tribunal looked at these matters afresh, this could unduly hamper the Commission in its inquiry work.

6.3.2   Reviewable matters

There are some eight decisions of the Commission which are simply 'reviewable' by the Tribunal and in these cases the Tribunal must apply the principles used by the High Court in an application for judicial review. The Tribunal would not therefore consider such cases afresh or take into account new evidence.

The 'reviewable matters' are:

- decisions to institute an inquiry in relation to a particular institution (1993 Act, s.8);
- decisions to open an inquiry in relation to a class of institutions (s.8);
- decisions not to make a common investment scheme (s.24);
- decisions not to make a common deposit scheme (s.25);
- decisions not to make an order authorising an action as expedient in the interests of the charity (s.26);
- decisions not to make an order authorising the disposal of land (s.36);
- decisions not to make an order authorising the mortgage of land (s.38); and
- orders requiring a charitable company's accounts to be investigated and audited by an auditor appointed by the Commission (s.69(1)).

6.3.3   Other provisions for reference to the Tribunal

New s.2A(4)(b) of and Sched.1D to the 1993 Act allow the Attorney-General to refer questions involving the operation or application of charity law to the Tribunal and the Commission (with the Attorney-General's consent) to refer questions relating to its functions as well as the operation or application of charity law. 'Charity law' is defined under para.7(1) of Sched.1D to include not only the 1993 Act, the 2006 Act, subordinate legislation and other legislation included in regulations by the Minster but also any rule of law which relates to charities, in other words the common law. These provisions could, therefore, be of considerable help in resolving arguments between charities or their professional advisers and the regulator of the charity sector.

Paragraphs 3 and 4 of Sched.1D provide for the suspension of the Commission's activities and relevant time-limits in relation to any matter affected by its reference, or that of the Attorney-General, to the Tribunal, until the case is concluded and the appeal process is exhausted.

6.3.4   Matters outside the Tribunal's remit

The government's response[1] to the Scrutiny Committee's report on the draft Charities Bill stated:

> The Government accepts that there should be a presumption in favour of including within the Tribunal's remit any decision of the Commission which there is no strong reason to exclude from the Tribunal's remit. A 'decision of the Commission' in this context means a decision to exercise, or not to exercise, a statutory power in relation to a charity (or, in some cases, in relation to a trustee, officer, employee or agent of a charity).

Notwithstanding that statement by the government, there are some significant omissions from the list of matters that may be referred to the Tribunal. Not all 'non-decisions' are subject to appeal or review and there are some curious inconsistencies. Whilst, for example, the Commission's decision to order a scheme to be made for the administration of a charity under s.16 of the 1993 Act, such as a cy-près scheme, may be appealed, an appeal does not lie against a refusal of the Commission to make an order for a scheme. In contrast, where the Commission is exercising its jurisdiction to give prior written consent to the alteration of the objects of a charitable company under s.64(2) of the 1993 Act, both the giving and the withholding of consent may be appealed.

Perhaps the most significant omission from the decisions and 'non-decisions' covered by the Tribunal is that of the Commission's refusal to exercise its powers under the new s.73D of the 1993 Act to relieve trustees and auditors, etc. from liability from breach of trust or a duty (see **Chapter 10**). An appeal against refusal must be made to the High Court.

---

1   *Government Reply to the Report from the Joint Committee on the Draft Charities Bill,* Cm 6440, Session 2003–04, 21 December 2004, see p.12.

6.4   COMPOSITION OF THE TRIBUNAL

The Tribunal is comprised of a President, legal members (one of whom may be appointed as deputy President) and lay members. All members are appointed, and may be removed, by the Lord Chancellor. The President and legal members are required to have a seven-year general qualification.[1] Ordinary members must have appropriate knowledge or experience relating to charities and, therefore, include not only other professionals concerned with charities, but also individuals who may have practical experience of working in the voluntary sector. Members of the Tribunal can be remunerated.

1   Courts and Legal Services Act 1990, s.71(3)(c) defines someone as having a general qualification if they have a 'right of audience in relation to any class of proceedings in any part of the Supreme Courts, or all proceedings in county courts or magistrates' courts'.

6.5   TRIBUNAL PROCEDURE AND POWERS

Reference to the Tribunal may be made in every case either by the Attorney-General or by the persons listed in column 2 of the Sched.1C Table against the decision, directions or order appealed against. In most cases this expressly includes the charity trustees or the charity itself (in the case of a corporate charity) as well as other persons who are or may be affected by the decision. There are some exceptions; for example, an order made under s.9 of the 1993 Act for the provision of information or documents can only be appealed by the person who is subject to the order and is required to supply the information or document concerned, not necessarily including either the charity or the charity trustees.

The Tribunal's powers in relation to appeals and reviewable matters are set out in column 3 of the Sched.1C Table. The Tribunal has the power to quash decisions, orders or directions and to remit matters to the Commission or, in some cases, to make a substitute or supplemental decision, direction or order. Under para.5, Sched.1C, a matter may be referred back to the Commission either generally or to be dealt with in accordance with a finding or direction of the Tribunal.

The Attorney-General may intervene in all proceedings before the Tribunal and the Tribunal may encourage such intervention by ordering that papers relating to the proceedings are sent to the Attorney-General.

Rules regulating appeals and concerning practice and procedure for Tribunal hearings will be made by the Lord Chancellor. The rules will, amongst other matters, set out the time-limits for an appeal or application to be made to the Tribunal following a Commission decision. The manner in which appeals and applications are to be made, and procedural matters such as the evidence and disclosure of documents, will also be covered by rules. It is also anticipated that rules will govern what decisions may be determined without an oral hearing and procedure for dealing with urgent cases.

The rules will also govern the award of costs. Under new s.2B(6) of the 1993 Act, the Tribunal may award costs against a party to the proceedings where it considers that party has acted 'vexatiously, frivolously or unreasonably'. Costs can be awarded against the Commission under s.2B(7) if the Tribunal considers that the decision, direction or order of the Commission which has been referred to the Tribunal was unreasonable.

The Scrutiny Committee recommended that the Commission be requested to confirm formally that it would not seek to recover costs from an unsuccessful applicant, except where the Tribunal decided that the appeal amounted to an abuse of process.[1] The Commission's response, recorded in the government's reply to the Scrutiny Committee report was that:

> The Charity Commission will not routinely ask for costs but the position would be very much governed by the facts of an individual case and the circumstances of the individual.[2]

The government rejected the Scrutiny Committee's recommendation to include in the 2006 Act a residuary power for ministers to make regulations enabling financial assistance to be given to parties to take a case before the Tribunal by way of a 'suitors' fund', in an attempt to ensure that access to the Tribunal was not limited by the cost of litigation. The government anticipated, perhaps unrealistically, that Tribunal users should be able to present evidence by themselves but that, where an appellant required legal representation, public funding might, exceptionally, be granted. We hope that the Attorney-General might be persuaded to intervene in proceedings where an applicant cannot afford legal representation to deal with a complex legal issue.

---

1   Joint Committee on the Draft Charities Bill, Vol.I, para.239.
2   *Government Reply to the Report from the Joint Committee on the Draft Charities Bill,* Cm 6440, Session 2003–04, 21 December 2004, see p.12.

6.6   THE LIKELY IMPACT OF THE TRIBUNAL

The Department for Constitutional Affairs is responsible for establishing the Tribunal but the task is not likely to be competed until well into 2008. Once operational, the Tribunal will be at the forefront of the development of charity law and practice, not least through the facility for the Commission to refer issues of charity law of general application to the Tribunal for consideration.

The Tribunal has also been widely welcomed as an accessible means of challenging Commission decisions but it remains to be seen how it will work in practice. At the very least the existence of the Tribunal to hear appeals or review decisions is likely to introduce a more focused approach to the Commission's procedures for the exercise of its powers and the recording and communication of its decisions.

7 SUPERVISION BY THE CHARITY COMMISSION AND REGULATION OF LAND TRANSACTIONS

7.1 SECTION 8 INQUIRIES

7.1.1 Complaints about charities

The Commission's stated objective in relation to what one might call consumer complaints is to help trustees of charities to function effectively and to try to resolve internally concerns or allegations which are brought to their attention by members of the public.[1] If, however, the Commission does receive a complaint then, unless the circumstances are exceptional, it will put the complaint to the charity's trustees and thereafter carry out a short evaluation to see whether the concerns or allegations do, on the face of it, stand up and should be investigated.

Under s.8 of the 1993 Act the Commission has power to investigate the activities of a particular charity or a group of charities. Each year the Commission carries out a little over 200 inquiries under s.8 of the 1993 Act, only about a quarter of those cases which it evaluates.

7.1.2 Proportionality and effectiveness of inquiries

There have been indications recently that the number of inquiries carried out by the Commission might reduce, because they are expensive in time and money for both the Commission and the charity. The 2006 Act now requires the Commission to be proportionate[2] in performing its duties and to perform its functions to act 'in the most efficient, effective and economic way';[3] further, since January 2006 investigations have been transferred to a single office of the Commission.

However, the Commission will, in consequence of the 2006 Act, have a significant number of additional charities to register and regulate, as they cease to be excepted or exempted (see **Chapter 3**), and will also have a regulatory role over exempt charities as and when requested by the principal regulator (see **Chapter 4**). It remains to be seen whether this additional group of 'clients' will have the effect of increasing the number of inquiries by the Commission.

Indeed, it is interesting to speculate whether the new whistle-blowing powers[4] given to auditors and independent examiners in circumstances which fall short of a duty to report[5] might have the effect of increasing the number of formal inquiries, simply because accountants may feel themselves under pressure to report even the minor errors of charity trustees to the Commission.

7.1.3 Existing Charity Commission powers

The 1993 Act gave the Commission in s.18(1) some useful powers to act for the protection of charities once a s.8 inquiry had been established, but only if it was satisfied *either* that the charity had suffered misconduct or mismanagement *or* that it was necessary or desirable to protect the charity's property or to secure its proper use. These powers were in short:

- to suspend trustees, employees or agents from their duties;
- to appoint additional trustees;
- to vest property in the Official Custodian for Charities;
- to freeze assets and bank accounts;
- to restrict a charity's transactions;
- to appoint a receiver and manager (now to be known as an interim manager).[6]

A further power in s.18(2) allowed the Commission to take the more permanent steps of removing trustees, employees or agents or establishing a scheme for the charity's future administration if the Commission reasonably believed *both* that there had been misconduct or mismanagement *and* that it was necessary or desirable to protect the charity's property or to secure its proper use; in other words a marginally harder test than for exercise of the s.18(1) powers.

---

1 *Complaints about Charities* (CC 47).
2 1993 Act, s.1D(2)4, inserted by 2006 Act, s.7.
3 1993 Act, s.1D(2)3.
4 1993 Act, s.44A(3), inserted by 2006 Act, s.29.
5 1993 Act, s.44(2).
6 See 2006 Act, Sched.8, para.111.

7.2 NEW SUPERVISORY POWERS

7.2.1 Power to remove trustees as members

A problem occasionally faced by the Commission was that it might in serious cases suspend or remove trustees and others from office using the s.18(2) power, only to find that the trustees, as the only or majority members of the charity, promptly reinstated themselves as trustees or were intent on hampering the longer-term stability of the charity by vetoing desirable constitutional changes. The new s.18A of the 1993 Act (introduced by s.19 of the 2006 Act) allows the Commission to move the matter forward by:

1. suspending a person's membership for so long as they are suspended from office; or
2. terminating a person's membership on removal from office and prohibiting reinstatement as a member without the Commission's consent. Consent to

reinstatement can be sought at any time but after five years have elapsed the Commission must allow reinstatement unless it is satisfied that there are special circumstances justifying refusal.

7.2.2   Powers to give specific directions about a charity

Stepping into the trustees' shoes

The Commission is prohibited by the new s.1E (replacing s.1(4)) of the 1993 Act from taking any step in the administration of a charity. If the Commission considers that the administration of a charity has broken down or that the trustees are not prepared, or able, to correct their perceived errors, the Commission has since 1993 had the power to appoint a receiver and manager under s.18(1)(vii) of the 1993 Act, usually to the exclusion of the trustees. In the decade since the passing of the 1993 Act the Commission appointed a little over 50 receivers and managers, mostly accountants and solicitors. In many cases such appointments successfully turned the problem charity around or at least ensured that the charity's assets could be given away to similar charities or used for similar purposes, but there were inevitably complaints about the expense of appointing professionals to manage charities, occasionally for several years.

In order to underline the temporary nature of the job whose purpose is either to get the charity back on its feet and into the hands of a refreshed body of trustees or to bring it to an end and apply its net assets for similar charitable purposes, the 2006 Act changes the job title from 'receiver and manager' to 'interim manager'.[1]

New options for the Commission

The Commission now has two new options where it has concerns, added by ss.20 and 21 of the 2006 Act which introduce, respectively, new ss.19A and 19B of the 1993 Act:

- The new s.19A of the 1993 Act gives the Commission the power to direct any charity trustee, or person holding as trustee for the charity, any officer or employee of the charity, or the charity itself if corporate, to take action which the Commission deems expedient in the interests of the charity. Such power allows the Commission to specify the action a charity should take and this would not be limited to protecting a charity's property; it could, for example, require the dismissal of an employee or a merger of the charity with another. This power is only available if the Commission has instituted an inquiry under s.8 of the 1993 Act, and is satisfied that there has been misconduct or mismanagement in the charity.
- The new s.19B of the 1993 Act allows the Commission to direct that a charity's property be used or transferred in a particular way if those in control of it refuse to use or apply the property for the purposes of the charity. Unlike the new s.19A power, this power does not have to be triggered by the institution of an inquiry. It is possible that the Commission could use this power to force

trustees to pursue policies offering greater public benefit, without having to go to the lengths of opening a s.8 inquiry.

In exercising either of these new powers the Commission cannot insist on any action which would break the law or be inimical to the charity's trusts or purposes. Nevertheless, a consequence of such a direction might be that a third party's rights would be compromised. For example, s.19A(5) ensures that third party rights cannot be affected by the Commission so the s.19A power, if used to dismiss an employee, might give rise to an unfair dismissal claim against the charity. It may be that in making such a direction the Commission will have to weigh up which is the lesser of two evils, namely to leave an errant employee in place and subject the charity to possible further damage or to direct the employee's dismissal and leave the charity open to a claim in the Employment Tribunal.

Whilst we can understand that there is sometimes frustration for the Commission in seeing a charity going wrong because its trustees will not change direction, it has to be said that both these new powers override the principle enshrined in what is now s.1E(2) of the 1993 Act, and often quoted by the Commission itself when asked to advise a charity what to do in difficult circumstances, namely that the Commission may not exercise the functions of a trustee of a charity or be directly involved in a charity's administration. So it must be hoped that the Commission will in practice use these new powers sparingly; in some cases the threat to use such powers might be sufficient to goad recalcitrant trustees into action. However, an interim manager who can act in place of the trustees may still be in a better position to chart the way forward for an errant charity than the, necessarily remote, regulator.

7.2.3   New power of entry

The power in the new s.31A of the 1993 Act (introduced by s.26 of the 2006 Act), to enter premises and seize documents as well as computer disks or other electronic storage devices, is entirely new. Doubtless nothing should be read into the fact that it follows on immediately from s.31 of the 1993 Act, which allows the Commission to tax a solicitors' bill. Nevertheless, the premises entered could be the offices of a solicitor or other professional, as the power is not confined to the premises of the charity involved.

There are stringent conditions attached to this significant new power and we sense that dramatic dawn raids on the premises of charities, their trustees or their professional advisers may be a rarity; however, the threat to use it may bring to heel trustees or advisers of charities who are being unreasonable in their refusal to hand over documents whose production has been ordered by the Commission.

The conditions set out in s.31A are briefly:

- A s.8 inquiry must have been instituted.
- A magistrate must have issued a warrant following evidence on oath from the Commission.

- The documents or information sought are believed to be on the premises and are relevant to the inquiry by virtue of s.9(1) of the 1993 Act.
- The Commission believes that its order for production of the information would not be complied with or that the information would be destroyed or concealed.
- The entry and search must be at a reasonable hour and no more than a month after the warrant has been issued.
- The documents or IT devices may be retained for only so long as is necessary (which may not be very long if a copy of the original is sufficient for the inquiry) and must thereafter be returned either to the person from whom it was taken or to the relevant charity trustees.
- The member of the Commission's staff who is authorised under the warrant must record in writing prescribed details of the entry on the premises and, if asked, supply a copy of that record to the occupier of the premises in question.

The member of the Commission's staff authorised to enter premises may under s.31A(3)(b) take others to assist him in carrying out the entry and search of the premises, for example a police officer, an accountant or a computer expert. The intentional obstruction of the exercise of the warrant is a criminal offence carrying a custodial sentence.

---

1   See 2006 Act, Sched.8, para.111.

7.3   MISCELLANEOUS ASSISTANCE TO CHARITIES

7.3.1   Publicity relating to schemes

The Commission has by virtue of s.16 of the 1993 Act concurrent jurisdiction with the High Court to establish schemes to alter the trusts of the charities, including altering objects cy-près (see **Chapter 8**). Public notice must be given of proposed orders establishing schemes inviting representations to be made to the Commission. The Commission's recent practice has been to make copies of schemes or proposed schemes available on its website **www.charitycommission. gov.uk** and to require charity trustees to arrange for newspaper publication, often in conjunction with the display of a notice in a public place. Under the 1993 Act public notice had to be given for at least one month before a scheme could be made. The 2006 Act substitutes a new s.20 into the 1993 Act to relax requirements for publicity, allowing flexibility in the timing of the public notice to be given prior to the making of such schemes or orders and flexibility to waive the publicity requirements where the Commission considers notice unnecessary. This should save cost, delay and a perhaps few trees.

The Commission must now ensure that any public notice inviting representations about the proposed scheme is sufficient and appropriate, including for example notice relating to a local charity being given to a parish council, but the previous absolute requirement of one month's publicity is abolished. The Commission has discretion as to the means, content and timing of the publicity. If it deems these publicity requirements to be unnecessary in the particular circumstances, it may dispense with publicity, allowing routine or non-controversial schemes to be processed more quickly. Where public notice is given, the Commission has to take into account any representation made within the specified period and may modify the scheme or simply proceed as proposed without giving further notice.

Once the scheme has been sealed it must be made available for public inspection for at least one month at the Commission and, unless the Commission considers it unnecessary, where the scheme concerns a local charity it must also be available at some convenient place in the local area.

There is in s.20A of the 1993 Act a similar relaxation in the requirements for giving public notice when the Commission exercises its powers in the context of a formal inquiry to make orders appointing, discharging or removing a charity trustee or someone acting as a trustee for a charity. There is no need for public notice where the order relates to the Official Custodian or where the order relates to the appointment of additional trustees during the course of a s.8 inquiry. However, where the Commission proposes to make an order to remove a charity trustee, or an officer, agent or employee of a charity without his or her consent, the individual concerned must be given not less than one month's notice inviting representations within a given period.

7.3.2   Common investment schemes

Common investment funds and common deposit funds are charities created by schemes under ss.24 and 25 of the 1993 Act. They are collective investment arrangements available exclusively to charities. Under s.23 of the 2006 Act the 1993 Act is amended so that these are now available not only to charities established in England and Wales but also to charities established in Scotland and Northern Ireland. The terms of common investment fund and common deposit fund schemes drawn up prior to the 2006 Act will almost certainly require amendment before charities established in Scotland and Northern Ireland can participate.

7.3.3   New advice and guidance powers

In s.29 of the 1993 Act the Commission was given the power to advise trustees on the performance of their duties in particular circumstances, provided that the Commission was given sufficient information. Because the trustees would be protected from an allegation of breach of their fiduciary duty if they acted in accordance with formal advice under s.29, the Commission has historically been cautious in giving such advice, preferring simply to make encouraging noises that trustees have the Commission's support in what they are doing, so long as they have taken proper professional advice.

The new s.29 of the 1993 Act, replaced by s.24 of the 2006 Act, is extended to the 'proper administration of the charity'. It may be that the Commission will be prepared to use this power more often and certainly many trustees of charities would welcome that.

In addition, the guidance may be given not only to a particular charity but to all charities or a group of charities (for example, on the Commission's website **www.charitycommission.gov.uk**) and trustees acting in accordance with such advice, if given formally under the new s.29, will be protected. The Commission is specifically encouraged by the new s.29(4) to give such advice pursuant to its general function to improve the administration of charities and in such case it does not have to wait to be asked by representatives of a charity to give advice.

Section 29 advice is an extension of the Commission's concurrent jurisdiction with the High Court and, given that there is no cost to the charity or the charity trustees or representatives being advised, is clearly to be preferred, but the Commission cannot give advice if a decision of the court has been made or is pending.

There has been a concern amongst some smaller charities that they do not know when they are being given advice by the Commission and when they are being directed to do something by the Commission as regulator. The distinction is sometimes blurred and suggestions were made during the parliamentary scrutiny process of the Charities Bill that the Commission should use different colours of letterhead according to whether it is advising or directing.[1] There is no current sign of colour coding of the Commission's letters.

7.3.4   Power to determine membership

Many charity constitutions give a role to the members if there is a need to change the charity's constitution, to approve accounts or to elect, even remove, trustees. Unfortunately, recording of the ebb and flow of membership in addition to trusteeship, even in charitable companies, is not always a priority for those who run charities and the question of whether successive decisions of general meetings had legal effect can be an expensive nightmare.

The new s.29A of the 1993 Act, inserted by s.25 of the 2006 Act, gives the Commission, or someone appointed by the Commission for the purpose, the power to decide who the charity's members are. The power to make such a determination can arise either at the request of the charity or once a formal inquiry into the charity has been instituted under s.8 of the 1993 Act. 'Members' in these circumstances are defined by s.97(1) of the 1993 Act as a body distinct from the charity trustees.[2]

---

1   *Report of the Joint Committee on the Draft Charities Bill*, September 2004, p.56, evidence of National Association of Councils for Voluntary Service.
2   See 2006 Act, Sched.8, para.174.

7.4   CHANGES TO THE REGIME FOR LAND TRANSACTIONS

7.4.1   Amendments to the section 36 procedure (disposal of land)

Prior to 1993 the general rule was that registered charities could not dispose of land without the consent of the Charity Commissioners or the court. Under s.36 of the 1993 Act charity trustees were permitted to dispose of land without such consent provided that:

- a report was obtained from a qualified surveyor acting solely for the charity and acted upon by the trustees with the purpose of achieving the best terms for the disposal that could reasonably be obtained; and
- the disposal of land was not made to a 'connected person' (defined by Sched.5 to the 1993 Act) or someone acting for a connected person.

This self-regulating regime has worked well and has in our experience ensured that disposals of land by charities can proceed promptly, are transparent and are dealt with on professional advice in the best interests of the charity. However, there have been uncertainties, for example about the meaning of 'sold' in the context of whether a sale takes place at the contract stage or on completion of the disposal. Further uncertainty amongst lawyers dealing with transactions involving charities was created by the *Bayoumi* case[1] in which it was decided that a contract for the disposal of land by trustees of a charity who had not gone through the s.36 procedure was unenforceable.

In consequence, amendments have been introduced by para.128, Sched.8 to the 2006 Act to s.36 of the 1993 Act, the effect of which is that:

- in s.36(1) the words 'conveyed' and 'transferred' have been substituted for 'sold' because *Bayoumi* made it clear that entering into a contract to dispose was not itself a disposal and 'sold' is often used in the context of entering into a contract of sale; and
- although the obligations to obtain a surveyor's report in s.36(3) and (5) of the 1993 Act had been regarded as freestanding and not linked to s.36(2) of that Act, they will henceforth be specifically linked to s.36(2) so that the failure to comply with subsections (3) or (5) does not mean that the agreement will be invalid, which arguably was the implication of *Bayoumi*. However, such an agreement for sale in the absence of a surveyor's report will only be able to take effect if an order under s.36(1) is made by the Commission prior to completion of the transaction.

In relation to the sale of land held on special trusts (for example, an almshouse) s.36(6) of the 1993 Act formerly provided that one month's prior notice of the proposed disposal had to be given publicly, in addition to any requirement for a surveyor's report under s.36(3) and (5). The amendments in para.128 of Sched.8 now make it clear that the one month's notice has to be prior to any *contractual* commitment by the trustees to the sale or disposal of the land. The reason is that it is not appropriate for charity trustees to enter into a contract for the sale of such land prior to public notice.

The self-regulating land disposal regime has since 1993 been backed by the requirement on the selling or acquiring charity trustees contained in s.37 of the 1993 Act to provide certain statements and certificates. As with the amendment to s.36(1) of the 1993 Act, the new s.37 now refers to 'conveyed' and 'transferred' rather than 'sold' which means that the relevant Commission order has to be obtained before completion of the transaction as opposed to before any contract for such a disposal.

It is a little puzzling that no attempt was made in the 2006 Act to extend the provisions of s.37 certificates of compliance with s.36(1) or (2) to the contract stage. To require the charity trustees to certify in the contract that they have complied with the s.36 processes by then would bring to the attention of the parties the requirement on the charity trustees to obtain a surveyor's advice prior to entering into any contract for disposal. Indeed, given the protection given to buyers by the provision of certificates of compliance in the documents effecting disposal (for example, the lease or the transfer itself), this would surely allow buyers to rely on a certificate of satisfaction in the contract, and would address issues of uncertainty between exchange of contracts and completion, which were demonstrated by *Bayoumi*.

The definition of 'connected person' in Sched.5 to the 1993 Act has been strengthened[2] to include:

- A person who is such either when the contract to dispose is made or when the disposal is completed – this change ensures that an order of the Commission under s.36(1) of the 1993 Act is still required if the person was a connected person at the date of the contract for sale but ceased to be so prior to completion of the sale.
- A person who is a business partner of a connected person.
- A person who is a civil partner of a connected person and also one who is living together with another person of the same sex as if they were civil partners.

When the new self-regulating regime for land disposals was introduced in 1992, s.36 of the 1992 Act provided that any provision in the trusts of a charity which required Charity Commission consent would cease to have effect. This particular section was retained within the rump of the 1992 Act when that Act was partially consolidated with the 1993 Act but has now been repealed by Sched.9 to the 2006 Act. Charities which still have express provisions requiring the Commission's consent to land disposals may be relieved to know that they will still be able to use the self-regulating regime, courtesy of the very last provision of the 2006 Act.[3]

7.4.2   Amendments to the section 38 procedure (mortgages of land)

Section 38 of the 1993 Act allows charities to mortgage their land without the need for authority from the Commission (or the court) provided that the trustees obtain and consider proper advice about the terms of the loan which is to be secured by the mortgage. The person giving such advice[4] should be someone who is qualified by ability and practical experience in financial matters, although not involved in making the loan; it could, for example, be a senior finance officer of the charity or one of the trustees or the charity's accountants.

Unfortunately this useful piece of self-regulation did not cover the situation where a grant was given to a charity and the obligations of the charity were required by the donor to be secured by a mortgage over the charity's land. Such mortgages will, by virtue of the amendments made to s.38 of the 1993 Act by s.27 of the 2006 Act, no longer require Charity Commission consent, provided that proper advice is obtained by the charity trustees. The proper advice is as to whether the terms of the grant are reasonable and within the ability of the charity to meet and also whether it is reasonable in the circumstances for the charity to undertake to discharge the obligations attached to the grant. The person giving that advice should have the same qualifications as one advising on a secured loan.[5]

The new regime also covers situations where after the mortgage is granted, future loans are made to the charity, to be secured on the same mortgage, for example on an 'all moneys due' basis. Again, no consent will be required of the Commission so long as proper advice is obtained by the charity trustees on each future loan transaction.

7.5   COMMENCEMENT

Many of the provisions in this chapter are due to be brought in by the third commencement order in early 2008. However, those relating to the relaxation of publicity surrounding schemes are due to be in force by early 2007. Further details can be found in the Implementation Plan in **Appendix 5**.

1   *Bayoumi v. Women's Total Abstinence Educational Union Ltd* [2004] 3 All ER 110.
2   See 2006 Act, Sched.8, para.178.
3   See 2006 Act, Sched.10, para.29(2)(b).
4   See 1993 Act, s.38(4), as amended.
5   Ibid.

8 ALTERATION OF GOVERNING DOCUMENTS

8.1 INTRODUCTION

Charities have to be responsive to the changing environment in which they operate. That means adapting not only to the changing needs of their beneficiaries but also to changing patterns of funding and, for some, changes in their role in public service delivery. Pressure to operate more efficiently or effectively can prompt charities to consider mergers, joint working arrangements or even hive-offs of parts of their activities to other organisations. Often, alteration of governing documents will be a prerequisite to making such changes.

The extent to which a charity can alter its governing documents depends upon the form of legal structure concerned. In some cases charity constitutions will confer express powers of variation on charity trustees. In the absence of any such powers, charitable trusts can only be altered by the court or the Charity Commission or by charity trustees under the statutory powers considered below. This chapter deals with changes under the 2006 Act to the powers to alter the objects of charitable trusts cy-près and the amended statutory powers for small charities to alter their objects and for charitable trusts generally to amend administrative provisions. The relaxation of restrictions on alteration of the memorandum and articles of association of charitable companies is also dealt with below.

8.2 CY-PRÈS ALTERATION OF THE PURPOSES OF CHARITABLE TRUSTS

8.2.1 The modern development of cy-près

Cy-près, from the Norman French phrase meaning 'as near as possible to it', is an expression used to refer to the alteration of the purposes of a charitable trust. Property can only be applied cy-près under a scheme of the court or the Charity Commission. In practice, almost all schemes are now made by the Commission. Cy-près schemes may be made not only for charitable trusts but also for charities established or regulated by Royal Charter (s.15(1) of the 1993 Act) or by statute (s.17 of the 1993 Act).

Since the law permits charitable trusts to continue in perpetuity, unlike non-charitable trusts, the doctrine of cy-près has a vital role in ensuring that charities can adapt to changing times. However, the doctrine has always been limited. Property can only be applied cy-près if a cy-près occasion has arisen. Before the 1960 Act, the only cy-près occasions were those where the objects had become impossible or impractical to carry out. A somewhat narrow interpretation of impossibility and impracticality was applied by the courts[1] with the result that the application of the doctrine was restricted. The 1960 Act extended cy-près by adding a list of other occasions in which property could be applied cy-près. It also dealt with the cy-près application of property given for a specific charitable purpose which had failed *ab initio*, that is where the gift had failed in its entirety from the outset.

8.2.2   The need for change

Over the years there have been many calls for the Commission to exercise its cy-près jurisdiction with greater flexibility. The Charity Commission's 1989 Annual Report contained the Commission's guidance on its application of the doctrine.[2] The Commission stated that its objective was to alter failing charitable purposes to the nearest practicable purpose that was both suitable and effective, bearing in mind the situation of the charity in the community and the needs of that community. An altered purpose might, for example, include purposes falling within other heads of charitable purpose, in particular where there was already adequate provision for the charitable head within which the original purpose was comprised. The Commission stated:

> In determining the new purposes, it is essential not to erect artificial barriers to a flexible use of the doctrine. Factors which are relevant but not overriding should not be rigidly applied as immutable legal rules or principles.

Despite the statements in the Commission's 1989 Annual Report, its approach to cy-près has in practice often been seen as restrictive and over legalistic. The Strategy Unit Report *Private Action, Public Benefit* called for a further review by the Commission of its application of its cy-près powers, with the aim of relaxing conditions for changing a charity's purposes. That review led to the inclusion in the 2006 Act of provisions intended to introduce more flexibility in the application of the doctrine. The 2006 Act both relaxes the conditions necessary to establish a cy-près occasion and alters the way in which property may be applied cy-près. The effect of the 2006 Act is to require the Commission (or the court) to take account of current circumstances, that is the current social and economic circumstances, when considering both when and how property may be applied cy-près. The 2006 Act also introduces new provisions to facilitate cy-près application of the proceeds of failed charity appeals. These changes are due to be brought into operation under the third commencement order under the 2006 Act, likely to be in early 2008.

1 'Where the directions of the testator do not offend against either law or public policy,
   the application of the cy près doctrine . . . is permissible only where the administration
   of the trust fund in accordance with the testamentary directions of the donor [is]
   practically impossible', per Kennedy L.J. in *Re Weir Hospital* [1910] 2 Ch 124.
2 Charity Commission Report 1989, paras.73–5.

8.3   CY-PRÈS OCCASIONS

The circumstances in which property could be applied cy-près were set out in
s.13(1) of the 1993 Act, re-enacting the provisions of the 1960 Act. Those provisions attached prime importance to the original purposes and the spirit of the original gift. The Act now places greater emphasis on current circumstances, coupling
most references to the *spirit of the gift* in s.13(1) of the 1993 Act, with reference to
the *social and economic circumstances prevailing at the time of the proposed alteration
of the original purposes*. The spirit of the gift concerned on the one hand and the
prevailing social and economic circumstances on the other are referred to as *the
appropriate considerations* (s.13(1A) of the 1993 Act as amended).

8.3.1   Cy-près occasions under the 2006 Act

Under s.13 of the 1993 Act as amended by the 2006 Act charitable property may
now be applied cy-près, in summary:

1. Where the original purposes, in whole or part:
    (a) have been as far as may be fulfilled; or
    (b) cannot be carried out, or not according to the directions given and to
         the spirit of the gift.
2. Where the original purposes provide a use for part only of the property.
3. Where the property available and other property applicable for similar chari-
    table purposes can more effectively be used in conjunction and to that end can
    suitably, having regard to the appropriate considerations, be made applicable
    to common purposes.
4. Where the original purposes were laid down by reference to an area which is
    no longer a unit for some other purpose, or by reference to a class of persons
    or to an area which has for any reason since ceased to be suitable, having
    regard to the appropriate considerations, or to be practical in administering
    the gift.
5. Where the original purposes, in whole or part, have:
    (a) been adequately provided for by other means; or
    (b) ceased, as being useless or harmful to the community or for other reasons
         to be in law charitable; or
    (c) ceased in any other way to provide a suitable and effective method of
         using the property, regard being had to the appropriate considerations.

8.3.2   The 'appropriate considerations'

The appropriate considerations must be taken into account where a value judgement has to be made as to the suitability or effectiveness of the use of charity property. That value judgement has previously been made by considering the *spirit of the gift* alone. The courts interpreted the spirit of the gift as equivalent to the *basic intention underlying the gift* as construed by reference to the governing document and any admissible evidence,[1] looking at substance rather than form.[2] Current social and economic circumstances now have to be weighed in the balance with the spirit of the gift.

The reference to *social and economic* considerations had its origins in the Strategy Unit Report. Although the term is not defined in the 2006 Act, it was used by the Strategy Unit when commenting on the need for the Charity Commission to take a wider view of charitable objects and the beneficiaries charities serve, rather than adopting a narrow regulatory focus on the internal operation of the charity in relation to its objects. In evidence to the Joint Committee, the Commission stated that 'We see social and economic impact as a modern interpretation of promoting the effective use of charitable resource'.[3]

Much of the pressure for relaxation of cy-près rules in the 2006 Act came from the need to enable charities to evolve and, particularly, to foster, rather than hamper, efforts by charities to merge or enter into joint working arrangements. Particularly helpful in this context is s.13(1)(c), which allows charitable objects to be amended so that property can be applied in conjunction with other property held for similar purposes. Prospective merger partners often have similar activities but different, albeit complementary, purposes. Merger may make strategic sense, yet may not fall within the spirit of the gift of the charities concerned. The requirement to consider prevailing social and economic circumstances should allow the Commission to be more flexible in facilitating mergers, assisted also by the changes to selection of altered purposes under the new s.14B of the 1993 Act (see **8.4.1** below).

---

1   *Re Lepton's Charity; Ambler v. Thomas* [1972] Ch 276.
2   See, e.g. *Varsani v. Jesani* [1999] Ch 219 per Morritt L.J. 'The Court is enjoined to have regard to the spirit of the gift . . . namely the basic intention underlying the gifts or the substance of the gift rather than the form of words used to express it or conditions imposed to effect it'.
3   Joint Committee on the Draft Charities Bill, Vol.III, Minutes of Evidence, Q.719.

8.4   CY-PRÈS SCHEMES

8.4.1   Principles for cy-près application

The guiding principle for the application of property cy-près, long established by case law, is that the new purposes should be as close as possible to the original purposes whilst also being both suitable and effective. The 2006 Act contains a new formulation of the principles for cy-près application. It requires consideration to be given to the suitability and effectiveness of the use of property to be applied cy-près, having regard to current social and economic circumstances. Under the new s.14B of the 1993 Act the power of application of property cy-près is now to be exercised having regard to:

- the spirit of the original gift;
- the desirability of securing that the property is applied for charitable purposes which are close to the original purposes; and
- the need for the charity concerned to have purposes which are suitable and effective in the light of current social and economic circumstances.

These factors reflect the inevitable tension between modernising reform and respect for an original charitable concept or the original donor's intentions. Proximity of purpose to the original charitable purpose is no longer to be paramount and equal weight has to be given to the need for the charity concerned to have purposes which are suitable and effective in current social and economic circumstances. This should encourage the Commission to be more flexible but it may also encourage trustees to be more creative in the ways in which they seek to develop the activities of their charities to pursue the needs of society.

8.4.2   Transfer of funds to other charities cy-près

A cy-près scheme can either set out new charitable purposes or can authorise the transfer of property to another charity with different charitable purposes. This latter provision is again particularly helpful where charities are merging, with the transfer of assets from one or more charities to another charity with suitable but distinct objects.

Where property is transferred cy-près to another charity, the scheme may impose a duty on the charity trustees of the recipient charity to ensure that the property is applied for purposes similar in character to the original purposes, insofar as reasonably practicable. Whilst this is helpful, in that it may encourage flexibility in the transfer of funds cy-près, the result of imposing conditions can be that the transferred funds are held as a restricted fund by the recipient charity, depriving the charity of some of the benefits of a full merger. Practical difficulties may also arise for the charity trustees, unless the scheme defines clearly the extent of the obligation to which they are subject.

8.5   CY-PRÈS AND GIFTS BY UNKNOWN OR DISCLAIMING DONORS

8.5.1   Failure at the outset of gifts for specific charitable purposes

Gifts for specific charitable purposes which fail at the outset can cause particular difficulties. Failure of this type often occurs where insufficient funds have been raised in response to a public appeal for a particular purpose or project. The funds cannot be applied cy-près unless a general charitable intention can be established, which is difficult where funds are given with a specific purpose in mind. Without such a general charitable intention, donors are entitled to the return of their donations if the project fails.

In practice, the problems can be easily prevented when drafting the terms of an appeal, by anticipating the possibility that the intended purpose may prove impossible to carry out. Provision can then be included for funds to be applied for other purposes by the charity concerned, broadening the purposes beyond the specific project for which the funds were raised.

As will be seen in **8.5.3** below, the 2006 Act encourages dealing with the possibility of failure when making appeals by introducing new provisions for gifts to be applied cy-près unless donors state that they want to be given the option to have their money back. If provision is not made in the appeal, however, then the default position is that, in the absence of a general charitable intention, the funds cannot be applied cy-près and are held on resulting trust for the donors. The practical difficulties that then arise in a typical appeal, where funds have been raised over a period of time and in a variety of ways, can readily be imagined.

8.5.2   Cy-près under section 14 of the 1993 Act and changes under the 2006 Act

To meet these difficulties the 1960 Act introduced provisions to allow property donated by unknown or disclaiming donors to be applied cy-près as if given for charitable purposes generally. These provisions, slightly extended in the 1992 Act, were then reproduced in s.14 of the 1993 Act.

Where donors are unidentified or cannot be found, an inquiry and advertisement procedure[1] must be followed but if no claim for the return of money donated is received, it can then be applied cy-près under s.14(1) of the 1993 Act. In some cases, however, the cumbersome advertisement and inquiry procedure need not be followed. Under s.14(3) of the 1993 Act the proceeds of cash collections from collecting boxes and funds raised by other means where one donation cannot be distinguished from another, are conclusively presumed to belong to donors who cannot be identified and so can be applied cy-près as if given for charitable purposes generally, even without advertisement and inquiry. In addition, under s.14(4) of the 1993 Act, the court has power to direct that other donations may be treated as belonging to unidentified donors so that they can be applied cy-près, again without inquiries and advertisement. The court must be satisfied that the value of the funds concerned does not justify the expense of advertising or that the donors could not reasonably expect a return of funds, given the nature, circumstances and amounts of the gifts and the time since they were made.

Under s.16 of the 2006 Act the Charity Commission is given the same powers as the court to give directions under s.14(4) of the 1993 Act. This will help to reduce the costs of dealing with a failed appeal. Unfortunately, the Commission's refusal of a direction under s.14(4) of the 1993 Act cannot be appealed to the Charity Tribunal; any appeal must be made to the High Court.

8.5.3   New provision for cy-près application of gifts made in response to appeals

Although s.14 of the 1993 Act is of some help in dealing with failed appeal funds, the procedures are nevertheless cumbersome and extremely time-consuming. It is always advisable to deal with the possible failure of an appeal in the terms of the appeal itself. This approach is encouraged by a welcome new provision under s.17 of the 2006 Act which introduces the new s.14A into the 1993 Act, providing for cy-près application of property given for specific charitable purposes which have failed. Reliance on the procedures in s.14 of the 1993 Act is no longer necessary so long as the appeal includes a statement dealing with the consequences of failure of the appeal, in accordance with new s.14A.

The new provisions apply to donations made in response to an appeal or solicitation for specific charitable purposes which has included a statement to the effect that if those purposes fail, the property will be applicable cy-près as if given for charitable purposes generally, unless the donor makes a *relevant declaration* at the time of making the gift.

In other words, donors are given the opportunity to say positively that their gift is for a particular charitable purpose and no other; if they do not make such a declaration, they cannot have their money back.

The new provisions apply to appeals for funds however made, covering not only donations made in response to written appeals, but also appeals on the television, radio or the Internet, at fundraising events and so forth.

If a donor makes a relevant declaration that he wishes the trustees to give him the opportunity to reclaim the property he has given (or a sum equal to its value at the time that the gift was made) then the property will not be applied cy-près. The trustees must then take the prescribed steps to:

- inform the donor of the failure of the specific charitable purposes for which the donation was made;
- enquire whether he wishes to request the return of the property donated; and
- return the property if he does indeed make such a request within the prescribed period.

The prescribed steps and the prescribed period are to be set out in regulations made by the Commission.

Where trustees have taken the prescribed steps and have either failed to find the donor, or the donor has not requested the return of the donated property within the prescribed period, then the property given can be applied cy-près under s.14(1) of the 1993 Act as if belonging to a donor who had disclaimed his right to have the property returned. Similarly, where specific charitable purposes have failed and the donor has not made a relevant declaration, the property can be applied cy-près under s.14(1) as if given by a donor who has disclaimed his right to the return of funds.

There is no prescribed wording for the relevant declaration to be made by donors. However, to ensure that the proceeds of failed appeals can be dealt with under s.14A, appeals should be accompanied by a simple statement that, if the intended purposes should fail, the property will be applied by the charity for other charitable purposes unless donors make a declaration when making the gift that they wish to be given the opportunity to ask for the return of their donations.

To avoid undue complication and to give the new provisions the widest possible application, where an appeal has been made on the basis of various solicitations, some of which are accompanied by statements within s.14A(2)(b) and some which are not, then a donor is taken to have responded to the solicitation which includes the statement, unless he can prove otherwise (see s.14A(8)(c)).

1   See the Charities (Cy-près Advertisements, Inquiries and Disclaimer) Regulations 1993.

8.6   POWER FOR SMALL UNINCORPORATED CHARITIES TO ALTER PURPOSES

8.6.1   Extension of powers under the 2006 Act

Power for small unincorporated charities to alter their purposes is contained in new s.74C of the 1993 Act. The provision will be brought into effect under the third commencement order under the 2006 Act, scheduled for early 2008. The power applies to charities with a gross income of £10,000 or less in the last financial year, replacing the limit of £5,000 under similar provisions in 1993 Act. The Minister may alter the annual income limit under s.74C(12). Unlike the equivalent powers under the 1993 Act, the new powers in s.74C apply to exempt charities and are therefore likely to be particularly useful in updating the purposes of subsidiary charities administered by exempt charities. The power to alter purposes does not, however, apply where a charity holds designated land, that is land held on trusts to be used for a particular purpose or purposes of the charity.

Where s.74C applies, charity trustees may amend their charity's purposes without the need to obtain a Charity Commission scheme under the Commission's cy-près powers.

8.6.2   When can small charities alter their purposes?

The statutory powers for small charities to amend their purposes, which originated in the Charities Act 1985 (1985 Act), have always been subject to less rigorous requirements than the cy-près powers. However, the application of the earlier provisions was limited by the requirement that the charity trustees had to be satisfied that the charity's existing purposes had ceased to be *conducive to a suitable and effective application of the charity's resources*. The new power is potentially more flexible, being based on what is expedient in the interests of the charity, albeit that what is in the interests of the charity has to be assessed on the basis of its existing objects.

The new power applies where a charity's trustees are satisfied that:

- it is expedient in the interests of the charity for the purposes to be replaced; and
- insofar as is reasonably practicable, the new purposes consist of or include purposes that are similar in character to those they replace.

Provided these conditions are met, the charity trustees may replace the charity's purposes with other charitable purposes which, so far as reasonably practicable, should consist of or include purposes similar in character to those they replace.

8.6.3   Procedure

The power must be exercised formally under a resolution, passed by a majority of not less than two-thirds of the charity trustees voting on the issue. Under s.74C(6), a copy of the resolution must then be sent to the Charity Commission, accompanied by a statement of the trustees' reasons.

Under s.74C(7), the Commission may require that public notice is given of the resolution and, if so, it must then take account of any representations made within 28 days. The Commission may also ask for additional information, concerning either the reasons for the resolution or the trustees' compliance with statutory procedures. Provided no objection is raised by the Commission, under s.74C(9) the trustees' resolution takes effect 60 days after its receipt by the Commission. The running of the 60-day period is, however, suspended whilst any public notice is given or additional information is provided under s.74A, as applied to these provisions by s.74C(10).

Appeal against the Commission's objection to a resolution under s.74C(2) may be made to the Charity Tribunal. The appeal may be brought either by the charity trustees or by any other person who may be affected by the decision. The Charity Tribunal has power to quash the Commission's decision.

8.7   POWER FOR UNINCORPORATED CHARITIES TO MODIFY POWERS OR PROCEDURES

8.7.1   Extension of trustees' powers under the 2006 Act

Under the new s.74D of the 1993 Act, the powers or procedures of any unincorporated charity may be amended by the charity trustees without seeking the approval of the Charity Commission. A similar power under the 1993 Act was previously only available to unincorporated charities with gross annual income below £5,000 and alterations only took effect if the Commission did not object. The new provisions extend the freedom to alter administrative provisions, without the Commission's consent, to all unincorporated charities, both large and small alike. The provisions are to be brought into operation under the first commencement order in early 2007.

8.7.2   What amendments may be made?

Like the previous power under the 1993 Act, the s.74D power allows alteration of any provision in the trusts of the charity:

- relating to any of the powers exercisable by the charity trustees in the administration of the charity; or
- regulating the procedure to be followed in connection with its administration.

Administrative powers arising by implication, such as a power to borrow in order to carry out the charity's purposes, as well as powers conferred by statute or under the general law, may be altered.[1]

Not all powers or procedures in the governing documents of an unincorporated charity are, however, regarded as within the scope of the power of amendment. Most important of all, the power cannot be used to benefit the charity trustees.[2] In addition, the Commission's Operational Guidance[3] relating to the previous powers under the 1993 Act concludes that the power cannot be used to introduce wholly new powers, only to modify administrative powers that the charity trustees have, whether express or implied, including statutory default powers. If this approach is carried through to the new provisions, it will significantly restrict the use of the new power, resulting in unincorporated charities being subject to greater regulation when modifying powers and procedures than charitable companies.

In addition, unincorporated charities, particularly trusts, have always offered freedom for settlors to entrench provisions as to the way a charity's objects might be carried out, for example, by prescribing the particular way an asset or premises may be used to further the charity's objects. Such provisions will not necessarily be part of a charity's charitable objects but nor are they clearly within s.74D. Charity trustees wishing to amend such 'hybrid' provisions may still require a Charity Commission scheme or order.

8.7.3   Procedure

Amendments under s.74D should be recorded by written resolution. If the charity is an unincorporated association, the resolution must be approved by the members of the association in general meeting, either by a majority of two-thirds of those voting on the matter, or by a decision taken without a vote but without any expression of dissent (s.74D(4)).

Although a copy of any resolution under s.74D should be sent to the Charity Commission to comply with s.3B(3)(a) and (b) of the 1993 Act as amended, the Commission's approval is not required. There is also no longer a requirement to give public notice of amendments.

---

1 See *Small Charities Provisions* (OG 201 B2), July 2006, para.3.2 which confirms this is the Commission's view under the similar powers in the 1993 Act.
2 *Re French Protestant Hospital* [1951] Ch 567 established that a power of amendment may not be used to confer a benefit on charity trustees unless this is contemplated in the power.
3 *Small Charities Provisions* (OG 201 B2), July 2006, para.3.6.

8.8   ALTERING THE CONSTITUTIONS OF CHARITABLE COMPANIES

8.8.1   Before the 2006 Act

Under the 1993 Act, the Commission's prior written consent was required to changes in a charitable company's objects clause and also to changes in any provision in its memorandum or articles of association directing or restricting the manner in which the company's property may be used or applied. This meant that prior consent was required for a wide range of changes, even of a modest character. Almost any change to a company's powers, for example, affects, directly or indirectly, the use or application of the company's assets and required consent. In operation, therefore, the 1993 Act put a veto on a wider range of alterations than was necessary in order to ensure that charitable companies could not use their powers of amendment in ways which conflict with the principles of charity law.

8.8.2   Relaxation of restrictions under the 2006 Act

The regulation of alterations of the memoranda and articles of association of charitable companies has now been relaxed under the 2006 Act. Only *regulated alterations* now require the prior written consent of the Charity Commission to be effective. Regulated alterations are defined under the new s.64(2A) of the 1993 Act as alterations of:

- the objects clause in the memorandum of association;
- any provision, whether in the memorandum or articles of association, directing the application of the company's assets on dissolution; and
- any provision where the alteration would provide authorisation for any benefit to be obtained by the company's directors or members or persons connected with them.

The Commission's approach to alteration of the objects of charitable companies prior to the 2006 Act was set out in its Operational Guidance.[1] Less stringent tests have been applied than for cy-près application prior to the 2006 Act. In practice, the Commission has required it to be established that there are good reasons in the best interests of the charity for making the change and that the changes are not so radical that they would not reasonably have been contemplated by those who supported the charity.

The Commission has treated additions and deletions as well as amendments as within the scope of *alterations* which required consent under the 1993 Act.[2] On this basis deletions and additions will constitute *regulated alterations* under the new provisions.

A *benefit* is widely defined under s.64(2B) to ensure that the Commission's prior written consent will be required for the provision of direct or indirect benefits of any nature, not just to directors, but also to members and connected persons. The test for connected persons is the same as that applying under the new s.73B(5) and (6) of the 1993 Act for the purposes of the new trustee remuneration powers (see **Chapter 10**).

The new provisions are more focused than those they replace but there remain instances where the prior consent of the Commission will be required for changes to powers or provisions of an essentially administrative character. For example, in the memoranda of older charitable companies it was common practice to set out the company's powers within the objects clause. An alteration of a power contained in the objects clause will continue to be a *regulated alteration* and will continue to require prior written consent. The memoranda of association of older charitable companies also frequently contain provisions requiring the Commission's prior consent to any amendment of the memorandum and articles of association, reflecting the pre-1982 requirements for charitable companies permitted to omit 'Limited' from their names. These provisions are not affected by the 2006 Act so consent will still be required. In practice the Commission is willing to agree to the removal of these provisions, which no longer serve any useful purpose, but that removal still entails obtaining the prior consent of the Commission.

Appeal against the Commission's decision to give or withhold consent to any regulated alteration under s.64(2) may be made to the Charity Tribunal. The appeal may be brought by the charity trustees, the charity itself or any other person who is, or may be, affected by the decision.

8.8.3   Companies Act 2006

A full discussion of the changes introduced by the Companies Act 2006 would require a separate book in itself, but it is necessary at this point to note the specific changes being introduced in connection with the memoranda and articles of association of companies. For new companies formed under the Companies Act 2006 the memorandum of association will, in effect, serve as a snapshot of the company at the date of its incorporation: the only information which it is required to contain is the list of subscribers and their shares/guarantees.

The objects will, in future, be contained within the articles, and the name of the company need only be recorded on the certificate of incorporation (although for the sake of practicality it will surely continue to be included on the face of new memoranda and articles of association). For existing companies the memorandum will be deemed to be incorporated into the articles of association, although there will be no need physically to do so.

1 See *Alterations to Governing Documents: Charitable Companies: When is Our Consent Required?* (OG 47 B2), September 2004, para.2.2.
2 See *Alterations to Governing Documents: Charitable Companies: The Legal Background* (OG 47 A1), December 2004, para.2.2.

8.9   AMENDMENT OF A CHARITABLE INCORPORATED ORGANISATION'S CONSTITUTION

A CIO[1] may amend its constitution by resolution of its members, subject to obtaining the prior written consent of the Charity Commission to the same range of changes as for charitable companies.

1 See **Chapter 11**.

9 POWERS TO SPEND CAPITAL AND MERGERS

9.1 INTRODUCTION

The Strategy Unit Report *Private Action, Public Benefit*[1] noted 'small but important barriers' in the way of charities wishing to change objects or update their constitutions, whether to allow organisations to develop and change or as a precursor to a merger. The report recommended that a package of legal measures be introduced to facilitate mergers and, more generally, the administrative running of charities. The focus of these measures was the promotion of the flexible use of charity endowments and practical assistance in carrying through mergers.

The new measures to relax restrictions on the alteration of governing documents were set out in **Chapter 8**. This chapter deals with the use of endowments, particularly permanent endowment, and then looks at specific provisions designed to make it easier for charities to merge.

---

1 See paras.4.57–4.68, pp.46–8.

9.2 PERMANENT ENDOWMENT

9.2.1 Practical difficulties with permanent endowment

Permanent endowment is charity property held on trusts[1] which restrict the expenditure of capital. It is unusual nowadays for a charity to be set up with permanent endowment but there are many long-established charities with substantial permanent endowment assets. However, it is not always obvious that a charity's funds are in fact permanent endowment. Under s.96(3) of the 1993 Act a charity is deemed for the purposes of that Act to have a permanent endowment unless all property held for the charity's purposes may be expended for those purposes without distinction between capital and income. The question of whether permanent endowment is held therefore involves the construction of the charity's governing document or, in the absence of a governing document, examination of any available extrinsic evidence.

Many permanently endowed charities hold investment funds generating income for the charity's purposes of which the capital, including capital gains, cannot be spent to support the charity's work. In other cases charities hold permanent endowment because they have assets which are settled on 'in-specie' trusts, that is trusts requiring their use for the charity's purposes. Land, for example, is often held for use for a charity's purposes, perhaps to found a school or an almshouse. Typically, the governing documents will set out powers to apply the charity's income but will not address the possibility that the land might ultimately be sold. In such cases there is usually no power to spend capital and the proceeds of sale can only be used to acquire other in-specie land or invested to generate income for the charity. This means, for example, that the proceeds of sale cannot be used to meet the costs of building on another part of the charity's in-specie land as a building is classified as a wasting asset, not a permanent asset of the charity.

In the context of charity restructuring and mergers, permanently endowed property cannot simply be decanted into another charity, winding up the permanently endowed charity, as this would amount to spending the endowment.[1] The solution is to transfer the trusteeship of permanent endowment property to the transferee charity or other corporate trustee. On an incorporation or merger this results in the transferee charity holding permanent endowment funds in subsidiary or linked charities. Very often, older charities or large charities which have developed through several mergers, will have innumerable permanently endowed subsidiaries, many of them relatively small. Although the funds can be administered and accounted for together with the main charity if a uniting direction[2] is obtained, this is nevertheless an unsatisfactory arrangement, with subsidiary funds seldom being used as efficiently as they might.

Permanent endowment also presents problems for charities wanting to invest on a total return basis, since capital gains of permanent endowment funds may not be spent as income. These well-publicised difficulties ultimately led to the introduction by the Charity Commission of its policy of sanctioning total return investment of permanent endowment funds by order.[3] The 2006 Act does not directly affect the total return issue and the Commission's policy and this aspect of permanent endowment is outside the scope of this book.[4]

9.2.2   Charity Commission powers to allow spending of permanent endowment before the 2006 Act

The Charity Commission in recent years has been prepared to exercise its power under s.26 of the 1993 Act to authorise expenditure of permanent endowment where it was satisfied that this was *expedient in the interests of the charity*. Where authority was given prior to the 2006 Act, this was almost invariably done on the basis that capital spent would be recouped out of income by instalments over a period of years, so that the capital was, in effect, an interest-free loan for that period. Inevitably, recoupment would often make substantial inroads into the charity's income and restrict its ability to carry on its charitable purposes. Trustees sometimes found the concept of 'borrowing' from their own charity difficult to understand.

9.2.3   The Charity Commission's new policy on spending and recoupment

The Commission has recently reviewed its policy on expenditure and recoupment of permanent endowment in the light of the wider changes to be introduced by the 2006 Act. In future, the Commission's powers will mainly be exercised in those situations where trustees do not wish to use the new powers in the 2006 Act allowing permanent endowment restrictions to be lifted, or where the Commission considers the charity has not established a case for the exercise of the powers applying to larger charities (see 9.5). The Commission now proposes to adopt a more flexible approach to expenditure and recoupment.

Each case will be considered on its own merits. The critical issue when the Commission considers expenditure of permanent endowment, is what is expedient in the interests of the charity, taking account of the nature of the expenditure and the expected benefits but also having regard to the availability of alternative funds and the spirit of the original gift.

Whether recoupment will be required should again be determined on the basis of what is expedient in the interests of the charity. The Commission will consider the nature of the charity's work and the likely long-term demands on its services, as well as the impact that recoupment would have on ongoing work. Recoupment is certainly appropriate if failure to recoup would unreasonably favour the charity's present beneficiaries at the expense of future beneficiaries. Where the benefits are long term, recoupment is less likely to be required, for example, where the proceeds of sale of in-specie land are to be used to provide buildings which have a substantial life on other in-specie land, recoupment may not be required. The Commission is understood to be more likely to require recoupment if the expenditure comes from permanently endowed investment funds, than from the proceeds of sale of in-specie land or other functional permanent endowment, as investment assets might be assumed to have been intended to sustain the long-term future of the charity.

---

1   Permanent endowment property is distinct from income or expendable capital set aside by charities in what they may call endowment or reserve funds. These funds are not permanent endowment but 'designated funds' which the trustees have reserved for a particular purpose.

2   *Re Faraker; Faraker v. Durrell* [1912] 2 Ch 488.

3   Uniting direction by the Charity Commission under 1993 Act, s.96(6).

4   See *Endowed Charities: A Total Return Approach to Investment Overview* (OG 83 A1), May 2001.

5   The Law Commission issued a Consultation Paper (Paper No. 175) *Capital and Income in Trusts: Classification and Apportionment* in 2004 concerning possible reform of traditional trust classification of income and capital. Final proposals are awaited.

9.3   OVERVIEW OF NEW POWERS TO SPEND PERMANENT ENDOWMENT

Powers allowing small charities to spend permanent endowment were first introduced in the 1985 Act, later extended in the 1992 Act and re-enacted in the 1993 Act. The 2006 Act replaces those provisions and confers powers for all charities to spend permanent endowment, subject to satisfying various conditions.

The rationale for these new powers is that there are innumerable permanent endowment funds held by charities where the income is too low to be used efficiently or satisfactorily. The new powers provide an opportunity to rationalise these funds and ensure their more effective use. In addition, the power to spend permanent endowment capital of larger funds provides a welcome degree of flexibility for the future.

The basic framework of the powers to spend permanent endowment is contained in the new s.75 of the 1993 Act. Additional provisions are grafted on to this basic regime for charities with permanent endowment capital of over £10,000 given for a particular purpose by a donor or group of donors. The powers relating to larger endowment funds are contained in s.75A with further provisions relating to special trusts in s.75B.

Permanent endowment is always held on trust, so cannot be part of the general funds of a corporate charity, so the powers apply only to unincorporated charities. The powers will, however, apply to special trusts held by incorporated charities under s.75B and to charities of which a corporate charity or other company acting as a trust corporation acts as sole trustee. This is a common arrangement, for example, following incorporation of an unincorporated charity holding permanent endowment funds.

The 2006 Act also extends powers under s.74 of the 1993 Act for small unincorporated charities, including those with permanent endowment, to transfer property to other charities. These powers are also likely to be helpful in rationalising charity structures and funds on the merger of charities with subsidiaries or linked charities. However, they will in practice be less useful than the powers to spend permanent endowment in the new s.75 of the 1993 Act. The powers under s.74 to transfer property apply only to small charities and also require funds to be transferred subject to existing restrictions, including permanent endowment provisions. In contrast, the powers to spend permanent endowment under s.75 allow permanent endowment restrictions to be lifted. The s.75 power can therefore be used to transfer funds to another charity outright, for example on a merger, or to provide funds for spending on the charity's work.

Originally, the new powers to spend capital contained in the Bill did not apply to in-specie land held on trust to be used for the charity's purposes. This would have significantly limited the usefulness of the new powers in practice. Following representations by the Charity Law Association, a change was introduced at the eleventh hour so that the power to spend permanent endowment capital was extended to cover in-specie land. This contrasts with the provisions under the new s.74 of the 1993 Act allowing small charities to transfer property (see **9.7**), where the power does not extend to any charity holding in-specie land.

The new powers in ss.74 and 75 are due to be brought into operation under the third commencement order under the 2006 Act, likely to be in early 2008.

9.4   GENERAL POWER TO SPEND PERMANENT ENDOWMENT

The general power to spend permanent endowment under the new s.75 of the 1993 Act applies to all permanent endowment funds except funds within the scope of s.75A, that is where the charity's gross income exceeds £1,000 and in addition the fund's value exceeds £10,000, and is entirely made up of contributions from a particular donor or grantor or group of donors or grantors *in pursuit of a common purpose* (as to which see **9.5.3** below).

Under the general powers in s.75, charity trustees may resolve to release the whole or any part of an 'available endowment fund' from restrictions on expenditure of capital, provided they are satisfied that the purposes for which the fund is held could be carried out more effectively if the capital of the fund, or the relevant part of it, could be spent as well as the income (s.75(4)).

The definition of 'available endowment fund' covers all the charity's permanent endowment held on the same trusts, or any permanent endowment which is subject to distinct trusts. It is therefore possible for a charity holding a number of permanent endowment funds to resolve to release some but not all of the funds from restriction on expenditure. Similarly, if a charity is exercising the power in relation to a number of permanent endowment funds held on different trusts, the charity trustees must be satisfied in each case that the purposes for which the funds are held could more effectively be carried out if the capital could be spent.

There is no requirement to obtain the Charity Commission's agreement to the exercise of the powers relating to small endowments under s.75.

9.5   RESTRICTIONS APPLYING TO LARGER ENDOWMENTS GIVEN FOR PARTICULAR PURPOSES

There is a more restrictive regime for expenditure of larger permanent endowment funds given for particular purposes, under the new s.75A of the 1993 Act. Where s.75A applies, the Charity Commission's agreement to spending of permanent endowment has to be obtained.

9.5.1   When does the regulated regime apply?

Under s.75A(1) and (2) this more regulated regime applies where:

- the capital of the fund consists entirely of property given:
    - by a particular individual (including by will);
    - by a particular institution (by way of grant or otherwise); or
    - by two or more individuals or institutions in pursuit of a common purpose, and
- the financial condition is met, namely:
    - the relevant charity's gross income in the last financial year exceeded £1,000; and
    - the market value of the endowment fund exceeds £10,000.

9.5.2   The financial condition

Although the 2006 Act refers to s.75A restrictions as applying to 'larger' charities, the thresholds in the financial condition are low. The market value threshold applies to the individual endowment funds concerned, so that where a charity has several separate endowment funds, the threshold is applied separately to each. However, the income threshold relates to the charity's gross income, not that of the individual endowment fund. Even small endowment funds, therefore, potentially fall within s.75A.

These thresholds will be included in the review of all thresholds to be undertaken a year after Royal Assent. The financial conditions may be varied by substitution of different sums by order made by the Minister. In theory, this could happen as the new section is brought into force.

9.5.3   Sole donors or donors with a common purpose

In addition to the financial condition, s.75A only applies if the capital of the endowment fund consists entirely of property given by a particular individual or institution (including by way of grant) or by two or more individuals or institutions 'in pursuit of a common purpose'. The requirement is for the capital to have been *entirely* given by the donor or donors concerned. Where capital given by a sole donor has been swelled by accumulation of the income or other accretions, it would nevertheless remain property given entirely by a particular individual or institution. However, if several donors have made contributions to permanent endowment, the fund will only fall within s.75A if all contributions were made 'in pursuit of a common purpose'.

When the powers to spend permanent endowment first appeared in the Bill, the restrictions applied only to cases where capital had been provided by a sole donor. The reference to several donors was introduced in response to criticism that the protection of the additional regulation under s.75A was appropriate not only in cases of a single donor but also where a family, family settlements or a group of individuals had together contributed to the fund.

The expression 'in pursuit of a common purpose' is not defined in the 2006 Act and was not clarified during consideration of the Bill. It gives rise to a number of questions.

The requirement for a *common purpose*, where two or more donors contribute to a permanent endowment fund, must be taken to add meaning and must therefore restrict the breadth of the provision without those words. Therefore, the mere fact that, over the years, several donors have all made contributions which are held on the same trusts, should not of itself be sufficient to bring s.75A into play. On the other hand, where donors act contemporaneously or in concert, this suggests they are acting in pursuit of a common purpose. Every case will have to be looked at on its own facts.

Cy-près alteration of an endowment fund's objects also gives rise to interesting questions. Whether donations made before and after a charity's objects have been altered cy-près can be said to be made in pursuit of a common purpose is not clear. This may depend on the nature of the cy-près occasion and extent of the alteration of the trusts. Again, every case will have to be considered on its own facts and in borderline cases, reference to the Commission is advisable.

9.5.4   Charity Commission concurrence and procedure

The charity trustees' powers under s.75A to free capital of available endowment funds largely mirror those of s.75; however, under s.75A, the completed resolution to release funds from restriction on expenditure must be sent to the Charity Commission with a statement of the trustees' reasons for passing it (s.75A(5)).

In considering whether or not to concur with the resolution, the Commission is required under s.75A(8) to take into account any available evidence as to the wishes of the donor or donors and any subsequent changes in circumstances, including the charity's financial position, the needs of its beneficiaries and the social, economic and legal environment within which the charity operates. The Commission may only concur with the resolution if it is satisfied that this would accord with the spirit of the gift (despite the fact that the donor's restriction on expenditure of capital would be lifted) and that the charity trustees have complied with the statutory procedures (see s.75A(9)).

The Commission can require the charity trustees to give public notice of the proposals. If so, it must then take account of any representations made by interested parties within 28 days of the public notice being given (s.75A(6)). The Commission may also require the charity trustees to provide additional information, either as to the circumstances behind their decision to exercise their powers, or as to their compliance with the statutory procedures (s.75A(7)).

The resolution comes into effect only once the Commission informs the charity trustees that it concurs with the resolution or, failing that, the deadline for the Commission to inform the charity trustees that it does not concur has passed (s.75A(12)). The deadline is the end of the three-month period beginning with

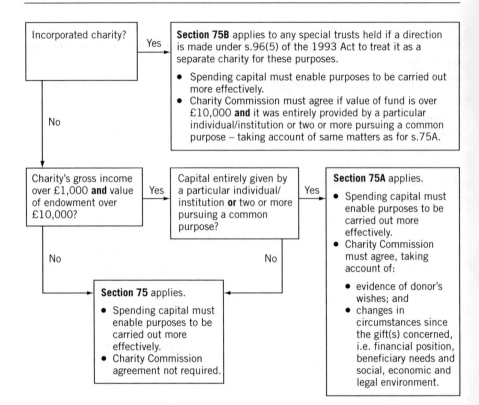

Figure 9.1   Spending permanent endowment under the new section 75 of the 1993 Act

the date on which public notice of the resolution was given or, if no notice was required to be given, then the earlier date on which the Commission received the copy of the resolution from the charity trustees.

A decision of the Commission not to concur with a resolution under s.75A may be appealed to the Charity Tribunal. The Tribunal has power to quash the decision and may refer the matter back to the Commission.

9.6   POWER TO SPEND CAPITAL SUBJECT TO SPECIAL TRUSTS

The term 'special trust' is used in the 1993 Act to mean 'property which is held and administered by or on behalf of a charity for any special purposes of the charity, and is so held and administered on separate trusts relating only to that property' (1993 Act, s.97(1)). For example, a fund given to a school for the repair of a particular building or war memorial might be a special trust. A special trust is not, by itself, a charity for the purposes of Part VI of the 1993 Act, that is for the purposes of charity accounts, reports and returns.

The power under the new s.75B of the 1993 Act applies to available endowment funds of any special trust for which the charity trustees have obtained a direction under s.96(5) of the 1993 Act, that the special trust is to be treated as a separate charity for the purpose of s.75B. This allows incorporated charities holding funds in special trusts to benefit from the new powers to spend capital.

Like the powers under s.75 and s.75A, the power under s.75B to spend permanent endowment capital held in special trusts applies where the charity trustees are satisfied that the purposes of the special trust could be carried out more effectively if all or part of the capital could be spent. The Charity Commission's agreement is required for larger funds with a value of over £10,000 where the capital was given by a particular individual or institution, or by two or more individuals or institutions pursuing a common purpose (s.75B(4)). Where concurrence of the Charity Commission is required, the same procedures and provisions apply as under s.75A.

As in the case of a resolution under s.75A, appeal against the non-concurrence of the Commission under s.75B may be made to the Charity Tribunal.

9.7   SMALL CHARITIES AND THE TRANSFER OF PROPERTY TO OTHER CHARITIES

9.7.1   Which charities can use the new powers?

For unincorporated charities with gross annual income not exceeding £10,000 the new s.74 of the 1993 Act allows the transfer of property to another charity or other charities. In contrast to the new s.75 powers these do not apply if the charity holds designated land, that is in-specie land held on trust to be used for the particular purpose or purposes of the charity.

There are two different regimes. One applies to charities with expendable capital only and the other to charities which are, in whole or part, permanently endowed. The basic provisions applying to charities with expendable endowment only are to be found in ss.74 and 74A. These provisions are modified under s.74B for charities holding permanent endowment.

9.7.2   When can property be transferred?

The powers build upon, and extend, similar powers under the original s.74 of the 1993 Act. The superseded powers could only be exercised where the transferor charity's purposes had ceased to be 'conducive to a suitable and effective application of the charity's resources', echoing elements of the cy-près regime.

In contrast, the new transfer powers apply where the transferor charity's trustees are satisfied that:

- the transfer is expedient in the interests of furthering the purposes for which the property concerned is held; and

- the purposes (or any of the purposes) of the transferee charity or charities are substantially similar to the purposes (or any of the purposes) of the transferor charity.

Not all the purposes of the transferor and transferee charities need be similar and a transferee charity may therefore have wider purposes. However, under s.74(10), the transfer must be made subject to any existing restrictions on expenditure and on the basis that it will be applied by the transferee charity for purposes substantially similar to those of the transferor charity. This is reinforced by s.74(11), which imposes that obligation on the charity trustees of the transferee charity or charities.

9.7.3   Charity Commission concurrence and procedure

Charity trustees must formally exercise their transfer powers by resolution, passed by a majority of not less than two-thirds of the charity trustees who vote. A copy of the resolution must then be sent to the Charity Commission with a statement of the reasons. There then follows a 60-day period before the resolution can take effect, allowing for consideration by the Commission.

During that period the Commission may ask for additional information, either as to the background circumstances or as to the trustees' compliance with the statutory procedures. If further information is asked for, the 60-day period is suspended, from the date on which the direction to provide the information is given to the date on which the information is provided.

The Commission may also require trustees to give public notice of the resolution. It must then take into account any representations made by interested parties within 28 days of the giving of public notice. If public notice has to be given, the 60-day period is suspended and resumes 42 days after the date on which public notice has been given.

The time-scale for provision of information and the giving of public notice is kept in check under s.74A(6) which provides that the resolution is treated as if it has never been passed if the 60-day period has been suspended for a period or periods of over 120 days.

Assuming no objection is raised by the Charity Commission, at the end of the 60-day period the resolution takes effect and the charity trustees must then transfer all the property of the transferor charity in accordance with the resolution and within a time-frame to be agreed between the transferor and transferee charity or charities. The Commission can be asked to make a vesting order to transfer property.

If the Commission objects to a proposed transfer under a resolution, it must notify the charity trustees in writing within the 60-day period. Objection may be based either on procedural grounds, that is if any of the requirements of s.74 have not been complied with, or on the merits of the proposals.

These time-scales are an administrative nightmare and unnecessarily complicated, particularly as they are designed to help small charities. Our advice is to take the initiative with the Commission to obtain its positive concurrence.

Appeal against the Commission's decision to object to a transfer resolution may be made to the Charity Tribunal. The appeal may be brought either by the charity trustees or by any other person who is or may be affected by the decision, therefore including the charity trustees of any proposed transferee charity. The Charity Tribunal has power to quash the Commission's decision.

9.7.4   Transfer powers where a charity has permanent endowment

Where a charity has permanent endowment, the operation of new s.74 of the 1993 Act is modified by s.74B. A permanently endowed charity will often also have non-permanent endowment or 'unrestricted' property. In that case the additional requirements only affect the permanent endowment property. The resolution under s.74 must, however, cover both the charity's permanent endowment and its unrestricted property.

The additional requirements for the transfer of permanent endowment property concern the matching of the purposes of the transferor and transferee charities and compliance with guidance provided by the Charity Commission.

Under s.74B(6) and (7), where permanent endowment property is transferred, the transferee charity must have purposes which are substantially similar to all the purposes of the transferor charity. Where permanent endowment is to be transferred to two or more charities, each of the transferee charities must have purposes substantially similar to one or more of the transferor charity's purposes and all the transferee charities together must have purposes which are substantially similar to all the purposes of the transferor charity.

Charity Commission guidance must be taken into account by the transferring charity trustees in any decision as to the division of their permanent endowment funds between proposed transferee charities. In addition, the charity trustees of any transferee charity must take account of the Commission's guidance on their obligations to ensure that the transferred property is applied for purposes that are substantially similar to those of the transferor charity.

Following a transfer under these powers, permanent endowment will remain subject to permanent endowment restrictions under s.74(10)(b). However, the property will be held as permanent endowment property of the transferee charity or charities and the transferor charity will cease to exist on the transfer. The main benefit of the new powers will therefore be in the ability to rationalise relatively small permanent endowment funds, amalgamating funds and easing administration.

Charity trustees proposing to use the s.74 powers to transfer to other charities should consider making resolutions under s.75 first to enable expenditure of permanent endowment.

9.8   MERGER OF CHARITIES

9.8.1   Before the 2006 Act

There are two significant practical problems faced when charities merge or incorporate (that is when an unincorporated charity transfers its activities and assets to a new corporate charity). One is the time and cost involved in the laborious transfer of assets and operations to the successor or transferee charity. The other is the risk that future gifts and legacies will be lost if a charity transferring its assets on a merger or incorporation is then wound up. In practice, charities which transfer their assets to a successor on a merger or incorporation are very often left on the charity register in 'shell' form to receive and apply any future gifts. This is nevertheless administratively inconvenient, not only for charity trustees but also for the Charity Commission and of course confusing to members of the public who consult the charity register.

9.8.2   The objectives of the 2006 Act

The 2006 Act provides for a new register of charity mergers to be set up by the Charity Commission. Provided a charity merger is registered, future gifts and legacies will transfer automatically to the successor charity following the merger. In addition, there is a new procedure intended to streamline transfers of title to property under a single pre-merger declaration, without the need for further documentation. Despite the register being called the register of charity mergers, it includes the merger of charities that occurs as part of the process of an unincorporated charity's incorporation. None of the provisions, however, applies to the amalgamation of CIOs which are dealt with by the new ss.69K–69M of the 1993 Act.[1]

9.8.3   Register of charity mergers

The new s.75C of the 1993 Act provides for the Commission to establish and maintain a register of charity mergers. The register will record details of every 'relevant charity merger' which is notified to the Commission.

A 'relevant charity merger' is defined under s.75C(4) as a merger of two or more charities where one (the transferee), acquires all the property of the other or others, each of which (the transferors) ceases to exist or will cease to exist following the transfer of its property. Alternatively, a relevant charity merger can be a merger of two or more charities into a new charity, with the transferor charities again ceasing to exist on or after the transfer of their property. This is modified for charities which hold permanent endowment in addition to other property, to reflect the fact that permanently endowed charities will not cease to exist and will only transfer non-permanent endowment property, along with the trusteeship of permanent endowment funds.

A charity merger can only be registered once the transfers of property to the transferee charity have taken place. However, a merger can be registered at any time after the transfer of property, so that mergers that took place long before the 2006 Act can be registered.

The requirements for the notification to the Commission of mergers are set out in s.75C(6)–(9). If the vesting declaration procedure is used (see **9.8.5** below), the merger must be registered under s.75C(7), otherwise registration of the merger is at the option of the charity trustees of the transferee charity. If they decide to register, then under s.75C(8), they must provide the Charity Commission with a notification:

- specifying the transfer or transfers of property involved and the relevant date or dates of transfers;
- including a statement that appropriate arrangements have been made for the discharge of liabilities of the transferor charity or charities; and
- in cases where notification is required because a vesting declaration has been entered into, giving details of the vesting declaration.

9.8.4   Contents of the mergers register

The new s.75D of the 1993 Act deals with the information that will be set out on the register. This will include the date when the transfer or transfers of property took place and whether or not a vesting declaration was made, together with any other information the Commission thinks fit. The mergers register is to be open to the public for inspection at all reasonable times. The register of charities is of course accessible on the Charity Commission website **www.charitycommission. gov.uk** without charge and the same arrangements may well be adopted for the mergers register.

9.8.5   Pre-merger vesting declaration

The vesting declaration procedure introduced under the new s.75E of the 1993 Act will provide a mechanism for transfer of title to a transferee charity on a merger. A vesting declaration must be made by deed by the charity trustees of the transferor and must provide for the transfer of all of the transferor charity's property to the transferee on a specified date. The declaration then operates to vest the legal title in the transferee without the need for any further document.

This is similar to the provisions of s.40 of the Trustee Act 1925 for the automatic vesting of property on changes of trustees. Like those provisions, s.75E also provides for some exceptions to automatic vesting. Under s.75E(3) the exceptions are:

- land held by the transferor charity as security;
- land subject to a covenant against assignment without the consent of some other person, such as landlord's consent to the assignment of a lease, unless the consent has been obtained before the specified date;
- any shares, stock, annuity or other property which is only transferable in books kept for the purpose, or is required by legislation to be transferred in some other particular manner.

Under s.75E(4) the transfer of title of registered land under a vesting declaration must still be registered with the Land Registry.

Looked at in the context of the overall arrangements between merging charities, the vesting declaration will have relatively limited scope. It only serves to vest title to property, so a transfer agreement will still be necessary to transfer beneficial ownership of the property, to record the consent of the transferee and to deal with the transferee's assumption of liabilities, the transfer of employees (under the TUPE Regulations[2]) and the benefit of contracts, the giving of warranties and indemnities.

Where the vesting declaration would appear to be most useful is in helping charities with registered land to cut down the number of separate transfer forms needed to be completed, albeit that separate applications to change the land register will have to be made.

Charities which do not cease to exist on a merger, for example where a consent required to the transfer of an asset (such as a lease) cannot be obtained, cannot make use of the vesting declaration procedure. In addition mergers which involve a transferor charity's property passing to more than one charity cannot register and vesting declarations cannot be used. The charity trustees could, however, apply to the Charity Commission for a vesting order under s.16 of the 1993 Act.

The limited scope of the vesting declaration under s.75E can be contrasted with the very much more comprehensive provisions applying to the amalgamation of CIOs under s.69M of the 1993 Act. Under s.69M, provision is made for the transfer of property, rights and liabilities on amalgamation of CIOs, automatically transferring not only legal title but beneficial entitlement. Unfortunately, the variety of possible legal structures involved in other charity mergers, with the differences in the way in which liabilities are incurred (whether by a corporate charity itself or by charity trustees of unincorporated charities), prevented a similar approach being taken to non-CIO amalgamations.

9.8.6   Registered charity mergers and future gifts and legacies

Under the new s.75F of the 1993 Act, where a merger is entered on the register of charity mergers, any gift to one or other of the transferor charities which takes effect once the merger is registered, will automatically take effect as a gift to the transferee charity. There is one exception, that of *excluded gifts*. These are gifts to a transferor charity with permanent endowment where the gift is intended to be held as part of the permanent endowment rather than part of its other property. The theory of this is that the permanent endowment fund will not have ceased to exist on the merger and any future gift would not be lost and will continue to be received into the permanent endowment fund; it is therefore important for charities to ensure that the existence of such funds is known and of course recorded in their accounts.

The automatic transfer of future gifts and legacies has been warmly welcomed. Charities which have long since merged, including those that have incorporated, but have decided not to wind up transferor charities for fear of losing legacies and gifts, will be able to register the merger and secure any future gifts. This will offer opportunities to rationalise old 'shell' charities, simplifying structures and administration.

---

1   See 11.9.
2   Transfer of Undertakings (Protection of Employment) Regulations 2006, SI 2006/246.

10 TRUSTEESHIP

The volunteer trustee who acts altruistically, without thought of benefiting himself, his family or friends, and who makes decisions solely in the best interests of the charity and those whom it is established to serve, remains a crucial element in the administration of charities in England and Wales. For this reason the Commission has for many years underlined the need for the selection of trustees with the appropriate set of skills, experience, qualifications, background and enthusiasm for each charity. The 2006 Act attempts to bolster this concept of the altruistic trustee by easing the personal burden of regulation, providing for the new CIO (see **Chapter 11**) and allowing for the payment of a minority of trustees, whilst ensuring that trustees avoid conflicts of interest.

10.1 WAIVER OF A TRUSTEE'S DISQUALIFICATION

Section 72 of the 1993 Act lists half a dozen events or scenarios in which a person would become disqualified from being a charity trustee. In short these are:

- if he has been convicted of any offence involving dishonesty or deception;
- if he has been adjudged bankrupt or made an arrangement with creditors;
- if he has been removed from the office of charity trustee or trustee for a charity by an order on the grounds of any misconduct or mismanagement in the administration of the charity; or
- if he is subject to a disqualification order under the Company Directors Disqualification Act 1986 or to an order made under s.429(2)(b) of the Insolvency Act 1986 (failure to pay under county court administration order).

Removal from office or disqualification as a director includes action taken by the courts under legislation in Scotland and Northern Ireland.

However, someone so disqualified had the right under s.72 to seek a waiver from the Commission, in relation either to a particular charity or to a type of charity. Section 35 of the 2006 Act introduces a new provision into s.72 of the 1993 Act which ensures that a person who has been disqualified for more than five years must be relieved from that disqualification unless the Commission decides that there is good reason not to do so.

As is the case with s.72, this rehabilitation of a disqualified trustee cannot be granted in relation to a charitable company where the person concerned is prohibited from acting as a director under the Company Directors Disqualification Act 1986 and leave has not been granted for him to act as a director of any other company.

10.2   REMUNERATION OF TRUSTEES

10.2.1   The principle of voluntary trusteeship

The essence of trusteeship, as developed for centuries by the courts, is that a trustee owes a duty of loyalty to the trust which should not be compromised. In the case of a private trust, that duty is owed to individual beneficiaries who can, if they have relevant capacity, waive that duty partially or even wholly. In the case of a charitable trust the trustee's duty is owed to the public on whose behalf the Charity Commission has been established as a watchdog. Payment of remuneration or any other valuable benefit to a trustee could compromise that duty of loyalty to the trust and is not permitted unless the constitution allows it.

Although the concept of loyalty to the charity has been developed under trust law, that duty is also owed by any person who is in a fiduciary relationship to the charity, that is one who is a 'charity trustee' as defined by the 1993 Act.[1] Use of diverse nomenclature does not always make for easy understanding, but such a person can be a director of a charitable company,[2] a member of the charity's council, board or management committee, a school governor or a trustee of one of the new CIOs.

It was clear from the debates leading up to the 2006 Act that the concern of many in the voluntary sector and in the legislature was that the principle of the volunteer trustee should remain at the heart of charities. In moving the second reading of the Bill in the House of Lords, the Minister[3] introduced the provision for trustees to be paid for certain types of service, provided that conditions were observed to ensure that any remuneration was proportionate and in the best interests of the charity and that conflicts of interest between the remunerated trustee and the charity were avoided. She continued:

> I emphasise that the Bill will not allow payment for carrying out the duties of trusteeship; nor will it allow a charity's paid employees to be trustees at the same time. It preserves the essence of the voluntary principle of trusteeship.

In addition to remuneration clauses, with which we deal below, there are some statutory provisions allowing remuneration of trustees in particular types of charity.[4] In addition, the Charity Commission has for many years had the power under s.26 of the 1993 Act to order a trustee to be paid for a particular purpose if it is expedient in the interests of the charity.

10.2.2   Remuneration clauses

It is commonplace in will-writing to include a charging clause to allow a professional executor to be paid for the services of himself or his firm on the same basis as if he were not an executor/trustee but was employed to act on behalf of the executors/trustees. There are two issues inherent in such a clause:

- The conflict of loyalties between the professional trustee and his trust remains, whatever the charging clause says, so the decision to appoint and remunerate him must be properly managed to ensure that he does not benefit from the trust to any greater extent than would another professional with similar skills employed to act on behalf of the trust.
- It should not be assumed that the professional's fellow executors/trustees would wish to employ him for all matters within the competence of his profession; they should be given the opportunity to decide whether some other professional would do all or part of the necessary professional work better, more efficiently or cheaply than their co-trustee, particularly where specialist skills are required.

It is therefore already common practice to provide in charity constitutions for the payment to a trustee for services or goods which he might provide to the charity, whether at full charge or at a discount. The better charging clauses[5] make it clear, precisely in order to manage the inevitable conflict of interest, that before it can be agreed that a trustee should be paid or otherwise take a benefit the following hurdles should be jumped:

- the goods or services in question must actually be required by the charity;
- the nature and level of remuneration is no more than reasonable;
- no more than a certain proportion (preferably one-third but certainly not more than half) of trustees should be subject to such an arrangement at any time; and
- whenever a trustee has a personal interest to be discussed at a meeting he must declare that interest, must withdraw from the meeting (unless expressly invited to remain to provide information), must not be counted in the quorum for the meeting during discussion of that issue and must not take part in any vote on the issue.

10.2.3   The new remuneration clause for trustees providing services

Trustees and other persons connected to the trustees (see 'Connected persons', p.64) will now be allowed under s.36 of the 2006 Act (introducing a new s.73A to the 1993 Act) to be remunerated for providing services if four conditions are satisfied:

- The amount of the remuneration is reasonable and is set out in writing (s.73A(3)).[6]

- The remaining trustees must be satisfied that it would be in the best interests of the charity for that trustee to provide the relevant services and for the agreed price (s.73A(4)).
- If more than one trustee is being remunerated they must collectively be in a minority (s.73A(5)).
- The charity's constitution must not contain any express provision against remuneration being paid to that trustee (s.73A(6)). Many charities have constitutions which contain the old standard clause which, whilst not completely barring remuneration, requires the consent of the Charity Commission; others have a complete bar on personal benefits to trustees. Either way, it may be that the Commission would be prepared to exercise its powers[7] to remove such a bar and thus allow the new statutory powers to be used.

The remuneration envisaged here is for trustees who are able to provide services to their charity. It does not include remuneration under a contract of employment or remuneration for being a trustee; in other words, unless the constitution so provides, the charity's paid staff still cannot be trustees and a trustee cannot be paid for sitting at a meeting or carrying out his functions as a trustee (s.73A(7)). However, a trustee will still be able to be remunerated (s.73A(8)) if:

- the constitution of the charity so allows; or
- the court or the Charity Commission has so ordered; or
- there is any other relevant statutory provision to that effect.

Supplementary provisions

Under s.73B the trustees must before entering into an agreement for the remuneration of one of their number:

- take account of guidance on the subject issued by the Charity Commission;[8] and
- exercise the duty of care in s.1(1) of the Trustee Act 2000, namely:

such care and skill as is reasonable in the circumstances, having regard in particular:

(a) to any special knowledge or experience that he has or holds himself out as having, and

(b) if he acts as trustee in the course of a business or profession, to any special knowledge or experience that it is reasonable to expect of a person acting in the course of that kind of business or profession.

The remuneration envisaged under the new s.73A of the 1993 Act is for services only and covers goods only insofar as they are supplied in connection with those services (s.73B(4)). So, a trustee who is a decorator might in consequence be able to paint his charity's premises and make a charge both for his time and for the paint used but a trustee who owns a DIY shop would not be able via the new procedure to make even a discounted charge for paint supplied to the charity. In the latter situation the Commission may be prepared to give authority under s.26 of the 1993 Act (see **10.2.1** above).

Connected persons

The provisions of s.73A of the 1993 Act allowing remuneration in certain circumstances would also cover 'connected' persons including close relatives of a trustee or their spouses, an institution controlled by the trustee or his close relatives or a company in which the trustee or his close relatives have a substantial interest (meaning 20 per cent or more of the equity or voting power). The rules to assist in defining such connected persons are set out in Sched.5 to the 1993 Act, which relates to the prohibition on disposal of land to connected persons without consent of the Charity Commission;[9] under Sched.5 as amended a connected person now includes a person who lives together with another of the same sex, even if that couple have not registered a civil partnership.

Disqualification of a trustee receiving remuneration under section 73A

The new s.73C of the 1993 Act (inserted by s.37 of the 2006 Act) introduces provisions to disqualify a trustee from involvement in decisions about any agreement allowing him remuneration. If a person, who would be entitled to receive remuneration under a remuneration agreement under s.73A, is disqualified from acting in relation to that agreement but in fact does so act, then his acts are not in themselves invalidated.

Repayment of remuneration by someone disqualified

However, a disqualified person can be ordered by the Charity Commission to repay all or part of any remuneration or benefit in kind he may have received. Furthermore, the trustee (or connected person) ceases to have any entitlement under the remuneration agreement if the Commission makes such an order. An appeal may be taken to the Charity Tribunal against an order of the Charity Commission to reimburse the charity any unauthorised remuneration:

- by the Attorney-General;
- by the person subject to that order;
- by the other trustees of the charity in question; or
- by any other person who might be affected.

The Tribunal may dismiss the appeal, quash the order (and refer the matter back to the Charity Commission) or substitute a different order of the kind that the Commission could have made.

---

1   1993 Act, s.97(1) defines 'charity trustee' as 'the persons having the general control and management of the administration of a charity'.
2   See *Bray v. Ford* [1896] AC 44 (HL).
3   Baroness Scotland of Asthal, Minister of State, Home Office, *Hansard*, 20 January 2005, col.888.
4   For example, Housing Act 1996 which allows remuneration of some trustees of charitable housing associations on conditions.
5   See, e.g. the Charity Law Association's model Memorandum of Association for a Charitable Company, cl.5.

6 Note that under s.73B(3) an agreement remains in force for this purpose so long as any obligations under the agreement have not been discharged by any party to it.

7 For example, a scheme under 1993 Act, s.16 (in respect of a trust) or consent under 1993 Act, s.64 (in respect of a charitable company).

8 See, e.g. *Payment of Charity Trustees* (Guidance Note CC 11).

9 See 1993 Act, s.36 and Sched.5, paras.2–4.

10.3   LIABILITY OF TRUSTEES FOR BREACH OF TRUST

As the guardians of the law of equity, the courts have assumed an equitable juris-diction to relieve a trustee from personal liability if the trustee has acted honestly and reasonably. In the *Exeter Corporation* case[1] the Lord Chancellor, Lord Eldon, stressed the need to be lenient towards charity trustees who had acted honestly and where the loss incurred arose from a mistake. 'To act on any other principle', he said, 'would be to deter all prudent persons from becoming trustees of charities'.

Bolstering equitable allowance or equitable relief by the High Court are two statu-tory provisions which have stood the test of time: s.61 of the Trustee Act 1925, which allows the court to grant full or partial relief to a trustee from liability for breach of trust if he has acted honestly and reasonably and ought fairly to be excused for the breach, and s.727 of the Companies Act 1985 which makes sim-ilar provision for company directors and therefore for the trustees of charitable companies. Under s.73E of the 1993 Act as amended the court can now grant this relief to charity trustees of a CIO. Relief is of course discretionary but courts are naturally reluctant to grant relief to a paid trustee.[2]

The Charity Commission does give both general and specific guidance to charity trustees through its website **www.charitycommission.gov.uk** and newsletters, as well as in letters addressed to trustees individually. However, our experience is that most trustees fall into breach of trust through a combination of honest ignor-ance and a lack of time during their busy lives to devote to the detail of their trusteeship responsibilities and of their charity's constitution. The difficulty in the past has been that the Charity Commission has, notwithstanding its concurrent jurisdiction with the courts in relation to charities, been unable of itself to grant equitable relief or allowance.

The result was that, where a charity trustee was allegedly in breach of trust the charity's trustees would, under pressure from the Commission, have to consider whether a claim might lie against that 'errant trustee' and consider what he said in his defence usually on legal advice; the errant trustee often had to take legal advice at his own cost to put forward a defence. Then, on further legal advice, the trustees would have to reach a conclusion as to whether or not the court would order full or partial restitution if proceedings were commenced against the errant trustee. The fact that a restitution case against a trustee is 'charity proceedings' for which Charity Commission consent is required under s.33 of the 1993 Act would only add to the complication and expense.

The Charity Commission now has power under s.73D of the 1993 Act (inserted by s.38 of the 2006 Act) to relieve a trustee who is or may be in breach of trust wholly or partially, provided 'that he has acted honestly and reasonably and ought fairly to be excused for the breach of trust or duty'.[3] Naturally, the new powers do not affect the existing powers of the court to relieve trustees of charities in these circumstances, but the process of obtaining relief from the Commission is likely to be easier and cheaper than asking the court to grant relief.

Unfortunately, if the Commission refuses to grant relief the issue cannot be referred to the Charity Tribunal but must be dealt with by appeal to the High Court (see **6.3.4**).

1 *Attorney-General* v. *Exeter Corporation* (1826) 2 Russ 45, 54.
2 See *Re Pauling's Settlement Trusts (No.1); Younghusband* v. *Coutts & Co. (No.1)* [1964] 1 Ch 303.
3 1993 Act, s.73D(2)(b).

10.4   LIABILITY OF AUDITORS

The Commission's powers to grant relief under the new s.73D of the 1993 Act also extend to auditors, independent examiners and reporting accountants for any breach of duty provided that they have acted honestly and reasonably and ought fairly to be excused for the breach of trust or duty. These powers are in addition to the whistleblowing protection granted to auditors, independent examiners and reporting accountants, included within s.68A(1) in the case of charitable companies and within s.44A(5) in the case of non-company charities (see **12.8**).

In addition, s.73E extends the statutory protection given under s.727 of the Companies Act 1985 (relief to directors and auditors of companies) and s.61 of the Trustee Act 1925 (relief to trustees) to enable the courts to grant protection for breach of duty or breach of trust to trustees, auditors, independent examiners and reporting accountants of all types of charity. This therefore removes anomalies of treatment, where previously auditors would only be offered protection if they were auditors of companies, while independent examiners and reporting accountants previously had no such protection.

10.5   TRUSTEE INDEMNITY INSURANCE

Trustee indemnity insurance (TII) is the equivalent in charity administration of directors and officers insurance in commercial entities. This insurance is not designed to insure the charity against the many third party claims to which any organisation doing business with the public may be subject, still less is it designed to relieve trustees of trusts and unincorporated charities from personal liability in the event of the charity not being able to pay its debts. Rather, TII is designed to give protection to individual trustees in respect of claims for breach of trust or breach of duty in their capacity as trustees, including any negligence or default in their capacity as directors of a corporate charity.

Claims on TII appear in our experience to be rare but many trustees nevertheless look to their charities to have such cover underwritten. Unfortunately, the Charity Commission has historically taken the view that TII benefits the individual trustee rather than his charity and that the charity cannot pay TII premiums unless the constitution so allowed or the Commission gave its consent, if necessary to amend the constitution. In recent years the Commission has simplified the procedure for obtaining such consent.[1]

Charity trustees will now be permitted by s.73F of the 1993 Act (introduced by s.39 of the 2006 Act) to pay TII premiums out of a charity's funds so long as the trustees decide that to do so is in the best interests of the charity.[2] It may well be in the charity's best interests because trustees would not otherwise be persuaded to join or remain on the board.

However, cover under the TII policy must not include:

- fines for criminal offences or penalties imposed by regulatory authorities for non-compliance;[3]
- costs of defending criminal proceedings where a trustee is convicted of an offence resulting from fraud, dishonesty or reckless misconduct; or
- liability of a trustee to his charity arising from conduct which he knew or ought to have known was not in the charity's interests.

The Minister is permitted to amend these exclusions by means of regulations approved by a positive order of both Houses of Parliament.

The new s.73F allows the purchase of TII, even if the charity's constitution prohibits, as is so often the case, the receipt of a personal benefit by a trustee. However, the new rule cannot override the much less common express prohibition in the charity's constitution against the purchase of insurance.

---

1   For example, under 1993 Act, s.26 to do something which is expedient in the interests of the charity or under s.64 of that Act to allow an amendment to a charitable company's memorandum and articles of association.
2   The trustees must have regard to the duty of care imposed on them by Trustee Act 2000, s.1(1).
3   For example, failure to pay employees' tax under PAYE regulations or submit an annual report and accounts to Companies House.

10.6   COMMENCEMENT

With the exception of 10.2 (the new power of remuneration of trustees providing services), these provisions are amongst those which are due to be brought in by the first commencement order in early 2007. The provisions relating to the remuneration of trustees are due to be included in the third commencement order in early 2008.

11 THE CHARITABLE INCORPORATED ORGANISATION

11.1 WHY IS A NEW CONSTITUTIONAL VEHICLE NECESSARY?

Section 34 of the 2006 Act is not very long, only 11 words to introduce the CIO; but it is the culmination of a dozen years of pressure, principally by the Charity Law Association, for a corporate legal structure designed for charities.

Charities have, more often unconsciously than consciously, used a variety of legal structures, from the express trust (which might be contained in a trust deed or a will or even in a conveyance or lease) to unincorporated associations and from companies limited by guarantee to Royal Charter corporations for the favoured few, but none of these has been specifically designed for charities. Indeed, there is usually a clear distinction between the rules which govern the charitable status of an organisation and the rules which govern the organisation itself. Let us take a quick look at these vehicles used by charities.

11.1.1 The trust

The perceived advantage of the express trust used to be the simplicity of the idea that a few people could come together to pursue charitable purposes which they would declare in the objects clause of the charity's governing instrument. The problems with it are that:

- Essentially, the trust is an obligation imposed in equity upon one or more persons holding property; there is not usually any provision about the operational activities of the charity.
- There is no implied power to accumulate income as capital; indeed powers to accumulate income are subject to statutory restrictions.[1]
- The trust has no separate legal existence from its trustees so changes of trustees have to incorporate procedures for the transfer of property.
- Above all, because the trust is not a legal person, third parties, whether they be employees, builders, bankers or customers, who deal with a charitable trust are at law dealing with the charity's individual trustees. Those individ-

ual trustees are, in consequence, personally liable to third parties for the charity's contractual or tortious acts. Whilst the individual trustees have an indemnity against the charity for expenditure properly incurred, including such claims, that is of little help if the charity has insufficient funds to meet its debts.

11.1.2   Part VII incorporation by the Charity Commission

Under the Charitable Trustees Incorporation Act 1872, replaced by Part VII of the 1993 Act, the Charity Commission has long since had power to incorporate the trustees of a charity, as opposed to incorporating the charity itself. This corporate body can hold property and investments, contract with third parties and sue and be sued in its own name.

However, incorporation by the Charity Commission does not limit the liability of the trustees, so has tended to be used largely by grant-making foundations, whose assets and activities might render limitation of liability unnecessary, and religious order charities whose trustees are likely to have taken a vow of personal poverty and who would not therefore be worth suing as individuals.

11.1.3   Unincorporated associations

Unincorporated associations are formed by groups of people coming together to pursue a common purpose. Like trusts, the unincorporated association can be registered as a charity under its constitution, but it has no separate legal existence from its members. An association's members might in some circumstances be personally liable to third parties to the extent that the association was unable to meet its liabilities, although there is a view that it is the members of the management committee who would primarily be in the firing line.

Governance of an unincorporated association can be a problem if the constitution does not carefully specify where control lies. Almost invariably there is a membership, consisting of supporters, even beneficiaries, who elect a management committee to run the association. The committee's members are the 'charity trustees'.[2]

In addition, the constitution very often provides for the appointment of a group of people called 'trustees' who are not the charity trustees but are simply appointed to hold the association's property to the order of its members through the committee. In practice, we find that the nomenclature gives rise to endless uncertainties in unincorporated associations and sometimes even in express trusts.

In the event of an unincorporated association being unable to pay its debts, the association's members could disappear with the wind, potentially leaving the committee of management exposed to liability to the association's creditors.

11.1.4   Corporate charities and sole corporate trustees

Corporate structures for charities are generally preferred. This is not only because of the limitation of liability for members and the charity trustees; other advantages are that:

- There is a single entity to hold property and other assets.
- There is no need to transfer those assets on appointment or removal of trustees – indeed the documentation required on change of directors/trustees is quite simple.
- The charitable activities can flow from a single structure.
- The regular review by the members of the activities of a corporation and its directors is in line with good practice for charities.

Incorporation of a charity under Royal Charter or by a specific Act of Parliament will provide these benefits, but they are available only to a select few. Therefore, incorporation of charities as private companies (usually as companies limited by guarantee) has been common for many years. A particular advantage for those many service-providing charities who operate beyond England and Wales is that the company structure is understood and accepted internationally; trusts or unincorporated associations are not universally understood and incorporation of the trustee body under Part VII of the 1993 Act is also seldom accepted in practice outside England and Wales.

The company format is generally used to encompass the charity itself, so that the company is the charity. However, the company can also be used to act as the trustee of an existing unincorporated charity where, because of its trusts, that charity has to remain in existence. Indeed, where the company is appointed the sole corporate trustee, then most of the advantages of incorporation of the charity itself are available – holding of assets, limitation of liability and regular review of activities and governance.

There have always been disadvantages to incorporation, not least because company law has not been drafted with charities in mind, so that there are two sets of statutory obligations to follow in terms of registration, holding of accounts and other documents. Also, a company cannot declare special trusts or endowments of its own funds, but must hold any restricted funds as trustee.

We also find that in practice it is difficult for many trustees of charities who are thinking of moving to a corporate structure to adjust to the nomenclature and the precise definition of roles. For example, those who promote a charitable company are likely to be *subscribers* and the initial *directors*; those directors might be called *trustees* and would for Charities Act purposes be *charity trustees* but could also be called *members of council*, *members of the management committee*, *members of the board* or even *governors*. There must be a minimum of one member for a private limited company[3] but there are likely to be a number of members in a charitable company; they could be limited to the trustees/directors for the time being or there could be a membership of many thousands or even the board of another organisation.

As the Scrutiny Committee pointed out, 'Company law is designed for profit-making enterprises and subject to European Union Law which does not fit easily with charities and charity law'.[4]

---

1 Law of Property Act 1925, s.164 and Perpetuities and Accumulations Act 1964, s.13. It should, however, be noted that retention of a charity's income by means of designated reserves, to be spent within a reasonable period, is not an accumulation.

2 Charity trustees are defined by 1993 Act, s.97(1) as 'the persons having the general control and management of the administration of a charity'.

3 Companies Act 1985, s.1(3A).

4 *Report of the Joint Committee of both Houses of Parliament*, September 2004, p.67.

11.2   ORIGINS OF THE CIO

The idea of the CIO, the new corporate structure established by the 2006 Act specifically to meet the needs of charities, although discussed over several years between the Charity Law Association and the Charity Commission, eventually received the stamp of government approval in the Department of Trade and Industry's review of company law in 2001.[1] Thankfully, perhaps, it was not left for inclusion in later company legislation. Nevertheless, it is to be hoped that the Commission will feel able to learn from the much-praised speed and efficiency of Companies House in relation to the registration and variation of company constitutions.

So, the CIO will be a corporate body with limited liability, coming into existence only on registration with the Charity Commission. It can be established as a new charity or it can be converted from another existing charitable vehicle. It will have one or more members who could be the existing charity trustees or a separate member group, inclusive of the trustees or not. It is potentially a very flexible vehicle in governance terms.

The CIO is introduced into law in a way beloved of parliamentary counsel:

- s.34 of the 2006 Act introduces:
- Sched.7 to the 2006 Act, which inserts:
  - in Part 1, a new Part 8A (ss.69A–69Q) and Sched.5B into the 1993 Act, and
  - in Part 2, a selection of miscellaneous amendments to the 1993 Act relating to CIOs.

---

1 *Modern Company Law: Final Report*, Department of Trade and Industry, 2001.

11.3   THE CONSTITUTION OF THE CIO

The CIO must be a body corporate with a constitution, a principal office in England or Wales, with one or more members who will either have no liability on the winding up of the organisation or liability limited to a specific maximum amount (s.69A). The convention with charitable companies limited by guarantee has been to limit the guarantee to a purely nominal figure, say £1, and it may be that members of new CIOs will opt for avoidance of any liability to third parties.

The CIO's constitution must, under s.69B, contain its name and purposes, the address of its principal office in England and Wales, what contribution (if any) its members must make to its assets if wound up, provisions for the eligibility of and method of appointing members and trustees and arrangements on dissolution. All of these provisions are of course generally to be found in the memorandum and articles of charitable companies but there are some helpful differences in nomenclature:

- The CIO will have a 'constitution' rather than memorandum and articles of association – s.69A(3).
- The CIO will have a 'principal office' rather than a registered office, although it has to be in England or Wales – s.69A(4).
- Those who control and manage the CIO are referred to as 'charity trustees' and may in practice be called 'trustees' but, as with companies limited by guarantee, the members and the trustees are distinct although they may or may not be the same people – s.69B(6).

The CIO's constitution will be in a form specified by the Commission. In practice, the form is unlikely to be imposed without extensive consultation by the Commission with the Charity Law Association and other relevant umbrella groups.

There are likely to be other requirements yet to be set out in regulations (s.69B(3)). This is curious, given the Commission's powers to prescribe the form of constitution. It is a provision which might worry all of us who care deeply about keeping charities independent of government, but in reality it is a useful method of updating legislation without the need for primary legislation.

11.4   ANNOUNCING THE STATUS OF THE CIO

The rules requiring CIOs to tell the world about their status (s.69C) mirror company legislation and go further than s.5 of the 1993 Act (announcing the status of a registered charity) by requiring the name of the CIO and its status to appear in legible characters on:

- its business letters;
- its notices and official publications;
- its cheques, bills of exchange, etc.;
- conveyances, leases and other deeds relating to land;
- bills, receipts, etc.

CIOs are encouraged by s.69C(3) to consider adding 'CIO', or the longer 'charitable incorporated organisation' to their name, because s.69C(5) requires all documents referred to above to include a statement announcing the fact that the body is a CIO.

The Welsh equivalent *sefydliad elusennol corfforedig* or SEC are alternatives which may be used only when the constitution is written in Welsh; the same applies to the statement under s.69C(5).

11.5   FAILURE TO ANNOUNCE CIO STATUS

Failure to comply with the 'flagging' of name and status of CIO is a criminal offence incurring the same potential penalty[1] as a failure to flag up the status of a registered charity under s.5 of the 1993 Act. However, there are two important differences:

- A trustee of the CIO is no less liable than the person (for example, a senior employee) who authorises the production of a non-compliant document.
- In the case of cheques or bills of exchange, etc. the CIO trustee or the person authorising the non-compliant document is, *in addition to* the fine mentioned above, 'personally liable to the holder of a cheque, bill of exchange, etc. for the amount of it, unless it is duly paid by the CIO' – s.69D(2)(b).

These potential penalties for non-compliance are little different from the penalties for failing to make clear the status of a company with limited liability but they are a stark reminder of the necessity of CIOs telling suppliers, customers and others with whom they deal that they are protecting their members and trustees from unlimited liability.

An offence is also committed under s.69D(3) by any person who holds out any body as a CIO when it is not, although there is a defence (s.69D(4)) of reasonable belief that the body was a CIO.

---

1   A fine on summary conviction not exceeding level 3 on the standard scale, currently £1,000.

11.6   REGISTRATION OF THE CIO

The application to the Charity Commission to create a CIO has a joint purpose, to constitute or incorporate the CIO and to register it as a charity – s.69E(1). The application form therefore is likely to be a variation of APP1 which has to be completed by any charity applying for registration.

However, there is one major difference in that the current registration at the Charity Commission is of a charitable organisation already in existence, for example a trust or company, whereas the CIO will not have any legal existence until it is registered. Furthermore, it will not be registered unless the Commission accepts that it would be a charity if it were registered (s.69E(3)(a)) and that its constitution complies with the s.69B requirements. The Charity Commission may also refuse registration of a CIO (s.69E(4)) if its name is the same as or similar to that of any other charity, registered or unregistered, or is likely to mislead the public as to its true purposes or activities, connections with central or local government or if the name is offensive.[1]

Section 69F confirms that once the application under s.69E has been granted, the CIO must be registered as a charity and that by virtue of that registration it is incorporated under the constitution and name referred to in the application.

Those who make the application are the first members of the CIO (s.69F(2)(c)) and any property vested in them on trust for the CIO's charitable purposes is automatically vested in the CIO on registration – s.69F(3).

The registration entry recorded at the Commission must include both the date of registration and the fact of its constitution as a CIO – s.69F(4). Finally, under s.69F(5), the CIO must be sent a copy of its entry on the register, to its principal office.

---

1   See 1993 Act, s.6 which allows the Charity Commission to direct a change of name if it is likely similarly to mislead the public.

11.7   CONVERSION OF AN EXISTING CHARITY TO CIO STATUS

A charitable company or an industrial and provident society (provided that if either is registered with a share capital those shares are fully paid) may apply for conversion to a CIO – s.69G – but not if it is an exempt charity.[1]

In addition to the documents and information required under s.69E(2) on application to constitute and register a CIO, the organisation wishing to convert must supply a copy of the resolution to convert to a CIO format and also a copy of the resolution adopting the proposed CIO constitution. Those resolutions must either be special resolutions,[2] or a unanimous written resolution signed by all members of the company or industrial and provident society entitled to vote. Doubtless, a written resolution would only be appropriate if the number of members of the organisation seeking incorporation as CIO was comparatively small.

If a company limited by guarantee applies for conversion to a CIO, the same liability of members on dissolution must be carried into the CIO's constitution, except where the liability of each member to contribute to assets on dissolution is of £10 or less, in which case the guarantee is automatically extinguished – s.69G(10). Given that the majority of charitable companies are limited by a guarantee of £1 per member, the likelihood is that on conversion CIOs will normally have a nil liability.

Uncertainty about the proposed name of the CIO and the fact that the proposed conversion might be considered 'inappropriate' would be reasons for denying registration of the CIO in these circumstances.

On the grant of an application for conversion of a charitable company or an industrial and provident society the registration of the CIO does not take effect until, respectively, the Registrar of Companies or the Financial Services Authority has registered the resolution to convert and that the registration of the CIO will cancel the pre-existing registration – s.69I. The Charity Commission will handle that part of the process with the appropriate registrar.

On conversion from a company or industrial and provident society which had a share capital, any shares previously held will be cancelled, although this would not affect any right which may have accrued in respect of such share prior to its cancellation.[3] It is, however, doubtful whether such shares would have had any real value which the shareholder was not willing to give away. In addition to the entry in the register of charities for the CIO there must be a note of the name of the pre-existing company or industrial and provident society – s.69I(7).

1   See **Chapter 4**.
2   See Industrial and Provident Societies Act 1965, s.52(3) and Companies Act 1985, s.378.
3   1993 Act, s.69I(5) and (6).

11.8   CONVERSION FROM A COMMUNITY INTEREST COMPANY TO A CIO

A community interest company (CIC)[1] is a company established for the purpose of pursuing social enterprise.

A CIC may not register as a charity but it is not beyond the bounds of possibility that the owner of a CIC might wish to give the value of their company for charitable purposes. This could be achieved by the owner simply passing his shares to one or more charities but converting the CIC itself into a charity will also be an option if the Minister makes regulations to that effect under s.69J.

1   See **11.16** for a description of the CIC and a comparison with the CIO.

11.9   AMALGAMATION OF CIOs

Any two or more CIOs may apply to the Charity Commission to be amalgamated and the formal process begins with a resolution by each of the existing CIOs to approve the proposed amalgamation and to adopt the constitution of the new CIO – s.69K(4). The resolutions referred to have to be passed by a 75 per cent majority of those voting in person (or by proxy or post assuming the CIO's constitution so permits) or unanimously if not at a general meeting – presumably by written resolution. If the latter method is used, the date of the resolution is a date deemed by the relevant CIO's constitution or under regulations[1] or by the date on which the last member agreed to the amalgamation, whichever is the later – s.69K(6).

The amalgamating CIOs must give reasonably wide notice to those who would most likely be affected by the amalgamation. The 2006 Act does not suggest who might be so affected but obviously donors and other supporters, customers, creditors and other stakeholders should be informed. The notice should invite all such stakeholders, if affected, to make written representations to the Charity

Commission. A copy of that notice should be sent to the Commission which will allow a time (specified in the notice) for representations to be made – s.69K(8).

The registration of the new CIO cancels the registration of the merging CIOs; the first members of the new CIO will be the members of the merging CIOs immediately before registration of the new CIO – s.69L(2). On cancellation of the registration of the merging CIOs all property, rights and liabilities of each of the merging CIOs will become the property, rights and liabilities of the new CIO and each of the merging CIOs will be dissolved – s.69L(3).

Although an application for amalgamation can be refused on a similar basis to that for refusal of an application for registration of a CIO (for example, because of a non-compliant constitution or because it would not be charitable if registered), the Commission may in addition refuse the application for amalgamation of two or more CIOs if there is a serious risk that the new, larger CIO would be unable properly to pursue its purposes – s.69K(9). In addition, it is open to the Commission to refuse an application to amalgamate CIOs if it is not satisfied that the new CIO would have substantially the same provisions as the amalgamating CIOs, covering what happens to the CIO's property on dissolution, benefits for trustees and connected persons – s.69K(10) and (11). As to the meaning of benefits and connected persons, see **Chapter 10**.

The entry in the register of charities for the new CIO created by an amalgamation will follow the style of the entry for the conversion from a charitable company or an industrial and provident society. As with the provisions for mergers of charities, a gift to one of the merging CIOs takes effect on registration of the new CIO as a gift to the new CIO (see **Chapter 9**).

1   Regulations made by the Minister for the Cabinet Office under s.69Q(1).

11.10   TRANSFER OF UNDERTAKING FROM ONE CIO TO ANOTHER

One CIO may resolve to transfer to another CIO its undertaking, in other words the second CIO takes over all its property, rights and liabilities. The process is similar to that for an amalgamation, except that both transferor CIO and transferee CIO must pass resolutions and the giving of public notice is a matter for the Charity Commission's discretion – s.69M. The resolution to transfer does not take effect until confirmed by the Charity Commission and, as with amalgamation, the Charity Commission has the right to refuse if there is a serious risk that the transferee CIO would be unable properly to pursue the purposes of the transferor CIO (s.69M(6)).

As with the amalgamation of CIOs – s.69K(11) – the Commission may refuse to confirm the resolutions if the constitution of the transferee CIO does not have substantially the same provisions as the transferor CIO in relation to purposes, property on dissolution and the benefits for trustees and connected persons.

Once the resolution is confirmed by the Charity Commission all the property, rights and liabilities pass to the transferee CIO and the transferor CIO is dissolved. Unless the Commission has already confirmed the resolution or refused to do so, the Commission's confirmation is deemed to have been made six months following its receipt. Reliance on a deemed confirmation seems fraught with difficulties, not least because the Commission may extend its period of consideration of the resolution for a further six months. This uncertainty would surely create considerable problems in the management of the ongoing operations of either CIO, not least its staff and compliance with the TUPE Regulations.[1] Common sense would indicate the necessity of a dialogue with the Commission on the proposed effective date of transfer of the undertaking from one organisation to the other.

A gift to the transferor CIO also takes effect as a gift to the transferee CIO on confirmation of the resolution. As with the provisions of mergers of charities this will be helpful in securing that legacies to the transferor CIO pass to the transferee CIO (see **Chapter 9**).

---

1   Transfer of Undertakings (Protection of Employment) Regulations 2006, SI 2006/246.

11.11   DISSOLUTION OF A CIO

The Minister has under s.69N been allotted the task of making regulations about the winding up, insolvency and dissolution of CIOs, as well as their revival and restoration to the register having been dissolved.

An indication of what those regulations might address can be seen in s.69N(2) which contains provisions designed to secure the proper charitable application of a CIO's property and assets, including disclaimer of property and the application of a CIO's property cy-près.

11.12   MISCELLANEOUS PROVISIONS

The power in s.74 of the 1993 Act for certain unincorporated charities to transfer all their property to another charity will allow such a charity to hand its property to one or more CIOs. However, under s.69O there is no restriction on the income size of the donor charity.[1]

Section 69Q allows the Minister to make regulations for the administration of CIOs, in particular about the execution of documents, communication with the Commission by electronic means, the maintenance of registers of members and trustees of CIOs and of charges over the assets of CIOs.

---

1   See 1993 Act, s.74 (as amended by 2006 Act, s.40) which otherwise limits the size of the transferor charity to an income of £10,000 p.a. See also **Chapter 9**.

11.13   CONSTITUTION AND OPERATION OF CIOs

In the new Sched.5B to the 1993 Act[1] there are further provisions relating to the constitutional and operational requirements affecting CIOs. The paragraphs in parentheses below are those of the new Sched.5B.

11.13.1   Powers (para.1)

Unless the CIO's constitution says otherwise, a CIO has the power to do anything to further its objects or that is conducive or incidental to its doing so. The CIO's charity trustees are given the responsibility of managing its affairs.

11.13.2   Constitution (paras.2–4)

The CIO must use its property in furtherance of its objects and in accordance with its constitution. If there is a provision that members are liable to contribute on the CIO being wound up (the equivalent of the members' guarantee in a company limited by guarantee), the duty to do so is enforceable as if it were contained in a contract between the CIO and each member (para.3). Further, any money payable by a member to the CIO is a specialty debt due by the member (para.4) which means that the debt remains enforceable for 12 years before the Limitation Act[2] affords a good defence to proceedings. It should be borne in mind that the guarantee of even a nominal sum (something of a legal fiction in companies limited by guarantee) is not likely to be used in practice for CIOs – see **11.7**.

11.13.3   Third parties (paras.5–8)

Third parties dealing with a CIO for value, in money or money's worth, cannot avoid obligations towards a CIO on the grounds that the CIO lacked 'constitutional capacity', in other words that it was acting outside its powers or that its trustees or representatives were acting without authority (para.5(3)), so long as the third parties were acting in good faith without knowing that the CIO or its trustees or representatives were unauthorised.

Furthermore, a party to a transaction with a CIO is not bound to enquire as to whether a CIO is operating within its powers or its trustees or representatives are properly authorised (para.5(5)). In any proceedings by a third party alleging lack of capacity or authority the burden of proof lies with the person making that allegation (para.5(7)), but a bona fide purchaser for value of an interest in property without notice that the CIO is exceeding its powers or that its trustees are unauthorised is protected (para.5(6)).

However, nothing in the third party rules set out in para.5 of Sched.5B will:

- block injunction proceedings to restrain a future action which is beyond the powers of a CIO or beyond the authority of its trustees or representatives (para.6(1)) provided that act is not being done to fulfil a legal obligation arising from a previous act of the CIO;

- prevent the Charity Commission from exercising any of its powers;
- limit a CIO trustee's liability for acting outside his powers (para.7);
- limit the duty of the CIO's trustees to act within the limits of its constitution and their powers (para.8).

11.13.4   Duties of CIO members and trustees (paras.9–10)

In line with the duties of care imposed on all trustees, including charity trustees, under the Trustee Act 2000 both members and trustees of CIOs are bound:

- to exercise powers (and other constitutional functions of a trustee) in good faith in the way in which they think would best further the objects of the CIO (para.9);
- to exercise reasonable care and skill having regard to their actual or reputed special knowledge or experience and in particular, if they are acting as a trustee in the course of a business or profession, having regard to the level of skill reasonably to be expected (para.10).

11.13.5   Personal benefits and payments (paras.11–12)

In a restatement of the existing law relating to payments and benefits to trustees, a CIO trustee may be paid or reimbursed expenses properly incurred in the performance of his functions (para.12) but under para.11(2) he may not benefit personally from any transaction.

The assumption made here is that CIO constitutions are likely to contain powers to remunerate or provide other benefits to CIO trustees and therefore para.11(1) requires that a trustee may not benefit personally from any arrangement or transaction entered into by the CIO unless he has previously disclosed to all co-trustees any direct or indirect material interest. In other words, if a trustee has a conflict of interest, however remote, he should declare it in advance or stand to lose whatever benefit or right he has. For the new rules in relation to trustee remuneration, see **Chapter 10**.

11.13.6   Procedural regulations (para.13)

The Minister has power to make regulations about procedures to be followed by CIOs; subject to those regulations and to any other statute a CIO may regulate its own procedure in accordance with its constitution.

However, para.13(3) does require certain provisions to be included in the CIO's constitution for general meetings of members. One cannot, of course, have members and not consult them, but that does beg the question as to whether such consultation can take place if the CIO's members are one and the same as its trustees.

Nevertheless, those who are familiar with the concept of trustees/directors of a charitable company also comprising the membership of that company should have little difficulty in accepting that people who are both members and trustees will be asked to perform two separate functions within a CIO. For those who are not so familiar with that concept there may be confusion over nomenclature.

11.13.7   Amendment of a CIO's constitution (para.14)

A CIO may amend its constitution by members' resolution. The voting requirement is 75 per cent of those voting (including by proxy or post if permitted) or a unanimous written resolution. Such a resolution would, if passed by written resolution or possibly by electronic means, be effective on the date on which regulations of the Minister[3] or the CIO's constitution deem it to have been passed or the date on which the last member agreed to it, whichever is the later (para.14(3)). Naturally, no amendment can be made which would have the effect of the CIO ceasing to be a charity (para.14(4)).

Mirroring the requirement for s.64 consent[4] prior to resolutions to alter key provisions in the memorandum and articles of association of a charitable company, a new resolution to make the following amendments will be ineffective unless the Charity Commission has given its prior written consent (para.14(5)):

- alteration to the objects;
- alteration of any provision as to the destination of a CIO's objects following dissolution;
- alterations to any provision which would have the effect of authorising trustees, members or connected persons to receive benefits[5] from the CIO.

However, it should be noted that para.15(5) allows the Commission to ignore the requirement for such prior consent and register the amendment anyway.

11.13.8   Registration of amendments to CIOs (para.15)

All resolutions to amend a CIO's constitution must be sent to the Charity Commission within 15 days after the passing of the resolution under para.14(3). Accompanying the resolution must be the constitution as amended and such other documents or information as the Commission may require; these might include an explanatory note or a note about the perceived effect of the amendment.

The Commission can refuse to register an amendment on the grounds that:

- the CIO has no power to make the amendment, for example, on the grounds that the effect would be that the CIO ceased to be a charity or that it was otherwise non-compliant with the 2006 Act or any other statute;
- that the amendment would change the name of the CIO to one which would be unacceptable on original application for the constitution and registration of the CIO.[6]

1   Added by 1993 Act, Part 8A, s.69P.
2   Limitation Act 1980, s.8(1).
3   Regulations made under 1993 Act, Sched.5B, para.13.
4   1993 Act, s.64 (as amended by the 2006 Act).
5   See **Chapter 10** as to the meaning of benefits.
6   See 1993 Act, s.69E(4).

11.14   CONSEQUENTIAL AMENDMENTS TO THE 1993 ACT

The arrival of the CIO on the scene has required several consequential amendments to certain provisions of the 1993 Act, in particular:

- **section 45** (annual reports): a CIO must submit to the Commission an annual report whatever its income;[1]
- **section 48** (annual returns): a CIO must produce an annual return whatever its income;[2]
- **section 86** (regulations and orders): confirms the authority for the Minister to make regulations pursuant to s.69N (winding up, insolvency and dissolution of CIOs) and s.69Q (administration of CIOs);
- **section 97(1)** (definitions): helpfully defines 'CIO' as charitable incorporated organisation.

1   Sections 45 and 48 otherwise do not require annual reports and annual returns (respectively) if the charity's gross income does not exceed a sum set from time to time by the Minister, currently £10,000 p.a.
2   Ibid.

11.15   WILL THE CIO BE WIDELY USED?

Certainly, the promoters of new charities and those unincorporated charities seeking the protection of limited liability or the other advantages of incorporation will wish to consider the CIO as a suitable vehicle. The same may well apply to two or more charities merging. Given the requirements for CIOs to produce annual reports and accounts it may be that very small charities will avoid CIOs as they now avoid company structures.

It seems less likely that existing charitable companies will rush to convert to a CIO structure unless they find that compliance with ever-changing company law becomes more difficult or expensive than it is already. By the same token it is unlikely that statutory or charter corporations would wish to throw out their much prized constitutions for the more prosaic CIO.

We are also concerned at the reaction of third parties to such new constitutions. Banks might, for instance, see an opportunity to request collateral security for loans by way of guarantees from trustees of CIOs; such requests should be refused.

Charities which regularly operate abroad, particularly if they purchase land or other assets in their own names, should check whether the law and legal practitioners in other countries would accept a CIO as an alternative to the company which is, after all, known worldwide as a business vehicle.

It may be that charities with existing corporate constitutions will wait a while to see how new CIOs fare before deciding to convert, unless of course a merger with another charitable company is in the offing, in which case the CIO may well be the best vehicle for the merged operation.

11.16   WHAT IS THE DIFFERENCE BETWEEN A COMMUNITY INTEREST COMPANY AND A CIO?

This question was raised during the examination passage of the draft Bill by the Scrutiny Committee[1] and it is perhaps worth answering anew, if only to say that the CIC has little similarity to and absolutely nothing to do with the CIO apart from the fact that it is another new corporate vehicle for use in the voluntary sector.

CICs were introduced by the Companies (Audit, Investigations and Community Enterprise) Act 2004 and are companies established to trade for the good of the community as a form of social enterprise. A CIC's promoters must certify that the company is formed to serve the community by pursuing a trade for social benefit, rather than with the motive of making private profit. The CIC must have 'asset lock' provisions which ensure that the company's assets and profits are always retained in the company and used for community benefit, although they can be transferred to a charity or another CIC.

Unlike a charity, the CIC can pay dividends on shares held by members but there will be a cap on such dividends, set by the CIC Regulator. In theory, a charity could, with consent of the Charity Commission, become a CIC but in doing so would lose its charitable status and the fiscal reliefs available to charities. As set out in 11.8 above a CIC could convert to a CIO and thus become a charity.

A CIC might be a useful alternative vehicle to a charity (corporate or not) where the promoters wish to pursue a social trade or enterprise and yet keep control of their organisation and be paid, as directors, for what they do. Whether such social entrepreneurs decide to establish a charity (including a CIO) or a CIC as the vehicle for their activity needs some thought. In the words of the CIC Regulator himself:

> In such cases, there may be a delicate balancing act to perform, weighing up the possible advantages of forming a CIC against the disadvantages of failing to attract the tax concessions open to . . . charities. There are no special tax advantages in being a CIC (though specific regional relief and access to Lottery and other funding may be open to CICs).[2]

---

1   Joint Committee of the Houses of Parliament which scrutinised the draft Bill.
2   Jim Hanlon, Community Interest Company Regulator, 23 May 2005, see **www. companieshouse.gov.uk/promotional/cics.shtml.**

11.17   COMMENCEMENT

The provisions of the 2006 Act relating to the establishment of CIOs are not likely to come into force before early 2008, being timetabled against the third implementation order.

12 AUDIT AND EXAMINATION OF ACCOUNTS

12.1 INTRODUCTION

The Strategy Unit Report, *Private Action, Public Benefit,* criticised the accessibility and quality of charity accounting information. The report pressed for higher standards and recommended the introduction of the Summary Information Return for larger charities. That recommendation has already been implemented.[1] In addition, the Charity Commission's initiative in displaying charity accounts alongside charity details on the register has certainly improved accessibility of information. The 2006 Act now brings in measures directed at improving the quality of information and extending the reach of the Charity Commission's monitoring. The focus is on larger charities, with smaller charities benefiting from some easing of requirements.

Strange as it now seems, it was not until the 1993 Act that the filing of annual returns was introduced and the Commission was able to carry out routine, systematic monitoring.[2] The 2006 Act strengthens the existing reporting and accounting framework in a number of ways. It rationalises the system, drawing the requirements for company and non-company accounts closer together. It simplifies thresholds for accounting requirements and external scrutiny. It also introduces important changes for auditors or examiners 'whistle-blowing' to the Charity Commission.

---

1 Summary Information Returns must now be filed annually with the Charity Commission by all charities with an annual income over £1 million.
2 The provisions contained in Part VI of the 1993 Act finally came into force in 1996 and required the filing of annual returns by all registered charities with an annual income or expenditure of over £10,000. See Table A on p.111.

12.2 HARMONISING COMPANY AND NON-COMPANY RULES

Whilst the requirements for annual reports and returns under Part VI of the 1993 Act apply to all registered charities, historically charity accounting obligations and external scrutiny requirements have varied according to the type of legal structure the charity adopts.

Non-company charities have been subject to the accounting regime provided under Part VI of the 1993 Act whilst charitable companies have been governed by Part VII of the Companies Act 1985. Both regimes established a framework with graduated, albeit different, requirements, relieving smaller organisations from the full rigour of regulation. These legal requirements are in turn supplemented by the Accounting and Reporting by Charities Statement of Recommended Practice (SORP). The SORP contains detailed recommendations as to the accounting practice and application of accounting standards in relation to charities (non-companies and companies alike) which prepare accruals accounts to give a true and fair view of financial activities and circumstances. For some reporting and accounting purposes, therefore, all charities of similar size have been treated alike, whilst for other purposes, requirements differ according to whether or not the charity is a company.

The protracted review of charity law regulation, which culminated in the 2006 Act, coincided with a major overhaul of company law and regulation. One welcome product of this was the recognition that charitable companies should be treated for accounting purposes primarily as charities, rather than as companies. Changes were introduced at a late stage in both Bills, paving the way for ministerial orders to be made aligning the two accounting regimes. The order-making power under s.77 of the 2006 Act is intended to allow the Minister to amend the 2006 Act and the 1993 Act to reflect the changes in company law to be made once the Companies Act 2006 comes into force. Under s.468 of the Companies Act 2006 power is reserved for that Act to be amended by order to allow alignment of the two regimes. The same reporting and accounting requirements and scrutiny will then extend to all charities, companies and non-companies alike. Similarly, the group accounting requirements will be harmonised, whether the group is headed by a company or a non-company charity.

12.3   AUDIT OR EXAMINATION FOR NON-COMPANY CHARITIES

Mention has already been made of the accounting and reporting framework for non-company charities contained in Part VI of the 1993 Act, underpinned by the Charities (Accounts and Reports) Regulations 2005, SI 2005/572.[1]

The legislation, regulations and the SORP all reflect the fact that accounting and reporting regulations can place a disproportionate burden on smaller charities by providing a less demanding regime for smaller charities. The 2006 Act adjusts existing thresholds for non-company accounting requirements and external scrutiny. It has been estimated that it will release as many as 3,000 smaller charities from the need to have a full audit.[2]

12.3.1   Audit

Under s.43(1) of the 1993 Act as amended by s.28(2) of the 2006 Act, non-company charities (including CIOs) must now have their accounts audited if:

- the charity's gross income exceeds £500,000 in the year in question; or
- the charity's gross income exceeds the accounts threshold and at the year end the aggregate assets of the charity before deduction of liabilities exceed £2.8 million.

The accounts threshold is the sum specified in s.42(3) of the 1993 Act as the gross income threshold for the preparation of accounts on the accruals basis, currently £100,000.

A charity's expenditure is no longer taken into account[3] and there is no longer any need to look at the charity's financial position in preceding years, only the year for which accounts are to be prepared. However, whilst the gross income threshold has been raised (from £250,000 to £500,000), the introduction of the asset value test for charities over the accounts threshold means that some charities with relatively low income but with substantial non-income producing functional assets may now require an audit for the first time. The asset value test is borrowed from company regulation but its suitability as a criterion for charity audit is more questionable, especially given the low level of the accounts threshold. Charities with subsidiaries under their control will also be required to have an audit if the group income threshold is exceeded (see **12.4** and **12.5** below), even if the parent charity's gross income does not exceed the threshold under s.43(1).

Where accounts must be audited, the auditor must satisfy the tests for eligibility to audit company accounts, under Part II of the Companies Act 1989 including as to the independence of the auditor.

12.3.2   Independent examination

For non-company charities with gross annual income over £10,000 but below £500,000, accounts must be subject to independent examination, if not audited. Charities below the audit threshold may, however, still opt for an audit and will need to do so if their governing document requires it or if an audit is a condition of their grant funding. Levels of expenditure are no longer taken into account for the purposes of the £10,000 threshold.

Charities having a gross income over £250,000, which have opted to have their accounts independently examined rather than audited, must now make sure that the independent examiner has a recognised qualification. The independent examiner must be a member of the Chartered Institute of Public Finance and Accountancy, a Fellow of the Association of Charity Independent Examiners or a member of any of the bodies listed in s.249D(3) of the Companies Act 1985 (which deals with professional qualifications of reporting accountants for company accounts).

Below the £250,000 threshold there is no requirement for the independent examiner to have a recognised qualification. It is only necessary that, as previously, an independent examiner is an independent person who is reasonably believed by the trustees to have the requisite ability and practical experience (s.43(3) of the 1993 Act as amended). The Charity Commission has issued guidance dealing with the selection of independent examiners.[4]

The income thresholds and asset value threshold in s.43 of the 1993 Act as amended can be varied by Order of the Minister. A comprehensive review of all thresholds in the 2006 Act is promised a year after Royal Assent.[5] In Standing Committee it was suggested that the £10,000 income threshold, in place since 1993, should be raised to £20,000. Although this was rejected, the issue is now being revisited, with a Charity Commission consultation underway in response to the Cabinet Office initiative to explore ways of cutting red tape. The £10,000 threshold is certainly out of kilter with company regulation which excludes charitable companies with gross income of less than £90,000 from the requirement to have external scrutiny of accounts.[6] Also, significantly, the Charity Commission's own policy in relation to the proportionate regulation of small charities defines small charities broadly by reference to income of less than £20,000.[7]

---

1 These replaced the Charities (Accounts and Reports) Regulations 1995, SI 1995/2724 and the Charities (Accounts and Reports) Regulations 2000, SI 2000/2868.
2 See the statements on Second Reading in the House of Commons by Hilary Armstrong, Minister for the Cabinet Office, *Hansard*, 26 June 2006, col.29.
3 Similarly expenditure is no longer taken into account under 1993 Act, s.45(3) (as amended) for the purposes of the requirement to file an annual report which is now mandatory simply where gross income exceeds £10,000.
4 *Independent Examination of Charity Accounts: Directions and Guidance Notes* (CC 63), October 2002, Appendix I.
5 See, e.g. the debates in the Standing Committee A, 11 July 2006 and the comments of Edward Miliband, the Parliamentary Secretary, Cabinet Office, *Hansard* HL, 11 July 2006, cols.195–8.
6 Companies Act 1985, s.249A(3).
7 *Small Charities – Principles of Commission Policy* (OG 200 A1), 5 July 2006.

12.4 AUDIT REQUIREMENTS FOR COMPANY CHARITIES

The 2006 Act makes changes to the thresholds for audit of charitable company accounts. Under s.249A(4) of the Companies Act 1985 as amended by s.32 of the 2006 Act, companies can opt for an accountant's report, instead of an audit, where:

*   gross income for the year in question does not exceed £500,000; and
*   the aggregate assets on the balance sheet before deduction of liabilities do not exceed £2.8 million.

There is no alteration in the £90,000 threshold below which company accounts do not require external scrutiny.

The group accounts thresholds in s.249B(1C) of the Companies Act 1985 are increased so that group accounts will not be required unless the group's aggregate income exceeds £700,000 net or £840,000 gross.

12.5   GROUP ACCOUNTS FOR NON-COMPANY GROUPS

In a move to harmonise the treatment of company and non-company charities, the 2006 Act introduces statutory requirements for group accounts for non-company groups. A non-company parent charity having subsidiaries under its control will usually be subject to the SORP requirements to prepare group accounts and the 2006 Act now provides this with a statutory basis. Companies (including charitable companies) that have subsidiaries are required to prepare group accounts under Part VII of the Companies Act 1985 in addition to their statutory accounts.

The framework for non-company group accounts is set out in new Sched.5A to the 1993 Act (inserted by s.30 of the 2006 Act) and will be fleshed out with detailed regulations made by order of the Minister. Regulations will cover matters including the form and contents of group accounts and the information to be provided in the parent charity's annual report concerning the activities of the subsidiaries. Group accounts must be submitted to the Commission with the annual report and the report of the auditor or independent examiner.

12.5.1   When are group accounts required?

Group accounts must be prepared for groups with a parent charity having subsidiary undertakings, whether these are charities or non-charities.

What is meant by a *parent* charity and *subsidiaries* for the purposes of Sched.5A is determined by reference to s.258 of and Sched.10A to the Companies Act 1985. Subsidiaries include entities over which the parent has the right to appoint a majority of its board or over which it exercises a dominant influence, including non-charities such as a charity's trading company. Subsidiaries do not include a charity's special trusts[1] nor any charity which is the subject of an accounts uniting direction under either s.96(5) or (6) of the 1993 Act, which will already be accounted for within the parent charity's accounts.

The requirement to prepare group accounts does not apply to exempt charities and there are further exceptions listed in para.4 of Sched.5A, where:

- the parent charity is itself a subsidiary of another charity;
- the aggregate group income is below the threshold fixed in the regulations to be made by the Minister; or
- the Minister makes regulations exempting or permitting charities to be exempted from the requirements.

Where a parent charity is required to prepare group accounts, the option to prepare its own accounts on the receipts and payments basis does not apply even where its income is below the accounts threshold in s.42(3) of the 1993 Act.

12.5.2   Audit or examination of group accounts

Group accounts must be audited, under para.6 of the new Sched.5A to the 1993 Act, if the parent charity's accounts fall to be audited or if the aggregate gross income and aggregate assets of the group exceed the thresholds laid down in regulations to be made by the Minister.

If the audit requirement does not apply, group accounts will be subject to independent examination, under para.7 of Sched.5A, if the aggregate gross income of the group in the year exceeds the thresholds set under s.43 of the 1993 Act for independent examination (currently £10,000).

Where a group's accounts are required to be audited or independently examined, then the parent charity's own accounts are also required to be audited or independently examined, as the case may be, irrespective of whether audit or independent examination would otherwise be required.

Schedule 5A also extends various provisions under Part VI of the 1993 Act, as amended, to group accounts. These provisions include those concerning the duties of auditors or reporting accountants to report matters to the Charity Commission and offences in connection with the accounts and report.

---

1   Special trusts are defined in 1993 Act, s.97(1) as property held for special purposes of the charity but not constituting a charity for the purposes of 1993 Act, Part VI relating to accounts, report and returns.

12.6   ANNUAL REPORTS AND RETURNS

The threshold for submission of annual reports and returns to the Charity Commission by all registered charities is now set at a gross income of £10,000 p.a. under s.45(3) and s.48(1A) of the 1993 Act as amended by Sched.8 to the 2006 Act. Levels of expenditure are no longer to be taken into account. The one exception to the £10,000 threshold is the CIO. A CIO must submit annual reports and returns whatever its level of gross income.

For the accounting regime in relation to exempt and excepted charities, see **Chapter 4**.

12.7   OFFENCES

The provisions of Part VI of the 1993 Act concerning the production and filing of annual reports and returns are backed up by offences for non-compliance under s.49. The 2006 Act amends s.49 to provide that charity trustees who have failed to take all reasonable steps to comply with their obligations are liable to a penalty which will increase according to the length of time the charity is in default. The basic penalty provided for under s.49 is a fine not exceeding level 4 on the standard scale (currently £2,500) and the daily default fine for continued contravention can be up to 10 per cent of level 4. The financial consequences of non-compliance for charity trustees are therefore now significantly more serious.

12.8   WHISTLE-BLOWING

Breaches of trust will often first come to light on audit or examination of accounts. Auditors and examiners therefore have a vital part to play in supporting the Commission's regulatory role. In an effort to make charity audits more effective and to encourage whistle-blowing, Part VI of the 1993 Act and the regulations made under it imposed a reporting obligation on non-company auditors who uncovered material abuse or breaches of trust. Reporting was required where a non-company auditor had reasonable cause to believe a matter would be 'of material significance' for the purposes of the exercise of the Charity Commission's functions under s.8 (power to institute inquiries) or s.18 (power to act for the protection of charities) of the 1993 Act. Auditors of non-company charities who were required to make a report would be protected against actions for breach of professional duty of confidentiality.

The 2006 Act casts the net far wider. It extends the whistle-blowing obligation to auditors of company accounts and to independent examiners under the new ss.44A and 68A of the 1993 Act. Whistle-blowing obligations are also imposed on the auditor or reporting accountant of non-company exempt charities – although in that case the report must be made to the charity's principal regulator rather than the Commission.

In an important new development, the whistle-blowing obligation is coupled with a new power to report concerns to the Commission under the new s.44A(3). This power applies to any matter which an auditor or independent examiner reasonably believes is likely to be relevant for the purpose of exercise of any of the Commission's functions. The Commission's functions under the new s.1C of the 1993 Act include not only regulatory functions, such as investigating and protecting against misconduct or mismanagement, but also its function to encourage and facilitate better administration of charities. It is difficult therefore to envisage concerns that would not fall within the scope of the new power.

All auditors and independent examiners are relieved under s.44A of the 1993 Act from breach of professional duty of confidence on whistle-blowing, including company auditors or reporting accountants (under the new s.68A of the 1993 Act). The relief from action for breach of professional duty applies to all whistle-blowing, whether there is a requirement to report or simply a power to do so. These changes look certain to encourage more widespread reporting to the Commission. The possibility that reports would leave auditors or examiners exposed to actions for breach of professional duty has effectively been removed.

Table A   Audit or examination of accounts

NON-COMPANY ACCOUNTS

Gross income	Requirement
£10,000 or less	Accounts to be filed only if requested by the Charity Commission
£10,001–£100,000	Independent examination
£100,001–£250,000	Independent examination unless aggregate assets before liabilities exceed £2.8m, in which case, audit
£250,001–£500,000	Independent examination by examiner with required qualification, unless aggregate assets before liabilities exceed £2.8m, in which case, audit
Over £500,000	Audit

COMPANY ACCOUNTS

Gross income	Requirement
Below £90,000	Audit exemption may be claimed
£90,001–£500,000	Accountant's report, unless aggregate assets on balance sheet before liabilities exceed £2.8m, in which case, audit
Over £500,000	Audit

Audit may also be required:

- where a charity is part of a group with aggregate gross income and assets exceeding the group audit threshold;
- under a charity's constitution or if a grant-funder requires it;
- for non-companies, where the Charity Commission requires it under s.43(4) of the 1993 Act;
- for companies where at least 10 per cent of the members vote for an audit.

An auditor or examiner will not be at risk even if the Commission ultimately decides not to follow up the report by opening a s.8 inquiry or taking any other protective action.

12.9   RELIEF OF LIABILITY FOR AUDITORS

The court has the power to grant relief to auditors against proceedings for negligence, default, breach of duty or breach of trust under s.727 of the Companies Act 1985 where the individual has acted honestly and reasonably and ought fairly to be excused. This power is extended by the new s.73E of the 1993 Act to include auditors, independent examiners and reporting accountants insofar as they are auditing, examining or reporting on charity accounts. This power now applies to charities whether or not they are companies.

The Charity Commission also now has a comparable power under s.73D of the 1993 Act to relieve an auditor, independent examiner or reporting accountant of an incorporated or unincorporated charity who is or may be in breach of trust or breach of duty. Again, relief will only be granted where the individual has acted honestly and ought fairly to be excused.

13 FUNDRAISING

13.1 THE BACKGROUND TO REFORM

The 2006 Act addresses some major concerns about the way in which public fundraising is conducted and regulated. The Strategy Unit Report, *Private Action, Public Benefit*[1] noted evidence of the public's less than positive view of fundraising and public criticism of under-regulation and lack of accountability. However, despite common perception, fundraising is in fact subject to considerable regulation, not least covering public charitable collections and relationships with professional fundraisers and commercial participators.[2] Public disenchantment appears to owe more to the failings in regulatory enforcement than lack of regulation.

Against this background, the proposal that a new self-regulatory scheme should be established to promote improvements in practice has been warmly endorsed by charities and fundraisers alike. The Fundraising Standards Board[3] has now been established to take this initiative forward. The government recognises, however, that to be effective, self-regulation needs to be supported by improvements in existing regulation, particularly in relation to public charitable collections.

The 2006 Act heralds a complete overhaul of regulation of public charitable collections and this is dealt with in detail in **Chapter 14**. This chapter is concerned with the other measures contained in the 2006 Act, concerning fundraising and charity funding, covering the new self-regulatory initiative and changes in relation to professional fundraisers and commercial participation.

The changes introduced in this connection are to Part II of the much-diminished 1992 Act.

1 At para.6.21, p.65.
2 As defined in 1992 Act, s.58(1).
3 See **www.fsboard.org.uk**.

13.2   THE SELF-REGULATORY INITIATIVE

13.2.1   The Fundraising Standards Board

In 2002, following the Strategy Unit Report, the Institute of Fundraising commissioned an independent report by Rodney Buse to look at possible models for a self-regulatory scheme. The Buse Commission's two reports[1] called for the establishment of a new body to act like an Office of Fair Trading for charities. The Fundraising Standards Board was set up well before the 2006 Act completed its parliamentary process, with a remit to encourage excellence in fundraising and to consider complaints from the public about fundraising activity.

The scheme is voluntary but all organisations engaged in fundraising will be encouraged to join, from charities and other philanthropic and voluntary sector organisations to fundraising businesses and consultants. As part of the scheme, members agree to follow the Institute of Fundraising's Codes of Fundraising Practice[2] and to keep the Board's Fundraising Promise. The Promise[3] focuses on commitment to high standards of honesty, accountability and reasonableness in fundraising. Members will be encouraged to use the Board's logo on all their fundraising materials, signalling adherence to the Board's scheme. The Board's strap-line is 'give with confidence' and it is hoped that, once public recognition is established, this will be a valuable, indeed essential, fundraising asset. All members of the scheme will be required to make their own complaints procedures publicly available but the Board will act as an arbiter of unresolved complaints.

13.2.2   Reserve power to control fundraising

The self-regulatory initiative is to operate on the best principle of 'carrot and stick'. The stick is the prospect that if charities and other potential members fail to enlist and self-regulation fails, the sector is likely to be subject to statutory regulation, probably of a more intensive and prescriptive nature, while the proffered carrot suggests a more supportive regime which will be responsive to changes in fundraising techniques and inevitable public concern. The carrot and stick approach received general support, including from the Institute of Fundraising.

Power for the Minister to intervene with statutory regulation has therefore been included at s.69 of the 2006 Act which introduces a new s.64A into the 1992 Act, to be brought into effect under the first commencement order under the 2006 Act in early 2007. The power allows the Minister to make such regulations as he considers 'necessary or desirable'. The trigger for statutory intervention has been left without further definition in the 2006 Act but consultation has already taken place and the government has responded outlining the criteria that will be used to assess the success of self-regulation.[4] These include the level of take-up of the Fundraising Standards Board scheme; the setting of a high standard of good practice, going beyond compliance with the law; sanctions for non-compliance and accountability of both the Fundraising Standards Board and its members. The scheme will be reviewed by the government on an annual basis according to agreed targets with a formal review of its success after five years to coincide with the review of the impact of the 2006 Act.

The reserve power allows the Minister to introduce regulations covering charity fundraising, defined under the new s.64A(2) of the 1992 Act so as to include fundraising not only for specific charities, but also for general charitable purposes and for benevolent or philanthropic purposes. It covers the activities of both the charity and its agents, so bringing a charity's activities through its volunteers and professional fundraisers within the scope of regulation. It does not, however, include primary purpose trading, that is trading in the course of carrying on the charity's objects or where the trade is carried out by the charity's beneficiaries.

The new provisions in s.64A of the 1992 Act anticipate the introduction of good practice requirements under which all reasonable steps must be taken to ensure that fundraising:

- does not unreasonably intrude on the privacy of potential donors;
- does not involve the making of unreasonably persistent approaches for donations;
- does not involve undue pressure being placed on potential donors; and
- does not involve false or misleading statements about the need for funds, the use to which funds will be put or the activities, achievements or finances of the recipient charity or connected company (s.64A(4) and (5)).

The Minister can provide that persistent compliance failure without reasonable excuse will be an offence.[5]

---

1   Phase I (August 2003) and Phase II (January 2004).
2   This can be seen at **www.institute-of-fundraising.org.uk**.
3   See **www.fsboard.org.uk/fundraising-promise.aspx**.
4   The consultation paper and government response are available at **www.cabinetoffice. gov.uk/third_sector/law_andregulation/fundraising_and_collections**.
5   On conviction, the offence could carry a fine not exceeding level 2 on the standard scale (currently £500).

13.3   CONTROLS OVER COMMERCIAL PARTICIPATORS AND PROFESSIONAL FUNDRAISERS

13.3.1   Regulation under the 1992 Act

The 1992 Act introduced the first regulation of charity relationships with professional fundraisers and commercial participators. The intention was to protect charity interests by ensuring that certain minimum standards would have to be met and to ensure that the public would not be misled about the benefits charities would receive from their donation or support.

The 1992 Act required written agreements to be in place between charities and the professional fundraisers or commercial participators they work with. In addition, when running an appeal or promotion, statements had to be made setting out the benefit passing to the charity and (in general terms) the remuneration or benefit taken by the professional fundraiser or commercial participator. In practice, these provisions proved to be unsatisfactory, with the statements made often providing the public with little meaningful information.

The 2006 Act revisits the existing statutory provisions, tightening the requirements for statements concerning remuneration or benefits that professional fundraisers or commercial participators receive. New provisions are also introduced for statements to be made when a charity's employees, officers and trustees are acting as fundraising collectors. These provisions will be brought into effect under the second commencement order under the 2006 Act, due in the second half of 2007.

13.3.2   New requirements for professional fundraisers and commercial participator statements

Under the 1992 Act, when conducting appeals for charitable, benevolent or philanthropic purposes, professional fundraisers had to state 'in general terms' the method by which their remuneration would be fixed. Under s.67(2) and (3) of the 2006 Act, professional fundraisers are now required to state the actual method by which their payment is fixed. In addition, they must disclose the 'notifiable amount' of their remuneration. This is the amount of their remuneration, if this is known and, if not, the estimated amount, calculated as accurately as is reasonably possible in the circumstances (see the new s.60(3A) of the 1992 Act).

The 2006 Act makes similar amendments to the information to be given by commercial participators. Under s.60 of the 1992 Act, a commercial participator was required to make a general statement outlining the method of fixing the benefit passing to the charity or charities concerned. A commercial participator's statement must now specify the notifiable amount passing to the institution concerned of:

* the consideration given for the goods or services, or
* the proceeds of the promotional venture, or
* the total donations,

as the case may be (see 1992 Act, s.60(3) as amended by 2006 Act, s.67(4)).

13.4   STATEMENTS TO BE MADE BY CHARITY EMPLOYEES, ETC. WHEN APPEALING FOR FUNDS

Under s.60 of the 1992 Act, professional fundraisers appealing for funds must make clear their relationship to the charity or charities concerned and the fact that they are paid. Officers, employees and trustees of the charity were expressly excluded from the 1992 Act definition of professional fundraiser but the Joint Committee on the Draft Bill[1] concluded that there was a public interest in knowing whether a collector was paid, in whatever capacity, and that the real distinction should lie between paid collectors, including employees and volunteers. This is now reflected in amendments under new s.60A of the 1992 Act so that, where a collector is an officer, employee or trustee of the charity or of a connected company such as its trading company and is being paid as such or for acting as a collector, he or she must state that fact. The amount of the payment does not have to be disclosed. Where an appeal is for charitable, benevolent or philanthropic purposes rather than for the benefit of the specific charity, then a similar statement has to be made. The appropriate forms of statement that might be used are to be set out in Cabinet Office guidance.

Collectors who receive only low levels of payment are excluded from the operation of these provisions under the new s.60B of the 1992 Act. This exclusion is similar to the exclusion of the lower paid professional fundraisers from regulation under s.58(3) of the 1992 Act. The earnings limit is set under s.60B at £500 for the collection concerned or more than £5 per day or £500 a year. These are the same limits as set under the 1992 Act for low paid professional fundraisers. The Minister, however, has power to vary the earnings limit under s.60B(6).

Collecting without complying with the new provisions is an offence under the new s.60A(8) of the 1992 Act, and similar provisions apply as for breach of the rules by professional fundraisers or commercial participators.[2] The defence under s.60(8) of the 1992 Act, that reasonable precautions have been taken and all due diligence exercised to avoid committing the offence, is extended to the new offences under s.60A.

---

1   Joint Committee on the Draft Charities Bill, Vol.I, para.330.
2   On conviction, the offence carries a fine not exceeding level 5 on the standard scale, currently up to £5,000.

14 PUBLIC CHARITABLE COLLECTIONS

14.1 INTRODUCTION

14.1.1 The current regime

Collections give voluntary organisations a very visible presence in our community but they are vulnerable to abuse and attract much negative publicity. Regulation has long been recognised as unsatisfactory, even lamentable. There was considerable pressure therefore for reform and the 2006 Act now introduces a wholly new regime.

The 2006 Act replaces regulation of street collections under the Police, Factories, Etc. (Miscellaneous Provisions) Act 1916 (1916 Act) and the House to House Collections Act 1939 (1939 Act). Under these Acts, regulation has largely rested with local authorities, except in London where the police have exercised control. Unfortunately, local authorities have not adopted a common approach to regulation. The 1916 Act conferred powers on local authorities to license street collections but did not require them to do so. The result has been that, although many authorities have assumed these functions, some have not. The 1939 Act made licensing of house-to-house collections mandatory but its enforcement has been patchy from authority to authority. There are also some curious inconsistencies between the street collections regime and that for house-to-house collections, for example, a refusal to license a house-to-house collection can be appealed but not the refusal of a street collection licence. An attempt was made in the 1992 Act to remedy matters by introducing a single unified system applying to all type of public charitable collections. However, concerns over the detailed workings of that regime as well as who would pay for it meant that it was never bought into operation.

14.1.2 Outline of the new regime

The 2006 Act will regulate public collections not only for charitable purposes but also for philanthropic or benevolent purposes. A two-stage system of regulation is to apply. Stage one involves obtaining a public collections certificate from the Charity Commission. The requirement for a certificate is to ensure that collections are being appropriately managed and are under suitable control. Stage two of the process involves obtaining permits or notifying the relevant local authority or authorities. The issue of permits enables local authorities to ensure that the timing and location of collections will not inconvenience the public, with too many collections taking place at the same time or in the same area.

The implementation of the new regime will require formulation of regulations and guidance following consultation as well as considerable preparation by the Charity Commission as the lead regulator. It is therefore unlikely to be before 2009. There are already fears that it will suffer the same fate as the regime proposed in the 1992 Act.

14.2   KEY DEFINITIONS

The scope of the regulatory framework is set by the definitions contained in ss.45–47 of the 2006 Act. Before turning to the detail of the new requirements for collections, it is helpful to refer briefly to the key definitions:

A *public charitable collection* is defined under s.45(2)(a) as a charitable appeal made (1) in any public place, or (2) by visits to houses or business premises, or both.

A *charitable appeal* is an appeal to the public, whether for money or for other property, accompanied by a representation that the whole or part of the proceeds of the collection will be applied for charitable, benevolent or philanthropic purposes. Under s.45(3)(a) of the 2006 Act a collection of money means the giving of money by whatever means, therefore including securing direct debit or standing order commitments. This clears up doubt that had existed under the previous regime as to whether the activities of the so-called 'chuggers' were covered by statutory regulation. Appeals under which donors receive something in return, be it a badge, a rose or a shoe shine, are also included if a representation is made that the proceeds will be applied for charitable, benevolent or philanthropic purposes.

A *public place* means a highway or any other place to which members of the public have access or are permitted access. The insides of buildings will not generally be treated as public places except where they are public areas such as stations, airports or shopping precincts. This remedies one of the deficiencies of the street collections regime under the 1916 Act which did not cover these locations, leaving a gaping hole in regulation. The definition of a public place, however, excludes places to which the public has access only on payment, or places to which the public has only been admitted for the purposes of the appeal (see s.45(5) and (6)). This will take many charity fundraising events outside regulation under the 2006 Act.

Also excluded from the definition of public charitable collections are charitable appeals made:

- in the course of public meetings;

- in churchyards or burial grounds, next to a place of worship or other land used in connection with, and next to, a place of worship, where the land is enclosed or substantially enclosed;
- on land to which the public have been allowed access or have statutory rights of access, for example, under the Countryside and Rights of Way Act 2000, where the promoter of the collection is the occupier of the land;
- by means of an unattended receptacle (that is, not attended by the person acting as collector in relation to the appeal). A typical example is that of collection boxes placed by shop tills.

A *collector* is a person who makes an appeal, alone or with others. It includes a person who is paid.

A *promoter* is a person who organises or controls the conduct of a charitable appeal, alone or with others and, again, it includes a person who receives payment. In the case of a corporate charity the promoter will usually be the charity itself. For an unincorporated charity the promoter will usually be a trustee or trustees. The collector is the promoter if no one else falls into this category.

14.3   REQUIREMENTS FOR CONDUCTING COLLECTIONS IN A PUBLIC PLACE

Under s.48 of the 2006 Act anyone promoting a collection in a public place must hold a public collections certificate issued by the Charity Commission. A local authority permit must also be obtained and the collection must be carried on in accordance with the permit. For charities launching collections nationally or over a wide area, a permit is required from every local authority concerned and this will represent a significant workload. It is an offence to carry on a collection other than an exempt collection without complying with s.48.[1] There is, however, an exemption for local, short-term collections under s.50 of the 2006 Act (see below).

This basic framework will be supplemented by regulations made by the Minister under s.63 of the 2006 Act. These regulations are to cover:

- the keeping and publication of accounts;
- the prevention of annoyance to the public;
- the use of badges and certificates of authority, their form, use and production on request; and
- the minimum age for collectors.

The regulations may also provide that breaches shall be a criminal offence.[2] The regulations will therefore ultimately establish minimum required standards. In the meantime, the Fundraising Standards Board is developing good practice standards under the self-regulatory initiative.

---

1   On conviction, the offence will carry a fine not exceeding level 5 on the standard scale, currently £5,000.

2   On conviction, breach of the regulation will carry a fine not exceeding level 2 on the standard scale, currently £500.

14.4   REQUIREMENTS FOR CONDUCTING DOOR-TO-DOOR COLLECTIONS

Under s.49 of the 2006 Act the promoters of any door-to-door collection must hold a public collections certificate issued by the Charity Commission. No local authority permit is required but the promoters must provide a copy of their certificate to each local authority concerned and inform them of the collection, its purpose, the time and place and any other matters required from time to time. It is an offence to carry on a door-to-door collection other than local, short-term collection without complying with s.49.[1] However, as with collections in a public place, there are exemptions for local short-term collections under s.50 of the 2006 Act.

The period for informing the local authority before a collection can take place will be prescribed by regulations made by the Minister under s.63 of the 2006 Act. It was clear from consultation on the draft Bill, which contained specific periods for notification, that charities will experience practical problems with over-prescriptive time-limits. For large charities with annual collecting programmes scheduled well in advance, it is important to be able to deal with notification at an early stage in the planning process. For other charities such as those operating locally and collecting goods for sale in charity shops, it is equally important to be able to launch a collection at short notice when stocks are low or storage space and volunteers are available.[2] Flexibility will be essential for the house-to-house collections regulations to be made workable.

1   On conviction, the offence carries a fine not exceeding level 5 on the standard rate, currently £5,000.
2   For a summary of the evidence see the Joint Committee on the Draft Charities Bill, Vol.I, paras.278–315.

14.5   EXEMPTION FOR LOCAL, SHORT-TERM COLLECTIONS

The 2006 Act recognises that regulation of all local, short-term collections would be disproportionately burdensome, not only for charities, but also no doubt for the Charity Commission and local authorities. Under s.50 of the 2006 Act collections are therefore exempt from regulation if they are local in character and short term, that is not exceeding the period to be prescribed by the Minister under regulations.

14.5.1   Requirements for local, short-term collections

No certificate or permit is required for local, short-term collections but the organisers will still have to notify the local authority or authorities concerned that the collection will take place. Failure to do so is an offence.[1] Details must be provided, including the purpose of the collection, the time and place and any other matters required by regulations. The local authority can reject a claim for treatment as an exempt collection, on the basis either that it considers the collection is not in fact local or short term in character or that the promoters have previously been in breach of fundraising regulations or have been convicted of fundraising offences or offences of dishonesty (as set out in s.53(2)(a)(i) to (vi) of the 2006 Act).

14.5.2   When is a collection local in character?

The factors to be taken into account by a local authority in deciding whether a collection is local in character will be covered by further regulations made by the Minister, but under s.63(2) of the 2006 Act these matters will include:

- the extent of the area to be covered by the appeal;
- whether the appeal is part of a series;
- the number of collectors to be involved and whether or not they will be paid;
- the financial resources of the charitable, benevolent or philanthropic institution for whose benefit the appeal is made; and
- where the promoters live or have a place of business.

14.5.3   Appeals against refusal of exemption

Where a local authority considers the exemption does not apply, it must serve notice to that effect giving its reasons. Appeals against a local authority's decision may be made to the magistrates' court under s.62 of the 2006 Act within 14 days of the service of the notice. In turn, an appeal from the magistrates' court may be brought to the Crown Court. The court may confirm, vary or reverse the local authority's decision and give directions, for example as to the date or dates on which the collection may be conducted.

---

1 On conviction, the offence carries a fine not exceeding level 3 on the standard scale, currently £1,000.

14.6   PUBLIC COLLECTIONS CERTIFICATES

14.6.1   Applying for a public collections certificate from the Charity Commission

Applications for certificates have to be made to the Charity Commission under s.51 of the 2006 Act. The Commission will make regulations concerning the form of the application and the period that must be allowed between the lodging of an application and the date of the collection. There is to be some flexibility in individual cases so that application made by made at shorter notice, for example, where a disaster appeal is launched. The regulations can also treat different types of cases differently, so the Commission should be able to meet the differing needs of large and small charities.

An application for a certificate can relate to a single collection or cover a series of collections but certificates cannot be in force for more than five years. Even the largest charities with major fundraising operations will therefore undergo review at least every five years.

Having received an application for a certificate, the Commission may make further enquiries and can call for information and documents to support the application. It must then either issue a certificate or refuse the application on the grounds set out in s.53(1) of the 2006 Act. Where an application is refused the Commission must give written notice setting out the reasons for the refusal and drawing attention to the right of appeal under s.57 and the time-limits that apply.

The Commission can issue a certificate subject to conditions, consistent with any regulations made by the Minister. Where a condition is imposed the Commission must give written notice of the reasons and of the right to appeal within the time-limit.

14.6.2   Refusal of certificates

The grounds on which the Commission may refuse to issue a public collections certificate are set out in s.53 of the 2006 Act and are, in brief that:

- the applicant has been convicted of a relevant offence (see below);
- the Commission is not satisfied that the applicant is authorised by or on behalf of the charity or benevolent or philanthropic institution concerned;[1]
- the applicant has previously failed to exercise due diligence in promoting other collections, including exempt local short-term collections and collections under the Scottish regulations;
- the Commission is not satisfied that the applicant will exercise due diligence in relation to the proposed collection;
- the amount to be devoted to charitable benevolent or philanthropic purposes is inadequate, given the likely proceeds of the collections;
- the applicant would be likely to receive excessive remuneration in relation to the collections;
- the applicant has failed to provide information including in relation to a previous application or in response to the Commission's request;
- the information provided is false or misleading in a material respect;
- the applicant has previously breached conditions attached to a certificate or has persistently breached conditions attached to a local authority permit; and
- the applicant or anyone authorised by him has breached any regulations made by the Minister in relation to the conduct of public charitable collections.

The *relevant offences* are described in s.53(2) of the 2006 Act and include not only offences under the new and previous statutory regimes for public charitable collections but also offences involving dishonesty and any offence which the

Commission considers would be likely to be assisted by the applicant obtaining a public collections certificate.

The *due diligence* required to be shown concerns matters such as ensuring that collectors are fit and proper persons and comply with the relevant regulations, as well as ensuring that anyone who is not authorised as a collector does not obtain badges or certificates of authority. What is appropriate due diligence will be a question of fact and degree. However, practices such as selecting collectors for street collections from the local telephone directory are unlikely to satisfy due diligence requirements.

14.6.3   Withdrawal or variation of certificates

The Commission has power under s.56 of the 2006 Act to withdraw a certificate or suspend a certificate for up to six months. In addition, it can vary conditions attaching to a certificate or introduce new conditions. These powers are exercisable where:

- circumstances have changed and the certificate would not have been issued in the changed circumstances;
- the certificate holder has unreasonably refused to provide information or documents requested by the Commission or the Commission has reason to believe that the applicant supplied false or misleading information when applying for the certificates; or
- the Commission has reason to believe there has been or there is likely to be a breach of conditions relating to a certificate.

The Commission must serve notice of its decision to withdraw or vary a certificate on the holder. There is a right of appeal to the Charity Tribunal. The Commission's decision takes effect on the expiry of the period for appeal or, if an appeal is brought, once the appeal is concluded. A certificate can, however, be withdrawn or varied with immediate effect if the Commission considers it is in the public interest, allowing for decisive action in cases of suspected abuse or fraud.

A certificate is not transferable except under s.55 of the 2006 Act, which allows the Commission to transfer certificates between trustees of an unincorporated charity, with the consent of the charity trustees as a whole.

14.6.4   Appealing against the Commission's decisions

The various rights of appeal to the Charity Tribunal on Commission decisions relating to public collections certificates are set out in s.57 of the 2006 Act.

A Commission decision under s.52 to reject an application for a certificate or to attach conditions can be appealed by the applicant. A certificate holder can also appeal Commission decisions under ss.55 and 56 not to transfer a certificate between trustees of an unincorporated charity and to withdraw or suspend a certificate or to attach or vary conditions respectively. The Attorney-General can also appeal Commission decisions relating to public collections certificates under s.57(4) of the 2006 Act.

All matters referred to the Tribunal are considered afresh by way of appeal and new evidence, not considered by the Commission, can be admitted. The Tribunal has powers to quash a decision, remitting it to the Commission or to make a substitute decision within the powers available to the Commission.

---

1   Unauthorised fundraising can be a significant problem for charities and this should assist in eliminating bogus fundraising and bringing fundraising under a charity's control. Under 1992 Act, s.62 a charity can apply to the court to prevent unauthorised fundraising but, in practice, this can be a costly exercise and is a last resort.

14.7   LOCAL AUTHORITY PERMITS

14.7.1   Applying for a permit from the local authority

As already mentioned, under s.58 of the 2006 Act any person intending to promote a public charitable collection (other than an exempt local, short-term collection) must obtain a permit from the local authority for the area concerned, in addition to holding a public collections certificate.

The application for a permit must set out the date or range of dates (not spanning more than 12 months) for which a permit is requested. Applications must also be accompanied by the promoter's public collections certificate and any additional information prescribed by regulations made by the Minister under s.63(1) of the 2006 Act. Regulations issued by the Minister will also cover matters including the period that must be allowed between making an application for a permit and the date, or first date, for the collection.

A permit may be issued with or without conditions. Conditions are intended to allow the local authority to take account of local circumstances and may cover:

* the day/week, date, time or frequency of the collection;
* the locality or localities in which the collection may take place;
* the manner in which the collection is to be conducted; and
* any other matter prescribed by the Minister.

The inclusion of conditions in a permit can be appealed (see **14.7.4** below).

14.7.2   Refusal of permits

A local authority may only refuse to issue a permit on the grounds set out in s.60(1) of the 2006 Act, namely that a collection would cause undue inconvenience to the public because of its timing, frequency or locations. Local authorities may take account of the fact that another public charitable collection or other collections, including exempt local, short-term collections, are already to be held in the locality on the same date or immediately before or after the date concerned. Otherwise, they have limited discretion. They may not favour one charity or type of charity over others and permits will come to be issued on the basis of 'first come, first served'. This will inevitably tend to favour larger charities with major fundraising programmes organised well in advance.

14.7.3   Withdrawal or variation of permits

Local authorities have power under s.61 of the 2006 Act to withdraw permits, to attach conditions or to vary any existing conditions. These powers can be exercised:

- where there has been a change in circumstances since the permit was issued or last varied and the local authority considers that it would not have issued the permit, or not without different or additional conditions, under the new circumstances; or
- the local authority has reason to believe that the application for the permit was false or misleading in a material respect; or
- the local authority has reason to believe that there has been, or is likely to be, a breach of any condition, or a breach of conditions is continuing.

The local authority has to serve notice of withdrawal or variation on the holder of the permit, giving reasons and referring to the right of appeal under s.62 and the time-limits that apply. The local authority's decision takes effect only once the time-limit for appeal has expired or the appeal is decided or abandoned.

When a permit is withdrawn, a local authority must also inform the Charity Commission, sending it a copy of the decision with reasons. This is an important part of the regulatory process, necessary if there is to be a co-ordinated response to abuse between local authorities and the Commission.

14.7.4   Appealing against local authority decisions

Appeals against local authority decisions may be made to the magistrates' court under s.62 of the 2006 Act within 14 days of service of the notice of the decision being appealed against. An appeal may be brought from the magistrates' court decision to the Crown Court. On appeal, the court may confirm, vary or reverse the local authority's decision and give directions as the court thinks fit (s.62(7)).

14.8   OTHER OFFENCES IN CONNECTION WITH COLLECTIONS

As already mentioned, there are offences of conducting public charitable collections otherwise than in accordance with the 2006 Act and regulations. In addition, under s.64 of the 2006 Act there are specific offences relating to:

- the improper use of badges or certificates of authority or the use of false badges or certificates; and

- the knowing or reckless provision of false or misleading information to the Charity Commission when applying for a public collections certificate or to the local authority in connection with door-to-door or local, short-term collections or applications for permits.[1]

In some circumstances where an offence is committed by a corporate body, its directors and other officers will themselves be guilty of an offence. Under s.65 of the 2006 Act, where a corporate body has committed an offence and it is established that a director, manager, secretary or other similar officer consented or connived in the offence, or that the offence is attributable to neglect on his or her part, then that individual is also guilty of the offence.

---

1   These offences carry fines not exceeding level 5 on the standard scale, currently £5,000.

14.9   HOW EFFECTIVE WILL THE NEW REGIME BE?

The new regime is universally acknowledged to be an improvement on the disjointed regulation of public charitable collections it will replace. Nevertheless, significant problems remain. Some collections escape regulation altogether, such as collections in unattended receptacles. In addition, as has been seen, collections of goods are generally treated to a lighter regime. The Scrutiny Committee heard evidence from some local authorities, however, expressing significant concerns about abuse associated with collections of goods and unattended clothing banks supposedly for charitable purposes.[1] The new regime will leave some gaps in regulation which are likely to be readily exploited by the unscrupulous, undermining public confidence generally.

At the same time concerns have been expressed about the burden the new regime imposes, not only on charities but also on local authorities and the Charity Commission. It is essential that the Commission should be properly resourced to allow it to carry out all appropriate checks on suitability for collection certificates. Equally, if the new system is to operate properly, local authorities and police forces will have to devote manpower and resources to maintaining a watchful eye so as to respond effectively to abuse. Achieving consistency of enforcement of the regulations at local level will be demanding. However, without a consistent approach, the regime as a whole will be seriously flawed.

Our view is that the man who stands on the street corner appealing for funds with a hand-written placard saying 'For the Cancer Hospice' is not likely to be a priority for the policeman on the beat unless he is causing a disturbance. The voluntary sector must surely set an example by ensuring that the public become aware of how well-run charities collect funds in public places, with collectors wearing tabards or other visible regalia bearing the Fundraising Standards Board's logo and using receptacles which prevent collectors or passers-by alike from helping themselves.

---

1   See, e.g. evidence from the Institute of Licensing in relation to bogus fundraising in Leeds, summarised in the Joint Committee on the Draft Charities Bill, Vol.I, p.81.

15 MISCELLANEOUS AMENDMENTS

15.1 GRANTS BY GOVERNMENT TO CHARITABLE BENEVOLENT OR PHILANTHROPIC INSTITUTIONS

There has been some doubt cast upon whether government may make general grants to charities and to other benevolent and philanthropic institutions, as opposed to grants made under specific statutory authority.[1] This power is now clarified by s.70 of the 2006 Act in relation to England and by s.71 in relation to Wales, the latter exercisable by the National Assembly for Wales. In addition to grants, loans, guarantees and specific expenditure are permitted.

Some of the terms and conditions which might reasonably be imposed in relation to the grant are set out in ss.70(4) and 71(4) respectively and include:

- the purposes for which the grants, loans and guarantees may be used and the circumstances in which they might have to be repaid;
- the keeping of accounts and records and reporting to the government departments in question as to the project being funded; and
- the onward transmission of the government financial assistance by way of loans and grants to others and the terms of such loans or grants.

The relevant Minister can also make arrangements for these grant-making powers to be exercised in whole or in part by other bodies.

There must be reports to Parliament or to the National Assembly for Wales, as appropriate, at the end of each financial year concerning the exercise of these powers.

---

1 Under the annual Appropriation Act.

15.2 EXCHANGE OF INFORMATION WITH THE NORTHERN IRELAND REGULATOR

As is already the case in Scotland, the reform of charity law is in progress in Northern Ireland and under s.72 of the 2006 Act the body which will regulate charities in Northern Ireland will be able, when established, to exchange information about charities with relevant public authorities under orders to be made by the Minister. The intention is to put the Northern Ireland charity regulator on a par with the Charity Commission and the Office of the Scottish Charity Regulator.

Disclosure of information by HMRC is subject to the same limits as are set out in s.10(2) of the 1993 Act (as amended), but unsurprisingly charities, benevolent and philanthropic institutions and their subsidiary trading companies are all bodies whose information can be disclosed to the Commission by HMRC.

Mutual disclosure apart from HMRC can be with departments of central and local government, the police and other charity regulators in the UK.

15.3   REVIEW OF THE ACT

The Minister is required by s.73 to establish a review of the operation of the 2006 Act within five years after Royal Assent (8 November 2006). The review must address, in particular, the effect of the 2006 Act on:

- excepted charities;
- public confidence in charities;
- the level of charitable donations; and
- the willingness of individuals to volunteer;

as well as the status of the Commission as a government department and other matters considered appropriate by the Minister.

In the final stages of the passage of the Bill through Parliament, government ministers indicated that they would be reviewing the public benefit issue within three years.

15.4   ORDERS, REGULATIONS, AMENDMENTS AND COMMENCEMENT

There are standard provisions in ss.74 and 75 of the 2006 Act giving the Minister for the Cabinet Office powers to make orders by statutory instrument to modify primary or secondary legislation for the purposes of the 2006 Act and to effect the repeal or modification of relevant legislation. Certain key amendments (for example, to regulations affecting exempt charities) may only be made by affirmative resolutions of both Houses of Parliament. Section 75 also introduces Scheds.8 to 10 into the 2006 Act which contain consequential amendments to legislation, repeal of enactments and other transitional provisions.

At the time of writing, the Minister for the Cabinet Office has indicated that consolidation of charity legislation could take place in 2008 and s.76 provides the Minister with the power to make orders facilitating consolidation, such orders to come into force immediately before the consolidated legislation.

As mentioned in **Chapter 12**, s.77 of the 2006 Act gives the Minister power (similar to that under s.468 of the Companies Act 2006) to allow for the report and accounts scrutiny regime for company and non-company charities to be harmonised.

Interpretation of words and phrases are dealt with in s.78 and of note are definitions of 'charity' by reference to s.1(1) and 'charitable purposes' by reference to s.2(6), as to which see **Chapter 2**.

Commencement of the 2006 Act will for the most part be dealt with in later commencement orders to be made by the Minister but certain provisions designed to facilitate the operation of the 2006 Act are already in force (see s.79). **Appendix 5** of this book contains the Implementation Plan for the 2006 Act produced in December 2006 by the Office of the Third Sector in the Cabinet Office. The Plan suggests that the 2006 Act will be brought into force by three separate commencement orders ending in 'early 2008'. Even then, some provisions relating to exempt and excepted charities and the voluntary registration of small charities (see **Chapter 3**) may not come into force until well into 2008 and the new licensing regime relating to public charitable collections (see **Chapter 14**) may well be delayed until 2009 and beyond.

Charity law and regulation in Scotland and Northern Ireland are now devolved to the legislatures of those countries so for the most part the 2006 Act extends only to England and Wales. However, for taxation purposes s.80 provides that ss.1, 2, 3 and 5 of the 2006 Act (relating to the meaning of charity, charitable purposes and public benefit) apply to Scotland and Northern Ireland as well.

APPENDIX 1
Recreational Charities Act 1958

[1958 c.17]

An Act to declare charitable under the law of England and Wales the provision in the interests of social welfare of facilities for recreation or other leisure-time occupation, to make similar provision as to certain trusts heretofore established for carrying out social welfare activities within the meaning of the Miners' Welfare Act 1952, to enable laws for corresponding purposes to be passed by the Parliament of Northern Ireland, and for purposes connected therewith

[13th March 1958]

BE IT ENACTED by the Queen's most Excellent Majesty, by and with the advice and consent of the Lords Spiritual and Temporal, and Commons, in this present Parliament assembled, and by the authority of the same, as follows:

1   **General provision as to recreational and similar trusts, etc.**

(1)   Subject to the provisions of this Act, it shall be and be deemed always to have been charitable to provide, or assist in the provision of, facilities for recreation or other leisure-time occupation, if the facilities are provided in the interests of social welfare:

Provided that nothing in this section shall be taken to derogate from the principle that a trust or institution to be charitable must be for the public benefit.

(2)   The requirement in subsection (1) that the facilities are provided in the interests of social welfare cannot be satisfied if the basic conditions are not met.

(2A)   The basic conditions are –

(a)   that the facilities are provided with the object of improving the conditions of life for the persons for whom the facilities are primarily intended; and

(b)   that either –

(i)   those persons have need of the facilities by reason of their youth, age, infirmity or disability, poverty, or social and economic circumstances, or

(ii)   the facilities are to be available to members of the public at large or to male, or to female, members of the public at large.

(3)   Subject to the said requirement, subsection (1) of this section applies in particular to the provision of facilities at village halls, community centres and women's institutes, and to the provision and maintenance of grounds and buildings to be used for purposes of recreation or leisure-time occupation, and extends to the provision of facilities for those purposes by the organising of any activity.

2   [. . .]

3   Savings and other provisions as to past transactions

(1)   Nothing in this Act shall be taken to restrict the purposes which are to be regarded as charitable independently of this Act.

(2)   Nothing in this Act –

(a)   shall apply to make charitable any trust, or validate any disposition, of property if before the seventeenth day of December, nineteen hundred and fifty-seven, that property or any property representing or forming part of it, or any income arising from any such property, has been paid or conveyed to, or applied for the benefit of, the persons entitled by reason of the invalidity of the trust or disposition; or

(b)   shall affect any order or judgment made or given (whether before or after the passing of this Act) in legal proceedings begun before that day; or

(c)   shall require anything properly done before that day, or anything done or to be done in pursuance of a contract entered into before that day, to be treated for any purpose as wrongful or ineffectual.

(3)   Nothing in this Act shall require anything to be treated for the purposes of any enactment as having been charitable at a time before the date of the passing of this Act, so as to invalidate anything done or any determination given before that date.

(4)–(5) [...]

4   [...]

5   Application to the Crown

This Act, and (except in so far as the contrary intention appears) any enactment of the Parliament of Northern Ireland passed for purposes similar to section one of this Act, shall bind the Crown.

6   Short title and extent

(1)   This Act may be cited as the Recreational Charities Act 1958.

(2)   Section 1 of this Act, as amended by section 5 of the Charities Act 2006, has the same effect in relation to the law of Scotland or Northern Ireland as section 5 of that Act has by virtue of section 80(3) to (6) of that Act.

(3)   Sections 1 and 2 of this Act, as in force before the commencement of section 5 of that Act, continue to have effect in relation to the law of Scotland or Northern Ireland so far as they affect the construction of any references to charities or charitable purposes which –

(a)   are to be construed in accordance with the law of England and Wales, but

(b)   are not contained in enactments relating to matters of the kind mentioned in section 80(4) or (6) of that Act.

APPENDIX 2
Charities Act 1992

[1992 c.41]

An Act to amend the Charities Act 1960 and make other provision with respect to charities; to regulate fund-raising activities carried on in connection with charities and other institutions; to make fresh provision with respect to public charitable collections; and for connected purposes.

[16th March 1992]

BE IT ENACTED by the Queen's most Excellent Majesty, by and with the advice and consent of the Lords Spiritual and Temporal, and Commons, in this present Parliament assembled, and by the authority of the same, as follows:–

PART I

1–57   [. . .]

PART II   CONTROL OF FUND-RAISING FOR CHARITABLE INSTITUTIONS

Preliminary

58   Interpretation of Part II

(1)   In this Part –

'charitable contributions', in relation to any representation made by any commercial participator or other person, means –

    (a)   the whole or part of –

        (i)   the consideration given for goods or services sold or supplied by him, or

        (ii)   any proceeds (other than such consideration) of a promotional venture undertaken by him, or

    (b)   sums given by him by way of donation in connection with the sale or supply of any such goods or services (whether the amount of such sums is determined by reference to the value of any such goods or services or otherwise);

'charitable institution' means a charity or an institution (other than a charity) which is established for charitable, benevolent or philanthropic purposes;

'charity' means a charity within the meaning of the Charities Act 1993;

'commercial participator', in relation to any charitable institution, means any person (apart from a company connected with the institution) who –

(a)   carries on for gain a business other than a fund-raising business, but

(b)   in the course of that business, engages in any promotional venture in the course of which it is represented that charitable contributions are to be given to or applied for the benefit of the institution;

'company' has the meaning given by section 97 of the Charities Act 1993;

'the court' means the High Court or a county court;

'credit card' means a card which is a credit-token within the meaning of the Consumer Credit Act 1974;

'debit card' means a card the use of which by its holder to make a payment results in a current account of his at a bank, or at any other institution providing banking services, being debited with the payment;

'fund-raising business' means any business carried on for gain and wholly or primarily engaged in soliciting or otherwise procuring money or other property for charitable, benevolent or philanthropic purposes;

'institution' includes any trust or undertaking;

'the Minister' means the Minister for the Cabinet Office;

'professional fund-raiser' means –

(a)   any person (apart from a charitable institution or a company connected with such an institution) who carries on a fund-raising business, or

(b)   any other person (apart from a person excluded by virtue of subsection (2) or (3)) who for reward solicits money or other property for the benefit of a charitable institution, if he does so otherwise than in the course of any fund-raising venture undertaken by a person falling within paragraph (a) above;

'promotional venture' means any advertising or sales campaign or any other venture undertaken for promotional purposes;

'radio or television programme' includes any item included in a programme service within the meaning of the Broadcasting Act 1990.

(2)   In subsection (1), paragraph (b) of the definition of 'professional fund-raiser' does not apply to any of the following, namely –

(a)   any charitable institution or any company connected with any such institution;

(b)   any officer or employee of any such institution or company, or any trustee of any such institution, acting (in each case) in his capacity as such;

(c)   any person acting as a collector in respect of a public charitable collection (apart from a person who is a promoter of such a collection as defined in section 47(1) of the Charities Act 2006);

(d)   any person who in the course of a relevant programme, that is to say a radio or television programme in the course of which a fund-raising venture is undertaken by –

(i)   a charitable institution, or

(ii)   a company connected with such an institution,

makes any solicitation at the instance of that institution or company; or

(e)   any commercial participator;

and for this purpose 'collector' and 'public charitable collection' have the same meaning as in Chapter 1 of Part 3 of the Charities Act 2006.

(3)   In addition, paragraph (b) of the definition of 'professional fund-raiser' does not apply to a person if he does not receive –

(a) more than –

    (i) £5 per day, or

    (ii) £500 per year,

by way of remuneration in connection with soliciting money or other property for the benefit of the charitable institution referred to in that paragraph; or

(b) more than £500 by way of remuneration in connection with any fund-raising venture in the course of which he solicits money or other property for the benefit of that institution.

(4) In this Part any reference to charitable purposes, where occurring in the context of a reference to charitable, benevolent or philanthropic purposes, is a reference to charitable purposes as defined by section 2(1) of the Charities Act 2006.

(5) For the purposes of this Part a company is connected with a charitable institution if –

(a) the institution, or

(b) the institution and one or more other charitable institutions, taken together,

is or are entitled (whether directly or through one or more nominees) to exercise, or control the exercise of, the whole of the voting power at any general meeting of the company.

(6) In this Part –

(a) 'represent' and 'solicit' mean respectively represent and solicit in any manner whatever, whether expressly or impliedly and whether done –

    (i) by speaking directly to the person or persons to whom the representation or solicitation is addressed (whether when in his or their presence or not), or

    (ii) by means of a statement published in any newspaper, film or radio or television programme,

or otherwise, and references to a representation or solicitation shall be construed accordingly; and

(b) any reference to soliciting or otherwise procuring money or other property is a reference to soliciting or otherwise procuring money or other property whether any consideration is, or is to be, given in return for the money or other property or not.

(7) Where –

(a) any solicitation of money or other property for the benefit of a charitable institution is made in accordance with arrangements between any person and that institution, and

(b) under those arrangements that person will be responsible for receiving on behalf of the institution money or other property given in response to the solicitation,

then (if he would not be so regarded apart from this subsection) that person shall be regarded for the purposes of this Part as soliciting money or other property for the benefit of the institution.

(8) Where any fund-raising venture is undertaken by a professional fund-raiser in the course of a radio or television programme, any solicitation which is made by a person in the course of the programme at the instance of the fund-raiser shall be regarded for the purposes of this Part as made by the fund-raiser and not by that person (and shall be so regarded whether or not the solicitation is made by that person for any reward).

(9) In this Part 'services' includes facilities, and in particular –

(a) access to any premises or event;

(b) membership of any organisation;

(c)   the provision of advertising space; and

(d)   the provision of any financial facilities;

and references to the supply of services shall be construed accordingly.

(10) The Minister may by order amend subsection (3) by substituting a different sum for any sum for the time being specified there.

Control of fund-raising

59   Prohibition on professional fund-raiser etc. raising funds for charitable institution without an agreement in prescribed form

(1)   It shall be unlawful for a professional fund-raiser to solicit money or other property for the benefit of a charitable institution unless he does so in accordance with an agreement with the institution satisfying the prescribed requirements.

(2)   It shall be unlawful for a commercial participator to represent that charitable contributions are to be given to or applied for the benefit of a charitable institution unless he does so in accordance with an agreement with the institution satisfying the prescribed requirements.

(3)   Where on the application of a charitable institution the court is satisfied –

(a)   that any person has contravened or is contravening subsection (1) or (2) in relation to the institution, and

(b)   that, unless restrained, any such contravention is likely to continue or be repeated,

the court may grant an injunction restraining the contravention; and compliance with subsection (1) or (2) shall not be enforceable otherwise than in accordance with this subsection.

(4)   Where –

(a)   a charitable institution makes any agreement with a professional fund-raiser or a commercial participator by virtue of which –

(i)   the professional fund-raiser is authorised to solicit money or other property for the benefit of the institution, or

(ii)   the commercial participator is authorised to represent that charitable contributions are to be given to or applied for the benefit of the institution,

as the case may be, but

(b)   the agreement does not satisfy the prescribed requirements in any respect,

the agreement shall not be enforceable against the institution except to such extent (if any) as may be provided by an order of the court.

(5)   A professional fund-raiser or commercial participator who is a party to such an agreement as is mentioned in subsection (4)(a) shall not be entitled to receive any amount by way of remuneration or expenses in respect of anything done by him in pursuance of the agreement unless –

(a)   he is so entitled under any provision of the agreement, and

(b)   either –

(i)   the agreement satisfies the prescribed requirements, or

(ii)   any such provision has effect by virtue of an order of the court under subsection (4).

(6)   In this section 'the prescribed requirements' means such requirements as are prescribed by regulations made by virtue of section 64(2)(a).

60 **Professional fund-raisers etc. required to indicate institutions benefiting and arrangements for remuneration**

(1) Where a professional fund-raiser solicits money or other property for the benefit of one or more particular charitable institutions, the solicitation shall be accompanied by a statement clearly indicating –

(a) the name or names of the institution or institutions concerned;

(b) if there is more than one institution concerned, the proportions in which the institutions are respectively to benefit; and

(c) the method by which the fund-raiser's remuneration in connection with the appeal is to be determined and the notifiable amount of that remuneration.

(2) Where a professional fund-raiser solicits money or other property for charitable, benevolent or philanthropic purposes of any description (rather than for the benefit of one or more particular charitable institutions), the solicitation shall be accompanied by a statement clearly indicating –

(a) the fact that he is soliciting money or other property for those purposes and not for the benefit of any particular charitable institution or institutions;

(b) the method by which it is to be determined how the proceeds of the appeal are to be distributed between different charitable institutions; and

(c) the method by which his remuneration in connection with the appeal is to be determined and the notifiable amount of that remuneration.

(3) Where any representation is made by a commercial participator to the effect that charitable contributions are to be given to or applied for the benefit of one or more particular charitable institutions, the representation shall be accompanied by a statement clearly indicating –

(a) the name or names of the institution or institutions concerned;

(b) if there is more than one institution concerned, the proportions in which the institutions are respectively to benefit; and

(c) the notifiable amount of whichever of the following sums is applicable in the circumstances –

(i) the sum representing so much of the consideration given for goods or services sold or supplied by him as is to be given to or applied for the benefit of the institution or institutions concerned,

(ii) the sum representing so much of any other proceeds of a promotional venture undertaken by him as is to be so given or applied, or

(iii) the sum of the donations by him in connection with the sale or supply of any such goods or services which are to be so given or supplied.

(3A) In subsections (1) to (3) a reference to the 'notifiable amount' of any remuneration or other sum is a reference –

(a) to the actual amount of the remuneration or sum, if that is known at the time when the statement is made; and

(b) otherwise to the estimated amount of the remuneration or sum, calculated as accurately as is reasonably possible in the circumstances.

(4) If any such solicitation or representation as is mentioned in any of subsections (1) to (3) is made –

(a) in the course of a radio or television programme, and

(b) in association with an announcement to the effect that payment may be made, in response to the solicitation or representation, by means of a credit or debit card,

the statement required by virtue of subsection (1), (2) or (3) (as the case may be) shall include full details of the right to have refunded under section 61(1) any payment of £50 or more which is so made.

(5)   If any such solicitation or representation as is mentioned in any of subsections (1) to (3) is made orally but is not made –

    (a)   by speaking directly to the particular person or persons to whom it is addressed and in his or their presence, or

    (b)   in the course of any radio or television programme,

the professional fund-raiser or commercial participator concerned shall, within seven days of any payment of £50 or more being made to him in response to the solicitation or representation, give to the person making the payment a written statement –

    (i)   of the matters specified in paragraphs (a) to (c) of that subsection; and

    (ii)   including full details of the right to cancel under section 61(2) an agreement made in response to the solicitation or representation, and the right to have refunded under section 61(2) or (3) any payment of £50 or more made in response thereto.

(6)   In subsection (5) above the reference to the making of a payment is a reference to the making of a payment of whatever nature and by whatever means, including a payment made by means of a credit card or a debit card; and for the purposes of that subsection –

    (a)   where the person making any such payment makes it in person, it shall be regarded as made at the time when it is so made;

    (b)   where the person making any such payment sends it by post, it shall be regarded as made at the time when it is posted; and

    (c)   where the person making any such payment makes it by giving, by telephone or by means of any other electronic communications apparatus, authority for an account to be debited with the payment, it shall be regarded as made at the time when any such authority is given.

(7)   Where any requirement of subsections (1) to (5) is not complied with in relation to any solicitation or representation, the professional fund-raiser or commercial participator concerned shall be guilty of an offence and liable on summary conviction to a fine not exceeding the fifth level on the standard scale.

(8)   It shall be a defence for a person charged with any such offence to prove that he took all reasonable precautions and exercised all due diligence to avoid the commission of the offence.

(9)   Where the commission by any person of an offence under subsection (7) is due to the act or default of some other person, that other person shall be guilty of the offence; and a person may be charged with and convicted of the offence by virtue of this subsection whether or not proceedings are taken against the first-mentioned person.

(10)   In this section –

'the appeal', in relation to any solicitation by a professional fund-raiser, means the campaign or other fund-raising venture in the course of which the solicitation is made;

[. . .]

60A   Other persons making appeals required to indicate institutions benefiting and arrangements for remuneration

(1)   Subsections (1) and (2) of section 60 apply to a person acting for reward as a collector in respect of a public charitable collection as they apply to a professional fund-raiser.

(2)   But those subsections do not so apply to a person excluded by virtue of –

    (a)   subsection (3) below, or

    (b)   section 60B(1) (exclusion of lower-paid collectors).

(3) Those subsections do not so apply to a person if –

    (a) section 60(1) or (2) applies apart from subsection (1) (by virtue of the exception in section 58(2)(c) for persons treated as promoters), or

    (b) subsection (4) or (5) applies,

in relation to his acting for reward as a collector in respect of the collection mentioned in subsection (1) above.

(4) Where a person within subsection (6) solicits money or other property for the benefit of one or more particular charitable institutions, the solicitation shall be accompanied by a statement clearly indicating –

    (a) the name or names of the institution or institutions for whose benefit the solicitation is being made;

    (b) if there is more than one such institution, the proportions in which the institutions are respectively to benefit;

    (c) the fact that he is an officer, employee or trustee of the institution or company mentioned in subsection (6); and

    (d) the fact that he is receiving remuneration as an officer, employee or trustee or (as the case may be) for acting as a collector.

(5) Where a person within subsection (6) solicits money or other property for charitable, benevolent or philanthropic purposes of any description (rather than for the benefit of one or more particular charitable institutions), the solicitation shall be accompanied by a statement clearly indicating –

    (a) the fact that he is soliciting money or other property for those purposes and not for the benefit of any particular charitable institution or institutions;

    (b) the method by which it is to be determined how the proceeds of the appeal are to be distributed between different charitable institutions;

    (c) the fact that he is an officer, employee or trustee of the institution or company mentioned in subsection (6); and

    (d) the fact that he is receiving remuneration as an officer, employee or trustee or (as the case may be) for acting as a collector.

(6) A person is within this subsection if –

    (a) he is an officer or employee of a charitable institution or a company connected with any such institution, or a trustee of any such institution,

    (b) he is acting as a collector in that capacity, and

    (c) he receives remuneration either in his capacity as officer, employee or trustee or for acting as a collector.

(7) But a person is not within subsection (6) if he is excluded by virtue of section 60B(4).

(8) Where any requirement of –

    (a) subsection (1) or (2) of section 60, as it applies by virtue of subsection (1) above, or

    (b) subsection (4) or (5) above,

is not complied with in relation to any solicitation, the collector concerned shall be guilty of an offence and liable on summary conviction to a fine not exceeding level 5 on the standard scale.

(9) Section 60(8) and (9) apply in relation to an offence under subsection (8) above as they apply in relation to an offence under section 60(7).

(10) In this section –

    'the appeal', in relation to any solicitation by a collector, means the campaign or other fund-raising venture in the course of which the solicitation is made;

    'collector' has the meaning given by section 47(1) of the Charities Act 2006;

    'public charitable collection' has the meaning given by section 45 of that Act.

60B   Exclusion of lower-paid collectors from provisions of section 60A

(1)   Section 60(1) and (2) do not apply (by virtue of section 60A(1)) to a person who is under the earnings limit in subsection (2) below.

(2)   A person is under the earnings limit in this subsection if he does not receive –

    (a)   more than –

        (i)   £5 per day, or

        (ii)   £500 per year,

        by way of remuneration for acting as a collector in relation to relevant collections, or

    (b)   more than £500 by way of remuneration for acting as a collector in relation to the collection mentioned in section 60A(1).

(3)   In subsection (2) 'relevant collections' means public charitable collections conducted for the benefit of –

    (a)   the charitable institution or institutions, or

    (b)   the charitable, benevolent or philanthropic purposes,

    for whose benefit the collection mentioned in section 60A(1) is conducted.

(4)   A person is not within section 60A(6) if he is under the earnings limit in subsection (5) below.

(5)   A person is under the earnings limit in this subsection if the remuneration received by him as mentioned in section 60A(6)(c) –

    (a)   is not more than –

        (i)   £5 per day, or

        (ii)   £500 per year, or

    (b)   if a lump sum, is not more than £500.

(6)   The Minister may by order amend subsections (2) and (5) by substituting a different sum for any sum for the time being specified there.

61   Cancellation of payments and agreements made in response to appeals

(1)   Where –

    (a)   a person ('the donor'), in response to any such solicitation or representation as is mentioned in any of subsections (1) to (3) of section 60 which is made in the course of a radio or television programme, makes any payment of £50 or more to the relevant fund-raiser by means of a credit card or a debit card, but

    (b)   before the end of the period of seven days beginning with the date of the solicitation or representation, the donor serves on the relevant fund-raiser a notice in writing which, however expressed, indicates the donor's intention to cancel the payment,

    the donor shall (subject to subsection (4) below) be entitled to have the payment refunded to him forthwith by the relevant fund-raiser.

(2)   Where –

    (a)   a person ('the donor'), in response to any solicitation or representation falling within subsection (5) of section 60, enters into an agreement with the relevant fund-raiser under which the donor is, or may be, liable to make any payment or payments to the relevant fund-raiser, and the amount or aggregate amount which the donor is, or may be, liable to pay to him under the agreement is £50 or more, but

    (b)   before the end of the period of seven days beginning with the date when he is given any such written statement as is referred to in that subsection, the donor serves on the relevant fund-raiser a notice in writing which, however expressed, indicates the donor's intention to cancel the agreement, the notice shall operate, as from the time when it is so served, to cancel the agreement and any liability of any person other than the donor in connection with the making of any such payment or payments, and the donor shall (subject to subsection (4) below) be entitled to have any payment of £50 or more made by him under the agreement refunded to him forthwith by the relevant fund-raiser.

(3) Where, in response to any solicitation or representation falling within subsection (5) of section 60, a person ('the donor') –

(a) makes any payment of £50 or more to the relevant fund-raiser, but
(b) does not enter into any such agreement as is mentioned in subsection (2) above,

then, if before the end of the period of seven days beginning with the date when the donor is given any such written statement as is referred to in subsection (5) of that section, the donor serves on the relevant fund-raiser a notice in writing which, however expressed, indicates the donor's intention to cancel the payment, the donor shall (subject to subsection (4) below) be entitled to have the payment refunded to him forthwith by the relevant fund-raiser.

(4) The right of any person to have a payment refunded to him under any of subsections (1) to (3) above –

(a) is a right to have refunded to him the amount of the payment less any administrative expenses reasonably incurred by the relevant fund-raiser in connection with –

(i) the making of the refund, or
(ii) (in the case of a refund under subsection (2)) dealing with the notice of cancellation served by that person; and

(b) shall, in the case of a payment for goods already received, be conditional upon restitution being made by him of the goods in question.

(5) Nothing in subsections (1) to (3) above has effect in relation to any payment made or to be made in respect of services which have been supplied at the time when the relevant notice is served.

(6) In this section any reference to the making of a payment is a reference to the making of a payment of whatever nature and (in the case of subsection (2) or (3)) a payment made by whatever means, including a payment made by means of a credit card or a debit card; and subsection (6) of section 60 shall have effect for determining when a payment is made for the purposes of this section as it has effect for determining when a payment is made for the purposes of subsection (5) of that section.

(7) In this section 'the relevant fund-raiser', in relation to any solicitation or representation, means the professional fund-raiser or commercial participator by whom it is made.

(8) The Minister may by order –

(a) amend any provision of this section by substituting a different sum for the sum for the time being specified there; and
(b) make such consequential amendments in section 60 as he considers appropriate.

62 Right of charitable institution to prevent unauthorised fund-raising

(1) Where on the application of any charitable institution –

(a) the court is satisfied that any person has done or is doing either of the following, namely –

(i) soliciting money or other property for the benefit of the institution, or
(ii) representing that charitable contributions are to be given to or applied for the benefit of the institution,

and that, unless restrained, he is likely to do further acts of that nature, and

(b) the court is also satisfied as to one or more of the matters specified in subsection (2), then (subject to subsection (3)) the court may grant an injunction restraining the doing of any such acts.

(2) The matters referred to in subsection (1)(b) are –

    (a) that the person in question is using methods of fund-raising to which the institution objects;

    (b) that that person is not a fit and proper person to raise funds for the institution; and

    (c) where the conduct complained of is the making of such representations as are mentioned in subsection (1)(a)(ii), that the institution does not wish to be associated with the particular promotional or other fund-raising venture in which that person is engaged.

(3) The power to grant an injunction under subsection (1) shall not be exercisable on the application of a charitable institution unless the institution has, not less than 28 days before making the application, served on the person in question a notice in writing –

    (a) requesting him to cease forthwith –

        (i)   soliciting money or other property for the benefit of the institution, or

        (ii) representing that charitable contributions are to be given to or applied for the benefit of the institution,

    as the case may be; and

    (b) stating that, if he does not comply with the notice, the institution will make an application under this section for an injunction.

(4) Where –

    (a) a charitable institution has served on any person a notice under subsection (3) ('the relevant notice') and that person has complied with the notice, but

    (b) that person has subsequently begun to carry on activities which are the same, or substantially the same, as those in respect of which the relevant notice was served,

    the institution shall not, in connection with an application made by it under this section in respect of the activities carried on by that person, be required by virtue of that subsection to serve a further notice on him, if the application is made not more than 12 months after the date of service of the relevant notice.

(5) This section shall not have the effect of authorising a charitable institution to make an application under this section in respect of anything done by a professional fund-raiser or commercial participator in relation to the institution.

63   False statements relating to institutions which are not registered charities

(1) Where –

    (a) a person solicits money or other property for the benefit of an institution in association with a representation that the institution is a registered charity, and

    (b) the institution is not such a charity,

    he shall be guilty of an offence and liable on summary conviction to a fine not exceeding the fifth level on the standard scale.

(1A) In any proceedings for an offence under subsection (1), it shall be a defence for the accused to prove that he believed on reasonable grounds that the institution was a registered charity.

(2) In this section 'registered charity' means a charity which is for the time being registered in the register of charities kept under section 3 of the Charities Act 1993.

Supplementary

64   Regulations about fund-raising

(1)   The Minister may make such regulations as appear to him to be necessary or desirable for any purposes connected with any of the preceding provisions of this Part.

(2)   Without prejudice to the generality of subsection (1), any such regulations may –

    (a)   prescribe the form and content of –

        (i)   agreements made for the purposes of section 59, and

        (ii)   notices served under section 62(3);

    (b)   require professional fund-raisers or commercial participators who are parties to such agreements with charitable institutions to make available to the institutions books, documents or other records (however kept) which relate to the institutions;

    (c)   specify the manner in which money or other property acquired by professional fund-raisers or commercial participators for the benefit of, or otherwise falling to be given to or applied by such persons for the benefit of, charitable institutions is to be transmitted to such institutions;

    (d)   provide for any provisions of section 60 or 61 having effect in relation to solicitations or representations made in the course of radio or television programmes to have effect, subject to any modifications specified in the regulations, in relation to solicitations or representations made in the course of such programmes –

        (i)   by charitable institutions, or

        (ii)   by companies connected with such institutions,

    and, in that connection, provide for any other provisions of this Part to have effect for the purposes of the regulations subject to any modifications so specified;

    (e)   make other provision regulating the raising of funds for charitable, benevolent or philanthropic purposes (whether by professional fund-raisers or commercial participators or otherwise).

(3)   In subsection (2)(c) the reference to such money or other property as is there mentioned includes a reference to money or other property which, in the case of a professional fund-raiser or commercial participator –

    (a)   has been acquired by him otherwise than in accordance with an agreement with a charitable institution, but

    (b)   by reason of any solicitation or representation in consequence of which it has been acquired, is held by him on trust for such an institution.

(4)   Regulations under this section may provide that any failure to comply with a specified provision of the regulations shall be an offence punishable on summary conviction by a fine not exceeding the second level on the standard scale.

64A   Reserve power to control fund-raising by charitable institutions

(1)   The Minister may make such regulations as appear to him to be necessary or desirable for or in connection with regulating charity fund-raising.

(2)   In this section 'charity fund-raising' means activities which are carried on by –

    (a)   charitable institutions,

    (b)   persons managing charitable institutions, or

    (c)   persons or companies connected with such institutions,

and involve soliciting or otherwise procuring funds for the benefit of such institutions or companies connected with them, or for general charitable, benevolent or philanthropic purposes.

But 'activities' does not include primary purpose trading.

(3)   Regulations under this section may, in particular, impose a good practice requirement on the persons managing charitable institutions in circumstances where –

(a)   those institutions,
(b)   the persons managing them, or
(c)   persons or companies connected with such institutions,

are engaged in charity fund-raising.

(4)   A 'good practice requirement' is a requirement to take all reasonable steps to ensure that the fund-raising is carried out in such a way that –

(a)   it does not unreasonably intrude on the privacy of those from whom funds are being solicited or procured;
(b)   it does not involve the making of unreasonably persistent approaches to persons to donate funds;
(c)   it does not result in undue pressure being placed on persons to donate funds;
(d)   it does not involve the making of any false or misleading representation about any of the matters mentioned in subsection (5).

(5)   The matters are –

(a)   the extent or urgency of any need for funds on the part of any charitable institution or company connected with such an institution;
(b)   any use to which funds donated in response to the fund-raising are to be put by such an institution or company;
(c)   the activities, achievements or finances of such an institution or company.

(6)   Regulations under this section may provide that a person who persistently fails, without reasonable excuse, to comply with any specified requirement of the regulations is to be guilty of an offence and liable on summary conviction to a fine not exceeding level 2 on the standard scale.

(7)   For the purposes of this section –

(a)   'funds' means money or other property;
(b)   'general charitable, benevolent or philanthropic purposes' means charitable, benevolent or philanthropic purposes other than those associated with one or more particular institutions;
(c)   the persons 'managing' a charitable institution are the charity trustees or other persons having the general control and management of the administration of the institution; and
(d)   a person is 'connected' with a charitable institution if he is an employee or agent of –

(i)   the institution,
(ii)   the persons managing it, or
(iii) a company connected with it,

or he is a volunteer acting on behalf of the institution or such a company.

(8)   In this section 'primary purpose trading', in relation to a charitable institution, means any trade carried on by the institution or a company connected with it where –

(a)   the trade is carried on in the course of the actual carrying out of a primary purpose of the institution; or
(b)   the work in connection with the trade is mainly carried out by beneficiaries of the institution.

PART III

ss.65–74 [. . .]

PART IV   GENERAL

Offences by bodies corporate

75   **Where any offence –**

(a)   under this Act or any regulations made under it, or

(b)   [. . .]

is committed by a body corporate and is proved to have been committed with the consent or connivance of, or to be attributable to any neglect on the part of, any director, manager, secretary or other similar officer of the body corporate, or any person who was purporting to act in any such capacity, he as well as the body corporate shall be guilty of that offence and shall be liable to be proceeded against and punished accordingly.

In relation to a body corporate whose affairs are managed by its members, 'director' means a member of the body corporate.

76   **Service of documents**

(1)   This section applies to –

    (a)   [. . .]

    (b)   any notice or other document required or authorised to be given or served under Part II of this Act; [. . .]

    (c)   [. . .]

(2)   A document to which this section applies may be served on or given to a person (other than a body corporate) –

    (a)   by delivering it to that person;

    (b)   by leaving it at his last known address in the United Kingdom; or

    (c)   by sending it by post to him at that address.

(3)   A document to which this section applies may be served on or given to a body corporate by delivering it or sending it by post –

    (a)   to the registered or principal office of the body in the United Kingdom, or

    (b)   if it has no such office in the United Kingdom, to any place in the United Kingdom where it carries on business or conducts its activities (as the case may be).

(4)   Any such document may also be served on or given to a person (including a body corporate) by sending it by post to that person at an address notified by that person for the purposes of this subsection to the person or persons by whom it is required or authorised to be served or given.

77   **Regulations and orders**

(1)   Any regulations or order of the Minister under this Act –

    (a)   shall be made by statutory instrument; and

    (b)   (subject to subsections (2) and (2A)) shall be subject to annulment in pursuance of a resolution of either House of Parliament.

(2)   Subsection (1)(b) does not apply –

    (a)–(c)   [. . .]

    (d)   to an order under section 79(2).

(2A) Subsection (1)(b) does not apply to regulations under section 64A, and no such regulations may be made unless a draft of the statutory instrument containing the regulations has been laid before, and approved by a resolution of, each House of Parliament.

(3)   Any regulations or order of the Minister under this Act may make –

  (a) different provision for different cases; and

  (b) such supplemental, incidental, consequential or transitional provision or savings as the Minister considers appropriate.

(4)   Before making any regulations under section 64 or 64A [. . .] the Minister shall consult such persons or bodies of persons as he considers appropriate.

78   Minor and consequential amendments and repeals

(1)   The enactments mentioned in Schedule 6 to this Act shall have effect subject to the amendments there specified (which are either minor amendments or amendments consequential on the provisions of this Act).

(2)   The enactments mentioned in Schedule 7 to this Act (which include some that are already spent or are no longer of practical utility) are hereby repealed to the extent specified in the third column of that Schedule.

79   Short title, commencement and extent

(1)   This Act may be cited as the Charities Act 1992.

(2)   This Act shall come into force on such day as the Minister may by order appoint; and different days may be so appointed for different provisions or for different purposes.

(3)   Subject to subsections (4) to (6) below, this Act extends only to England and Wales.

(4)–(5) [. . .]

(6)   The amendments in Schedule 6, and [. . .] the repeals in Schedule 7, have the same extent as the enactments to which they refer, and section 78 extends accordingly.

(7)   [. . .]

SCHEDULES

SCHEDULES 1–4 [. . .]

SCHEDULE 5 [. . .]

SCHEDULE 6 MINOR AND CONSEQUENTIAL AMENDMENTS
Section 78(1)

Clergy Pensions Measure 1961 (No.3)

1.   In section 33 (preservation of restrictions on certain transactions) –

   (a) for 'section twenty-nine of the Charities Act 1960' substitute 'section 32 of the Charities Act 1992'; and

   (b) for 'said Act' substitute 'Charities Act 1960'.

Finance Act 1963 (c.25)

2.   [. . .]

Cathedrals Measure 1963 (No.2)

3.   In section 20(2)(iii) (consents to disposal of land by cathedral bodies), for 'section twenty-nine of the Charities Act 1960' substitute 'section 32 of the Charities Act 1992'.

Leasehold Reform Act 1967 (c.88)

4.   In section 23(4) (grant of new tenancy), for 'section 29 of the Charities Act 1960' substitute 'section 32 of the Charities Act 1992'.

Sharing of Church Buildings Act 1969 (c.38)

5.   In section 8(3) (shared buildings), for the words from the beginning to 'Commissioners)' substitute 'Section 32 of the Charities Act 1992 (restrictions on dispositions of charity land)'.

Local Government Act 1972 (c.70)

6.   In section 131(3) (savings) –

   (a) for the words from 'section 29' to 'property)' substitute 'section 32 of the Charities Act 1992 (restrictions on disposition of charity land)'; and

   (b) for 'subsection (3)(a) of that section' substitute 'section 32(9)(a) of that Act'.

Fire Precautions (Loans) Act 1973 (c.11)

7.   In section 1(7) (loans to meet certain expenditure), for the words from the beginning to 'property)' substitute 'Section 34 of the Charities Act 1992 (which restricts the charging of charity property)'.

Theatres Trust Act 1976 (c.27)

8.   In section 2(2)(d) (powers of trustees), for 'section 29 of the Charities Act 1960' substitute 'sections 32 and 34 of the Charities Act 1992'.

Local Government (Miscellaneous Provisions) Act 1982 (c.30)

9.   [. . .]

Civic Government (Scotland) Act 1982 (c.45)

10.   [. . .]

Companies Act 1985 (c.6)

11.   In each of the following provisions, namely –

    (a)   section 209(1)(c) (interests to be disregarded for purposes of general disclosure provisions), and

    (b)   paragraph 11(b) of Schedule 13 (interests to be disregarded for purposes of provisions relating to disclosure by directors etc.),

    after 'section 22' insert 'or 22A'.

Housing Act 1985 (c.68)

12.   For paragraph 12 of Schedule 1 substitute

    '12.   A licence to occupy a dwelling-house is not a secure tenancy if –

        (a)   the dwelling-house is an almshouse, and

        (b)   the licence was granted by or on behalf of a charity which –

            (i)   is authorised under its trusts to maintain the dwelling-house as an almshouse, and

            (ii)   has no power under its trusts to grant a tenancy of the dwelling-house;

    and in this paragraph 'almshouse' means any premises maintained as an almshouse, whether they are called an almshouse or not; and 'trusts', in relation to a charity, means the provisions establishing it as a charity and regulating its purposes and administration, whether those provisions take effect by way of trust or not.'

Housing Associations Act 1985 (c.69)

13.   (1)   In section 10(1) (excepted dispositions), for 'section 29 of the Charities Act 1960' substitute 'sections 32 and 34 of the Charities Act 1992'.

    (2)   [. . .]

    (3)   In section 35(2)(c) (power to transfer housing to local housing authority), for the words from 'section' to 'Commissioners)' substitute 'section 32 of the Charities Act 1992 (restrictions on dispositions of charity land)'.

Financial Services Act 1986 (c.60)

14.   In section 45(1)(j) (miscellaneous exemptions), after 'section 22' insert 'or 22A'.

Coal Industry Act 1987 (c.3)

15.   In section 5 (power of Commissioners to make schemes relating to coal industry trusts), for subsection (8) substitute –

    '(8)   Sections 18(3), (8), (10) to (12), 19(1) to (5) and (7) and 21 of the Charities Act 1960 shall apply in relation to the powers of the Charity Commissioners and the making of schemes under this section as they apply in relation to their powers and the making of schemes under that Act; and sections 40(1) to (4), 40A and 42 of that Act shall apply to orders and decisions under this section as they apply to orders and decisions under that Act.

    (8A) The Commissioners shall not proceed under section 19 of that Act (as applied by subsection (8) above) without the like application, and the like notice to the trustees of the trust in question, as would be required if they were proceeding under subsection (1) above; but on any application made with a view to a scheme under subsection (1) above the Commissioners may proceed under that subsection or under section 19 of that Act (as so applied) as appears to them appropriate.'

Reverter of Sites Act 1987 (c.15)

16.   In section 4(4) (supplementary provisions), after 'sections 40' insert ',40A'.

Income and Corporation Taxes Act 1988 (c.1)

17.   After paragraph 3 of Schedule 20 (charities: qualifying investments and loans) insert –

'3A. Any investment in a common deposit fund established under section 22A of the Charities Act 1960 or in any similar fund established for the exclusive benefit of charities by or under any enactment relating to any particular charities or class of charities.'

SCHEDULE 7   REPEALS   Section 78(2)

Chapter	Short title	Extent of repeal
1872 c.24.	Charitable Trustees Incorporation Act 1872.	In section 2, the words from '; and all' onwards. In section 4, the words from '; and the appointment' onwards. In section 5, the words from '; and nothing' onwards. In section 7, the words from '; and there' onwards. The Schedule.
[. . .]	[. . .]	[. . .]
1939 c.44.	House to House Collections Act 1939.	The whole Act.
1940 c.31.	War Charities Act 1940.	The whole Act.
1948 c.29.	National Assistance Act 1948.	Section 41.
1958 c.49.	Trading Representations (Disabled Persons) Act 1958.	Section 1(2)(b).
1959 c.72.	Mental Health Act 1959.	Section 8(3).
1960 c.58.	Charities Act 1960.	In section 4(6), the words from 'and any person' onwards. Section 6(6) and (9). Section 7(4). [. . .] Section 16(2).

Chapter	Short title	Extent of repeal
		In section 19(6), the words 'or the like reference from the Secretary of State'.
		In section 22, subsection (6) and, in subsection (9), the words from ', and the' to 'endowment' (where last occurring).
		Section 27.
		Section 29.
		In section 30C(1)(c), the words 'by or'.
		Section 31.
		Section 44.
		In section 45(3), the words 'Subject to subsection (9) of section twenty-two of this Act,'.
		In section 46, the words ', subject to subsection (9) of section twenty-two of this Act,'.
		In Schedule 1, in paragraph 1(3), the words 'Subject to sub-paragraph (6) below,'.
		In Schedule 6, the entry relating to the War Charities Act 1940.
1966 c.42.	Local Government Act 1966.	In Schedule 3, in column 1 of Part II, paragraph 20.
1968 c.60.	Theft Act 1968.	In Schedule 2, in Part III, the entry relating to the House to House Collections Act 1939.
1970 c.42.	Local Authority Social Services Act 1970.	In Schedule 1, the entry relating to section 41 of the National Assistance Act 1948.
1972 c.70.	Local Government Act 1972.	Section 210(8). In Schedule 29, paragraphs 22 and 23.
1983 c.41.	Health and Social Services and Social Security Adjudications Act 1983.	Section 30(3).

Chapter	Short title	Extent of repeal
1983 c.47.	National Heritage Act 1983.	In Schedule 4, paragraphs 13 and 14.
1985 c.9.	Companies Consolidation (Consequential Provisions) Act 1985.	In Schedule 2, the entry relating to section 30(1) of the Charities Act 1960.
[. . .]	[. . .]	[. . .]
1986 c.41.	Finance Act 1986.	Section 33.

APPENDIX 3
Charities Act 1993

1993 Chapter c.10

An Act to consolidate the Charitable Trustees Incorporation Act 1872 and, except for certain spent or transitional provisions, the Charities Act 1960 and Part I of the Charities Act 1992.

[27th May 1993]

Be it enacted by the Queen's most Excellent Majesty, by and with the advice and consent of the Lords Spiritual and Temporal, and Commons, in this present Parliament assembled, and by the authority of the same, as follows:

PART I   THE CHARITY COMMISSION AND THE OFFICIAL CUSTODIAN FOR CHARITIES

1   [. . .]

1A   The Charity Commission

(1)   There shall be a body corporate to be known as the Charity Commission for England and Wales (in this Act referred to as 'the Commission').
(2)   In Welsh the Commission shall be known as 'Comisiwn Elusennau Cymru a Lloegr'.
(3)   The functions of the Commission shall be performed on behalf of the Crown.
(4)   In the exercise of its functions the Commission shall not be subject to the direction or control of any Minister of the Crown or other government department.
(5)   But subsection (4) above does not affect –

   (a)   any provision made by or under any enactment;
   (b)   any administrative controls exercised over the Commission's expenditure by the Treasury.

(6)   The provisions of Schedule 1A to this Act shall have effect with respect to the Commission.

1B   The Commission's objectives

(1)   The Commission has the objectives set out in subsection (2).
(2)   The objectives are –

   1.   The public confidence objective.
   2.   The public benefit objective.
   3.   The compliance objective.
   4.   The charitable resources objective.
   5.   The accountability objective.

(3)   Those objectives are defined as follows –

1.   The public confidence objective is to increase public trust and confidence in charities.
2.   The public benefit objective is to promote awareness and understanding of the operation of the public benefit requirement.
3.   The compliance objective is to promote compliance by charity trustees with their legal obligations in exercising control and management of the administration of their charities.
4.   The charitable resources objective is to promote the effective use of charitable resources.
5.   The accountability objective is to enhance the accountability of charities to donors, beneficiaries and the general public.

(4)   In this section 'the public benefit requirement' means the requirement in section 2(1)(b) of the Charities Act 2006 that a purpose falling within section 2(2) of that Act must be for the public benefit if it is to be a charitable purpose.

1C   The Commission's general functions

(1)   The Commission has the general functions set out in subsection (2).
(2)   The general functions are –

1.   Determining whether institutions are or are not charities.
2.   Encouraging and facilitating the better administration of charities.
3.   Identifying and investigating apparent misconduct or mismanagement in the administration of charities and taking remedial or protective action in connection with misconduct or mismanagement therein.
4.   Determining whether public collections certificates should be issued, and remain in force, in respect of public charitable collections.
5.   Obtaining, evaluating and disseminating information in connection with the performance of any of the Commission's functions or meeting any of its objectives.
6.   Giving information or advice, or making proposals, to any Minister of the Crown on matters relating to any of the Commission's functions or meeting any of its objectives.

(3)   The Commission's fifth general function includes (among other things) the maintenance of an accurate and up-to-date register of charities under section 3 below.
(4)   The Commission's sixth general function includes (among other things) complying, so far as is reasonably practicable, with any request made by a Minister of the Crown for information or advice on any matter relating to any of its functions.
(5)   In this section 'public charitable collection' and 'public collections certificate' have the same meanings as in Chapter 1 of Part 3 of the Charities Act 2006.

1D   The Commission's general duties

(1)   The Commission has the general duties set out in subsection (2).
(2)   The general duties are –

1.   So far as is reasonably practicable the Commission must, in performing its functions, act in a way –

    (a)   which is compatible with its objectives, and
    (b)   which it considers most appropriate for the purpose of meeting those objectives.

2.   So far as is reasonably practicable the Commission must, in performing its functions, act in a way which is compatible with the encouragement of –

    (a)   all forms of charitable giving, and
    (b)   voluntary participation in charity work.

3. In performing its functions the Commission must have regard to the need to use its resources in the most efficient, effective and economic way.

4. In performing its functions the Commission must, so far as relevant, have regard to the principles of best regulatory practice (including the principles under which regulatory activities should be proportionate, accountable, consistent, transparent and targeted only at cases in which action is needed).

5. In performing its functions the Commission must, in appropriate cases, have regard to the desirability of facilitating innovation by or on behalf of charities.

6. In managing its affairs the Commission must have regard to such generally accepted principles of good corporate governance as it is reasonable to regard as applicable to it.

1E   The Commission's incidental powers

(1) The Commission has power to do anything which is calculated to facilitate, or is conducive or incidental to, the performance of any of its functions or general duties.

(2) However, nothing in this Act authorises the Commission –

(a) to exercise functions corresponding to those of a charity trustee in relation to a charity, or

(b) otherwise to be directly involved in the administration of a charity.

(3) Subsection (2) does not affect the operation of section 19A or 19B below (power of Commission to give directions as to action to be taken or as to application of charity property).

2   The official custodian for charities

(1) There shall continue to be an officer known as the official custodian for charities (in this Act referred to as 'the official custodian') whose function it shall be to act as trustee for charities in the cases provided for by this Act; and the official custodian shall be by that name a corporation sole having perpetual succession and using an official seal which shall be officially and judicially noticed.

(2) Such individual as the Commission may from time to time designate shall be the official custodian.

(3) The official custodian shall perform his duties in accordance with such general or special directions as may be given him by the Commission, and his expenses (except those reimbursed to him or recovered by him as trustee for any charity) shall be defrayed by the Commission.

(4) Anything which is required to or may be done by, to or before the official custodian may be done by, to or before any member of the staff of the Commission generally or specially authorised by it to act for him during a vacancy in his office or otherwise.

(5) The official custodian shall not be liable as trustee for any charity in respect of any loss or of the misapplication of any property unless it is occasioned by or through the wilful neglect or default of the custodian or of any person acting for him; but the Consolidated Fund shall be liable to make good to a charity any sums for which the custodian may be liable by reason of any such neglect or default.

(6) The official custodian shall keep such books of account and such records in relation thereto as may be directed by the Treasury and shall prepare accounts in such form, in such manner and at such times as may be so directed.

(7) The accounts so prepared shall be examined and certified by the Comptroller and Auditor General.

(8) The Comptroller and Auditor General shall send to the Commission a copy of the accounts as certified by him together with his report on them.

(9) The Commission shall publish and lay before Parliament a copy of the documents sent to it under subsection (8) above.

PART 1A   THE CHARITY TRIBUNAL

2A   The Charity Tribunal

(1) There shall be a tribunal to be known as the Charity Tribunal (in this Act referred to as 'the Tribunal').

(2) In Welsh the Tribunal shall be known as 'Tribiwnlys Elusennau'.

(3) The provisions of Schedule 1B to this Act shall have effect with respect to the constitution of the Tribunal and other matters relating to it.

(4) The Tribunal shall have jurisdiction to hear and determine –

    (a) such appeals and applications as may be made to the Tribunal in accordance with Schedule 1C to this Act, or any other enactment, in respect of decisions, orders or directions of the Commission, and

    (b) such matters as may be referred to the Tribunal in accordance with Schedule 1D to this Act by the Commission or the Attorney General.

(5) Such appeals, applications and matters shall be heard and determined by the Tribunal in accordance with those Schedules, or any such enactment, taken with section 2B below and rules made under that section.

2B   Practice and procedure

(1) The Lord Chancellor may make rules –

    (a) regulating the exercise of rights to appeal or to apply to the Tribunal and matters relating to the making of references to it;

    (b) about the practice and procedure to be followed in relation to proceedings before the Tribunal.

(2) Rules under subsection (1)(a) above may, in particular, make provision –

    (a) specifying steps which must be taken before appeals, applications or references are made to the Tribunal (and the period within which any such steps must be taken);

    (b) specifying the period following the Commission's final decision, direction or order within which such appeals or applications may be made;

    (c) requiring the Commission to inform persons of their right to appeal or apply to the Tribunal following a final decision, direction or order of the Commission;

    (d) specifying the manner in which appeals, applications or references to the Tribunal are to be made.

(3) Rules under subsection (1)(b) above may, in particular, make provision –

    (a) for the President or a legal member of the Tribunal (see paragraph 1(2)(b) of Schedule 1B to this Act) to determine preliminary, interlocutory or ancillary matters;

    (b) for matters to be determined without an oral hearing in specified circumstances;

    (c) for the Tribunal to deal with urgent cases expeditiously;

    (d) about the disclosure of documents;

    (e) about evidence;

    (f) about the admission of members of the public to proceedings;

    (g) about the representation of parties to proceedings;

    (h) about the withdrawal of appeals, applications or references;

    (i) about the recording and promulgation of decisions;

    (j) about the award of costs.

(4) Rules under subsection (1)(a) or (b) above may confer a discretion on –

    (a) the Tribunal,

    (b) a member of the Tribunal, or

    (c) any other person.

(5)   The Tribunal may award costs only in accordance with subsections (6) and (7) below.

(6)   If the Tribunal considers that any party to proceedings before it has acted vexatiously, frivolously or unreasonably, the Tribunal may order that party to pay to any other party to the proceedings the whole or part of the costs incurred by that other party in connection with the proceedings.

(7)   If the Tribunal considers that a decision, direction or order of the Commission which is the subject of proceedings before it was unreasonable, the Tribunal may order the Commission to pay to any other party to the proceedings the whole or part of the costs incurred by that other party in connection with the proceedings.

(8)   Rules of the Lord Chancellor under this section –

(a)   shall be made by statutory instrument, and

(b)   shall be subject to annulment in pursuance of a resolution of either House of Parliament.

(9)   Section 86(3) below applies in relation to rules of the Lord Chancellor under this section as it applies in relation to regulations and orders of the Minister under this Act.

2C   Appeal from Tribunal

(1)   A party to proceedings before the Tribunal may appeal to the High Court against a decision of the Tribunal.

(2)   Subject to subsection (3) below, an appeal may be brought under this section against a decision of the Tribunal only on a point of law.

(3)   In the case of an appeal under this section against a decision of the Tribunal which determines a question referred to it by the Commission or the Attorney General, the High Court –

(a)   shall consider afresh the question referred to the Tribunal, and

(b)   may take into account evidence which was not available to the Tribunal.

(4)   An appeal under this section may be brought only with the permission of –

(a)   the Tribunal, or

(b)   if the Tribunal refuses permission, the High Court.

(5)   For the purposes of subsection (1) above –

(a)   the Commission and the Attorney General are to be treated as parties to all proceedings before the Tribunal, and

(b)   rules under section 2B(1) above may include provision as to who else is to be treated as being (or not being) a party to proceedings before the Tribunal.

2D   Intervention by Attorney General

(1)   This section applies to any proceedings –

(a)   before the Tribunal, or

(b)   on an appeal from the Tribunal,

to which the Attorney General is not a party.

(2)   The Tribunal or, in the case of an appeal from the Tribunal, the court may at any stage of the proceedings direct that all the necessary papers in the proceedings be sent to the Attorney General.

(3)   A direction under subsection (2) may be made by the Tribunal or court –

(a)   of its own motion, or

(b)   on the application of any party to the proceedings.

(4)   The Attorney General may –

(a)   intervene in the proceedings in such manner as he thinks necessary or expedient, and

(b) argue before the Tribunal or court any question in relation to the proceedings which the Tribunal or court considers it necessary to have fully argued.

(5) Subsection (4) applies whether or not the Tribunal or court has given a direction under subsection (2).

PART II   REGISTRATION AND NAMES OF CHARITIES

Registration of charities

3   Register of charities

(1) There shall continue to be a register of charities, which shall be kept by the Commission.

(2) The register shall be kept by the Commission in such manner as it thinks fit.

(3) The register shall contain –

    (a) the name of every charity registered in accordance with section 3A below (registration), and

    (b) such other particulars of, and such other information relating to, every such charity as the Commission thinks fit.

(4) The Commission shall remove from the register –

    (a) any institution which it no longer considers is a charity, and

    (b) any charity which has ceased to exist or does not operate.

(5) If the removal of an institution under subsection (4)(a) above is due to any change in its trusts, the removal shall take effect from the date of that change.

(6) A charity which is for the time being registered under section 3A(6) below (voluntary registration) shall be removed from the register if it so requests.

(7) The register (including the entries cancelled when institutions are removed from the register) shall be open to public inspection at all reasonable times.

(8) Where any information contained in the register is not in documentary form, subsection (7) above shall be construed as requiring the information to be available for public inspection in legible form at all reasonable times.

(9) If the Commission so determines, subsection (7) shall not apply to any particular information contained in the register that is specified in the determination.

(10) Copies (or particulars) of the trusts of any registered charity as supplied to the Commission under section 3B below (applications for registration etc.) shall, so long as the charity remains on the register –

    (a) be kept by the Commission, and

    (b) be open to public inspection at all reasonable times.

3A   Registration of charities

(1) Every charity must be registered in the register of charities unless subsection (2) below applies to it.

(2) The following are not required to be registered –

    (a) any exempt charity (see Schedule 2 to this Act);

    (b) any charity which for the time being –

        (i) is permanently or temporarily excepted by order of the Commission, and

        (ii) complies with any conditions of the exception,

    and whose gross income does not exceed £100,000;

    (c) any charity which for the time being –

        (i) is, or is of a description, permanently or temporarily excepted by regulations made by the Secretary of State, and

      (ii)   complies with any conditions of the exception,

      and whose gross income does not exceed £100,000; and

  (d)   any charity whose gross income does not exceed £5,000.

(3)   For the purposes of subsection (2)(b) above –

  (a)   any order made or having effect as if made under section 3(5)(b) of this Act (as originally enacted) and in force immediately before the appointed day has effect as from that day as if made under subsection (2)(b) (and may be varied or revoked accordingly); and

  (b)   no order may be made under subsection (2)(b) so as to except on or after the appointed day any charity that was not excepted immediately before that day.

(4)   For the purposes of subsection (2)(c) above –

  (a)   any regulations made or having effect as if made under section 3(5)(b) of this Act (as originally enacted) and in force immediately before the appointed day have effect as from that day as if made under subsection (2)(c) (and may be varied or revoked accordingly);

  (b)   such regulations shall be made under subsection (2)(c) as are necessary to secure that all of the formerly specified institutions are excepted under that provision (subject to compliance with any conditions of the exception and the financial limit mentioned in that provision); but

  (c)   otherwise no regulations may be made under subsection (2)(c) so as to except on or after the appointed day any description of charities that was not excepted immediately before that day.

(5)   In subsection (4)(b) above 'formerly specified institutions' means –

  (a)   any institution falling within section 3(5B)(a) or (b) of this Act as in force immediately before the appointed day (certain educational institutions); or

  (b)   any institution ceasing to be an exempt charity by virtue of section 11 of the Charities Act 2006 or any order made under that section.

(6)   A charity within –

  (a)   subsection (2)(b) or (c) above, or

  (b)   subsection (2)(d) above,

must, if it so requests, be registered in the register of charities.

(7)   The Minister may by order amend –

  (a)   subsection (2)(b) and (c) above, or

  (b)   subsection (2)(d) above,

by substituting a different sum for the sum for the time being specified there.

(8)   The Minister may only make an order under subsection (7) above –

  (a)   so far as it amends subsection (2)(b) and (c), if he considers it expedient to so with a view to reducing the scope of the exception provided by those provisions;

  (b)   so far as it amends subsection (2)(d), if he considers it expedient to do so in consequence of changes in the value of money or with a view to extending the scope of the exception provided by that provision,

and no order may be made by him under subsection (7)(a) unless a copy of a report under section 73 of the Charities Act 2006 (report on operation of that Act) has been laid before Parliament in accordance with that section.

(9)   In this section 'the appointed day' means the day on which subsections (1) to (5) above come into force by virtue of an order under section 79 of the Charities Act 2006 relating to section 9 of that Act (registration of charities).

(10) In this section any reference to a charity's 'gross income' shall be construed, in relation to a particular time –

  (a)   as a reference to the charity's gross income in its financial year immediately preceding that time, or

(b) if the Commission so determines, as a reference to the amount which the Commission estimates to be the likely amount of the charity's gross income in such financial year of the charity as is specified in the determination.

(11) The following provisions of this section –

(a) subsection (2)(b) and (c),
(b) subsections (3) to (5), and
(c) subsections (6)(a), (7)(a), (8)(a) and (9),

shall cease to have effect on such day as the Minister may by order appoint for the purposes of this subsection.

3B   Duties of trustees in connection with registration

(1) Where a charity required to be registered by virtue of section 3A(1) above is not registered, it is the duty of the charity trustees –

(a) to apply to the Commission for the charity to be registered, and
(b) to supply the Commission with the required documents and information.

(2) The 'required documents and information' are –

(a) copies of the charity's trusts or (if they are not set out in any extant document) particulars of them,
(b) such other documents or information as may be prescribed by regulations made by the Minister, and
(c) such other documents or information as the Commission may require for the purposes of the application.

(3) Where an institution is for the time being registered, it is the duty of the charity trustees (or the last charity trustees) –

(a) to notify the Commission if the institution ceases to exist, or if there is any change in its trusts or in the particulars of it entered in the register, and
(b) (so far as appropriate), to supply the Commission with particulars of any such change and copies of any new trusts or alterations of the trusts.

(4) Nothing in subsection (3) above requires a person –

(a) to supply the Commission with copies of schemes for the administration of a charity made otherwise than by the court,
(b) to notify the Commission of any change made with respect to a registered charity by such a scheme, or
(c) if he refers the Commission to a document or copy already in the possession of the Commission, to supply a further copy of the document.

(5) Where a copy of a document relating to a registered charity –

(a) is not required to be supplied to the Commission as the result of subsection (4) above, but
(b) is in the possession of the Commission,

a copy of the document shall be open to inspection under section 3(10) above as if supplied to the Commission under this section.

4   Effect of, and claims and objections to, registration

(1) An institution shall for all purposes other than rectification of the register be conclusively presumed to be or to have been a charity at any time when it is or was on the register of charities.

(2) Any person who is or may be affected by the registration of an institution as a charity may, on the ground that it is not a charity, object to its being entered by the Commission in the register, or apply to the Commission for it to be removed from the register; and provision may be made by regulations made by the Secretary of State as

to the manner in which any such objection or application is to be made, prosecuted or dealt with.

(3)   [. . .]

(4)   If there is an appeal to the Tribunal against any decision of the Commission to enter an institution in the register, or not to remove an institution from the register, then until the Commission is satisfied whether the decision of the Commission is or is not to stand, the entry in the register shall be maintained, but shall be in suspense and marked to indicate that it is in suspense; and for the purposes of subsection (1) above an institution shall be deemed not to be on the register during any period when the entry relating to it is in suspense under this subsection.

(5)   Any question affecting the registration or removal from the register of an institution may, notwithstanding that it has been determined by a decision on appeal under Schedule 1C to this Act, be considered afresh by the Commission and shall not be concluded by that decision, if it appears to the Commission that there has been a change of circumstances or that the decision is inconsistent with a later judicial decision.

5   **Status of registered charity (other than small charity) to appear on official publications etc.**

(1)   This section applies to a registered charity if its gross income in its last financial year exceeded £10,000.

(2)   Where this section applies to a registered charity, the fact that it is a registered charity shall be stated in legible characters –

(a)   in all notices, advertisements and other documents issued by or on behalf of the charity and soliciting money or other property for the benefit of the charity;

(b)   in all bills of exchange, promissory notes, endorsements, cheques and orders for money or goods purporting to be signed on behalf of the charity; and

(c)   in all bills rendered by it and in all its invoices, receipts and letters of credit.

(2A) The statement required by subsection (2) above shall be in English, except that, in the case of a document which is otherwise wholly in Welsh, the statement may be in Welsh if it consists of or includes the words 'elusen cofrestredig' (the Welsh equivalent of 'registered charity').

(3)   Subsection (2)(a) above has effect whether the solicitation is express or implied, and whether the money or other property is to be given for any consideration or not.

(4)   If, in the case of a registered charity to which this section applies, any person issues or authorises the issue of any document falling within paragraph (a) or (c) of subsection (2) above which does not contain the statement required by that subsection, he shall be guilty of an offence and liable on summary conviction to a fine not exceeding level 3 on the standard scale.

(5)   If, in the case of any such registered charity, any person signs any document falling within paragraph (b) of subsection (2) above which does not contain the statement required by that subsection, he shall be guilty of an offence and liable on summary conviction to a fine not exceeding level 3 on the standard scale.

(6)   The Secretary of State may by order amend subsection (1) above by substituting a different sum for the sum for the time being specified there.

Charity names

6   **Power of Commission to require charity's name to be changed**

(1)   Where this subsection applies to a charity, the Commission may give a direction requiring the name of the charity to be changed, within such period as is specified in the direction, to such other name as the charity trustees may determine with the approval of the Commission.

(2) Subsection (1) above applies to a charity if –

   (a) it is a registered charity and its name ('the registered name') –

      (i) is the same as, or

      (ii) is in the opinion of the Commission too like,

     the name, at the time when the registered name was entered in the register in respect of the charity, of any other charity (whether registered or not);

   (b) the name of the charity is in the opinion of the Commission likely to mislead the public as to the true nature –

      (i) of the purposes of the charity as set out in its trusts, or

      (ii) of the activities which the charity carries on under its trusts in pursuit of those purposes;

   (c) the name of the charity includes any word or expression for the time being specified in regulations made by the Secretary of State and the inclusion in its name of that word or expression is in the opinion of the Commission likely to mislead the public in any respect as to the status of the charity;

   (d) the name of the charity is in the opinion of the Commission likely to give the impression that the charity is connected in some way with Her Majesty's Government or any local authority, or with any other body of persons or any individual, when it is not so connected; or

   (e) the name of the charity is in the opinion of the Commission offensive;

   and in this subsection any reference to the name of a charity is, in relation to a registered charity, a reference to the name by which it is registered.

(3) Any direction given by virtue of subsection (2)(a) above must be given within twelve months of the time when the registered name was entered in the register in respect of the charity.

(4) Any direction given under this section with respect to a charity shall be given to the charity trustees; and on receiving any such direction the charity trustees shall give effect to it notwithstanding anything in the trusts of the charity.

(5) Where the name of any charity is changed under this section, then (without prejudice to section 3B(3)) it shall be the duty of the charity trustees forthwith to notify the Commission of the charity's new name and of the date on which the change occurred.

(6) A change of name by a charity under this section does not affect any rights or obligations of the charity; and any legal proceedings that might have been continued or commenced by or against it in its former name may be continued or commenced by or against it in its new name.

(7) Section 26(3) of the Companies Act 1985 (minor variations in names to be disregarded) shall apply for the purposes of this section as if the reference to section 26(1)(c) of that Act were a reference to subsection (2)(a) above.

(8) Any reference in this section to the charity trustees of a charity shall, in relation to a charity which is a company, be read as a reference to the directors of the company.

(9) [. . .]

7 Effect of direction under s.6 where charity is a company

(1) Where any direction is given under section 6 above with respect to a charity which is a company, the direction shall be taken to require the name of the charity to be changed by resolution of the directors of the company.

(2) Section 380 of the Companies Act 1985 (registration etc. of resolutions and agreements) shall apply to any resolution passed by the directors in compliance with any such direction.

(3) Where the name of such a charity is changed in compliance with any such direction, the registrar of companies –

(a) shall, subject to section 26 of the Companies Act 1985 (prohibition on registration of certain names), enter the new name on the register of companies in place of the former name, and

(b) shall issue a certificate of incorporation altered to meet the circumstances of the case;

and the change of name has effect from the date on which the altered certificate is issued.

PART III   INFORMATION POWERS

8   General power to institute inquiries

(1) The Commission may from time to time institute inquiries with regard to charities or a particular charity or class of charities, either generally or for particular purposes, but no such inquiry shall extend to any exempt charity except where this has been requested by its principal regulator.

(2) The Commission may either conduct such an inquiry itself or appoint a person to conduct it and make a report to the Commission.

(3) For the purposes of any such inquiry the Commission, or a person appointed by the Commission to conduct it, may direct any person (subject to the provisions of this section) –

(a) to furnish accounts and statements in writing with respect to any matter in question at the inquiry, being a matter on which he has or can reasonably obtain information, or to return answers in writing to any questions or inquiries addressed to him on any such matter, and to verify any such accounts, statements or answers by statutory declaration;

(b) to furnish copies of documents in his custody or under his control which relate to any matter in question at the inquiry, and to verify any such copies by statutory declaration;

(c) to attend at a specified time and place and give evidence or produce any such documents.

(4) For the purposes of any such inquiry evidence may be taken on oath, and the person conducting the inquiry may for that purpose administer oaths, or may instead of administering an oath require the person examined to make and subscribe a declaration of the truth of the matters about which he is examined.

(5) The Commission may pay to any person the necessary expenses of his attendance to give evidence or produce documents for the purpose of an inquiry under this section, and a person shall not be required in obedience to a direction under paragraph (c) of subsection (3) above to go more than ten miles from his place of residence unless those expenses are paid or tendered to him.

(6) Where an inquiry has been held under this section, the Commission may either –

(a) cause the report of the person conducting the inquiry, or such other statement of the results of the inquiry as the Commission thinks fit, to be printed and published, or

(b) publish any such report or statement in some other way which is calculated in the Commission's opinion to bring it to the attention of persons who may wish to make representations to the Commission about the action to be taken.

(7) The council of a county or district, the Common Council of the City of London and the council of a London borough may contribute to the expenses of the Commission in connection with inquiries under this section into local charities in the council's area.

9   Power to call for documents and search records

(1)   The Commission may by order –

(a)   require any person to furnish the Commission with any information in his possession which relates to any charity and is relevant to the discharge of the Commission's functions or of the functions of the official custodian;

(b)   require any person who has in his custody or under his control any document which relates to any charity and is relevant to the discharge of the Commission's functions or of the functions of the official custodian –

(i)   to furnish them with a copy of or extract from the document, or

(ii)   (unless the document forms part of the records or other documents of a court or of a public or local authority) to transmit the document itself to the Commission for its inspection.

(2)   Any member of the staff of the Commission, if so authorised by it, shall be entitled without payment to inspect and take copies of or extracts from the records or other documents of any court, or of any public registry or office of records, for any purpose connected with the discharge of the functions of the Commission or of the official custodian.

(3)   The Commission shall be entitled without payment to keep any copy or extract furnished to it under subsection (1) above; and where a document transmitted to the Commission under that subsection for it to inspect relates only to one or more charities and is not held by any person entitled as trustee or otherwise to the custody of it, the Commission may keep it or may deliver it to the charity trustees or to any other person who may be so entitled.

(4)   [. . .]

(5)   The rights conferred by subsection (2) above shall, in relation to information recorded otherwise than in legible form, include the right to require the information to be made available in legible form for inspection or for a copy or extract to be made of or from it.

(6)   In subsection (2) the reference to a member of the staff of the Commission includes the official custodian even if he is not a member of the staff of the Commission.

10   Disclosure of information to Commission

(1)   Any relevant public authority may disclose information to the Commission if the disclosure is made for the purpose of enabling or assisting the Commission to discharge any of its functions.

(2)   But Revenue and Customs information may be disclosed under subsection (1) only if it relates to an institution, undertaking or body falling within one (or more) of the following paragraphs –

(a)   a charity;

(b)   an institution which is established for charitable, benevolent or philanthropic purposes;

(c)   an institution by or in respect of which a claim for exemption has at any time been made under section 505(1) of the Income and Corporation Taxes Act 1988;

(d)   a subsidiary undertaking of a charity;

(e)   a body entered in the Scottish Charity Register which is managed or controlled wholly or mainly in or from England or Wales.

(3)   In subsection (2)(d) above 'subsidiary undertaking of a charity' means an undertaking (as defined by section 259(1) of the Companies Act 1985) in relation to which –

(a)   a charity is (or is to be treated as) a parent undertaking in accordance with the provisions of section 258 of, and Schedule 10A to, the Companies Act 1985, or

(b)   two or more charities would, if they were a single charity, be (or be treated as) a parent undertaking in accordance with those provisions.

(4)   For the purposes of the references to a parent undertaking –

    (a)   in subsection (3) above, and

    (b)   in section 258 of, and Schedule 10A to, the Companies Act 1985 as they apply for the purposes of that subsection,

    'undertaking' includes a charity which is not an undertaking as defined by section 259(1) of that Act.

10A Disclosure of information by Commission

(1)   Subject to subsections (2) and (3) below, the Commission may disclose to any relevant public authority any information received by the Commission in connection with any of the Commission's functions –

    (a)   if the disclosure is made for the purpose of enabling or assisting the relevant public authority to discharge any of its functions, or

    (b)   if the information so disclosed is otherwise relevant to the discharge of any of the functions of the relevant public authority.

(2)   In the case of information disclosed to the Commission under section 10(1) above, the Commission's power to disclose the information under subsection (1) above is exercisable subject to any express restriction subject to which the information was disclosed to the Commission.

(3)   Subsection (2) above does not apply in relation to Revenue and Customs information disclosed to the Commission under section 10(1) above; but any such information may not be further disclosed (whether under subsection (1) above or otherwise) except with the consent of the Commissioners for Her Majesty's Revenue and Customs.

(4)   Any responsible person who discloses information in contravention of subsection (3) above is guilty of an offence and liable –

    (a)   on summary conviction, to imprisonment for a term not exceeding 12 months or to a fine not exceeding the statutory maximum, or both;

    (b)   on conviction on indictment, to imprisonment for a term not exceeding two years or to a fine, or both.

(5)   It is a defence for a responsible person charged with an offence under subsection (4) above of disclosing information to prove that he reasonably believed –

    (a)   that the disclosure was lawful, or

    (b)   that the information had already and lawfully been made available to the public.

(6)   In the application of this section to Scotland or Northern Ireland, the reference to 12 months in subsection (4) is to be read as a reference to 6 months.

(7)   In this section 'responsible person' means a person who is or was –

    (a)   a member of the Commission,

    (b)   a member of the staff of the Commission,

    (c)   a person acting on behalf of the Commission or a member of the staff of the Commission, or

    (d)   a member of a committee established by the Commission.

10B Disclosure to and by principal regulators of exempt charities

(1)   Sections 10 and 10A above apply with the modifications in subsections (2) to (4) below in relation to the disclosure of information to or by the principal regulator of an exempt charity.

(2)   References in those sections to the Commission or to any of its functions are to be read as references to the principal regulator of an exempt charity or to any of the functions of that body or person as principal regulator in relation to the charity.

(3)   Section 10 above has effect as if for subsections (2) and (3) there were substituted –

'(2)   But Revenue and Customs information may be disclosed under subsection (1) only if it relates to –

   (a)   the exempt charity in relation to which the principal regulator has functions as such, or
   (b)   a subsidiary undertaking of the exempt charity.

(3)   In subsection (2)(b) above 'subsidiary undertaking of the exempt charity' means an undertaking (as defined by section 259(1) of the Companies Act 1985) in relation to which –

   (a)   the exempt charity is (or is to be treated as) a parent undertaking in accordance with the provisions of section 258 of, and Schedule 10A to, the Companies Act 1985, or
   (b)   the exempt charity and one or more other charities would, if they were a single charity, be (or be treated as) a parent undertaking in accordance with those provisions.'

(4)   Section 10A above has effect as if for the definition of 'responsible person' in sub-section (7) there were substituted a definition specified by regulations under section 13(4)(b) of the Charities Act 2006 (regulations prescribing principal regulators).

(5)   Regulations under section 13(4)(b) of that Act may also make such amendments or other modifications of any enactment as the Secretary of State considers appropriate for securing that any disclosure provisions that would otherwise apply in relation to the principal regulator of an exempt charity do not apply in relation to that body or person in its or his capacity as principal regulator.

(6)   In subsection (5) above 'disclosure provisions' means provisions having effect for authorising, or otherwise in connection with, the disclosure of information by or to the principal regulator concerned.

10C   Disclosure of information: supplementary

(1)   In sections 10 and 10A above 'relevant public authority' means –

   (a)   any government department (including a Northern Ireland department),
   (b)   any local authority,
   (c)   any constable, and
   (d)   any other body or person discharging functions of a public nature (including a body or person discharging regulatory functions in relation to any description of activities).

(2)   In section 10A above 'relevant public authority' also includes any body or person within subsection (1)(d) above in a country or territory outside the United Kingdom.

(3)   In sections 10 to 10B above and this section –

   'enactment' has the same meaning as in the Charities Act 2006;
   'Revenue and Customs information' means information held as mentioned in section 18(1) of the Commissioners for Revenue and Customs Act 2005.

(4)   Nothing in sections 10 and 10A above (or in those sections as applied by section 10B(1) to (4) above) authorises the making of a disclosure which –

   (a)   contravenes the Data Protection Act 1998, or
   (b)   is prohibited by Part 1 of the Regulation of Investigatory Powers Act 2000.

11   Supply of false or misleading information to Commission, etc.

(1)   Any person who knowingly or recklessly provides the Commission with information which is false or misleading in a material particular shall be guilty of an offence if the information –

(a) is provided in purported compliance with a requirement imposed by or under this Act; or

(b) is provided otherwise than as mentioned in paragraph (a) above but in circumstances in which the person providing the information intends, or could reasonably be expected to know, that it would be used by the Commission for the purpose of discharging its functions under this Act.

(2) Any person who wilfully alters, suppresses, conceals or destroys any document which he is or is liable to be required, by or under this Act, to produce to the Commission shall be guilty of an offence.

(3) Any person guilty of an offence under this section shall be liable –

(a) on summary conviction, to a fine not exceeding the statutory maximum;

(b) on conviction on indictment, to imprisonment for a term not exceeding two years or to a fine, or both.

(4) In this section references to the Commission include references to any person conducting an inquiry under section 8 above.

12   [. . .]

PART IV   APPLICATION OF PROPERTY CY-PRÈS AND ASSISTANCE AND SUPERVISION OF CHARITIES BY COURT AND COMMISSION

Extended powers of court and variation of charters

13   Occasions for applying property cy-près

(1) Subject to subsection (2) below, the circumstances in which the original purposes of a charitable gift can be altered to allow the property given or part of it to be applied cy-près shall be as follows –

(a) where the original purposes, in whole or in part –

(i)   have been as far as may be fulfilled; or

(ii)   cannot be carried out, or not according to the directions given and to the spirit of the gift; or

(b) where the original purposes provide a use for part only of the property available by virtue of the gift; or

(c) where the property available by virtue of the gift and other property applicable for similar purposes can be more effectively used in conjunction, and to that end can suitably, regard being had to the appropriate considerations, be made applicable to common purposes; or

(d) where the original purposes were laid down by reference to an area which then was but has since ceased to be a unit for some other purpose, or by reference to a class of persons or to an area which has for any reason since ceased to be suitable, regard being had to the appropriate considerations, or to be practical in administering the gift; or

(e) where the original purposes, in whole or in part, have, since they were laid down, –

(i)   been adequately provided for by other means; or

(ii)   ceased, as being useless or harmful to the community or for other reasons, to be in law charitable; or

(iii) ceased in any other way to provide a suitable and effective method of using the property available by virtue of the gift, regard being had to the appropriate considerations.

(1A) In subsection (1) above 'the appropriate considerations' means –

  (a) (on the one hand) the spirit of the gift concerned, and
  (b) (on the other) the social and economic circumstances prevailing at the time of the proposed alteration of the original purposes.

(2) Subsection (1) above shall not affect the conditions which must be satisfied in order that property given for charitable purposes may be applied cy-près except in so far as those conditions require a failure of the original purposes.

(3) References in the foregoing subsections to the original purposes of a gift shall be construed, where the application of the property given has been altered or regulated by a scheme or otherwise, as referring to the purposes for which the property is for the time being applicable.

(4) Without prejudice to the power to make schemes in circumstances falling within subsection (1) above, the court may by scheme made under the court's jurisdiction with respect to charities, in any case where the purposes for which the property is held are laid down by reference to any such area as is mentioned in the first column in Schedule 3 to this Act, provide for enlarging the area to any such area as is mentioned in the second column in the same entry in that Schedule.

(5) It is hereby declared that a trust for charitable purposes places a trustee under a duty, where the case permits and requires the property or some part of it to be applied cy-près, to secure its effective use for charity by taking steps to enable it to be so applied.

14   Application cy-près of gifts of donors unknown or disclaiming

(1) Property given for specific charitable purposes which fail shall be applicable cy-près as if given for charitable purposes generally, where it belongs –

  (a) to a donor who after –

     (i) the prescribed advertisements and inquiries have been published and made, and
     (ii) the prescribed period beginning with the publication of those advertisements has expired,

     cannot be identified or cannot be found; or

  (b) to a donor who has executed a disclaimer in the prescribed form of his right to have the property returned.

(2) Where the prescribed advertisements and inquiries have been published and made by or on behalf of trustees with respect to any such property, the trustees shall not be liable to any person in respect of the property if no claim by him to be interested in it is received by them before the expiry of the period mentioned in subsection (1)(a)(ii) above.

(3) For the purposes of this section property shall be conclusively presumed (without any advertisement or inquiry) to belong to donors who cannot be identified, in so far as it consists –

  (a) of the proceeds of cash collections made by means of collecting boxes or by other means not adapted for distinguishing one gift from another; or
  (b) of the proceeds of any lottery, competition, entertainment, sale or similar money-raising activity, after allowing for property given to provide prizes or articles for sale or otherwise to enable the activity to be undertaken.

(4) The court or the Commission may by order direct that property not falling within subsection (3) above shall for the purposes of this section be treated (without any advertisement or inquiry) as belonging to donors who cannot be identified where it appears to the court or the Commission either –

  (a) that it would be unreasonable, having regard to the amounts likely to be returned to the donors, to incur expense with a view to returning the property; or

(b) that it would be unreasonable, having regard to the nature, circumstances and amounts of the gifts, and to the lapse of time since the gifts were made, for the donors to expect the property to be returned.

(5) Where property is applied cy-près by virtue of this section, the donor shall be deemed to have parted with all his interest at the time when the gift was made; but where property is so applied as belonging to donors who cannot be identified or cannot be found, and is not so applied by virtue of subsection (3) or (4) above –

(a) the scheme shall specify the total amount of that property; and

(b) the donor of any part of that amount shall be entitled, if he makes a claim not later than six months after the date on which the scheme is made, to recover from the charity for which the property is applied a sum equal to that part, less any expenses properly incurred by the charity trustees after that date in connection with claims relating to his gift; and

(c) the scheme may include directions as to the provision to be made for meeting any such claim.

(6) Where –

(a) any sum is, in accordance with any such directions, set aside for meeting any such claims, but

(b) the aggregate amount of any such claims actually made exceeds the relevant amount,

then, if the Commission so directs, each of the donors in question shall be entitled only to such proportion of the relevant amount as the amount of his claim bears to the aggregate amount referred to in paragraph (b) above; and for this purpose 'the relevant amount' means the amount of the sum so set aside after deduction of any expenses properly incurred by the charity trustees in connection with claims relating to the donors' gifts.

(7) For the purposes of this section, charitable purposes shall be deemed to 'fail' where any difficulty in applying property to those purposes makes that property or the part not applicable cy-près available to be returned to the donors.

(8) In this section 'prescribed' means prescribed by regulations made by the Commission; and such regulations may, as respects the advertisements which are to be published for the purposes of subsection (1)(a) above, make provision as to the form and content of such advertisements as well as the manner in which they are to be published.

(9) Any regulations made by the Commission under this section shall be published by the Commission in such manner as it thinks fit.

(10) In this section, except in so far as the context otherwise requires, references to a donor include persons claiming through or under the original donor, and references to property given include the property for the time being representing the property originally given or property derived from it.

(11) This section shall apply to property given for charitable purposes, notwithstanding that it was so given before the commencement of this Act.

14A Application cy-près of gifts made in response to certain solicitations

(1) This section applies to property given –

(a) for specific charitable purposes, and

(b) in response to a solicitation within subsection (2) below.

(2) A solicitation is within this subsection if –

(a) it is made for specific charitable purposes, and

(b) it is accompanied by a statement to the effect that property given in response to it will, in the event of those purposes failing, be applicable cy-près as if given for charitable purposes generally, unless the donor makes a relevant declaration at the time of making the gift.

(3)   A 'relevant declaration' is a declaration in writing by the donor to the effect that, in the event of the specific charitable purposes failing, he wishes the trustees holding the property to give him the opportunity to request the return of the property in question (or a sum equal to its value at the time of the making of the gift).

(4)   Subsections (5) and (6) below apply if –

   (a)   a person has given property as mentioned in subsection (1) above,
   (b)   the specific charitable purposes fail, and
   (c)   the donor has made a relevant declaration.

(5)   The trustees holding the property must take the prescribed steps for the purpose of –

   (a)   informing the donor of the failure of the purposes,
   (b)   enquiring whether he wishes to request the return of the property (or a sum equal to its value), and
   (c)   if within the prescribed period he makes such a request, returning the property (or such a sum) to him.

(6)   If those trustees have taken all appropriate prescribed steps but –

   (a)   they have failed to find the donor, or
   (b)   the donor does not within the prescribed period request the return of the property (or a sum equal to its value),

   section 14(1) above shall apply to the property as if it belonged to a donor within paragraph (b) of that subsection (application of property where donor has disclaimed right to return of property).

(7)   If –

   (a)   a person has given property as mentioned in subsection (1) above,
   (b)   the specific charitable purposes fail, and
   (c)   the donor has not made a relevant declaration,

   section 14(1) above shall similarly apply to the property as if it belonged to a donor within paragraph (b) of that subsection.

(8)   For the purposes of this section –

   (a)   'solicitation' means a solicitation made in any manner and however communicated to the persons to whom it is addressed,
   (b)   it is irrelevant whether any consideration is or is to be given in return for the property in question, and
   (c)   where any appeal consists of both solicitations that are accompanied by statements within subsection (2)(b) and solicitations that are not so accompanied, a person giving property as a result of the appeal is to be taken to have responded to the former solicitations and not the latter, unless he proves otherwise.

(9)   In this section 'prescribed' means prescribed by regulations made by the Commission, and any such regulations shall be published by the Commission in such manner as it thinks fit.

(10) Subsections (7) and (10) of section 14 shall apply for the purposes of this section as they apply for the purposes of section 14.

14B   Cy-près schemes

(1)   The power of the court or the Commission to make schemes for the application of property cy-près shall be exercised in accordance with this section.

(2)   Where any property given for charitable purposes is applicable cy-près, the court or the Commission may make a scheme providing for the property to be applied –

   (a)   for such charitable purposes, and
   (b)   (if the scheme provides for the property to be transferred to another charity) by or on trust for such other charity,

   as it considers appropriate, having regard to the matters set out in subsection (3).

(3)   The matters are –

    (a)   the spirit of the original gift,

    (b)   the desirability of securing that the property is applied for charitable purposes which are close to the original purposes, and

    (c)   the need for the relevant charity to have purposes which are suitable and effective in the light of current social and economic circumstances.

The 'relevant charity' means the charity by or on behalf of which the property is to be applied under the scheme.

(4)   If a scheme provides for the property to be transferred to another charity, the scheme may impose on the charity trustees of that charity a duty to secure that the property is applied for purposes which are, so far as is reasonably practicable, similar in character to the original purposes.

(5)   In this section references to property given include the property for the time being representing the property originally given or property derived from it.

(6)   In this section references to the transfer of property to a charity are references to its transfer –

    (a)   to the charity, or

    (b)   to the charity trustees, or

    (c)   to any trustee for the charity, or

    (d)   to a person nominated by the charity trustees to hold it in trust for the charity,

as the scheme may provide.

15   Charities governed by charter, or by or under statute

(1)   Where a Royal charter establishing or regulating a body corporate is amendable by the grant and acceptance of a further charter, a scheme relating to the body corporate or to the administration of property held by the body (including a scheme for the cy-près application of any such property) may be made by the court under the court's jurisdiction with respect to charities notwithstanding that the scheme cannot take effect without the alteration of the charter, but shall be so framed that the scheme, or such part of it as cannot take effect without the alteration of the charter, does not purport to come into operation unless or until Her Majesty thinks fit to amend the charter in such manner as will permit the scheme or that part of it to have effect.

(2)   Where under the court's jurisdiction with respect to charities or the corresponding jurisdiction of a court in Northern Ireland, or under powers conferred by this Act or by any Northern Ireland legislation relating to charities, a scheme is made with respect to a body corporate, and it appears to Her Majesty expedient, having regard to the scheme, to amend any Royal charter relating to that body, Her Majesty may, on the application of that body, amend the charter accordingly by Order in Council in any way in which the charter could be amended by the grant and acceptance of a further charter; and any such Order in Council may be revoked or varied in like manner as the charter it amends.

(3)   The jurisdiction of the court with respect to charities shall not be excluded or restricted in the case of a charity of any description mentioned in Schedule 4 to this Act by the operation of the enactments or instruments there mentioned in relation to that description, and a scheme established for any such charity may modify or supersede in relation to it the provision made by any such enactment or instrument as if made by a scheme of the court, and may also make any such provision as is authorised by that Schedule.

Powers of Commission to make schemes and act for protection of charities etc.

16   Concurrent jurisdiction with High Court for certain purposes

(1)   Subject to the provisions of this Act, the Commission may by order exercise the same jurisdiction and powers as are exercisable by the High Court in charity proceedings for the following purposes –

(a)   establishing a scheme for the administration of a charity;

(b)   appointing, discharging or removing a charity trustee or trustee for a charity, or removing an officer or employee;

(c)   vesting or transferring property, or requiring or entitling any person to call for or make any transfer of property or any payment.

(2)   Where the court directs a scheme for the administration of a charity to be established, the court may by order refer the matter to the Commission for it to prepare or settle a scheme in accordance with such directions (if any) as the court sees fit to give, and any such order may provide for the scheme to be put into effect by order of the Commission as if prepared under subsection (1) above and without any further order of the court.

(3)   The Commission shall not have jurisdiction under this section to try or determine the title at law or in equity to any property as between a charity or trustee for a charity and a person holding or claiming the property or an interest in it adversely to the charity, or to try or determine any question as to the existence or extent of any charge or trust.

(4)   Subject to the following subsections, the Commission shall not exercise its jurisdiction under this section as respects any charity, except –

(a)   on the application of the charity; or

(b)   on an order of the court under subsection (2) above; or

(c)   on the application of the Attorney General.

(5)   In the case of a charity whose gross income does not exceed £500 a year, the Commission may exercise its jurisdiction under this section on the application –

(a)   of any one or more of the charity trustees; or

(b)   of any person interested in the charity; or

(c)   of any two or more inhabitants of the area of the charity if it is a local charity.

(6)   Where in the case of a charity, other than an exempt charity, the Commission is satisfied that the charity trustees ought in the interests of the charity to apply for a scheme, but have unreasonably refused or neglected to do so and the Commission has given the charity trustees an opportunity to make representations to them, the Commission may proceed as if an application for a scheme had been made by the charity but the Commission shall not have power in a case where it acts by virtue of this subsection to alter the purposes of a charity, unless forty years have elapsed from the date of its foundation.

(7)   Where –

(a)   a charity cannot apply to the Commission for a scheme by reason of any vacancy among the charity trustees or the absence or incapacity of any of them, but

(b)   such an application is made by such number of the charity trustees as the Commission considers appropriate in the circumstances of the case,

the Commission may nevertheless proceed as if the application were an application made by the charity.

(8)   The Commission may on the application of any charity trustee or trustee for a charity exercise its jurisdiction under this section for the purpose of discharging him from his trusteeship.

(9)   Before exercising any jurisdiction under this section otherwise than on an order of the court, the Commission shall give notice of its intention to do so to each of the charity trustees, except any that cannot be found or has no known address in the

United Kingdom or who is party or privy to an application for the exercise of the jurisdiction; and any such notice may be given by post, and, if given by post, may be addressed to the recipient's last known address in the United Kingdom.

(10) The Commission shall not exercise its jurisdiction under this section in any case (not referred to them by order of the court) which, by reason of its contentious character, or of any special question of law or of fact which it may involve, or for other reasons, the Commission may consider more fit to be adjudicated on by the court.

(11) [...]

(12) [...]

(13) [...]

(14) [...]

(15) If the Secretary of State thinks it expedient to do so –

(a) in consequence of changes in the value of money, or

(b) with a view to increasing the number of charities in respect of which the Commission may exercise its jurisdiction under this section in accordance with subsection (5) above,

he may by order amend that subsection by substituting a different sum for the sum for the time being specified there.

17   Further powers to make schemes or alter application of charitable property

(1) Where it appears to the Commission that a scheme should be established for the administration of a charity, but also that it is necessary or desirable for the scheme to alter the provision made by an Act of Parliament establishing or regulating the charity or to make any other provision which goes or might go beyond the powers exercisable by the Commission apart from this section, or that it is for any reason proper for the scheme to be subject to parliamentary review, then (subject to subsection (6) below) the Commission may settle a scheme accordingly with a view to its being given effect under this section.

(2) A scheme settled by the Commission under this section may be given effect by order of the Secretary of State, and a draft of the order shall be laid before Parliament.

(3) Without prejudice to the operation of section 6 of the Statutory Instruments Act 1946 in other cases, in the case of a scheme which goes beyond the powers exercisable apart from this section in altering a statutory provision contained in or having effect under any public general Act of Parliament, the order shall not be made unless the draft has been approved by resolution of each House of Parliament.

(4) Subject to subsection (5) below, any provision of a scheme brought into effect under this section may be modified or superseded by the court or the Commission as if it were a scheme brought into effect by order of the Commission under section 16 above.

(5) Where subsection (3) above applies to a scheme, the order giving effect to it may direct that the scheme shall not be modified or superseded by a scheme brought into effect otherwise than under this section, and may also direct that that subsection shall apply to any scheme modifying or superseding the scheme to which the order gives effect.

(6) The Commission shall not proceed under this section without the like application and the like notice to the charity trustees, as would be required if the Commission was proceeding (without an order of the court) under section 16 above; but on any application for a scheme, or in a case where it acts by virtue of subsection (6) or (7) of that section, the Commission may proceed under this section or that section as appears to it appropriate.

(7) Notwithstanding anything in the trusts of a charity, no expenditure incurred in preparing or promoting a Bill in Parliament shall without the consent of the court or the Commission be defrayed out of any moneys applicable for the purposes of a charity.

(8) Where the Commission is satisfied –

    (a) that the whole of the income of a charity cannot in existing circumstances be effectively applied for the purposes of the charity; and

    (b) that, if those circumstances continue, a scheme might be made for applying the surplus cy-près; and

    (c) that it is for any reason not yet desirable to make such a scheme;

    then the Commission may by order authorise the charity trustees at their discretion (but subject to any conditions imposed by the order) to apply any accrued or accruing income for any purposes for which it might be made applicable by such a scheme, and any application authorised by the order shall be deemed to be within the purposes of the charity.

(9) An order under subsection (8) above shall not extend to more than £300 out of income accrued before the date of the order, nor to income accruing more than three years after that date, nor to more than £100 out of the income accruing in any of those three years.

18 Power to act for protection of charities

(1) Where, at any time after it has instituted an inquiry under section 8 above with respect to any charity, the Commission is satisfied –

    (a) that there is or has been any misconduct or mismanagement in the administration of the charity; or

    (b) that it is necessary or desirable to act for the purpose of protecting the property of the charity or securing a proper application for the purposes of the charity of that property or of property coming to the charity,

    the Commission may of its own motion do one or more of the following things –

    (i) by order suspend any trustee, charity trustee, officer, agent or employee of the charity from the exercise of his office or employment pending consideration being given to his removal (whether under this section or otherwise);

    (ii) by order appoint such number of additional charity trustees as it considers necessary for the proper administration of the charity;

    (iii) by order vest any property held by or in trust for the charity in the official custodian, or require the persons in whom any such property is vested to transfer it to him, or appoint any person to transfer any such property to him;

    (iv) order any person who holds any property on behalf of the charity, or of any trustee for it, not to part with the property without the approval of the Commission;

    (v) order any debtor of the charity not to make any payment in or towards the discharge of his liability to the charity without the approval of the Commission;

    (vi) by order restrict (notwithstanding anything in the trusts of the charity) the transactions which may be entered into, or the nature or amount of the payments which may be made, in the administration of the charity without the approval of the Commission;

    (vii) by order appoint (in accordance with section 19 below) an interim manager, who shall act as receiver and manager in respect of the property and affairs of the charity.

(2) Where, at any time after it has instituted an inquiry under section 8 above with respect to any charity, the Commission is satisfied –

    (a) that there is or has been any misconduct or mismanagement in the administration of the charity; and

    (b) that it is necessary or desirable to act for the purpose of protecting the property of the charity or securing a proper application for the purposes of the charity of that property or of property coming to the charity, the Commission may of its own motion do either or both of the following things –

   (i) by order remove any trustee, charity trustee, officer, agent or employee of the charity who has been responsible for or privy to the misconduct or mismanagement or has by his conduct contributed to it or facilitated it;

   (ii) by order establish a scheme for the administration of the charity.

(3) The references in subsection (1) or (2) above to misconduct or mismanagement shall (notwithstanding anything in the trusts of the charity) extend to the employment for the remuneration or reward of persons acting in the affairs of the charity, or for other administrative purposes, of sums which are excessive in relation to the property which is or is likely to be applied or applicable for the purposes of the charity.

(4) The Commission may also remove a charity trustee by order made of its own motion –

   (a) where, within the last five years, the trustee –

      (i) having previously been adjudged bankrupt or had his estate sequestrated, has been discharged, or

      (ii) having previously made a composition or arrangement with, or granted a trust deed for, his creditors, has been discharged in respect of it;

   (b) where the trustee is a corporation in liquidation;

   (c) where the trustee is incapable of acting by reason of mental disorder within the meaning of the Mental Health Act 1983;

   (d) where the trustee has not acted, and will not declare his willingness or unwillingness to act;

   (e) where the trustee is outside England and Wales or cannot be found or does not act, and his absence or failure to act impedes the proper administration of the charity.

(5) The Commission may by order made of its own motion appoint a person to be a charity trustee –

   (a) in place of a charity trustee removed by the Commission under this section or otherwise;

   (b) where there are no charity trustees, or where by reason of vacancies in their number or the absence or incapacity of any of their number the charity cannot apply for the appointment;

   (c) where there is a single charity trustee, not being a corporation aggregate, and the Commission is of opinion that it is necessary to increase the number for the proper administration of the charity;

   (d) where the Commission is of opinion that it is necessary for the proper administration of the charity to have an additional charity trustee because one of the existing charity trustees who ought nevertheless to remain a charity trustee either cannot be found or does not act or is outside England and Wales.

(6) The powers of the Commission under this section to remove or appoint charity trustees of its own motion shall include power to make any such order with respect to the vesting in or transfer to the charity trustees of any property as the Commission could make on the removal or appointment of a charity trustee by it under section 16 above.

(7) Any order under this section for the removal or appointment of a charity trustee or trustee for a charity, or for the vesting or transfer of any property, shall be of the like effect as an order made under section 16 above.

(8) [. . .]

(9) [. . .]

(10) [. . .]

(11) The power of the Commission to make an order under subsection (1)(i) above shall not be exercisable so as to suspend any person from the exercise of his office or employment for a period of more than twelve months; but (without prejudice to the generality of section 89(1) below), any such order made in the case of any person

may make provision as respects the period of his suspension for matters arising out of it, and in particular for enabling any person to execute any instrument in his name or otherwise act for him and, in the case of a charity trustee, for adjusting any rules governing the proceedings of the charity trustees to take account of the reduction in the number capable of acting.

(12) Before exercising any jurisdiction under this section otherwise than by virtue of subsection (1) above, the Commission shall give notice of its intention to do so to each of the charity trustees, except any that cannot be found or has no known address in the United Kingdom; and any such notice may be given by post and, if given by post, may be addressed to the recipient's last known address in the United Kingdom.

(13) The Commission shall, at such intervals as it thinks fit, review any order made by it under paragraph (i), or any of paragraphs (iii) to (vii), of subsection (1) above; and, if on any such review it appears to the Commission that it would be appropriate to discharge the order in whole or in part, the Commission shall so discharge it (whether subject to any savings or other transitional provisions or not).

(14) If any person contravenes an order under subsection (1)(iv), (v) or (vi) above, he shall be guilty of an offence and liable on summary conviction to a fine not exceeding level 5 on the standard scale.

(15) Subsection (14) above shall not be taken to preclude the bringing of proceedings for breach of trust against any charity trustee or trustee for a charity in respect of a contravention of an order under subsection (1)(iv) or (vi) above (whether proceedings in respect of the contravention are brought against him under subsection (14) above or not).

(16) In this section –

(a) subsections (1) to (3) apply in relation to an exempt charity, and

(b) subsections (4) to (6) apply in relation to such a charity at any time after the Commission have instituted an inquiry under section 8 with respect to it,

and the other provisions of this section apply accordingly.

18A Power to suspend or remove trustees etc. from membership of charity

(1) This section applies where the Commission makes –

(a) an order under section 18(1) above suspending from his office or employment any trustee, charity trustee, officer, agent or employee of a charity, or

(b) an order under section 18(2) above removing from his office or employment any officer, agent or employee of a charity,

and the trustee, charity trustee, officer, agent or employee (as the case may be) is a member of the charity.

(2) If the order suspends the person in question from his office or employment, the Commission may also make an order suspending his membership of the charity for the period for which he is suspended from his office or employment.

(3) If the order removes the person in question from his office or employment, the Commission may also make an order –

(a) terminating his membership of the charity, and

(b) prohibiting him from resuming his membership of the charity without the Commission's consent.

(4) If an application for the Commission's consent under subsection (3)(b) above is made five years or more after the order was made, the Commission must grant the application unless satisfied that, by reason of any special circumstances, it should be refused.

19 Supplementary provisions relating to interim manager appointed for a charity

(1) The Commission may under section 18(1)(vii) above appoint to be interim manager in respect of a charity such person (other than a member of its staff) as it thinks fit.

(2)   Without prejudice to the generality of section 89(1) below, any order made by the Commission under section 18(1)(vii) above may make provision with respect to the functions to be discharged by the interim manager appointed by the order; and those functions shall be discharged by him under the supervision of the Commission.

(3)   In connection with the discharge of those functions any such order may provide –

(a)   for the interim manager appointed by the order to have such powers and duties of the charity trustees of the charity concerned (whether arising under this Act or otherwise) as are specified in the order;

(b)   for any powers or duties exercisable or falling to be performed by the interim manager by virtue of paragraph (a) above to be exercisable or performed by him to the exclusion of those trustees.

(4)   Where a person has been appointed interim manager by any such order –

(a)   section 29 below shall apply to him and to his functions as a person so appointed as it applies to a charity trustee of the charity concerned and to his duties as such; and

(b)   the Commission may apply to the High Court for directions in relation to any particular matter arising in connection with the discharge of those functions.

(5)   The High Court may on an application under subsection (4)(b) above –

(a)   give such directions, or

(b)   make such orders declaring the rights of any persons (whether before the court or not),

as it thinks just; and the costs of any such application shall be paid by the charity concerned.

(6)   Regulations made by the Secretary of State may make provision with respect to –

(a)   the appointment and removal of persons appointed in accordance with this section;

(b)   the remuneration of such persons out of the income of the charities concerned;

(c)   the making of reports to the Commission by such persons.

(7)   Regulations under subsection (6) above may, in particular, authorise the Commission –

(a)   to require security for the due discharge of his functions to be given by a person so appointed;

(b)   to determine the amount of such a person's remuneration;

(c)   to disallow any amount of remuneration in such circumstances as are prescribed by the regulations.

19A   Power to give specific directions for protection of charity

(1)   This section applies where, at any time after the Commission has instituted an inquiry under section 8 above with respect to any charity, it is satisfied as mentioned in section 18(1)(a) or (b) above.

(2)   The Commission may by order direct –

(a)   the charity trustees,

(b)   any trustee for the charity,

(c)   any officer or employee of the charity, or

(d)   (if a body corporate) the charity itself,

to take any action specified in the order which the Commission considers to be expedient in the interests of the charity.

(3)   An order under this section –

(a)   may require action to be taken whether or not it would otherwise be within the powers exercisable by the person or persons concerned, or by the charity, in relation to the administration of the charity or to its property, but

(b) may not require any action to be taken which is prohibited by any Act of Parliament or expressly prohibited by the trusts of the charity or is inconsistent with its purposes.

(4) Anything done by a person or body under the authority of an order under this section shall be deemed to be properly done in the exercise of the powers mentioned in subsection (3)(a) above.

(5) Subsection (4) does not affect any contractual or other rights arising in connection with anything which has been done under the authority of such an order.

19B Power to direct application of charity property

(1) This section applies where the Commission is satisfied –

(a) that a person or persons in possession or control of any property held by or on trust for a charity is or are unwilling to apply it properly for the purposes of the charity, and

(b) that it is necessary or desirable to make an order under this section for the purpose of securing a proper application of that property for the purposes of the charity.

(2) The Commission may by order direct the person or persons concerned to apply the property in such manner as is specified in the order.

(3) An order under this section –

(a) may require action to be taken whether or not it would otherwise be within the powers exercisable by the person or persons concerned in relation to the property, but

(b) may not require any action to be taken which is prohibited by any Act of Parliament or expressly prohibited by the trusts of the charity.

(4) Anything done by a person under the authority of an order under this section shall be deemed to be properly done in the exercise of the powers mentioned in subsection (3)(a) above.

(5) Subsection (4) does not affect any contractual or other rights arising in connection with anything which has been done under the authority of such an order.

19C Copy of order under section 18, 18A, 19A or 19B, and Commission's reasons, to be sent to charity

(1) Where the Commission makes an order under section 18, 18A, 19A or 19B, it must send the documents mentioned in subsection (2) below –

(a) to the charity concerned (if a body corporate), or

(b) (if not) to each of the charity trustees.

(2) The documents are –

(a) a copy of the order, and

(b) a statement of the Commission's reasons for making it.

(3) The documents must be sent to the charity or charity trustees as soon as practicable after the making of the order.

(4) The Commission need not, however, comply with subsection (3) above in relation to the documents, or (as the case may be) the statement of its reasons, if it considers that to do so –

(a) would prejudice any inquiry or investigation, or

(b) would not be in the interests of the charity;

but, once the Commission considers that this is no longer the case, it must send the documents, or (as the case may be) the statement, to the charity or charity trustees as soon as practicable.

(5) Nothing in this section requires any document to be sent to a person who cannot be found or who has no known address in the United Kingdom.

(6) Any documents required to be sent to a person under this section may be sent to, or otherwise served on, that person in the same way as an order made by the Commission under this Act could be served on him in accordance with section 91 below.

20   Publicity relating to schemes

(1) The Commission may not –

   (a) make any order under this Act to establish a scheme for the administration of a charity, or

   (b) submit such a scheme to the court or the Minister for an order giving it effect,

   unless, before doing so, the Commission has complied with the publicity requirements in subsection (2) below.

   This is subject to any disapplication of those requirements under subsection (4) below.

(2) The publicity requirements are –

   (a) that the Commission must give public notice of its proposals, inviting representations to be made to it within a period specified in the notice; and

   (b) that, in the case of a scheme relating to a local charity (other than an ecclesiastical charity) in a parish or in a community in Wales, the Commission must communicate a draft of the scheme to the parish or community council (or, where a parish has no council, to the chairman of the parish meeting).

(3) The time when any such notice is given or any such communication takes place is to be decided by the Commission.

(4) The Commission may determine that either or both of the publicity requirements is or are not to apply in relation to a particular scheme if it is satisfied that –

   (a) by reason of the nature of the scheme, or

   (b) for any other reason,

   compliance with the requirement or requirements is unnecessary.

(5) Where the Commission gives public notice of any proposals under this section, the Commission –

   (a) must take into account any representations made to it within the period specified in the notice, and

   (b) may (without further notice) proceed with the proposals either without modifications or with such modifications as it thinks desirable.

(6) Where the Commission makes an order under this Act to establish a scheme for the administration of a charity, a copy of the order must be available, for at least a month after the order is published, for public inspection at all reasonable times –

   (a) at the Commission's office, and

   (b) if the charity is a local charity, at some convenient place in the area of the charity.

   Paragraph (b) does not apply if the Commission is satisfied that for any reason it is unnecessary for a copy of the scheme to be available locally.

(7) Any public notice of any proposals which is to be given under this section –

   (a) is to contain such particulars of the proposals, or such directions for obtaining information about them, as the Commission thinks sufficient and appropriate, and

   (b) is to be given in such manner as the Commission thinks sufficient and appropriate.

20A Publicity for orders relating to trustees or other individuals

(1) The Commission may not make any order under this Act to appoint, discharge or remove a charity trustee or trustee for a charity, other than –

    (a) an order relating to the official custodian, or

    (b) an order under section 18(1)(ii) above,

unless, before doing so, the Commission has complied with the publicity requirement in subsection (2) below.

This is subject to any disapplication of that requirement under subsection (4) below.

(2) The publicity requirement is that the Commission must give public notice of its proposals, inviting representations to be made to it within a period specified in the notice.

(3) The time when any such notice is given is to be decided by the Commission.

(4) The Commission may determine that the publicity requirement is not to apply in relation to a particular order if it is satisfied that for any reason compliance with the requirement is unnecessary.

(5) Before the Commission makes an order under this Act to remove without his consent –

    (a) a charity trustee or trustee for a charity, or

    (b) an officer, agent or employee of a charity,

the Commission must give him not less than one month's notice of its proposals, inviting representations to be made to it within a period specified in the notice.

This does not apply if the person cannot be found or has no known address in the United Kingdom.

(6) Where the Commission gives notice of any proposals under this section, the Commission –

    (a) must take into account any representations made to it within the period specified in the notice, and

    (b) may (without further notice) proceed with the proposals either without modifications or with such modifications as it thinks desirable.

(7) Any notice of any proposals which is to be given under this section –

    (a) is to contain such particulars of the proposals, or such directions for obtaining information about them, as the Commission thinks sufficient and appropriate, and

    (b) (in the case of a public notice) is to be given in such manner as the Commission thinks sufficient and appropriate.

(8) Any notice to be given under subsection (5) –

    (a) may be given by post, and

    (b) if given by post, may be addressed to the recipient's last known address in the United Kingdom.

Property vested in official custodian

21 Entrusting charity property to official custodian, and termination of trust

(1) The court may by order –

    (a) vest in the official custodian any land held by or in trust for a charity;

    (b) authorise or require the persons in whom any such land is vested to transfer it to him; or

    (c) appoint any person to transfer any such land to him;

but this subsection does not apply to any interest in land by way of mortgage or other security.

(2)   Where property is vested in the official custodian in trust for a charity, the court may make an order discharging him from the trusteeship as respects all or any of that property.

(3)   Where the official custodian is discharged from his trusteeship of any property, or the trusts on which he holds any property come to an end, the court may make such vesting orders and give such directions as may seem to the court to be necessary or expedient in consequence.

(4)   No person shall be liable for any loss occasioned by his acting in conformity with an order under this section or by his giving effect to anything done in pursuance of such an order, or be excused from so doing by reason of the order having been in any respect improperly obtained.

22   Supplementary provisions as to property vested in official custodian

(1)   Subject to the provisions of this Act, where property is vested in the official custodian in trust for a charity, he shall not exercise any powers of management, but he shall as trustee of any property have all the same powers, duties and liabilities, and be entitled to the same rights and immunities, and be subject to the control and orders of the court, as a corporation appointed custodian trustee under section 4 of the Public Trustee Act 1906 except that he shall have no power to charge fees.

(2)   Subject to subsection (3) below, where any land is vested in the official custodian in trust for a charity, the charity trustees shall have power in his name and on his behalf to execute and do all assurances and things which they could properly execute or do in their own name and on their own behalf if the land were vested in them.

(3)   If any land is so vested in the official custodian by virtue of an order under section 18 above, the power conferred on the charity trustees by subsection (2) above shall not be exercisable by them in relation to any transaction affecting the land, unless the transaction is authorised by order of the court or of the Commission.

(4)   Where any land is vested in the official custodian in trust for a charity, the charity trustees shall have the like power to make obligations entered into by them binding on the land as if it were vested in them; and any covenant, agreement or condition which is enforceable by or against the custodian by reason of the land being vested in him shall be enforceable by or against the charity trustees as if the land were vested in them.

(5)   In relation to a corporate charity, subsections (2), (3) and (4) above shall apply with the substitution of references to the charity for references to the charity trustees.

(6)   Subsections (2), (3) and (4) above shall not authorise any charity trustees or charity to impose any personal liability on the official custodian.

(7)   Where the official custodian is entitled as trustee for a charity to the custody of securities or documents of title relating to the trust property, he may permit them to be in the possession or under the control of the charity trustees without thereby incurring any liability.

23   Divestment in the case of land subject to Reverter of Sites Act 1987

(1)   Where –

(a)   any land is vested in the official custodian in trust for a charity, and

(b)   it appears to the Commission that section 1 of the Reverter of Sites Act 1987 (right of reverter replaced by trust) will, or is likely to, operate in relation to the land at a particular time or in particular circumstances,

the jurisdiction which, under section 16 above, is exercisable by the Commission for the purpose of discharging a trustee for a charity may, at any time before section 1 of that Act ('the 1987 Act') operates in relation to the land, be exercised by the Commission of its own motion for the purpose of –

(i)   making an order discharging the official custodian from his trusteeship of the land, and

    (ii) making such vesting orders and giving such directions as appear to the Commission to be necessary or expedient in consequence.

(2) Where –

    (a) section 1 of the 1987 Act has operated in relation to any land which, immediately before the time when that section so operated, was vested in the official custodian in trust for a charity, and

    (b) the land remains vested in him but on the trust arising under that section,

the court or the Commission (of its own motion) may –

    (i) make an order discharging the official custodian from his trusteeship of the land, and

    (ii) (subject to the following provisions of this section) make such vesting orders and give such directions as appear to it to be necessary or expedient in consequence.

(3) Where any order discharging the official custodian from his trusteeship of any land –

    (a) is made by the court under section 21(2) above, or by the Commission under section 16 above, on the grounds that section 1 of the 1987 Act will, or is likely to, operate in relation to the land, or

    (b) is made by the court or the Commission under subsection (2) above,

the persons in whom the land is to be vested on the discharge of the official custodian shall be the relevant charity trustees (as defined in subsection (4) below), unless the court or (as the case may be) the Commission is satisfied that it would be appropriate for it to be vested in some other persons.

(4) In subsection (3) above 'the relevant charity trustees' means –

    (a) in relation to an order made as mentioned in paragraph (a) of that subsection, the charity trustees of the charity in trust for which the land is vested in the official custodian immediately before the time when the order takes effect, or

    (b) in relation to an order made under subsection (2) above, the charity trustees of the charity in trust for which the land was vested in the official custodian immediately before the time when section 1 of the 1987 Act operated in relation to the land.

(5) Where –

    (a) section 1 of the 1987 Act has operated in relation to any such land as is mentioned in subsection (2)(a) above, and

    (b) the land remains vested in the official custodian as mentioned in subsection (2)(b) above,

then (subject to subsection (6) below), all the powers, duties and liabilities that would, apart from this section, be those of the official custodian as trustee of the land shall instead be those of the charity trustees of the charity concerned; and those trustees shall have power in his name and on his behalf to execute and do all assurances and things which they could properly execute or do in their own name and on their own behalf if the land were vested in them.

(6) Subsection (5) above shall not be taken to require or authorise those trustees to sell the land at a time when it remains vested in the official custodian.

(7) Where –

    (a) the official custodian has been discharged from his trusteeship of any land by an order under subsection (2) above, and

    (b) the land has, in accordance with subsection (3) above, been vested in the charity trustees concerned or (as the case may be) in any persons other than those trustees,

the land shall be held by those trustees, or (as the case may be) by those persons, as trustees on the terms of the trust arising under section 1 of the 1987 Act.

(8)   The official custodian shall not be liable to any person in respect of any loss or mis-application of any land vested in him in accordance with that section unless it is occasioned by or through any wilful neglect or default of his or of any person acting for him; but the Consolidated Fund shall be liable to make good to any person any sums for which the official custodian may be liable by reason of any such neglect or default.

(9)   In this section any reference to section 1 of the 1987 Act operating in relation to any land is a reference to a trust arising in relation to the land under that section.

Establishment of common investment or deposit funds

24   Schemes to establish common investment funds

(1)   The court or the Commission may by order make and bring into effect schemes (in this section referred to as 'common investment schemes') for the establishment of common investment funds under trusts which provide –

  (a)   for property transferred to the fund by or on behalf of a charity participating in the scheme to be invested under the control of trustees appointed to manage the fund; and

  (b)   for the participating charities to be entitled (subject to the provisions of the scheme) to the capital and income of the fund in shares determined by reference to the amount or value of the property transferred to it by or on behalf of each of them and to the value of the fund at the time of the transfers.

(2)   The court or the Commission may make a common investment scheme on the application of any two or more charities.

(3)   A common investment scheme may be made in terms admitting any charity to participate, or the scheme may restrict the right to participate in any manner.

(3A) A common investment scheme may provide for appropriate bodies to be admitted to participate in the scheme (in addition to the participating charities) to such extent as the trustees appointed to manage the fund may determine.

(3B) In this section 'appropriate body' means –

  (a)   a Scottish recognised body, or

  (b)   a Northern Ireland charity,

and, in the application of the relevant provisions in relation to a scheme which contains provisions authorised by subsection (3A) above, 'charity' includes an appropriate body. 'The relevant provisions' are subsections (1) and (4) to (6) and (in relation only to a charity within paragraph (b)) subsection (7).

(4)   A common investment scheme may make provision for, and for all matters connected with, the establishment, investment, management and winding up of the common investment fund, and may in particular include provision –

  (a)   for remunerating persons appointed trustees to hold or manage the fund or any part of it, with or without provision authorising a person to receive the remuneration notwithstanding that he is also a charity trustee of or trustee for a participating charity;

  (b)   for restricting the size of the fund, and for regulating as to time, amount or otherwise the right to transfer property to or withdraw it from the fund, and for enabling sums to be advanced out of the fund by way of loan to a participating charity pending the withdrawal of property from the fund by the charity;

  (c)   for enabling income to be withheld from distribution with a view to avoiding fluctuations in the amounts distributed, and generally for regulating distributions of income;

  (d)   for enabling money to be borrowed temporarily for the purpose of meeting payments to be made out of the funds;

(e) for enabling questions arising under the scheme as to the right of a charity to participate, or as to the rights of participating charities, or as to any other matter, to be conclusively determined by the decision of the trustees managing the fund or in any other manner;

(f) for regulating the accounts and information to be supplied to participating charities.

(5) A common investment scheme, in addition to the provision for property to be transferred to the fund on the basis that the charity shall be entitled to a share in the capital and income of the fund, may include provision for enabling sums to be deposited by or on behalf of a charity on the basis that (subject to the provisions of the scheme) the charity shall be entitled to repayment of the sums deposited and to interest thereon at a rate determined by or under the scheme; and where a scheme makes any such provision it shall also provide for excluding from the amount of capital and income to be shared between charities participating otherwise than by way of deposit such amounts (not exceeding the amounts properly attributable to the making of deposits) as are from time to time reasonably required in respect of the liabilities of the fund for the repayment of deposits and for the interest on deposits, including amounts required by way of reserve.

(6) Except in so far as a common investment scheme provides to the contrary, the rights under it of a participating charity shall not be capable of being assigned or charged, nor shall any trustee or other person concerned in the management of the common investment fund be required or entitled to take account of any trust or other equity affecting a participating charity or its property or rights.

(7) The powers of investment of every charity shall include power to participate in common investment schemes unless the power is excluded by a provision specifically referring to common investment schemes in the trusts of the charity.

(8) A common investment fund shall be deemed for all purposes to be a charity [. . .].

(9) Subsection (8) above shall apply not only to common investment funds established under the powers of this section, but also to any similar fund established for the exclusive benefit of charities by or under any enactment relating to any particular charities or class of charity.

25 Schemes to establish common deposit funds

(1) The court or the Commission may by order make and bring into effect schemes (in this section referred to as 'common deposit schemes') for the establishment of common deposit funds under trusts which provide –

(a) for sums to be deposited by or on behalf of a charity participating in the scheme and invested under the control of trustees appointed to manage the fund; and

(b) for any such charity to be entitled (subject to the provisions of the scheme) to repayment of any sums so deposited and to interest thereon at a rate determined under the scheme.

(2) Subject to subsection (3) below, the following provisions of section 24 above, namely –

(a) subsections (2), (3) and (4), and

(b) subsections (6) to (9),

shall have effect in relation to common deposit schemes and common deposit funds as they have effect in relation to common investment schemes and common investment funds.

(3) In its application in accordance with subsection (2) above, subsection (4) of that section shall have effect with the substitution for paragraphs (b) and (c) of the following paragraphs –

'(b) for regulating as to time, amount or otherwise the right to repayment of sums deposited in the fund;

(c)   for authorising a part of the income for any year to be credited to a reserve account maintained for the purpose of counteracting any losses accruing to the fund, and generally for regulating the manner in which the rate of interest on deposits is to be determined from time to time;'

(4)   A common deposit scheme may provide for appropriate bodies to be admitted to participate in the scheme (in addition to the participating charities) to such extent as the trustees appointed to manage the fund may determine.

(5)   In this section 'appropriate body' means –

(a)   a Scottish recognised body, or

(b)   a Northern Ireland charity,

and, in the application of the relevant provisions in relation to a scheme which contains provisions authorised by subsection (4) above, 'charity' includes an appropriate body.

(6)   'The relevant provisions' are –

(a)   subsection (1) above, and

(b)   subsections (4) and (6) of section 24 above, as they apply in accordance with subsections (2) and (3) above, and

(c)   (in relation only to a charity within subsection (5)(b) above) subsection (7) of that section, as it so applies.

25A   Meaning of 'Scottish recognised body' and 'Northern Ireland charity' in sections 24 and 25

(1)   In sections 24 and 25 above 'Scottish recognised body' means a body –

(a)   established under the law of Scotland, or

(b)   managed or controlled wholly or mainly in or from Scotland,

to which the Commissioners for Her Majesty's Revenue and Customs have given intimation, which has not subsequently been withdrawn, that relief is due under section 505 of the Income and Corporation Taxes Act 1988 in respect of income of the body which is applicable and applied to charitable purposes only.

(2)   In those sections 'Northern Ireland charity' means an institution –

(a)   which is a charity under the law of Northern Ireland, and

(b)   to which the Commissioners for Her Majesty's Revenue and Customs have given intimation, which has not subsequently been withdrawn, that relief is due under section 505 of the Income and Corporation Taxes Act 1988 in respect of income of the institution which is applicable and applied to charitable purposes only.'

Additional powers of Commission

26   Power to authorise dealings with charity property etc.

(1)   Subject to the provisions of this section, where it appears to the Commission that any action proposed or contemplated in the administration of a charity is expedient in the interests of the charity, the Commission may by order sanction that action, whether or not it would otherwise be within the powers exercisable by the charity trustees in the administration of the charity; and anything done under the authority of such an order shall be deemed to be properly done in the exercise of those powers.

(2)   An order under this section may be made so as to authorise a particular transaction, compromise or the like, or a particular application of property, or so as to give a more general authority, and (without prejudice to the generality of subsection (1) above) may authorise a charity to use common premises, or employ a common staff, or otherwise combine for any purpose of administration, with any other charity.

(3) An order under this section may give directions as to the manner in which any expenditure is to be borne and as to other matters connected with or arising out of the action thereby authorised; and where anything is done in pursuance of an authority given by any such order, any directions given in connection therewith shall be binding on the charity trustees for the time being as if contained in the trusts of the charity; but any such directions may on the application of the charity be modified or superseded by a further order.

(4) Without prejudice to the generality of subsection (3) above, the directions which may be given by an order under this section shall in particular include directions for meeting any expenditure out of a specified fund, for charging any expenditure to capital or to income, for requiring expenditure charged to capital to be recouped out of income within a specified period, for restricting the costs to be incurred at the expense of the charity, or for the investment of moneys arising from any transaction.

(5) An order under this section may authorise any act notwithstanding that it is prohibited by any of the disabling Acts mentioned in subsection (6) below or that the trusts of the charity provide for the act to be done by or under the authority of the court; but no such order shall authorise the doing of any act expressly prohibited by Act of Parliament other than the disabling Acts or by the trusts of the charity or shall extend or alter the purposes of the charity.

(5A) In the case of a charity that is a company, an order under this section may authorise an act notwithstanding that it involves the breach of a duty imposed on a director of the company under Chapter 2 of Part 10 of the Companies Act 2006 (general duties of directors).

(6) The Acts referred to in subsection (5) above as the disabling Acts are the Ecclesiastical Leases Act 1571, the Ecclesiastical Leases Act 1572, the Ecclesiastical Leases Act 1575 and the Ecclesiastical Leases Act 1836.

(7) An order under this section shall not confer any authority in relation to a building which has been consecrated and of which the use or disposal is regulated, and can be further regulated, by a scheme having effect under the Union of Benefices Measures 1923 to 1952, the Reorganisation Areas Measures 1944 and 1954, the Pastoral Measure 1968 or the Pastoral Measure 1983, the reference to a building being taken to include part of a building and any land which under such a scheme is to be used or disposed of with a building to which the scheme applies.

27   Power to authorise ex gratia payments etc.

(1) Subject to subsection (3) below, the Commission may by order exercise the same power as is exercisable by the Attorney General to authorise the charity trustees of a charity –

   (a) to make any application of property of the charity, or
   (b) to waive to any extent, on behalf of the charity, its entitlement to receive any property,

   in a case where the charity trustees –

   (i)   (apart from this section) have no power to do so, but
   (ii) in all the circumstances regard themselves as being under a moral obligation to do so.

(2) The power conferred on the Commission by subsection (1) above shall be exercisable by the Commission under the supervision of, and in accordance with such directions as may be given by, the Attorney General; and any such directions may in particular require the Commission, in such circumstances as are specified in the directions –

   (a) to refrain from exercising that power; or
   (b) to consult the Attorney General before exercising it.

(3) Where –

   (a) an application is made to the Commission for it to exercise that power in a case where it is not precluded from doing so by any such directions, but

(b) the Commission considers that it would nevertheless be desirable for the application to be entertained by the Attorney General rather than by the Commission,

the Commission shall refer the application to the Attorney General.

(4) It is hereby declared that where, in the case of any application made to the Commission as mentioned in subsection (3)(a) above, the Commission determines the application by refusing to authorise charity trustees to take any action falling within subsection (1)(a) or (b) above, that refusal shall not preclude the Attorney General, on an application subsequently made to him by the trustees, from authorising the trustees to take that action.

28   Power to give directions about dormant bank accounts of charities

(1) Where the Commission –

(a) is informed by a relevant institution –

(i) that it holds one or more accounts in the name of or on behalf of a particular charity ('the relevant charity'), and

(ii) that the account, or (if it so holds two or more accounts) each of the accounts, is dormant, and

(b) is unable, after making reasonable inquiries, to locate that charity or any of its trustees,

it may give a direction under subsection (2) below.

(2) A direction under this subsection is a direction which –

(a) requires the institution concerned to transfer the amount, or (as the case may be) the aggregate amount, standing to the credit of the relevant charity in the account or accounts in question to such other charity as is specified in the direction in accordance with subsection (3) below; or

(b) requires the institution concerned to transfer to each of two or more other charities so specified in the direction such part of that amount or aggregate amount as is there specified in relation to that charity.

(3) The Commission may specify in a direction under subsection (2) above such other charity or charities as it considers appropriate, having regard, in a case where the purposes of the relevant charity are known to the Commission, to those purposes and to the purposes of the other charity or charities; but the Commission shall not so specify any charity unless it has received from the charity trustees written confirmation that those trustees are willing to accept the amount proposed to be transferred to the charity.

(4) Any amount received by a charity by virtue of this section shall be received by the charity on terms that –

(a) it shall be held and applied by the charity for the purposes of the charity, but

(b) it shall, as property of the charity, nevertheless be subject to any restrictions on expenditure to which it was subject as property of the relevant charity.

(5) Where –

(a) the Commission has been informed as mentioned in subsection (1)(a) above by any relevant institution, and

(b) before any transfer is made by the institution in pursuance of a direction under subsection (2) above, the institution has, by reason of any circumstances, cause to believe that the account, or (as the case may be) any of the accounts, held by it in the name of or on behalf of the relevant charity is no longer dormant,

the institution shall forthwith notify those circumstances in writing to the Commission; and, if it appears to the Commission that the account or accounts in question is or are no longer dormant, it shall revoke any direction under subsection

(2) above which has previously been given by it to the institution with respect to the relevant charity.

(6) The receipt of any charity trustees or trustee for a charity in respect of any amount received from a relevant institution by virtue of this section shall be a complete discharge of the institution in respect of that amount.

(7) No obligation as to secrecy or other restriction on disclosure (however imposed) shall preclude a relevant institution from disclosing any information to the Commission for the purpose of enabling the Commission to discharge its functions under this section.

(8) For the purposes of this section –

    (a) an account is dormant if no transaction, other than –

        (i) a transaction consisting in a payment into the account, or

        (ii) a transaction which the institution holding the account has itself caused to be effected,

    has been effected in relation to the account within the period of five years immediately preceding the date when the Commission is informed as mentioned in paragraph (a) of subsection (1) above;

    (b) a 'relevant institution' means –

        (i) the Bank of England;

        (ii) a person who has permission under Part 4 of the Financial Services and Markets Act 2000 to accept deposits;

        (iii) an EEA firm of the kind mentioned in paragraph 5(b) of Schedule 3 to that Act which has permission under paragraph 15 of that Schedule (as a result of qualifying for authorisation under paragraph 12(1) of that Schedule) to accept deposits; or

        (iv) such other person who may lawfully accept deposits in the United Kingdom as may be prescribed by the Secretary of State;

    (c) references to the transfer of any amount to a charity are references to its transfer –

        (i) to the charity trustees, or

        (ii) to any trustee for the charity,

    as the charity trustees may determine (and any reference to any amount received by a charity shall be construed accordingly).

(8A) Sub-paragraphs (ii) to (iv) of the definition of 'relevant institution' in subsection (8)(b) must be read with –

    (a) section 22 of the Financial Services and Markets Act 2000;

    (b) any relevant order under that section; and

    (c) Schedule 2 to that Act.

(9) For the purpose of determining the matters in respect of which any of the powers conferred by section 8 or 9 above may be exercised it shall be assumed that the Commission has no functions under this section in relation to accounts to which this subsection applies (with the result that, for example, a relevant institution shall not, in connection with the functions of the Commission under this section, be required under section 8(3)(a) above to furnish any statements, or answer any questions or inquiries, with respect to any such accounts held by the institution).

This subsection applies to accounts which are dormant accounts by virtue of subsection (8)(a) above but would not be such accounts if sub-paragraph (i) of that provision were omitted.

(10) [. . .]

29   Power to give advice and guidance

(1) The Commission may, on the written application of any charity trustee or trustee for a charity, give that person its opinion or advice in relation to any matter –

(a) relating to the performance of any duties of his, as such a trustee, in relation to the charity concerned, or

(b) otherwise relating to the proper administration of the charity.

(2) A charity trustee or trustee for a charity who acts in accordance with any opinion or advice given by the Commission under subsection (1) above (whether to him or to another trustee) is to be taken, as regards his responsibility for so acting, to have acted in accordance with his trust.

(3) But subsection (2) above does not apply to a person if, when so acting, either –

(a) he knows or has reasonable cause to suspect that the opinion or advice was given in ignorance of material facts, or

(b) a decision of the court or the Tribunal has been obtained on the matter or proceedings are pending to obtain one.

(4) The Commission may, in connection with its second general function mentioned in section 1C(2) above, give such advice or guidance with respect to the administration of charities as it considers appropriate.

(5) Any advice or guidance so given may relate to –

(a) charities generally,

(b) any class of charities, or

(c) any particular charity,

and may take such form, and be given in such manner, as the Commission considers appropriate.

29A   Power to determine membership of charity

(1) The Commission may –

(a) on the application of a charity, or

(b) at any time after the institution of an inquiry under section 8 above with respect to a charity,

determine who are the members of the charity.

(2) The Commission's power under subsection (1) may also be exercised by a person appointed by the Commission for the purpose.

(3) In a case within subsection (1)(b) the Commission may, if it thinks fit, so appoint the person appointed to conduct the inquiry.

30   Powers for preservation of charity documents

(1) The Commission may provide books in which any deed, will or other document relating to a charity may be enrolled.

(2) The Commission may accept for safe keeping any document of or relating to a charity, and the charity trustees or other persons having the custody of documents of or relating to a charity (including a charity which has ceased to exist) may with the consent of the Commission deposit them with the Commission for safe keeping, except in the case of documents required by some other enactment to be kept elsewhere.

(3) Where a document is enrolled by the Commission or is for the time being deposited with the Commission under this section, evidence of its contents may be given by means of a copy certified by any member of the staff of the Commission generally or specially authorised by the Commission to act for this purpose; and a document purporting to be such a copy shall be received in evidence without proof of the official position, authority or handwriting of the person certifying it or of the original document being enrolled or deposited as aforesaid.

(4) Regulations made by the Secretary of State may make provision for such documents deposited with the Commission under this section as may be prescribed by the regulation to be destroyed or otherwise disposed of after such period or in such circumstances as may be so prescribed.

(5) Subsections (3) and (4) above shall apply to any document transmitted to the Commission under section 9 above and kept by the Commission under subsection (3) of that section, as if the document had been deposited with the Commission for safe keeping under this section.

31 Power to order taxation of solicitor's bill

(1) The Commission may order that a solicitor's bill of costs for business done for a charity, or for charity trustees or trustees for a charity, shall be taxed, together with the costs of the taxation, by a taxing officer in such division of the High Court as may be specified in the order, or by the taxing officer of any other court having jurisdiction to order the taxation of the bill.

(2) On any order under this section for the taxation of a solicitor's bill the taxation shall proceed, and the taxing officer shall have the same powers and duties, and the costs of the taxation shall be borne, as if the order had been made, on the application of the person chargeable with the bill, by the court in which the costs are taxed.

(3) No order under this section for the taxation of a solicitor's bill shall be made after payment of the bill unless the Commission is of opinion that it contains exorbitant charges; and no such order shall in any case be made where the solicitor's costs are not subject to taxation on an order of the High Court by reason either of an agreement as to his remuneration or the lapse of time since payment of the bill.

31A Power to enter premises

(1) A justice of the peace may issue a warrant under this section if satisfied, on information given on oath by a member of the Commission's staff, that there are reasonable grounds for believing that each of the conditions in subsection (2) below is satisfied.

(2) The conditions are –

(a) that an inquiry has been instituted under section 8 above;

(b) that there is on the premises to be specified in the warrant any document or information relevant to that inquiry which the Commission could require to be produced or furnished under section 9(1) above; and

(c) that, if the Commission were to make an order requiring the document or information to be so produced or furnished –

(i) the order would not be complied with, or

(ii) the document or information would be removed, tampered with, concealed or destroyed.

(3) A warrant under this section is a warrant authorising the member of the Commission's staff who is named in it –

(a) to enter and search the premises specified in it;

(b) to take such other persons with him as the Commission considers are needed to assist him in doing anything that he is authorised to do under the warrant;

(c) to take possession of any documents which appear to fall within subsection (2)(b) above, or to take any other steps which appear to be necessary for preserving, or preventing interference with, any such documents;

(d) to take possession of any computer disk or other electronic storage device which appears to contain information falling within subsection (2)(b), or information contained in a document so falling, or to take any other steps which appear to be necessary for preserving, or preventing interference with, any such information;

(e) to take copies of, or extracts from, any documents or information falling within paragraph (c) or (d);

(f) to require any person on the premises to provide an explanation of any such document or information or to state where any such documents or information may be found;

(g) to require any such person to give him such assistance as he may reasonably require for the taking of copies or extracts as mentioned in paragraph (e) above.

(4) Entry and search under such a warrant must be at a reasonable hour and within one month of the date of its issue.

(5) The member of the Commission's staff who is authorised under such a warrant ('the authorised person') must, if required to do so, produce –

(a) the warrant, and

(b) documentary evidence that he is a member of the Commission's staff,

for inspection by the occupier of the premises or anyone acting on his behalf.

(6) The authorised person must make a written record of –

(a) the date and time of his entry on the premises;

(b) the number of persons (if any) who accompanied him onto the premises, and the names of any such persons;

(c) the period for which he (and any such persons) remained on the premises;

(d) what he (and any such persons) did while on the premises; and

(e) any document or device of which he took possession while there.

(7) If required to do so, the authorised person must give a copy of the record to the occupier of the premises or someone acting on his behalf.

(8) Unless it is not reasonably practicable to do so, the authorised person must comply with the following requirements before leaving the premises, namely –

(a) the requirements of subsection (6), and

(b) any requirement made under subsection (7) before he leaves the premises.

(9) Where possession of any document or device is taken under this section –

(a) the document may be retained for so long as the Commission considers that it is necessary to retain it (rather than a copy of it) for the purposes of the relevant inquiry under section 8 above, or

(b) the device may be retained for so long as the Commission considers that it is necessary to retain it for the purposes of that inquiry,

as the case may be.

(10) Once it appears to the Commission that the retention of any document or device has ceased to be so necessary, it shall arrange for the document or device to be returned as soon as is reasonably practicable –

(a) to the person from whose possession it was taken, or

(b) to any of the charity trustees of the charity to which it belonged or related.

(11) A person who intentionally obstructs the exercise of any rights conferred by a warrant under this section is guilty of an offence and liable on summary conviction –

(a) to imprisonment for a term not exceeding 51 weeks, or

(b) to a fine not exceeding level 5 on the standard scale,

or to both.

Legal proceedings relating to charities

32   Proceedings by Commission

(1) Subject to subsection (2) below, the Commission may exercise the same powers with respect to –

(a) the taking of legal proceedings with reference to charities or the property or affairs of charities, or

(b) the compromise of claims with a view to avoiding or ending such proceedings,

as are exercisable by the Attorney General acting ex officio.

(2) Subsection (1) above does not apply to the power of the Attorney General under section 63(1) below to present a petition for the winding up of a charity.

(3) The practice and procedure to be followed in relation to any proceedings taken by the Commission under subsection (1) above shall be the same in all respects (and in particular as regards costs) as if they were proceedings taken by the Attorney General acting ex officio.

(4) No rule of law or practice shall be taken to require the Attorney General to be a party to any such proceedings.

(5) The powers exercisable by the Commission by virtue of this section shall be exercisable by the Commission of its own motion, but shall be exercisable only with the agreement of the Attorney General on each occasion.

33   Proceedings by other persons

(1) Charity proceedings may be taken with reference to a charity either by the charity, or by any of the charity trustees, or by any person interested in the charity, or by any two or more inhabitants of the area of the charity if it is a local charity, but not by any other person.

(2) Subject to the following provisions of this section, no charity proceedings relating to a charity shall be entertained or proceeded with in any court unless the taking of the proceedings is authorised by order of the Commission.

(3) The Commission shall not, without special reasons, authorise the taking of charity proceedings where in its opinion the case can be dealt with by the Commission under the powers of this Act other than those conferred by section 32 above.

(4) This section shall not require any order for the taking of proceedings in a pending cause or matter or for the bringing of any appeal.

(5) Where the foregoing provisions of this section require the taking of charity proceedings to be authorised by an order of the Commission, the proceedings may nevertheless be entertained or proceeded with if, after the order had been applied for and refused, leave to take the proceedings was obtained from one of the judges of the High Court attached to the Chancery Division.

(6) Nothing in the foregoing subsections shall apply to the taking of proceedings by the Attorney General, with or without a relator, or to the taking of proceedings by the Commission in accordance with section 32 above.

(7) Where it appears to the Commission, on an application for an order under this section or otherwise, that it is desirable for legal proceedings to be taken with reference to any charity or its property or affairs, and for the proceedings to be taken by the Attorney General, the Commission shall so inform the Attorney General, and send him such statements and particulars as the Commission thinks necessary to explain the matter.

(8) In this section 'charity proceedings' means proceedings in any court in England or Wales brought under the court's jurisdiction with respect to charities, or brought under the court's jurisdiction with respect to trusts in relation to the administration of a trust for charitable purposes.

34   Report of s.8 inquiry to be evidence in certain proceedings

(1) A copy of the report of the person conducting an inquiry under section 8 above shall, if certified by the Commission to be a true copy, be admissible in any proceedings to which this section applies –

  (a) as evidence of any fact stated in the report; and
  (b) as evidence of the opinion of that person as to any matter referred to in it.

(2) This section applies to –

  (a) any legal proceedings instituted by the Commission under this Part of this Act; and
  (b) any legal proceedings instituted by the Attorney General in respect of a charity.

(3)   A document purporting to be a certificate issued for the purposes of subsection (1) above shall be received in evidence and be deemed to be such a certificate, unless the contrary is proved.

Meaning of 'trust corporation'

35   Application of provisions to trust corporations appointed under s.16 or 18

(1)   In the definition of 'trust corporation' contained in the following provisions –

    (a)   section 117(xxx) of the Settled Land Act 1925,

    (b)   section 68(18) of the Trustee Act 1925,

    (c)   section 205(xxviii) of the Law of Property Act 1925,

    (d)   section 55(xxvi) of the Administration of Estates Act 1925, and

    (e)   section 128 of the Supreme Court Act 1981,

the reference to a corporation appointed by the court in any particular case to be a trustee includes a reference to a corporation appointed by the Commission under this Act to be a trustee.

(2)   This section shall be deemed always to have had effect; but the reference to section 128 of the Supreme Court Act 1981 shall, in relation to any time before 1st January 1982, be construed as a reference to section 175(1) of the Supreme Court of Judicature (Consolidation) Act 1925.

PART V   CHARITY LAND

36   Restrictions on dispositions

(1)   Subject to the following provisions of this section and section 40 below, no land held by or in trust for a charity shall be conveyed, transferred, leased or otherwise disposed of without an order of the court or of the Commission.

(2)   Subsection (1) above shall not apply to a disposition of such land if –

    (a)   the disposition is made to a person who is not –

        (i)   a connected person (as defined in Schedule 5 to this Act), or

        (ii)   a trustee for, or nominee of, a connected person; and

    (b)   the requirements of subsection (3) or (5) below have been complied with in relation to it.

(3)   Except where the proposed disposition is the granting of such a lease as is mentioned in subsection (5) below, the requirements mentioned in subsection (2)(b) above are that the charity trustees must, before entering into an agreement for the sale, or (as the case may be) for a lease or other disposition, of the land –

    (a)   obtain and consider a written report on the proposed disposition from a qualified surveyor instructed by the trustees and acting exclusively for the charity;

    (b)   advertise the proposed disposition for such period and in such manner as the surveyor has advised in his report (unless he has there advised that it would not be in the best interests of the charity to advertise the proposed disposition); and

    (c)   decide that they are satisfied, having considered the surveyor's report, that the terms on which the disposition is proposed to be made are the best that can reasonably be obtained for the charity.

(4)   For the purposes of subsection (3) above a person is a qualified surveyor if –

    (a)   he is a fellow or professional associate of the Royal Institution of Chartered Surveyors or of the Incorporated Society of Valuers and Auctioneers or satisfies such other requirement or requirements as may be prescribed by regulations made by the Secretary of State; and

(b) he is reasonably believed by the charity trustees to have ability in, and experience of, the valuation of land of the particular kind, and in the particular area,
in question;

and any report prepared for the purposes of that subsection shall contain such information, and deal with such matters, as may be prescribed by regulations so made.

(5) Where the proposed disposition is the granting of a lease for a term ending not more
than seven years after it is granted (other than one granted wholly or partly in consideration of a fine), the requirements mentioned in subsection (2)(b) above are that
the charity trustees must, before entering into an agreement for the lease –

   (a) obtain and consider the advice on the proposed disposition of a person who is
reasonably believed by the trustees to have the requisite ability and practical
experience to provide them with competent advice on the proposed disposition;
and

   (b) decide that they are satisfied, having considered that person's advice, that the
terms on which the disposition is proposed to be made are the best that can
reasonably be obtained for the charity.

(6) Where –

   (a) any land is held by or in trust for a charity, and

   (b) the trusts on which it is so held stipulate that it is to be used for the purposes,
or any particular purposes, of the charity,

then (subject to subsections (7) and (8) below and without prejudice to the operation
of the preceding provisions of this section) the land shall not be conveyed, transferred,
leased or otherwise disposed of unless the charity trustees have before the relevant
time –

   (i) given public notice of the proposed disposition, inviting representations to be
made to them within a time specified in the notice, being not less than one
month from the date of the notice; and

   (ii) taken into consideration any representations made to them within that time
about the proposed disposition.

(6A) In subsection (6) above 'the relevant time' means –

   (a) where the charity trustees enter into an agreement for the sale, or (as the case
may be) for the lease or other disposition, the time when they enter into that
agreement, and

   (b) in any other case, the time of the disposition.

(7) Subsection (6) above shall not apply to any such disposition of land as is there
mentioned if –

   (a) the disposition is to be effected with a view to acquiring by way of replacement
other property which is to be held on the trusts referred to in paragraph (b) of
that subsection; or

   (b) the disposition is the granting of a lease for a term ending not more than two
years after it is granted (other than one granted wholly or partly in consideration
of a fine).

(8) The Commission may direct –

   (a) that subsection (6) above shall not apply to dispositions of land held by or in
trust for a charity or class of charities (whether generally or only in the case of
a specified class of dispositions or land, or otherwise as may be provided in the
direction), or

   (b) that that subsection shall not apply to a particular disposition of land held by or
in trust for a charity,

if, on an application made to them in writing by or on behalf of the charity or charities in question, the Commission is satisfied that it would be in the interests of the
charity or charities for the Commission to give the direction.

(9) The restrictions on disposition imposed by this section apply notwithstanding
anything in the trusts of a charity; but nothing in this section applies –

(a) to any disposition for which general or special authority is expressly given
(without the authority being made subject to the sanction of an order of the
court) by any statutory provision contained in or having effect under an Act of
Parliament or by any scheme legally established; or

(b) to any disposition of land held by or in trust for a charity which –

(i)   is made to another charity otherwise than for the best price that can
reasonably be obtained, and

(ii) is authorised to be so made by the trusts of the first-mentioned charity; or

(c) to the granting, by or on behalf of a charity and in accordance with its trusts, of
a lease to any beneficiary under those trusts where the lease –

(i)   is granted otherwise than for the best rent that can reasonably be obtained;
and

(ii) is intended to enable the demised premises to be occupied for the purposes,
or any particular purposes, of the charity.

(10) Nothing in this section applies –

(a) to any disposition of land held by or in trust for an exempt charity;

(b) to any disposition of land by way of mortgage or other security; or

(c) to any disposition of an advowson.

(11) In this section 'land' means land in England or Wales.

37   Supplementary provisions relating to dispositions

(1) Any of the following instruments, namely –

(a) any contract for the sale, or for a lease or other disposition, of land which is held
by or in trust for a charity, and

(b) any conveyance, transfer, lease or other instrument effecting a disposition of
such land,

shall state –

(i)   that the land is held by or in trust for a charity,

(ii) whether the charity is an exempt charity and whether the disposition is one
falling within paragraph (a), (b) or (c) of subsection (9) of section 36 above, and

(iii) if it is not an exempt charity and the disposition is not one falling within any of
those paragraphs, that the land is land to which the restrictions on disposition
imposed by that section apply.

(2) Where any land held by or in trust for a charity is conveyed, transferred, leased or
otherwise disposed of by a disposition to which subsection (1) or (2) of section 36
above applies, the charity trustees shall certify in the instrument by which the
disposition is effected –

(a) (where subsection (1) of that section applies) that the disposition has been sanctioned by an order of the court or of the Commission (as the case may be), or

(b) (where subsection (2) of that section applies) that the charity trustees have
power under the trusts of the charity to effect the disposition, and that they have
complied with the provisions of that section so far as applicable to it.

(3) Where subsection (2) above has been complied with in relation to any disposition of
land, then in favour of a person who (whether under the disposition or afterwards)
acquires an interest in the land for money or money's worth, it shall be conclusively
presumed that the facts were as stated in the certificate.

(4) Where –

    (a) any land held by or in trust for a charity is conveyed, transferred, leased or otherwise disposed of by a disposition to which subsection (1) or (2) of section 36 above applies, but

    (b) subsection (2) above has not been complied with in relation to the disposition,

then in favour of a person who (whether under the disposition or afterwards) in good faith acquires an interest in the land for money or money's worth, the disposition shall be valid whether or not –

    (i) the disposition has been sanctioned by an order of the court or of the Commission, or

    (ii) the charity trustees have power under the trusts of the charity to effect the disposition and have complied with the provisions of that section so far as applicable to it.

(5) Any of the following instruments, namely –

    (a) any contract for the sale, or for a lease or other disposition, of land which will, as a result of the disposition, be held by or in trust for a charity, and

    (b) any conveyance, transfer, lease or other instrument effecting a disposition of such land,

shall state –

    (i) that the land will, as a result of the disposition, be held by or in trust for a charity,

    (ii) whether the charity is an exempt charity, and

    (iii) if it is not an exempt charity, that the restrictions on disposition imposed by section 36 above will apply to the land (subject to subsection (9) of that section).

(6) [. . .]

(7) Where the disposition to be effected by any such instrument as is mentioned in subsection (1)(b) or (5)(b) above will be –

    (a) a registrable disposition, or

    (b) a disposition which triggers the requirement of registration,

the statement which, by virtue of subsection (1) or (5) above, is to be contained in the instrument shall be in such form as may be prescribed by land registration rules.

(8) Where the registrar approves an application for registration of –

    (a) a disposition of registered land, or

    (b) a person's title under a disposition of unregistered land,

and the instrument effecting the disposition contains a statement complying with subsections (5) and (7) above, he shall enter in the register a restriction reflecting the limitation under section 36 above on subsequent disposal.

(9) Where –

    (a) any such restriction is entered in the register in respect of any land, and

    (b) the charity by or in trust for which the land is held becomes an exempt charity,

the charity trustees shall apply to the registrar for the removal of the entry; and on receiving any application duly made under this subsection the registrar shall remove the entry.

(10) Where –

    (a) any registered land is held by or in trust for an exempt charity and the charity ceases to be an exempt charity, or

    (b) any registered land becomes, as a result of a declaration of trust by the registered proprietor, land held in trust for a charity (other than an exempt charity),

the charity trustees shall apply to the registrar for such a restriction as is mentioned in subsection (8) above to be entered in the register in respect of the land; and on receiving any application duly made under this subsection the registrar shall enter such a restriction in the register in respect of the land.

(11) In this section –

    (a) references to a disposition of land do not include references to –

        (i)   a disposition of land by way of mortgage or other security,

        (ii) any disposition of an advowson, or

        (iii) any release of a rentcharge falling within section 40(1) below; and

    (b) 'land' means land in England or Wales;

and subsections (7) to (10) above shall be construed as one with the Land Registration Act 2002.

38   Restrictions on mortgaging

(1) Subject to subsection (2) below, no mortgage of land held by or in trust for a charity shall be granted without an order of the court or of the Commission.

(2) Subsection (1) above shall not apply to a mortgage of any such land if the charity trustees have, before executing the mortgage, obtained and considered proper advice, given to them in writing, on the relevant matters or matter mentioned in subsection (3) or (3A) below (as the case may be).

(3) In the case of a mortgage to secure the repayment of a proposed loan or grant, the relevant matters are –

    (a) whether the loan or grant is necessary in order for the charity trustees to be able to pursue the particular course of action in connection with which they are seeking the loan or grant;

    (b) whether the terms of the loan or grant are reasonable having regard to the status of the charity as the prospective recipient of the loan or grant; and

    (c) the ability of the charity to repay on those terms the sum proposed to be paid by way of loan or grant.

(3A) In the case of a mortgage to secure the discharge of any other proposed obligation, the relevant matter is whether it is reasonable for the charity trustees to undertake to discharge the obligation, having regard to the charity's purposes.

(3B) Subsection (3) or (as the case may be) subsection (3A) above applies in relation to such a mortgage as is mentioned in that subsection whether the mortgage –

    (a) would only have effect to secure the repayment of the proposed loan or grant or the discharge of the proposed obligation, or

    (b) would also have effect to secure the repayment of sums paid by way of loan or grant, or the discharge of other obligations undertaken, after the date of its execution.

(3C) Subsection (3D) below applies where –

    (a) the charity trustees of a charity have executed a mortgage of land held by or in trust for a charity in accordance with subsection (2) above, and

    (b) the mortgage has effect to secure the repayment of sums paid by way of loan or grant, or the discharge of other obligations undertaken, after the date of its execution.

(3D) In such a case, the charity trustees must not after that date enter into any transaction involving –

    (a) the payment of any such sums, or

    (b) the undertaking of any such obligations,

unless they have, before entering into the transaction, obtained and considered proper advice, given to them in writing, on the matters or matter mentioned in subsection (3)(a) to (c) or (3A) above (as the case may be).

(4)　For the purposes of this section proper advice is the advice of a person –

  (a)　who is reasonably believed by the charity trustees to be qualified by his ability in and practical experience of financial matters; and

  (b)　who has no financial interest in relation to the loan, grant or other transaction in connection with which his advice is given;

  and such advice may constitute proper advice for those purposes notwithstanding that the person giving it does so in the course of his employment as an officer or employee of the charity or of the charity trustees.

(5)　This section applies notwithstanding anything in the trusts of a charity; but nothing in this section applies to any mortgage for which general or special authority is given as mentioned in section 36(9)(a) above.

(6)　In this section –

  'land' means land in England or Wales;
  'mortgage' includes a charge.

(7)　Nothing in this section applies to an exempt charity.

39　Supplementary provisions relating to mortgaging

(1)　Any mortgage of land held by or in trust for a charity shall state –

  (a)　that the land is held by or in trust for a charity,

  (b)　whether the charity is an exempt charity and whether the mortgage is one falling within subsection (5) of section 38 above, and

  (c)　if it is not an exempt charity and the mortgage is not one falling within that subsection, that the mortgage is one to which the restrictions imposed by that section apply;

  and where the mortgage will be a registered disposition any such statement shall be in such form as may be prescribed by land registration rules.

(1A)　Where any such mortgage will be one to which section 4(1)(g) of the Land Registration Act 2002 applies –

  (a)　the statement required by subsection (1) above shall be in such form as may be prescribed by land registration rules; and

  (b)　if the charity is not an exempt charity, the mortgage shall also contain a statement, in such form as may be prescribed by land registration rules, that the restrictions on disposition imposed by section 36 above apply to the land (subject to subsection (9) of that section).

(1B)　Where –

  (a)　the registrar approves an application for registration of a person's title to land in connection with such a mortgage as is mentioned in subsection (1A) above,

  (b)　the mortgage contains statements complying with subsections (1) and (1A) above, and

  (c)　the charity is not an exempt charity,

  the registrar shall enter in the register a restriction reflecting the limitation under section 36 above on subsequent disposal.

(1C)　Section 37(9) above shall apply in relation to any restriction entered under subsection (1B) as it applies in relation to any restriction entered under section 37(8).

(2)　Where subsection (1) or (2) of section 38 above applies to any mortgage of land held by or in trust for a charity, the charity trustees shall certify in the mortgage –

  (a)　(where subsection (1) of that section applies) that the mortgage has been sanctioned by an order of the court or of the Commission (as the case may be), or

  (b)　(where subsection (2) of that section applies) that the charity trustees have power under the trusts of the charity to grant the mortgage, and that they have obtained and considered such advice as is mentioned in that subsection.

(3)   Where subsection (2) above has been complied with in relation to any mortgage, then in favour of a person who (whether under the mortgage or afterwards) acquires an interest in the land in question for money or money's worth, it shall be conclusively presumed that the facts were as stated in the certificate.

(4)   Where –

(a)   subsection (1) or (2) of section 38 above applies to any mortgage of land held by or in trust for a charity, but

(b)   subsection (2) above has not been complied with in relation to the mortgage,

then in favour of a person who (whether under the mortgage or afterwards) in good faith acquires an interest in the land for money or money's worth, the mortgage shall be valid whether or not –

(i)   the mortgage has been sanctioned by an order of the court or of the Commission, or

(ii)   the charity trustees have power under the trusts of the charity to grant the mortgage and have obtained and considered such advice as is mentioned in subsection (2) of that section.

(4A)   Where subsection (3D) of section 38 above applies to any mortgage of land held by or in trust for a charity, the charity trustees shall certify in relation to any transaction falling within that subsection that they have obtained and considered such advice as is mentioned in that subsection.

(4B)   Where subsection (4A) above has been complied with in relation to any transaction, then, in favour of a person who (whether under the mortgage or afterwards) has acquired or acquires an interest in the land for money or money's worth, it shall be conclusively presumed that the facts were as stated in the certificate.

(5)   [. . .]

(6)   In this section –

'mortgage' includes a charge, and 'mortgagee' shall be construed accordingly;

'land' means land in England or Wales;

and subsections (1) to (1B) above shall be construed as one with the Land Registration Act 2002.

40   Release of charity rentcharges

(1)   Section 36(1) above shall not apply to the release by a charity of a rentcharge which it is entitled to receive if the release is given in consideration of the payment of an amount which is not less than ten times the annual amount of the rentcharge.

(2)   Where a charity which is entitled to receive a rentcharge releases it in consideration of the payment of an amount not exceeding £500, any costs incurred by the charity in connection with proving its title to the rentcharge shall be recoverable by the charity from the person or persons in whose favour the rentcharge is being released.

(3)   Neither section 36(1) nor subsection (2) above applies where a rentcharge which a charity is entitled to receive is redeemed under sections 8 to 10 of the Rentcharges Act 1977.

(4)   The Secretary of State may by order amend subsection (2) above by substituting a different sum for the sum for the time being specified there.

PART VI   CHARITY ACCOUNTS, REPORTS AND RETURNS

41   Duty to keep accounting records

(1)   The charity trustees of a charity shall ensure that accounting records are kept in respect of the charity which are sufficient to show and explain all the charity's transactions, and which are such as to –

(a) disclose at any time, with reasonable accuracy, the financial position of the charity at that time, and

(b) enable the trustees to ensure that, where any statements of accounts are prepared by them under section 42(1) below, those statements of accounts comply with the requirements of regulations under that provision.

(2) The accounting records shall in particular contain –

(a) entries showing from day to day all sums of money received and expended by the charity, and the matters in respect of which the receipt and expenditure takes place; and

(b) a record of the assets and liabilities of the charity.

(3) The charity trustees of a charity shall preserve any accounting records made for the purposes of this section in respect of the charity for at least six years from the end of the financial year of the charity in which they are made.

(4) Where a charity ceases to exist within the period of six years mentioned in subsection (3) above as it applies to any accounting records, the obligation to preserve those records in accordance with that subsection shall continue to be discharged by the last charity trustees of the charity, unless the Commission consents in writing to the records being destroyed or otherwise disposed of.

(5) Nothing in this section applies to a charity which is a company.

42   Annual statements of accounts

(1) The charity trustees of a charity shall (subject to subsection (3) below) prepare in respect of each financial year of the charity a statement of accounts complying with such requirements as to its form and contents as may be prescribed by regulations made by the Secretary of State.

(2) Without prejudice to the generality of subsection (1) above, regulations under that subsection may make provision –

(a) for any such statement to be prepared in accordance with such methods and principles as are specified or referred to in the regulations;

(b) as to any information to be provided by way of notes to the accounts;

and regulations under that subsection may also make provision for determining the financial years of a charity for the purposes of this Act and any regulations made under it.

(2A) Such regulations may, however, not impose on the charity trustees of a charity that is a charitable trust created by any person ('the settlor') any requirement to disclose, in any statement of accounts prepared by them under subsection (1) –

(a) the identities of recipients of grants made out of the funds of the charity, or

(b) the amounts of any individual grants so made,

if the disclosure would fall to be made at a time when the settlor or any spouse or civil partner of his was still alive.

(3) Where a charity's gross income in any financial year does not exceed £100,000, the charity trustees may, in respect of that year, elect to prepare the following, namely –

(a) a receipts and payments account, and

(b) a statement of assets and liabilities,

instead of a statement of accounts under subsection (1) above.

(4) The charity trustees of a charity shall preserve –

(a) any statement of accounts prepared by them under subsection (1) above, or

(b) any account and statement prepared by them under subsection (3) above,

for at least six years from the end of the financial year to which any such statement relates or (as the case may be) to which any such account and statement relate.

(5)   Subsection (4) of section 41 above shall apply in relation to the preservation of any such statement or account and statement as it applies in relation to the preservation of any accounting records (the references to subsection (3) of that section being read as references to subsection (4) above).

(6)   The Secretary of State may by order amend subsection (3) above by substituting a different sum for the sum for the time being specified there.

(7)   Nothing in this section applies to a charity which is a company.

(8)   Provisions about the preparation of accounts in respect of groups consisting of certain charities and their subsidiary undertakings, and about other matters relating to such groups, are contained in Schedule 5A to this Act (see section 49A below).

43   Annual audit or examination of charity accounts

(1)   Subsection (2) below applies to a financial year of a charity if –

(a)   the charity's gross income in that year exceeds £500,000; or

(b)   the charity's gross income in that year exceeds the accounts threshold and at the end of the year the aggregate value of its assets (before deduction of liabilities) exceeds £2.8 million.

'The accounts threshold' means £100,000 or such other sum as is for the time being specified in section 42(3) above.

(2)   If this subsection applies to a financial year of a charity, the accounts of the charity for that year shall be audited by a person who –

(a)   would be eligible for appointment as auditor of the charity under Part 2 of the Companies Act 1989 if the charity were a company, or

(b)   is a member of a body for the time being specified in regulations under section 44 below and is under the rules of that body eligible for appointment as auditor of the charity.

(3)   If subsection (2) above does not apply to a financial year of a charity but its gross income in that year exceeds £10,000, the accounts of the charity for that year shall, at the election of the charity trustees, either –

(a)   be examined by an independent examiner, that is to say an independent person who is reasonably believed by the trustees to have the requisite ability and practical experience to carry out a competent examination of the accounts, or

(b)   be audited by such a person as is mentioned in subsection (2) above.

This is subject to the requirements of subsection (3A) below where the gross income exceeds £250,000, and to any order under subsection (4) below.

(3A) If subsection (3) above applies to the accounts of a charity for a year and the charity's gross income in that year exceeds £250,000, a person qualifies as an independent examiner for the purposes of paragraph (a) of that subsection if (and only if) he is an independent person who is –

(a)   a member of a body for the time being specified in section 249D(3) of the Companies Act 1985 (reporting accountants);

(b)   a member of the Chartered Institute of Public Finance and Accountancy; or

(c)   a Fellow of the Association of Charity Independent Examiners.

(4)   Where it appears to the Commission –

(a)   that subsection (2), or (as the case may be) subsection (3) above, has not been complied with in relation to a financial year of a charity within ten months from the end of that year, or

(b)   that, although subsection (2) above does not apply to a financial year of a charity, it would nevertheless be desirable for the accounts of the charity for that year to be audited by such a person as is mentioned in that subsection,

the Commission may by order require the accounts of the charity for that year to be audited by such a person as is mentioned in that subsection.

(5)   If the Commission makes an order under subsection (4) above with respect to a charity, then unless –

   (a) the order is made by virtue of paragraph (b) of that subsection, and

   (b) the charity trustees themselves appoint an auditor in accordance with the order,

   the auditor shall be a person appointed by the Commission.

(6)   The expenses of any audit carried out by an auditor appointed by the Commission under subsection (5) above, including the auditor's remuneration, shall be recoverable by the Commission –

   (a) from the charity trustees of the charity concerned, who shall be personally liable, jointly and severally, for those expenses; or

   (b) to the extent that it appears to the Commission not to be practical to seek recovery of those expenses in accordance with paragraph (a) above, from the funds of the charity.

(7)   The Commission may –

   (a) give guidance to charity trustees in connection with the selection of a person for appointment as an independent examiner;

   (b) give such directions as it thinks appropriate with respect to the carrying out of an examination in pursuance of subsection (3)(a) above;

   and any such guidance or directions may either be of general application or apply to a particular charity only.

(8)   The Minister may by order –

   (a) amend subsection (1)(a) or (b), (3) or (3A) above by substituting a different sum for any sum for the time being specified there;

   (b) amend subsection (3A) by adding or removing a description of person to or from the list in that subsection or by varying any entry for the time being included in that list.

(9)   Nothing in this section applies to a charity which is a company.

(10) Nothing in this section applies in relation to a financial year of a charity where, at any time in the year, a charity is an English National Health Service charity or Welsh National Health Service charity (as defined in sections 43A and 43B respectively).

43A   Annual audit or examination of English National Health Service charity accounts

(1)   This section applies in relation to a financial year of a charity where, at any time in the year, the charity is an English National Health Service charity.

(2)   In any case where paragraph (a) or (b) of section 43(1) is satisfied in relation to a financial year of an English National Health Service charity, the accounts of the charity for that financial year shall be audited by a person appointed by the Audit Commission.

(3)   In any other case, the accounts of the charity for that financial year shall, at the election of the Audit Commission, be –

   (a) audited by a person appointed by the Audit Commission; or

   (b) examined by a person so appointed.

(4)   Section 3 of the Audit Commission Act 1998 (c.18) applies in relation to any appointment under subsection (2) or (3)(a).

(5)   The Commission may give such directions as it thinks appropriate with respect to the carrying out of an examination in pursuance of subsection (3)(b); and any such directions may either be of general application or apply to a particular charity only.

(6)   The Comptroller and Auditor General may at any time examine and inspect –

   (a) the accounts of the charity for the financial year;

   (b) any records relating to those accounts; and

   (c) any report of a person appointed under subsection (2) or (3) to audit or examine those accounts.

(7)   In this section –

'Audit Commission' means the Audit Commission for Local Authorities and the National Health Service in England and Wales; and

'English National Health Service charity' means a charitable trust, the trustees of which are –

(a)   a Strategic Health Authority;

(b)   a Primary Care Trust;

(c)   a National Health Service trust all or most of whose hospitals, establishments and facilities are situated in England;

(d)   trustees appointed in pursuance of section 11 of the National Health Service and Community Care Act 1990 (c.19), or special trustees appointed in pursuance of section 29(1) of the National Health Service Reorganisation Act 1973 (c.32) and section 95(1) of the National Health Service Act 1977 (c.49), for a National Health Service trust falling within paragraph (c); or

(e)   trustees for a Primary Care Trust appointed in pursuance of section 96B of the National Health Service Act 1977.

43B   Annual audit or examination of Welsh National Health Service charity accounts

(1)   This section applies in relation to a financial year of a charity where, at any time in the year, the charity is a Welsh National Health Service charity.

(2)   In any case where paragraph (a) or (b) of section 43(1) is satisfied in relation to a financial year of a Welsh National Health Service charity, the accounts of the charity for that financial year shall be audited by the Auditor General for Wales.

(3)   In any other case, the accounts of the charity for that financial year shall, at the election of the Auditor General for Wales, be audited or examined by the Auditor General for Wales.

(4)   In this section –

'Welsh National Health Service charity' means a charitable trust, the trustees of which are –

(a)   a Local Health Board;

(b)   a National Health Service trust all or most of whose hospitals, establishments and facilities are situated in Wales; or

(c)   trustees appointed in pursuance of section 11 of the National Health Service and Community Care Act 1990 (c.19), or special trustees appointed in pursuance of section 29(1) of the National Health Service Reorganisation Act 1973 (c.32) and section 95(1) of the National Health Service Act 1977 (c.49), for a National Health Service trust falling within paragraph (b).

(5)   References in this Act to an auditor or an examiner have effect in relation to this section as references to the Auditor General for Wales acting under this section as an auditor or examiner.

44   Supplementary provisions relating to audits etc.

(1)   The Secretary of State may by regulations make provision –

(a)   specifying one or more bodies for the purposes of section 43(2)(b) above;

(b)   with respect to the duties of an auditor carrying out an audit under section 43, 43A or 43B above, including provision with respect to the making by him of a report on –

(i)   the statement of accounts prepared for the financial year in question under section 42(1) above, or

(ii)   the account and statement so prepared under section 42(3) above,

as the case may be;

(c) with respect to the making of a report –

    (i) by an independent examiner in respect of an examination carried out by him under section 43 above; or

    (ii) by an examiner in respect of an examination carried out by him under section 43A or 43B above;

(d) conferring on such an auditor or on an independent examiner or examiner a right of access with respect to books, documents and other records (however kept) which relate to the charity concerned;

(e) entitling such an auditor or an independent examiner or examiner to require, in the case of a charity, information and explanations from past or present charity trustees or trustees for the charity, or from past or present officers or employees of the charity;

(f) enabling the Commission, in circumstances specified in the regulations, to dispense with the requirements of section 43(2) or (3) above in the case of a particular charity or in the case of any particular financial year of a charity.

(2) If any person fails to afford an auditor or an independent examiner or examiner any facility to which he is entitled by virtue of subsection (1)(d) or (e) above, the Commission may by order give –

(a) to that person, or

(b) to the charity trustees for the time being of the charity concerned,

such directions as the Commission thinks appropriate for securing that the default is made good.

(3) [. . .]

44A Duty of auditors etc. to report matters to Commission

(1) This section applies to –

(a) a person acting as an auditor or independent examiner appointed by or in relation to a charity under section 43 above,

(b) a person acting as an auditor or examiner appointed under section 43A(2) or (3) above, and

(c) the Auditor General for Wales acting under section 43B(2) or (3) above.

(2) If, in the course of acting in the capacity mentioned in subsection (1) above, a person to whom this section applies becomes aware of a matter –

(a) which relates to the activities or affairs of the charity or of any connected institution or body, and

(b) which he has reasonable cause to believe is likely to be of material significance for the purposes of the exercise by the Commission of its functions under section 8 or 18 above,

he must immediately make a written report on the matter to the Commission.

(3) If, in the course of acting in the capacity mentioned in subsection (1) above, a person to whom this section applies becomes aware of any matter –

(a) which does not appear to him to be one that he is required to report under subsection (2) above, but

(b) which he has reasonable cause to believe is likely to be relevant for the purposes of the exercise by the Commission of any of its functions,

he may make a report on the matter to the Commission.

(4) Where the duty or power under subsection (2) or (3) above has arisen in relation to a person acting in the capacity mentioned in subsection (1), the duty or power is not affected by his subsequently ceasing to act in that capacity.

(5)   Where a person makes a report as required or authorised by subsection (2) or (3), no duty to which he is subject is to be regarded as contravened merely because of any information or opinion contained in the report.

(6)   In this section 'connected institution or body', in relation to a charity, means –

(a)   an institution which is controlled by, or
(b)   a body corporate in which a substantial interest is held by,

the charity or any one or more of the charity trustees acting in his or their capacity as such.

(7)   Paragraphs 3 and 4 of Schedule 5 to this Act apply for the purposes of subsection (6) above as they apply for the purposes of provisions of that Schedule.

45   Annual reports

(1)   The charity trustees of a charity shall prepare in respect of each financial year of the charity an annual report containing –

(a)   such a report by the trustees on the activities of the charity during that year, and
(b)   such other information relating to the charity or to its trustees or officers,

as may be prescribed by regulations made by the Secretary of State.

(2)   Without prejudice to the generality of subsection (1) above, regulations under that subsection may make provision –

(a)   for any such report as is mentioned in paragraph (a) of that subsection to be prepared in accordance with such principles as are specified or referred to in the regulations;
(b)   enabling the Commission to dispense with any requirement prescribed by virtue of subsection (1)(b) above in the case of a particular charity or a particular class of charities, or in the case of a particular financial year of a charity or of any class of charities.

(3)   Where a charity's gross income in any financial year exceeds £10,000, a copy of the annual report required to be prepared under this section in respect of that year shall be transmitted to the Commission by the charity trustees –

(a)   within ten months from the end of that year, or
(b)   within such longer period as the Commissioners may for any special reason allow in the case of that report.

(3A) Where a charity's gross income in any financial year does not exceed £10,000, a copy of the annual report required to be prepared under this section in respect of that year shall, if the Commission so requests, be transmitted to it by the charity trustees –

(a)   in the case of a request made before the end of seven months from the end of the financial year to which the report relates, within ten months from the end of that year, and
(b)   in the case of a request not so made, within three months from the date of the request,

or, in either case, within such longer period as the Commission may for any special reason allow in the case of that report.

(3B) But in the case of a charity which is constituted as a CIO –

(a)   the requirement imposed by subsection (3) applies whatever the charity's gross income is, and
(b)   subsection (3A) does not apply.

(4)   Subject to subsection (5) below, any copy of an annual report transmitted to the Commission under this section shall have attached to it a copy of the statement of accounts prepared for the financial year in question under section 42(1) above or (as the case may be) a copy of the account and statement so prepared under section 42(3) above, together with –

(a) where the accounts of the charity for that year have been audited under section 43, 43A or 43B above, a copy of the report made by the auditor on that statement of accounts or (as the case may be) on that account and statement;

(b) where the accounts of the charity for that year have been examined under section 43, 43A or 43B above, a copy of the report made by the person carrying out the examination.

(5) Subsection (4) above does not apply to a charity which is a company, and any copy of an annual report transmitted by the charity trustees of such a charity under this section shall instead have attached to it a copy of the charity's annual accounts prepared for the financial year in question under Part VII of the Companies Act 1985, together with a copy of any auditors' report or report made for the purposes of section 249A(2) of that Act on those accounts.

(6) Any copy of an annual report transmitted to the Commission under this section, together with the documents attached to it, shall be kept by the Commission for such period as it thinks fit.

(7) The charity trustees of a charity shall preserve, for at least six years from the end of the financial year to which it relates, any annual report prepared by them under subsection (1) above of which they have not been required to transmit a copy to the Commission.

(8) Subsection (4) of section 41 above shall apply in relation to the preservation of any such annual report as it applies in relation to the preservation of any accounting records (the references to subsection (3) of that section being read as references to subsection (7) above).

(9) The Secretary of State may by order amend subsection (3) or (3A) above by substituting a different sum for the sum for the time being specified there.

46   Special provision as respects accounts and annual reports of exempt and other excepted charities

(1) Nothing in sections 41 to 44 or section 45 above applies to any exempt charity; but the charity trustees of an exempt charity shall keep proper books of account with respect to the affairs of the charity, and if not required by or under the authority of any other Act to prepare periodical statements of account shall prepare consecutive statements of account consisting on each occasion of an income and expenditure account relating to a period of not more than fifteen months and a balance sheet relating to the end of that period.

(2) The books of accounts and statements of account relating to an exempt charity shall be preserved for a period of six years at least unless the charity ceases to exist and the Commission consents in writing to their being destroyed or otherwise disposed of.

(2A) Section 44A(2) to (7) above shall apply in relation to a person appointed to audit, or report on, the accounts of an exempt charity which is not a company as they apply in relation to a person such as is mentioned in section 44A(1).

(2B) But section 44A(2) to (7) so apply with the following modifications –

(a) any reference to a person acting in the capacity mentioned in section 44A(1) is to be read as a reference to his acting as a person appointed as mentioned in subsection (2A) above; and

(b) any reference to the Commission or to any of its functions is to be read as a reference to the charity's principal regulator or to any of that person's functions in relation to the charity as such.

(3) Except in accordance with subsections (3A) and (3B) below, nothing in section 43, 44, 44A or 45 applies to any charity which –

(a) falls within section 3A(2)(d) above (whether or not it also falls within section 3A(2)(b) or (c)), and

(b) is not registered.

(3A) Section 44A above applies in accordance with subsections (2A) and (2B) above to a charity mentioned in subsection (3) above which is also an exempt charity.

(3B) Sections 44 and 44A above apply to a charity mentioned in subsection (3) above which is also an English National Health Service charity or a Welsh National Health Service charity (as defined in sections 43A and 43B above).

(4) Except in accordance with subsection (7) below, nothing in section 45 above applies to any charity which –

(a) falls within section 3A(2)(b) or (c) above but does not fall within section 3A(2)(d), and

(b) is not registered.

(5) If requested to do so by the Commission, the charity trustees of any such charity as is mentioned in subsection (4) above shall prepare an annual report in respect of such financial year of the charity as is specified in the Commission's request.

(6) Any report prepared under subsection (5) above shall contain –

(a) such a report by the charity trustees on the activities of the charity during the year in question, and

(b) such other information relating to the charity or to its trustees or officers,

as may be prescribed by regulations made under section 45(1) above in relation to annual reports prepared under that provision.

(7) The following provisions of section 45 above shall apply in relation to any report required to be prepared under subsection (5) above as if it were an annual report required to be prepared under subsection (1) of that section –

(a) subsection (3), with the omission of the words preceding 'a copy of the annual report', and

(b) subsections (4) to (6).

(8) [. . .]

47   Public inspection of annual reports etc.

(1) Any document kept by the Commission in pursuance of section 45(6) above shall be open to public inspection at all reasonable times –

(a) during the period for which it is so kept; or

(b) if the Commission so determines, during such lesser period as it may specify.

(2) Where any person –

(a) requests the charity trustees of a charity in writing to provide him with a copy of the charity's most recent accounts or (if subsection (4) below applies) of its most recent annual report, and

(b) pays them such reasonable fee (if any) as they may require in respect of the costs of complying with the request,

those trustees shall comply with the request within the period of two months beginning with the date on which it is made.

(3) In subsection (2) above the reference to a charity's most recent accounts is –

(a) [. . .]

(b) in the case of a charity other than one falling within paragraph (c) or (d) below, a reference to the statement of accounts or account and statement prepared in pursuance of section 42(1) or (3) above in respect of the last financial year of the charity in respect of which a statement of accounts or account and statement has or have been so prepared;

(c) in the case of a charity which is a company, a reference to the most recent annual accounts of the company prepared under Part VII of the Companies Act 1985 in relation to which any of the following conditions is satisfied –

- (i)   they have been audited;
- (ii) a report required for the purposes of section 249A(2) of that Act has been made in respect of them; or
- (iii) they relate to a year in respect of which the company is exempt from audit by virtue of section 249A(1) of that Act; and

- (d) in the case of an exempt charity, a reference to the accounts of the charity most recently audited in pursuance of any statutory or other requirement or, if its accounts are not required to be audited, the accounts most recently prepared in respect of the charity.

(4)   This subsection applies if an annual report has been prepared in respect of any financial year of a charity in pursuance of section 45(1) or 46(5) above.

(5)   In subsection (2) above the reference to a charity's most recent annual report is a reference to the annual report prepared in pursuance of section 45(1) or 46(5) in respect of the last financial year of the charity in respect of which an annual report has been so prepared.

48   Annual returns by registered charities

(1)   Subject to subsection (1A) below, every registered charity shall prepare in respect of each of its financial years an annual return in such form, and containing such information, as may be prescribed by regulations made by the Commission.

(1A) Subsection (1) above shall not apply in relation to any financial year of a charity in which the charity's gross income does not exceed £10,000 (but this subsection does not apply if the charity is constituted as a CIO).

(2)   Any such return shall be transmitted to the Commission by the date by which the charity trustees are, by virtue of section 45(3) above, required to transmit to the Commission the annual report required to be prepared in respect of the financial year in question.

(3)   The Commission may dispense with the requirements of subsection (1) above in the case of a particular charity or a particular class of charities, or in the case of a particular financial year of a charity or of any class of charities.

(4)   The Secretary of State may by order amend subsection (1A) above by substituting a different sum for the sum for the time being specified there.

49   Offences

(1)   If any requirement imposed –

- (a) by section 45(3) or (3A) above (taken with section 45(3B), (4) and (5), as applicable), or
- (b) by section 47(2) or 48(2) above,

is not complied with, each person who immediately before the date for compliance specified in the section in question was a charity trustee of the charity shall be guilty of an offence and liable on summary conviction to the penalty mentioned in subsection (2).

(2)   The penalty is –

- (a) a fine not exceeding level 4 on the standard scale, and
- (b) for continued contravention, a daily default fine not exceeding 10% of level 4 on the standard scale for so long as the person in question remains a charity trustee of the charity.

(3)   It is a defence for a person charged with an offence under subsection (1) to prove that he took all reasonable steps for securing that the requirement in question would be complied with in time.

49A Group accounts

The provisions of Schedule 5A to this Act shall have effect with respect to –

    (a)   the preparation and auditing of accounts in respect of groups consisting of parent charities and their subsidiary undertakings (within the meaning of that Schedule), and

    (b)   other matters relating to such groups.

PART VII   INCORPORATION OF CHARITY TRUSTEES

50   Incorporation of trustees of a charity

(1)   Where –

    (a)   the trustees of a charity, in accordance with section 52 below, apply to the Commission for a certificate of incorporation of the trustees as a body corporate, and

    (b)   the Commission considers that the incorporation of the trustees would be in the interests of the charity,

the Commission may grant such a certificate, subject to such conditions or directions as the Commission thinks fit to insert in it.

(2)   The Commission shall not, however, grant such a certificate in a case where the charity appears to the Commission to be required to be registered in accordance with section 3A above but is not so registered.

(3)   On the grant of such a certificate –

    (a)   the trustees of the charity shall become a body corporate by such name as is specified in the certificate; and

    (b)   (without prejudice to the operation of section 54 below) any relevant rights or liabilities of those trustees shall become rights or liabilities of that body.

(4)   After their incorporation the trustees –

    (a)   may sue and be sued in their corporate name; and

    (b)   shall have the same powers, and be subject to the same restrictions and limitations, as respects the holding, acquisition and disposal of property for or in connection with the purposes of the charity as they had or were subject to while unincorporated;

and any relevant legal proceedings that might have been continued or commenced by or against the trustees may be continued or commenced by or against them in their corporate name.

(5)   A body incorporated under this section need not have a common seal.

(6)   In this section –

    'relevant rights or liabilities' means rights or liabilities in connection with any property vesting in the body in question under section 51 below; and

    'relevant legal proceedings' means legal proceedings in connection with any such property.

51   Estate to vest in body corporate

The certificate of incorporation shall vest in the body corporate all real and personal estate, of whatever nature or tenure, belonging to or held by any person or persons in trust for the charity, and thereupon any person or persons in whose name or names any stocks, funds or securities are standing in trust for the charity, shall transfer them into the name of the body corporate, except that the foregoing provisions shall not apply to property vested in the official custodian.

52   Applications for incorporation

(1)   Every application to the Commission for a certificate of incorporation under this Part of this Act shall –

(a)   be in writing and signed by the trustees of the charity concerned; and

(b)   be accompanied by such documents or information as the Commission may require for the purpose of the application.

(2)   The Commission may require –

(a)   any statement contained in any such application, or

(b)   any document or information supplied under subsection (1)(b) above,

to be verified in such manner as it may specify.

53   Nomination of trustees, and filling up vacancies

(1)   Before a certificate of incorporation is granted under this Part of this Act, trustees of the charity must have been effectually appointed to the satisfaction of the Commission.

(2)   Where a certificate of incorporation is granted vacancies in the number of the trustees of the charity shall from time to time be filled up so far as required by the constitution or settlement of the charity, or by any conditions or directions in the certificate, by such legal means as would have been available for the appointment of new trustees of the charity if no certificate of incorporation had been granted, or otherwise as required by such conditions or directions.

54   Liability of trustees and others, notwithstanding incorporation

After a certificate of incorporation has been granted under this Part of this Act all trustees of the charity, notwithstanding their incorporation, shall be chargeable for such property as shall come into their hands, and shall be answerable and accountable for their own acts, receipts, neglects, and defaults, and for the due administration of the charity and its property, in the same manner and to the same extent as if no such incorporation had been effected.

55   Certificate to be evidence of compliance with requirements for incorporation

A certificate of incorporation granted under this Part of this Act shall be conclusive evidence that all the preliminary requirements for incorporation under this Part of this Act have been complied with, and the date of incorporation mentioned in the certificate shall be deemed to be the date at which incorporation has taken place.

56   Power of Commission to amend certificate of incorporation

(1)   The Commission may amend a certificate of incorporation either on the application of the incorporated body to which it relates or of the Commission's own motion.

(2)   Before making any such amendment of its own motion, the Commission shall by notice in writing –

(a)   inform the trustees of the relevant charity of its proposals, and

(b)   invite those trustees to make representations to it within a time specified in the notice, being not less than one month from the date of the notice.

(3)   The Commission shall take into consideration any representations made by those trustees within the time so specified, and may then (without further notice) proceed with its proposals either without modification or with such modifications as appear to it to be desirable.

(4)   The Commission may amend a certificate of incorporation either –

(a)   by making an order specifying the amendment; or

(b)   by issuing a new certificate of incorporation taking account of the amendment.

57   Records of applications and certificates

(1)   The Commission shall keep a record of all applications for, and certificates of, incorporation under this Part of this Act and shall preserve all documents sent to it under this Part of this Act.

(2)   Any person may inspect such documents, under the direction of the Commission, and any person may require a copy or extract of any such document to be certified by a certificate signed by a member of staff of the Commission.

58   Enforcement of orders and directions

All conditions and directions inserted in any certificate of incorporation shall be binding upon and performed or observed by the trustees as trusts of the charity, and section 88 below shall apply to any trustee who fails to perform or observe any such condition or direction as it applies to a person guilty of disobedience to any such order of the Commission as is mentioned in that section.

59   Gifts to charity before incorporation to have same effect afterwards

After the incorporation of the trustees of any charity under this Part of this Act every donation, gift and disposition of property, real or personal, lawfully made before the incorporation but not having actually taken effect, or thereafter lawfully made, by deed, will or otherwise to or in favour of the charity, or the trustees of the charity, or otherwise for the purposes of the charity, shall take effect as if made to or in favour of the incorporated body or otherwise for the like purposes.

60   Execution of documents by incorporated body

(1)   This section has effect as respects the execution of documents by an incorporated body.

(2)   If an incorporated body has a common seal, a document may be executed by the body by the affixing of its common seal.

(3)   Whether or not it has a common seal, a document may be executed by an incorporated body either –

    (a)   by being signed by a majority of the trustees of the relevant charity and expressed (in whatever form of words) to be executed by the body; or

    (b)   by being executed in pursuance of an authority given under subsection (4) below.

(4)   For the purposes of subsection (3)(b) above the trustees of the relevant charity in the case of an incorporated body may, subject to the trusts of the charity, confer on any two or more of their number –

    (a)   a general authority, or

    (b)   an authority limited in such manner as the trustees think fit,

to execute in the name and on behalf of the body documents for giving effect to transactions to which the body is a party.

(5)   An authority under subsection (4) above –

    (a)   shall suffice for any document if it is given in writing or by resolution of a meeting of the trustees of the relevant charity, notwithstanding the want of any formality that would be required in giving an authority apart from that subsection;

    (b)   may be given so as to make the powers conferred exercisable by any of the trustees, or may be restricted to named persons or in any other way;

    (c)   subject to any such restriction, and until it is revoked, shall, notwithstanding any change in the trustees of the relevant charity, have effect as a continuing authority given by the trustees from time to time of the charity and exercisable by such trustees.

(6)   In any authority under subsection (4) above to execute a document in the name and on behalf of an incorporated body there shall, unless the contrary intention appears, be implied authority also to execute it for the body in the name and on behalf of the official custodian or of any other person, in any case in which the trustees could do so.

(7)   A document duly executed by an incorporated body which makes it clear on its face that it is intended by the person or persons making it to be a deed has effect, upon delivery, as a deed; and it shall be presumed, unless a contrary intention is proved, to be delivered upon its being so executed.

(8)   In favour of a purchaser a document shall be deemed to have been duly executed by such a body if it purports to be signed –

(a) by a majority of the trustees of the relevant charity, or

(b) by such of the trustees of the relevant charity as are authorised by the trustees of that charity to execute it in the name and on behalf of the body,

and, where the document makes it clear on its face that it is intended by the person or persons making it to be a deed, it shall be deemed to have been delivered upon its being executed.

For this purpose 'purchaser' means a purchaser in good faith for valuable consideration and includes a lessee, mortgagee or other person who for valuable consideration acquires an interest in property.

61   Power of Commission to dissolve incorporated body

(1)   Where the Commission is satisfied –

(a) that an incorporated body has no assets or does not operate, or

(b) that the relevant charity in the case of an incorporated body has ceased to exist, or

(c) that the institution previously constituting, or treated by the Commission as constituting, any such charity has ceased to be, or (as the case may be) was not at the time of the body's incorporation, a charity, or

(d) that the purposes of the relevant charity in the case of an incorporated body have been achieved so far as is possible or are in practice incapable of being achieved,

the Commission may of its own motion make an order dissolving the body as from such date as is specified in the order.

(2)   Where the Commission is satisfied, on the application of the trustees of the relevant charity in the case of an incorporated body, that it would be in the interests of the charity for that body to be dissolved, the Commission may make an order dissolving the body as from such date as is specified in the order.

(3)   Subject to subsection (4) below, an order made under this section with respect to an incorporated body shall have the effect of vesting in the trustees of the relevant charity, in trust for that charity, all property for the time being vested –

(a) in the body, or

(b) in any other person (apart from the official custodian),

in trust for that charity.

(4)   If the Commission so directs in the order –

(a) all or any specified part of that property shall, instead of vesting in the trustees of the relevant charity, vest –

(i)   in a specified person as trustee for, or nominee of, that charity, or

(ii) in such persons (other than the trustees of the relevant charity) as may be specified;

(b) any specified investments, or any specified class or description of investments, held by any person in trust for the relevant charity shall be transferred –

(i)   to the trustees of that charity, or

      (ii)   to any such person or persons as is or are mentioned in paragraph (a)(i) or (ii) above;

    and for this purpose 'specified' means specified by the Commission in the order.

(5)   Where an order to which this subsection applies is made with respect to an incorporated body –

    (a)   any rights or liabilities of the body shall become rights or liabilities of the trustees of the relevant charity; and

    (b)   any legal proceedings that might have been continued or commenced by or against the body may be continued or commenced by or against those trustees.

(6)   Subsection (5) above applies to any order under this section by virtue of which –

    (a)   any property vested as mentioned in subsection (3) above is vested –

        (i)   in the trustees of the relevant charity, or

        (ii)   in any person as trustee for, or nominee of, that charity; or

    (b)   any investments held by any person in trust for the relevant charity are required to be transferred –

        (i)   to the trustees of that charity, or

        (ii)   to any person as trustee for, or nominee of, that charity.

(7)   [. . .]

62   Interpretation of Part VII

In this Part of this Act –

    'incorporated body' means a body incorporated under section 50 above;

    'the relevant charity', in relation to an incorporated body, means the charity the trustees of which have been incorporated as that body;

    'the trustees', in relation to a charity, means the charity trustees.

PART VIII   CHARITABLE COMPANIES

63   Winding up

(1)   Where a charity may be wound up by the High Court under the Insolvency Act 1986, a petition for it to be wound up under that Act by any court in England or Wales having jurisdiction may be presented by the Attorney General, as well as by any person authorised by that Act.

(2)   Where a charity may be so wound up by the High Court, such a petition may also be presented by the Commission if, at any time after it has instituted an inquiry under section 8 above with respect to the charity, it is satisfied as mentioned in section 18(1)(a) or (b) above.

(3)   Where a charitable company is dissolved, the Commission may make an application under section 651 of the Companies Act 1985 (power of court to declare dissolution of company void) for an order to be made under that section with respect to the company; and for this purpose subsection (1) of that section shall have effect in relation to a charitable company as if the reference to the liquidator of the company included a reference to the Commission.

(4)   Where a charitable company's name has been struck off the register of companies under section 652 of the Companies Act 1985 (power of registrar to strike defunct company off register), the Commission may make an application under section 653(2) of that Act (objection to striking off by person aggrieved) for an order restoring the company's name to that register; and for this purpose section 653(2) shall have effect in relation to a charitable company as if the reference to any such person aggrieved as is there mentioned included a reference to the Commission.

(5)   The powers exercisable by the Commission by virtue of this section shall be exercisable by the Commission of its own motion, but shall be exercisable only with the agreement of the Attorney General on each occasion.

(6)   In this section 'charitable company' means a company which is a charity.

64   Alteration of objects clause

(1)   Where a charity is a company or other body corporate having power to alter the instruments establishing or regulating it as a body corporate, no exercise of that power which has the effect of the body ceasing to be a charity shall be valid so as to affect the application of –

   (a)   any property acquired under any disposition or agreement previously made otherwise than for full consideration in money or money's worth, or any property representing property so acquired,

   (b)   any property representing income which has accrued before the alteration is made, or

   (c)   the income from any such property as aforesaid.

(2)   Where a charity is a company, any regulated alteration by the company –

   (a)   requires the prior written consent of the Commission, and

   (b)   is ineffective if such consent has not been obtained.

(2A)   The following are 'regulated alterations' –

   (a)   any alteration of the objects clause in the company's memorandum of association,

   (b)   any alteration of any provision of its memorandum or articles of association directing the application of property of the company on its dissolution, and

   (c)   any alteration of any provision of its memorandum or articles of association where the alteration would provide authorisation for any benefit to be obtained by directors or members of the company or persons connected with them.

(2B)   For the purposes of subsection (2A) above –

   (a)   'benefit' means a direct or indirect benefit of any nature, except that it does not include any remuneration (within the meaning of section 73A below) whose receipt may be authorised under that section; and

   (b)   the same rules apply for determining whether a person is connected with a director or member of the company as apply, in accordance with section 73B(5) and (6) below, for determining whether a person is connected with a charity trustee for the purposes of section 73A.

(3)   Where a company has made a regulated alteration in accordance with subsection (2) above and –

   (a)   in connection with the alteration is required by virtue of –

      (i)   section 6(1) of the Companies Act 1985 (delivery of documents following alteration of objects), or

      (ii)   that provision as applied by section 17(3) of that Act (alteration of condition in memorandum which could have been contained in articles),

   to deliver to the registrar of companies a printed copy of its memorandum, as altered, or

   (b)   is required by virtue of section 380(1) of that Act (registration etc. of resolutions and agreements) to forward to the registrar a printed or other copy of the special resolution effecting the alteration,

   the copy so delivered or forwarded by the company shall be accompanied by a copy of the Commission's consent.

(4)   Section 6(3) of that Act (offences) shall apply to any default by a company in complying with subsection (3) above as it applies to any such default as is mentioned in that provision.

65   Invalidity of certain transactions

(1)   Sections 35 and 35A of the Companies Act 1985 (capacity of company not limited by its memorandum; power of directors to bind company) do not apply to the acts of a company which is a charity except in favour of a person who –

(a)   gives full consideration in money or money's worth in relation to the act in question, and

(b)   does not know that the act is not permitted by the company's memorandum or, as the case may be, is beyond the powers of the directors,

or who does not know at the time the act is done that the company is a charity.

(2)   However, where such a company purports to transfer or grant an interest in property, the fact that the act was not permitted by the company's memorandum or, as the case may be, that the directors in connection with the act exceeded any limitation on their powers under the company's constitution, does not affect the title of a person who subsequently acquires the property or any interest in it for full consideration without actual notice of any such circumstances affecting the validity of the company's act.

(3)   In any proceedings arising out of subsection (1) above the burden of proving –

(a)   that a person knew that an act was not permitted by the company's memorandum or was beyond the powers of the directors, or

(b)   that a person knew that the company was a charity,

lies on the person making that allegation.

(4)   Where a company is a charity, the ratification of an act under section 35(3) of the Companies Act 1985, or the ratification of a transaction to which section 322A of that Act applies (invalidity of certain transactions to which directors or their associates are parties), is ineffective without the prior written consent of the Commission.

66   Consent of Commission required for approval etc. by members of charitable companies

(1)   Where a company is a charity –

(a)   any approval given by the members of the company under any provision of Chapter 4 of Part 10 of the Companies Act 2006 (transactions with directors requiring approval by members) listed in subsection (2) below, and

(b)   any affirmation given by members of the company under section 196 or 214 of that Act (affirmation of unapproved property transactions and loans), is ineffective without the prior written consent of the Commission.

(2)   The provisions are –

(a)   section 188 (directors' long-term service contracts);

(b)   section 190 (substantial property transactions with directors etc.);

(c)   section 197, 198 or 200 (loans and quasi-loans to directors etc.);

(d)   section 201 (credit transactions for benefit of directors etc.);

(e)   section 203 (related arrangements);

(f)   section 217 (payments to directors for loss of office);

(g)   section 218 (payments to directors for loss of office: transfer of undertaking etc.).

66A   Consent of Commission required for certain acts of charitable company

(1)   A company that is a charity may not do an act to which this section applies without the prior written consent of the Commission.

(2)   This section applies to an act that –

(a)   does not require approval under a listed provision of Chapter 4 of Part 10 of the Companies Act 2006 (transactions with directors) by the members of the company, but

(b)   would require such approval but for an exemption in the provision in question that disapplies the need for approval on the part of the members of a body corporate which is a wholly owned subsidiary of another body corporate.

(3) The reference to a listed provision is a reference to a provision listed in section 66(2) above.

(4) If a company acts in contravention of this section, the exemption referred to in subsection (2)(b) shall be treated as of no effect in relation to the act.

67 Name to appear on correspondence etc.

Section 30(7) of the Companies Act 1985 (exemption from requirements relating to publication of name etc.) shall not, in its application to any company which is a charity, have the effect of exempting the company from the requirements of section 349(1) of that Act (company's name to appear in its correspondence etc.).

68 Status to appear on correspondence etc.

(1) Where a company is a charity and its name does not include the word 'charity' or the word 'charitable' then, subject to subsection (1A), the fact that the company is a charity shall be stated in legible characters –

    (a) in all business letters of the company,
    (b) in all its notices and other official publications,
    (c) in all bills of exchange, promissory notes, endorsements, cheques and orders for money or goods purporting to be signed on behalf of the company,
    (d) in all conveyances purporting to be executed by the company, and
    (e) in all bills rendered by it and in all its invoices, receipts, and letters of credit.

(1A) Where a company's name includes the word 'elusen' or the word 'elusennol' (the Welsh equivalents of the words 'charity' and 'charitable'), subsection (1) above shall not apply in relation to any document which is wholly in Welsh.

(1B) The statement required by subsection (1) above shall be in English, except that, in the case of a document which is otherwise wholly in Welsh, the statement may be in Welsh if it consists of or includes the word 'elusen' or the word 'elusennol'.

(2) In subsection (1)(d) above 'conveyance' means any instrument creating, transferring, varying or extinguishing an interest in land.

(3) Subsections (2) to (4) of section 349 of the Companies Act 1985 (offences in connection with failure to include required particulars in business letters etc.) shall apply in relation to a contravention of subsection (1) above, taking the reference in subsection (3)(b) of that section to a bill of parcels as a reference to any such bill as is mentioned in subsection (1)(e) above.

68A Duty of charity's auditors etc. to report matters to Commission

(1) Section 44A(2) to (7) above shall apply in relation to a person acting as –

    (a) an auditor of a charitable company appointed under Chapter 5 of Part 11 of the Companies Act 1985 (auditors), or
    (b) a reporting accountant appointed by a charitable company for the purposes of section 249C of that Act (report required instead of audit),

as they apply in relation to a person such as is mentioned in section 44A(1).

(2) For this purpose any reference in section 44A to a person acting in the capacity mentioned in section 44A(1) is to be read as a reference to his acting in the capacity mentioned in subsection (1) of this section.

(3) In this section 'charitable company' means a charity which is a company.

69 Investigation of accounts

(1) In the case of a charity which is a company the Commission may by order require that the condition and accounts of the charity for such period as the Commission thinks fit shall be investigated and audited by an auditor appointed by the Commission, being a person eligible for appointment as a company auditor under section 25 of the Companies Act 1989.

(2) An auditor acting under subsection (1) above –

    (a) shall have a right of access to all books, accounts and documents relating to the charity which are in the possession or control of the charity trustees or to which the charity trustees have access;

    (b) shall be entitled to require from any charity trustee, past or present, and from any past or present officer or employee of the charity such information and explanation as he thinks necessary for the performance of his duties;

    (c) shall at the conclusion or during the progress of the audit make such reports to the Commission about the audit or about the accounts or affairs of the charity as he thinks the case requires, and shall send a copy of any such report to the charity trustees.

(3) The expenses of any audit under subsection (1) above, including the remuneration of the auditor, shall be paid by the Commission.

(4) If any person fails to afford an auditor any facility to which he is entitled under subsection (2) above the Commission may by order give to that person or to the charity trustees for the time being such directions as the Commission thinks appropriate for securing that the default is made good.

PART 8A   CHARITABLE INCORPORATED ORGANISATIONS

Nature and constitution

69A Charitable incorporated organisations

(1) In this Act, a charitable incorporated organisation is referred to as a 'CIO'.

(2) A CIO shall be a body corporate.

(3) A CIO shall have a constitution.

(4) A CIO shall have a principal office, which shall be in England or in Wales.

(5) A CIO shall have one or more members.

(6) The members may be either –

    (a) not liable to contribute to the assets of the CIO if it is wound up, or

    (b) liable to do so up to a maximum amount each.

69B Constitution

(1) A CIO's constitution shall state –

    (a) its name,

    (b) its purposes,

    (c) whether its principal office is in England or in Wales, and

    (d) whether or not its members are liable to contribute to its assets if it is wound up, and (if they are) up to what amount.

(2) A CIO's constitution shall make provision –

    (a) about who is eligible for membership, and how a person becomes a member,

    (b) about the appointment of one or more persons who are to be charity trustees of the CIO, and about any conditions of eligibility for appointment, and

    (c) containing directions about the application of property of the CIO on its dissolution.

(3) A CIO's constitution shall also provide for such other matters, and comply with such requirements, as are specified in regulations made by the Minister.

(4) A CIO's constitution –

    (a) shall be in English if its principal office is in England,

    (b) may be in English or in Welsh if its principal office is in Wales.

(5) A CIO's constitution shall be in the form specified in regulations made by the Commission, or as near to that form as the circumstances admit.

(6) Subject to anything in a CIO's constitution: a charity trustee of the CIO may, but need not, be a member of it; a member of the CIO may, but need not, be one of its charity trustees; and those who are members of the CIO and those who are its charity trustees may, but need not, be identical.

69C Name and status

(1) The name of a CIO shall appear in legible characters –

  (a) in all business letters of the CIO,
  (b) in all its notices and other official publications,
  (c) in all bills of exchange, promissory notes, endorsements, cheques and orders for money or goods purporting to be signed on behalf of the CIO,
  (d) in all conveyances purporting to be executed by the CIO, and
  (e) in all bills rendered by it and in all its invoices, receipts, and letters of credit.

(2) In subsection (1)(d), 'conveyance' means any instrument creating, transferring, varying or extinguishing an interest in land.

(3) Subsection (5) applies if the name of a CIO does not include –

  (a) 'charitable incorporated organisation', or
  (b) 'CIO', with or without full stops after each letter, or
  (c) a Welsh equivalent mentioned in subsection (4) (but this option applies only if the CIO's constitution is in Welsh),

  and it is irrelevant, in any such case, whether or not capital letters are used.

(4) The Welsh equivalents referred to in subsection (3)(c) are –

  (a) 'sefydliad elusennol corfforedig', or
  (b) 'SEC', with or without full stops after each letter.

(5) If this subsection applies, the fact that a CIO is a CIO shall be stated in legible characters in all the documents mentioned in subsection (1).

(6) The statement required by subsection (5) shall be in English, except that in the case of a document which is otherwise wholly in Welsh, the statement may be in Welsh.

69D Offences connected with name and status

(1) A charity trustee of a CIO or a person on the CIO's behalf who issues or authorises the issue of any document referred to in paragraph (a), (b), (d) or (e) of section 69C(1) above which fails to comply with the requirements of section 69C(1), (5) or (6) is liable on summary conviction to a fine not exceeding level 3 on the standard scale.

(2) A charity trustee of a CIO or a person on the CIO's behalf who signs or authorises to be signed on behalf of the CIO any document referred to in paragraph (c) of section 69C(1) above which fails to comply with the requirements of section 69C(1), (5) or (6) –

  (a) is liable on summary conviction to a fine not exceeding level 3 on the standard scale, and
  (b) is personally liable to the holder of the bill of exchange (etc.) for the amount of it, unless it is duly paid by the CIO.

(3) A person who holds any body out as being a CIO when it is not (however he does this) is guilty of an offence and is liable on summary conviction to a fine not exceeding level 3 on the standard scale.

(4) It is a defence for a person charged with an offence under subsection (3) to prove that he believed on reasonable grounds that the body was a CIO.

Registration

69E Application for registration

(1) Any one or more persons ('the applicants') may apply to the Commission for a CIO to be constituted and for its registration as a charity.

(2) The applicants shall supply the Commission with –

(a) a copy of the proposed constitution of the CIO,

(b) such other documents or information as may be prescribed by regulations made by the Minister, and

(c) such other documents or information as the Commission may require for the purposes of the application.

(3) The Commission shall refuse such an application if –

(a) it is not satisfied that the CIO would be a charity at the time it would be registered, or

(b) the CIO's proposed constitution does not comply with one or more of the requirements of section 69B above and any regulations made under that section.

(4) The Commission may refuse such an application if –

(a) the proposed name of the CIO is the same as, or is in the opinion of the Commission too like, the name of any other charity (whether registered or not), or

(b) the Commission is of the opinion referred to in any of paragraphs (b) to (e) of section 6(2) above (power of Commission to require change in charity's name) in relation to the proposed name of the CIO (reading paragraph (b) as referring to the proposed purposes of the CIO and to the activities which it is proposed it should carry on).

69F Effect of registration

(1) If the Commission grants an application under section 69E above it shall register the CIO to which the application relates as a charity in the register of charities.

(2) Upon the registration of the CIO in the register of charities, it becomes by virtue of the registration a body corporate –

(a) whose constitution is that proposed in the application,

(b) whose name is that specified in the constitution, and

(c) whose first member is, or first members are, the applicants referred to in section 69E above.

(3) All property for the time being vested in the applicants (or, if more than one, any of them) on trust for the charitable purposes of the CIO (when incorporated) shall by virtue of this subsection become vested in the CIO upon its registration.

(4) The entry relating to the charity's registration in the register of charities shall include –

(a) the date of the charity's registration, and

(b) a note saying that it is constituted as a CIO.

(5) A copy of the entry in the register shall be sent to the charity at the principal office of the CIO.

Conversion, amalgamation and transfer

69G Conversion of charitable company or registered industrial and provident society

(1) The following may apply to the Commission to be converted into a CIO, and for the CIO's registration as a charity, in accordance with this section –

(a) a charitable company,

(b) a charity which is a registered society within the meaning of the Industrial and Provident Societies Act 1965.

(2) But such an application may not be made by –

  (a) a company or registered society having a share capital if any of the shares are not fully paid up, or

  (b) an exempt charity.

(3) Such an application is referred to in this section and sections 69H and 69I below as an 'application for conversion'.

(4) The Commission shall notify the following of any application for conversion –

  (a) the appropriate registrar, and

  (b) such other persons (if any) as the Commission thinks appropriate in the particular case.

(5) The company or registered society shall supply the Commission with –

  (a) a copy of a resolution of the company or registered society that it be converted into a CIO,

  (b) a copy of the proposed constitution of the CIO,

  (c) a copy of a resolution of the company or registered society adopting the proposed constitution of the CIO,

  (d) such other documents or information as may be prescribed by regulations made by the Minister, and

  (e) such other documents or information as the Commission may require for the purposes of the application.

(6) The resolution referred to in subsection (5)(a) shall be –

  (a) a special resolution of the company or registered society, or

  (b) a unanimous written resolution signed by or on behalf of all the members of the company or registered society who would be entitled to vote on a special resolution.

(7) In the case of a registered society, 'special resolution' has the meaning given in section 52(3) of the Industrial and Provident Societies Act 1965.

(8) In the case of a company limited by guarantee which makes an application for conversion (whether or not it also has a share capital), the proposed constitution of the CIO shall (unless subsection (10) applies) provide for the CIO's members to be liable to contribute to its assets if it is wound up, and for the amount up to which they are so liable.

(9) That amount shall not be less than the amount up to which they were liable to contribute to the assets of the company if it was wound up.

(10) If the amount each member of the company is liable to contribute to its assets on its winding up is £10 or less, the guarantee shall be extinguished on the conversion of the company into a CIO, and the requirements of subsections (8) and (9) do not apply.

(11) In subsection (4), and in sections 69H and 69I below, 'the appropriate registrar' means –

  (a) in the case of an application for conversion by a charitable company, the registrar of companies,

  (b) in the case of an application for conversion by a registered society, the Financial Services Authority.

(12) In this section, 'charitable company' means a company which is a charity.

69H Conversion: consideration of application

(1) The Commission shall consult those to whom it has given notice of an application for conversion under section 69G(4) above about whether the application should be granted.

(2)   The Commission shall refuse an application for conversion if –

    (a)   it is not satisfied that the CIO would be a charity at the time it would be registered,

    (b)   the CIO's proposed constitution does not comply with one or more of the requirements of section 69B above and any regulations made under that section, or

    (c)   in the case of an application for conversion made by a company limited by guarantee, the CIO's proposed constitution does not comply with the requirements of subsections (8) and (9) of section 69G above.

(3)   The Commission may refuse an application for conversion if –

    (a)   the proposed name of the CIO is the same as, or is in the opinion of the Commission too like, the name of any other charity (whether registered or not),

    (b)   the Commission is of the opinion referred to in any of paragraphs (b) to (e) of section 6(2) above (power of Commission to require change in charity's name) in relation to the proposed name of the CIO (reading paragraph (b) as referring to the proposed purposes of the CIO and to the activities which it is proposed it should carry on), or

    (c)   having considered any representations received from those whom it has consulted under subsection (1), the Commission considers (having regard to any regulations made under subsection (4)) that it would not be appropriate to grant the application.

(4)   The Minister may make provision in regulations about circumstances in which it would not be appropriate to grant an application for conversion.

(5)   If the Commission refuses an application for conversion, it shall so notify the appropriate registrar (see section 69G(11) above).

69I   Conversion: supplementary

(1)   If the Commission grants an application for conversion, it shall –

    (a)   register the CIO to which the application related in the register of charities, and

    (b)   send to the appropriate registrar (see section 69G(11) above) a copy of each of the resolutions of the converting company or registered society referred to in section 69G(5)(a) and (c) above, and a copy of the entry in the register relating to the CIO.

(2)   The registration of the CIO in the register shall be provisional only until the appropriate registrar cancels the registration of the company or registered society as required by subsection (3)(b).

(3)   The appropriate registrar shall –

    (a)   register the documents sent to him under subsection (1)(b), and

    (b)   cancel the registration of the company in the register of companies, or of the society in the register of friendly societies,

    and shall notify the Commission that he has done so.

(4)   When the appropriate registrar cancels the registration of the company or of the registered society, the company or registered society is thereupon converted into a CIO, being a body corporate –

    (a)   whose constitution is that proposed in the application for conversion,

    (b)   whose name is that specified in the constitution, and

    (c)   whose first members are the members of the converting company or society immediately before the moment of conversion.

(5)   If the converting company or registered society had a share capital, upon the conversion of the company or registered society all the shares shall by virtue of this subsection be cancelled, and no former holder of any cancelled share shall have any right in respect of it after its cancellation.

(6) Subsection (5) does not affect any right which accrued in respect of a share before its cancellation.

(7) The entry relating to the charity's registration in the register shall include –

    (a) a note that it is constituted as a CIO,

    (b) the date on which it became so constituted, and

    (c) a note of the name of the company or society which was converted into the CIO,

but the matters mentioned in paragraphs (a) and (b) are to be included only when the appropriate registrar has notified the Commission as required by subsection (3).

(8) A copy of the entry in the register shall be sent to the charity at the principal office of the CIO.

(9) The conversion of a charitable company or of a registered society into a CIO does not affect, in particular, any liability to which the company or registered society was subject by virtue of its being a charitable company or registered society.

69J Conversion of community interest company

(1) The Minister may by regulations make provision for the conversion of a community interest company into a CIO, and for the CIO's registration as a charity.

(2) The regulations may, in particular, apply, or apply with modifications specified in the regulations, or disapply, anything in sections 53 to 55 of the Companies (Audit, Investigations and Community Enterprise) Act 2004 or in sections 69G to 69I above.

69K Amalgamation of CIOs

(1) Any two or more CIOs ('the old CIOs') may, in accordance with this section, apply to the Commission to be amalgamated, and for the incorporation and registration as a charity of a new CIO ('the new CIO') as their successor.

(2) Such an application is referred to in this section and section 69L below as an 'application for amalgamation'.

(3) Subsections (2) to (4) of section 69E above apply in relation to an application for amalgamation as they apply to an application for a CIO to be constituted, but in those subsections –

    (a) 'the applicants' shall be construed as meaning the old CIOs, and

    (b) references to the CIO are to the new CIO.

(4) In addition to the documents and information referred to in section 69E(2) above, the old CIOs shall supply the Commission with –

    (a) a copy of a resolution of each of the old CIOs approving the proposed amalgamation, and

    (b) a copy of a resolution of each of the old CIOs adopting the proposed constitution of the new CIO.

(5) The resolutions referred to in subsection (4) must have been passed –

    (a) by a 75% majority of those voting at a general meeting of the CIO (including those voting by proxy or by post, if voting that way is permitted), or

    (b) unanimously by the CIO's members, otherwise than at a general meeting.

(6) The date of passing of such a resolution is –

    (a) the date of the general meeting at which it was passed, or

    (b) if it was passed otherwise than at a general meeting, the date on which provision in the CIO's constitution or in regulations made under paragraph 13 of Schedule 5B to this Act deems it to have been passed (but that date may not be earlier than that on which the last member agreed to it).

(7) Each old CIO shall –

(a) give notice of the proposed amalgamation in the way (or ways) that in the opinion of its charity trustees will make it most likely to come to the attention of those who would be affected by the amalgamation, and

(b) send a copy of the notice to the Commission.

(8) The notice shall invite any person who considers that he would be affected by the proposed amalgamation to make written representations to the Commission not later than a date determined by the Commission and specified in the notice.

(9) In addition to being required to refuse it on one of the grounds mentioned in section 69E(3) above as applied by subsection (3) of this section, the Commission shall refuse an application for amalgamation if it considers that there is a serious risk that the new CIO would be unable properly to pursue its purposes.

(10) The Commission may refuse an application for amalgamation if it is not satisfied that the provision in the constitution of the new CIO about the matters mentioned in subsection (11) is the same, or substantially the same, as the provision about those matters in the constitutions of each of the old CIOs.

(11) The matters are –

(a) the purposes of the CIO,

(b) the application of property of the CIO on its dissolution, and

(c) authorisation for any benefit to be obtained by charity trustees or members of the CIO or persons connected with them.

(12) For the purposes of subsection (11)(c) –

(a) 'benefit' means a direct or indirect benefit of any nature, except that it does not include any remuneration (within the meaning of section 73A below) whose receipt may be authorised under that section, and

(b) the same rules apply for determining whether a person is connected with a charity trustee or member of the CIO as apply, in accordance with section 73B(5) and (6) below, for determining whether a person is connected with a charity trustee for the purposes of section 73A.

69L Amalgamation: supplementary

(1) If the Commission grants an application for amalgamation, it shall register the new CIO in the register of charities.

(2) Upon the registration of the new CIO it thereupon becomes by virtue of the registration a body corporate –

(a) whose constitution is that proposed in the application for amalgamation,

(b) whose name is that specified in the constitution, and

(c) whose first members are the members of the old CIOs immediately before the new CIO was registered.

(3) Upon the registration of the new CIO –

(a) all the property, rights and liabilities of each of the old CIOs shall become by virtue of this subsection the property, rights and liabilities of the new CIO, and

(b) each of the old CIOs shall be dissolved.

(4) Any gift which –

(a) is expressed as a gift to one of the old CIOs, and

(b) takes effect on or after the date of registration of the new CIO,

takes effect as a gift to the new CIO.

(5) The entry relating to the registration in the register of the charity constituted as the new CIO shall include –

(a) a note that it is constituted as a CIO,

(b) the date of the charity's registration, and

(c) a note that the CIO was formed following amalgamation, and of the name of each of the old CIOs.

(6) A copy of the entry in the register shall be sent to the charity at the principal office of the new CIO.

69M Transfer of CIO's undertaking

(1) A CIO may resolve that all its property, rights and liabilities should be transferred to another CIO specified in the resolution.

(2) Where a CIO has passed such a resolution, it shall send to the Commission –

    (a) a copy of the resolution, and
    (b) a copy of a resolution of the transferee CIO agreeing to the transfer to it.

(3) Subsections (5) and (6) of section 69K above apply to the resolutions referred to in subsections (1) and (2)(b) as they apply to the resolutions referred to in section 69K(4).

(4) Having received the copy resolutions referred to in subsection (2), the Commission –

    (a) may direct the transferor CIO to give public notice of its resolution in such manner as is specified in the direction, and
    (b) if it gives such a direction, must take into account any representations made to it by persons appearing to it to be interested in the transferor CIO, where those representations are made to it within the period of 28 days beginning with the date when public notice of the resolution is given by the transferor CIO.

(5) The resolution shall not take effect until confirmed by the Commission.

(6) The Commission shall refuse to confirm the resolution if it considers that there is a serious risk that the transferee CIO would be unable properly to pursue the purposes of the transferor CIO.

(7) The Commission may refuse to confirm the resolution if it is not satisfied that the provision in the constitution of the transferee CIO about the matters mentioned in section 69K(11) above is the same, or substantially the same, as the provision about those matters in the constitution of the transferor CIO.

(8) If the Commission does not notify the transferor CIO within the relevant period that it is either confirming or refusing to confirm the resolution, the resolution is to be treated as confirmed by the Commission on the day after the end of that period.

(9) Subject to subsection (10), 'the relevant period' means –

    (a) in a case where the Commission directs the transferor CIO under subsection (4) to give public notice of its resolution, the period of six months beginning with the date when that notice is given, or
    (b) in any other case, the period of six months beginning with the date when both of the copy resolutions referred to in subsection (2) have been received by the Commission.

(10) The Commission may at any time within the period of six months mentioned in subsection (9)(a) or (b) give the transferor CIO a notice extending the relevant period by such period (not exceeding six months) as is specified in the notice.

(11) A notice under subsection (10) must set out the Commission's reasons for the extension.

(12) If the resolution is confirmed (or treated as confirmed) by the Commission –

    (a) all the property, rights and liabilities of the transferor CIO shall become by virtue of this subsection the property, rights and liabilities of the transferee CIO in accordance with the resolution, and
    (b) the transferor CIO shall be dissolved.

(13) Any gift which –

    (a) is expressed as a gift to the transferor CIO, and
    (b) takes effect on or after the date on which the resolution is confirmed (or treated as confirmed),

takes effect as a gift to the transferee CIO.

Winding up, insolvency and dissolution

69N Regulations about winding up, insolvency and dissolution

(1) The Minister may by regulations make provision about –

    (a) the winding up of CIOs,

    (b) their insolvency,

    (c) their dissolution, and

    (d) their revival and restoration to the register following dissolution.

(2) The regulations may, in particular, make provision –

    (a) about the transfer on the dissolution of a CIO of its property and rights (including property and rights held on trust for the CIO) to the official custodian or another person or body,

    (b) requiring any person in whose name any stocks, funds or securities are standing in trust for a CIO to transfer them into the name of the official custodian or another person or body,

    (c) about the disclaiming, by the official custodian or other transferee of a CIO's property, of title to any of that property,

    (d) about the application of a CIO's property cy-près,

    (e) about circumstances in which charity trustees may be personally liable for contributions to the assets of a CIO or for its debts,

    (f) about the reversal on a CIO's revival of anything done on its dissolution.

(3) The regulations may –

    (a) apply any enactment which would not otherwise apply, either without modification or with modifications specified in the regulations,

    (b) disapply, or modify (in ways specified in the regulations) the application of, any enactment which would otherwise apply.

(4) In subsection (3), 'enactment' includes a provision of subordinate legislation within the meaning of the Interpretation Act 1978.

Miscellaneous

69O Power to transfer all property of unincorporated charity to one or more CIOs

Section 74 below (power to transfer all property of unincorporated charity) applies with the omission of paragraph (a) of subsection (1) in relation to a resolution by the charity trustees of a charity to transfer all its property to a CIO or to divide its property between two or more CIOs.

69P Further provision about CIOs

The provisions of Schedule 5B to this Act shall have effect with respect to CIOs.

69Q Regulations

(1) The Minister may by regulations make further provision about applications for registration of CIOs, the administration of CIOs, the conversion of charitable companies, registered societies and community interest companies into CIOs, the amalgamation of CIOs, and in relation to CIOs generally.

(2) The regulations may, in particular, make provision about –

    (a) the execution of deeds and documents,

    (b) the electronic communication of messages or documents relevant to a CIO or to any dealing with the Commission in relation to one,

    (c) the maintenance of registers of members and of charity trustees,

    (d) the maintenance of other registers (for example, a register of charges over the CIO's assets).

(3) The regulations may, in relation to charities constituted as CIOs –

    (a) disapply any of sections 3 to 4 above,

    (b) modify the application of any of those sections in ways specified in the regulations.

(4) Subsections (3) and (4) of section 69N above apply for the purposes of this section as they apply for the purposes of that.

PART IX   MISCELLANEOUS

70–71   [. . .]

Charity trustees

72   Persons disqualified for being trustees of a charity

(1) Subject to the following provisions of this section, a person shall be disqualified for being a charity trustee or trustee for a charity if –

    (a) he has been convicted of any offence involving dishonesty or deception;

    (b) he has been adjudged bankrupt or sequestration of his estate has been awarded and (in either case) he has not been discharged or he is the subject of a bankruptcy restrictions order or an interim order;

    (c) he has made a composition or arrangement with, or granted a trust deed for, his creditors and has not been discharged in respect of it;

    (d) he has been removed from the office of charity trustee or trustee for a charity by an order made –

        (i) by the Commission or Commissioners under section 18(2)(i) above, or

        (ii) by the Commissioners under section 20(1A)(i) of the Charities Act 1960 (power to act for protection of charities) or under section 20(1)(i) of that Act (as in force before the commencement of section 8 of the Charities Act 1992), or

        (iii) by the High Court,

    on the grounds of any misconduct or mismanagement in the administration of the charity for which he was responsible or to which he was privy, or which he by his conduct contributed to or facilitated;

    (e) he has been removed, under section 7 of the Law Reform (Miscellaneous Provisions) (Scotland) Act 1990 (powers of Court of Session to deal with management of charities) or section 34(5)(e) of the Charities and Trustee Investment (Scotland) Act 2005 (powers of the Court of Session), from being concerned in the management or control of any body;

    (f) he is subject to a disqualification order or disqualification undertaking under the Company Directors Disqualification Act 1986 to a disqualification order under Part II of the Companies (Northern Ireland) Order 1989 or disqualification undertaking under the Company Directors Disqualification (Northern Ireland) Order 2002 or to an order made under section 429(2)(b) of the Insolvency Act 1986 (failure to pay under county court administration order).

(2) In subsection (1) above –

    (a) paragraph (a) applies whether the conviction occurred before or after the commencement of that subsection, but does not apply in relation to any conviction which is a spent conviction for the purposes of the Rehabilitation of Offenders Act 1974;

    (b) paragraph (b) applies whether the adjudication of bankruptcy or the sequestration or the making of a bankruptcy restrictions order or an interim order occurred before or after the commencement of that subsection;

(c)   paragraph (c) applies whether the composition or arrangement was made, or the trust deed was granted, before or after the commencement of that subsection; and

(d)   paragraphs (d) to (f) apply in relation to orders made and removals effected before or after the commencement of that subsection.

(3)   Where (apart from this subsection) a person is disqualified under subsection (1)(b) above for being a charity trustee or trustee for any charity which is a company, he shall not be so disqualified if leave has been granted under section 11 of the Company Directors Disqualification Act 1986 (undischarged bankrupts) for him to act as director of the charity; and similarly a person shall not be disqualified under subsection (1)(f) above for being a charity trustee or trustee for such a charity if –

(a)   in the case of a person subject to a disqualification order or disqualification undertaking under the Company Directors Disqualification Act 1986, leave for the purposes of section 1(1)(a) or 1A(1)(a) of that Act has been granted for him to act as director of the charity,

(aa) in the case of a person subject to a disqualification order under Part II of the Companies (Northern Ireland) Order 1989 or disqualification undertaking under the Company Directors Disqualification (Northern Ireland) Order 2002, leave has been granted by the High Court in Northern Ireland for him to act as director of the charity,

(b)   in the case of a person subject to an order under section 429(2)(b) of the Insolvency Act 1986, leave has been granted by the court which made the order for him to so act.

(4)   The Commission may, on the application of any person disqualified under subsection (1) above, waive his disqualification either generally or in relation to a particular charity or a particular class of charities; but no such waiver may be granted in relation to any charity which is a company if –

(a)   the person concerned is for the time being prohibited, by virtue of –

(i)   a disqualification order or disqualification undertaking under the Company Directors Disqualification Act 1986, or

(ii)   section 11(1), 12(2), 12A or 12B of that Act (undischarged bankrupts; failure to pay under county court administration order; Northern Irish disqualification orders; Northern Irish disqualification undertakings),

from acting as director of the charity; and

(b)   leave has not been granted for him to act as director of any other company.

(4A) If –

(a)   a person disqualified under subsection (1)(d) or (e) makes an application under subsection (4) above five years or more after the date on which his disqualification took effect, and

(b)   the Commission is not prevented from granting the application by virtue of paragraphs (a) and (b) of subsection (4),

the Commission must grant the application unless satisfied that, by reason of any special circumstances, it should be refused.

(5)   Any waiver under subsection (4) above shall be notified in writing to the person concerned.

(6)   For the purposes of this section the Commission shall keep, in such manner as it thinks fit, a register of all persons who have been removed from office as mentioned in subsection (1)(d) above either –

(a)   by an order of the Commission or the Commissioners made before or after the commencement of subsection (1) above, or

(b)   by an order of the High Court made after the commencement of section 45(1) of the Charities Act 1992;

and, where any person is so removed from office by an order of the High Court, the court shall notify the Commission of his removal.

(7) The entries in the register kept under subsection (6) above shall be available for public inspection in legible form at all reasonable times.

(8) In this section 'the Commissioners' means the Charity Commissioners for England and Wales.

73   Person acting as charity trustee while disqualified

(1) Subject to subsection (2) below, any person who acts as a charity trustee or trustee for a charity while he is disqualified for being such a trustee by virtue of section 72 above shall be guilty of an offence and liable –

   (a) on summary conviction, to imprisonment for a term not exceeding six months or to a fine not exceeding the statutory maximum, or both;

   (b) on conviction on indictment, to imprisonment for a term not exceeding two years or to a fine, or both.

(2) Subsection (1) above shall not apply where –

   (a) the charity concerned is a company; and

   (b) the disqualified person is disqualified by virtue only of paragraph (b) or (f) of section 72(1) above.

(3) Any acts done as charity trustee or trustee for a charity by a person disqualified for being such a trustee by virtue of section 72 above shall not be invalid by reason only of that disqualification.

(4) Where the Commission is satisfied –

   (a) that any person has acted as charity trustee or trustee for a charity while disqualified for being such a trustee by virtue of section 72 above, and

   (b) that, while so acting, he has received from the charity any sums by way of remuneration or expenses, or any benefit in kind, in connection with his acting as charity trustee or trustee for the charity,

   the Commission may by order direct him to repay to the charity the whole or part of any such sums, or (as the case may be) to pay to the charity the whole or part of the monetary value (as determined by the Commission) of any such benefit.

(5) Subsection (4) above does not apply to any sums received by way of remuneration or expenses in respect of any time when the person concerned was not disqualified for being a charity trustee or trustee for the charity.

73A   Remuneration of trustees etc. providing services to charity

(1) This section applies to remuneration for services provided by a person to or on behalf of a charity where –

   (a) he is a charity trustee or trustee for the charity, or

   (b) he is connected with a charity trustee or trustee for the charity and the remuneration might result in that trustee obtaining any benefit.

   This is subject to subsection (7) below.

(2) If conditions A to D are met in relation to remuneration within subsection (1), the person providing the services ('the relevant person') is entitled to receive the remuneration out of the funds of the charity.

(3) Condition A is that the amount or maximum amount of the remuneration –

   (a) is set out in an agreement in writing between –

      (i) the charity or its charity trustees (as the case may be), and

      (ii) the relevant person,

      under which the relevant person is to provide the services in question to or on behalf of the charity, and

(b) does not exceed what is reasonable in the circumstances for the provision by that person of the services in question.

(4) Condition B is that, before entering into that agreement, the charity trustees decided that they were satisfied that it would be in the best interests of the charity for the services to be provided by the relevant person to or on behalf of the charity for the amount or maximum amount of remuneration set out in the agreement.

(5) Condition C is that if immediately after the agreement is entered into there is, in the case of the charity, more than one person who is a charity trustee and is –

(a) a person in respect of whom an agreement within subsection (3) above is in force, or

(b) a person who is entitled to receive remuneration out of the funds of the charity otherwise than by virtue of such an agreement, or

(c) a person connected with a person falling within paragraph (a) or (b) above,

the total number of them constitute a minority of the persons for the time being holding office as charity trustees of the charity.

(6) Condition D is that the trusts of the charity do not contain any express provision that prohibits the relevant person from receiving the remuneration.

(7) Nothing in this section applies to –

(a) any remuneration for services provided by a person in his capacity as a charity trustee or trustee for a charity or under a contract of employment, or

(b) any remuneration not within paragraph (a) which a person is entitled to receive out of the funds of a charity by virtue of any provision or order within subsection (8).

(8) The provisions or orders within this subsection are –

(a) any provision contained in the trusts of the charity,

(b) any order of the court or the Commission,

(c) any statutory provision contained in or having effect under an Act of Parliament other than this section.

(9) Section 73B below applies for the purposes of this section.

73B Supplementary provisions for purposes of section 73A

(1) Before entering into an agreement within section 73A(3) the charity trustees must have regard to any guidance given by the Commission concerning the making of such agreements.

(2) The duty of care in section 1(1) of the Trustee Act 2000 applies to a charity trustee when making such a decision as is mentioned in section 73A(4).

(3) For the purposes of section 73A(5) an agreement within section 73A(3) is in force so long as any obligations under the agreement have not been fully discharged by a party to it.

(4) In section 73A –

'benefit' means a direct or indirect benefit of any nature;

'maximum amount', in relation to remuneration, means the maximum amount of the remuneration whether specified in or ascertainable under the terms of the agreement in question;

'remuneration' includes any benefit in kind (and 'amount' accordingly includes monetary value);

'services', in the context of remuneration for services, includes goods that are supplied in connection with the provision of services.

(5) For the purposes of section 73A the following persons are 'connected' with a charity trustee or trustee for a charity –

(a) a child, parent, grandchild, grandparent, brother or sister of the trustee;

    (b) the spouse or civil partner of the trustee or of any person falling within paragraph (a);

    (c) a person carrying on business in partnership with the trustee or with any person falling within paragraph (a) or (b);

    (d) an institution which is controlled –

        (i) by the trustee or by any person falling within paragraph (a), (b) or (c), or

        (ii) by two or more persons falling within sub-paragraph (i), when taken together;

    (e) a body corporate in which –

        (i) the trustee or any connected person falling within any of paragraphs (a) to (c) has a substantial interest, or

        (ii) two or more persons falling within sub-paragraph (i), when taken together, have a substantial interest.

(6) Paragraphs 2 to 4 of Schedule 5 to this Act apply for the purposes of subsection (5) above as they apply for the purposes of provisions of that Schedule.

73C Disqualification of trustee receiving remuneration under section 73A

(1) This section applies to any charity trustee or trustee for a charity –

    (a) who is or would be entitled to remuneration under an agreement or proposed agreement within section 73A(3) above, or

    (b) who is connected with a person who is or would be so entitled.

(2) The charity trustee or trustee for a charity is disqualified from acting as such in relation to any decision or other matter connected with the agreement.

(3) But any act done by such a person which he is disqualified from doing by virtue of subsection (2) above shall not be invalid by reason only of that disqualification.

(4) Where the Commission is satisfied –

    (a) that a person ('the disqualified trustee') has done any act which he was disqualified from doing by virtue of subsection (2) above, and

    (b) that the disqualified trustee or a person connected with him has received or is to receive from the charity any remuneration under the agreement in question,

    it may make an order under subsection (5) or (6) below (as appropriate).

(5) An order under this subsection is one requiring the disqualified trustee –

    (a) to reimburse to the charity the whole or part of the remuneration received as mentioned in subsection (4)(b) above;

    (b) to the extent that the remuneration consists of a benefit in kind, to reimburse to the charity the whole or part of the monetary value (as determined by the Commission) of the benefit in kind.

(6) An order under this subsection is one directing that the disqualified trustee or (as the case may be) connected person is not to be paid the whole or part of the remuneration mentioned in subsection (4)(b) above.

(7) If the Commission makes an order under subsection (5) or (6) above, the disqualified trustee or (as the case may be) connected person accordingly ceases to have any entitlement under the agreement to so much of the remuneration (or its monetary value) as the order requires him to reimburse to the charity or (as the case may be) as it directs is not to be paid to him.

(8) Subsections (4) to (6) of section 73B above apply for the purposes of this section as they apply for the purposes of section 73A above.

73D Power to relieve trustees, auditors etc. from liability for breach of trust or duty

(1) This section applies to a person who is or has been –

    (a) a charity trustee or trustee for a charity,

(b)   a person appointed to audit a charity's accounts (whether appointed under an enactment or otherwise), or

(c)   an independent examiner, reporting accountant or other person appointed to examine or report on a charity's accounts (whether appointed under an enactment or otherwise).

(2)   If the Commission considers –

(a)   that a person to whom this section applies is or may be personally liable for a breach of trust or breach of duty committed in his capacity as a person within paragraph (a), (b) or (c) of subsection (1) above, but

(b)   that he has acted honestly and reasonably and ought fairly to be excused for the breach of trust or duty,

the Commission may make an order relieving him wholly or partly from any such liability.

(3)   An order under subsection (2) above may grant the relief on such terms as the Commission thinks fit.

(4)   Subsection (2) does not apply in relation to any personal contractual liability of a charity trustee or trustee for a charity.

(5)   For the purposes of this section and section 73E below –

(a)   subsection (1)(b) above is to be read as including a reference to the Auditor General for Wales acting as auditor under section 43B above, and

(b)   subsection (1)(c) above is to be read as including a reference to the Auditor General for Wales acting as examiner under that section;

and in subsection (1)(b) and (c) any reference to a charity's accounts is to be read as including any group accounts prepared by the charity trustees of a charity.

(6)   This section does not affect the operation of –

(a)   section 61 of the Trustee Act 1925 (power of court to grant relief to trustees),

(b)   section 727 of the Companies Act 1985 (power of court to grant relief to officers or auditors of companies), or

(c)   section 73E below (which extends section 727 to auditors etc. of charities which are not companies).

73E   Court's power to grant relief to apply to all auditors etc. of charities which are not companies

(1)   Section 727 of the Companies Act 1985 (power of court to grant relief to officers or auditors of companies) shall have effect in relation to a person to whom this section applies as it has effect in relation to a person employed as an auditor by a company.

(2)   This section applies to –

(a)   a person acting in a capacity within section 73D(1)(b) or (c) above in a case where, apart from this section, section 727 would not apply in relation to him as a person so acting, and

(b)   a charity trustee of a CIO.

73F   Trustees' indemnity insurance

(1)   The charity trustees of a charity may arrange for the purchase, out of the funds of the charity, of insurance designed to indemnify the charity trustees or any trustees for the charity against any personal liability in respect of –

(a)   any breach of trust or breach of duty committed by them in their capacity as charity trustees or trustees for the charity, or

(b)   any negligence, default, breach of duty or breach of trust committed by them in their capacity as directors or officers of the charity (if it is a body corporate) or of any body corporate carrying on any activities on behalf of the charity.

(2)   The terms of such insurance must, however, be so framed as to exclude the provision of any indemnity for a person in respect of –

    (a)   any liability incurred by him to pay –

        (i)   a fine imposed in criminal proceedings, or

        (ii)   a sum payable to a regulatory authority by way of a penalty in respect of non-compliance with any requirement of a regulatory nature (however arising);

    (b)   any liability incurred by him in defending any criminal proceedings in which he is convicted of an offence arising out of any fraud or dishonesty, or wilful or reckless misconduct, by him; or

    (c)   any liability incurred by him to the charity that arises out of any conduct which he knew (or must reasonably be assumed to have known) was not in the interests of the charity or in the case of which he did not care whether it was in the best interests of the charity or not.

(3)   For the purposes of subsection (2)(b) above –

    (a)   the reference to any such conviction is a reference to one that has become final;

    (b)   a conviction becomes final –

        (i)   if not appealed against, at the end of the period for bringing an appeal, or

        (ii)   if appealed against, at the time when the appeal (or any further appeal) is disposed of; and

    (c)   an appeal is disposed of –

        (i)   if it is determined and the period for bringing any further appeal has ended, or

        (ii)   if it is abandoned or otherwise ceases to have effect.

(4)   The charity trustees of a charity may not purchase insurance under this section unless they decide that they are satisfied that it is in the best interests of the charity for them to do so.

(5)   The duty of care in section 1(1) of the Trustee Act 2000 applies to a charity trustee when making such a decision.

(6)   The Minister may by order make such amendments of subsections (2) and (3) above as he considers appropriate.

(7)   No order may be made under subsection (6) above unless a draft of the order has been laid before and approved by a resolution of each House of Parliament.

(8)   This section –

    (a)   does not authorise the purchase of any insurance whose purchase is expressly prohibited by the trusts of the charity, but

    (b)   has effect despite any provision prohibiting the charity trustees or trustees for the charity receiving any personal benefit out of the funds of the charity.

Miscellaneous powers of charities

74   Power to transfer all property of unincorporated charity

(1)   This section applies to a charity if –

    (a)   its gross income in its last financial year did not exceed £10,000,

    (b)   it does not hold any designated land, and

    (c)   it is not a company or other body corporate.

'Designated land' means land held on trusts which stipulate that it is to be used for the purposes, or any particular purposes, of the charity.

(2)   The charity trustees of such a charity may resolve for the purposes of this section –

     (a) that all the property of the charity should be transferred to another charity specified in the resolution, or

     (b) that all the property of the charity should be transferred to two or more charities specified in the resolution in accordance with such division of the property between them as is so specified.

(3) Any charity so specified may be either a registered charity or a charity which is not required to be registered.

(4) But the charity trustees of a charity ('the transferor charity') do not have power to pass a resolution under subsection (2) above unless they are satisfied –

     (a) that it is expedient in the interests of furthering the purposes for which the property is held by the transferor charity for the property to be transferred in accordance with the resolution, and

     (b) that the purposes (or any of the purposes) of any charity to which property is to be transferred under the resolution are substantially similar to the purposes (or any of the purposes) of the transferor charity.

(5) Any resolution under subsection (2) above must be passed by a majority of not less than two-thirds of the charity trustees who vote on the resolution.

(6) Where charity trustees have passed a resolution under subsection (2), they must send a copy of it to the Commission, together with a statement of their reasons for passing it.

(7) Having received the copy of the resolution, the Commission –

     (a) may direct the charity trustees to give public notice of the resolution in such manner as is specified in the direction, and

     (b) if it gives such a direction, must take into account any representations made to it by persons appearing to it to be interested in the charity, where those representations are made to it within the period of 28 days beginning with the date when public notice of the resolution is given by the charity trustees.

(8) The Commission may also direct the charity trustees to provide the Commission with additional information or explanations relating to –

     (a) the circumstances in and by reference to which they have decided to act under this section, or

     (b) their compliance with any obligation imposed on them by or under this section in connection with the resolution.

(9) Subject to the provisions of section 74A below, a resolution under subsection (2) above takes effect at the end of the period of 60 days beginning with the date on which the copy of it was received by the Commission.

(10) Where such a resolution has taken effect, the charity trustees must arrange for all the property of the transferor charity to be transferred in accordance with the resolution, and on terms that any property so transferred –

     (a) is to be held by the charity to which it is transferred ('the transferee charity') in accordance with subsection (11) below, but

     (b) when so held is nevertheless to be subject to any restrictions on expenditure to which it was subject as property of the transferor charity;

and the charity trustees must arrange for the property to be so transferred by such date after the resolution takes effect as they agree with the charity trustees of the transferee charity or charities concerned.

(11) The charity trustees of any charity to which property is transferred under this section must secure, so far as is reasonably practicable, that the property is applied for such of its purposes as are substantially similar to those of the transferor charity.

But this requirement does not apply if those charity trustees consider that complying with it would not result in a suitable and effective method of applying the property.

(12) For the purpose of enabling any property to be transferred to a charity under this section, the Commission may, at the request of the charity trustees of that charity, make orders vesting any property of the transferor charity –

    (a) in the transferee charity, in its charity trustees or in any trustee for that charity, or

    (b) in any other person nominated by those charity trustees to hold property in trust for that charity.

(13) The Minister may by order amend subsection (1) above by substituting a different sum for the sum for the time being specified there.

(14) In this section references to the transfer of property to a charity are references to its transfer –

    (a) to the charity, or

    (b) to the charity trustees, or

    (c) to any trustee for the charity, or

    (d) to a person nominated by the charity trustees to hold it in trust for the charity,

as the charity trustees may determine.

(15) Where a charity has a permanent endowment, this section has effect in accordance with section 74B.

74A Resolution not to take effect or to take effect at later date

(1) This section deals with circumstances in which a resolution under section 74(2) above either –

    (a) does not take effect under section 74(9) above, or

    (b) takes effect at a time later than that mentioned in section 74(9).

(2) A resolution does not take effect under section 74(9) above if before the end of –

    (a) the period of 60 days mentioned in section 74(9) ('the 60-day period'), or

    (b) that period as modified by subsection (3) or (4) below,

the Commission notifies the charity trustees in writing that it objects to the resolution, either on procedural grounds or on the merits of the proposals contained in the resolution.

'On procedural grounds' means on the grounds that any obligation imposed on the charity trustees by or under section 74 above has not been complied with in connection with the resolution.

(3) If under section 74(7) above the Commission directs the charity trustees to give public notice of a resolution, the running of the 60-day period is suspended by virtue of this subsection –

    (a) as from the date on which the direction is given to the charity trustees, and

    (b) until the end of the period of 42 days beginning with the date on which public notice of the resolution is given by the charity trustees.

(4) If under section 74(8) above the Commission directs the charity trustees to provide any information or explanations, the running of the 60-day period is suspended by virtue of this subsection –

    (a) as from the date on which the direction is given to the charity trustees, and

    (b) until the date on which the information or explanations is or are provided to the Commission.

(5) Subsection (6) below applies once the period of time, or the total period of time, during which the 60-day period is suspended by virtue of either or both of subsections (3) and (4) above exceeds 120 days.

(6) At that point the resolution (if not previously objected to by the Commission) is to be treated as if it had never been passed.

74B Transfer where charity has permanent endowment

(1) This section provides for the operation of section 74 above where a charity within section 74(1) has a permanent endowment (whether or not the charity's trusts contain provision for the termination of the charity).

(2) In such a case section 74 applies as follows –

    (a) if the charity has both a permanent endowment and other property ('unrestricted property') –

        (i) a resolution under section 74(2) must relate to both its permanent endowment and its unrestricted property, and

        (ii) that section applies in relation to its unrestricted property in accordance with subsection (3) below and in relation to its permanent endowment in accordance with subsections (4) to (11) below;

    (b) if all of the property of the charity is comprised in its permanent endowment, that section applies in relation to its permanent endowment in accordance with subsections (4) to (11) below.

(3) Section 74 applies in relation to unrestricted property of the charity as if references in that section to all or any of the property of the charity were references to all or any of its unrestricted property.

(4) Section 74 applies in relation to the permanent endowment of the charity with the following modifications.

(5) References in that section to all or any of the property of the charity are references to all or any of the property comprised in its permanent endowment.

(6) If the property comprised in its permanent endowment is to be transferred to a single charity, the charity trustees must (instead of being satisfied as mentioned in section 74(4)(b)) be satisfied that the proposed transferee charity has purposes which are substantially similar to all of the purposes of the transferor charity.

(7) If the property comprised in its permanent endowment is to be transferred to two or more charities, the charity trustees must (instead of being satisfied as mentioned in section 74(4)(b)) be satisfied –

    (a) that the proposed transferee charities, taken together, have purposes which are substantially similar to all of the purposes of the transferor charity, and

    (b) that each of the proposed transferee charities has purposes which are substantially similar to one or more of the purposes of the transferor charity.

(8) In the case of a transfer to which subsection (7) above applies, the resolution under section 74(2) must provide for the property comprised in the permanent endowment of the charity to be divided between the transferee charities in such a way as to take account of such guidance as may be given by the Commission for the purposes of this section.

(9) The requirement in section 74(11) shall apply in the case of every such transfer, and in complying with that requirement the charity trustees of a transferee charity must secure that the application of property transferred to the charity takes account of any such guidance.

(10) Any guidance given by the Commission for the purposes of this section may take such form and be given in such manner as the Commission considers appropriate.

(11) For the purposes of sections 74 and 74A above, any reference to any obligation imposed on the charity trustees by or under section 74 includes a reference to any obligation imposed on them by virtue of any of subsections (6) to (8) above.

(12) Section 74(14) applies for the purposes of this section as it applies for the purposes of section 74.

74C Power to replace purposes of unincorporated charity

(1) This section applies to a charity if –

    (a) its gross income in its last financial year did not exceed £10,000,

(b) it does not hold any designated land, and

(c) it is not a company or other body corporate.

'Designated land' means land held on trusts which stipulate that it is to be used for the purposes, or any particular purposes, of the charity.

(2) The charity trustees of such a charity may resolve for the purposes of this section that the trusts of the charity should be modified by replacing all or any of the purposes of the charity with other purposes specified in the resolution.

(3) The other purposes so specified must be charitable purposes.

(4) But the charity trustees of a charity do not have power to pass a resolution under subsection (2) above unless they are satisfied –

(a) that it is expedient in the interests of the charity for the purposes in question to be replaced, and

(b) that, so far as is reasonably practicable, the new purposes consist of or include purposes that are similar in character to those that are to be replaced.

(5) Any resolution under subsection (2) above must be passed by a majority of not less than two-thirds of the charity trustees who vote on the resolution.

(6) Where charity trustees have passed a resolution under subsection (2), they must send a copy of it to the Commission, together with a statement of their reasons for passing it.

(7) Having received the copy of the resolution, the Commission –

(a) may direct the charity trustees to give public notice of the resolution in such manner as is specified in the direction, and

(b) if it gives such a direction, must take into account any representations made to it by persons appearing to it to be interested in the charity, where those representations are made to it within the period of 28 days beginning with the date when public notice of the resolution is given by the charity trustees.

(8) The Commission may also direct the charity trustees to provide the Commission with additional information or explanations relating to –

(a) the circumstances in and by reference to which they have decided to act under this section, or

(b) their compliance with any obligation imposed on them by or under this section in connection with the resolution.

(9) Subject to the provisions of section 74A above (as they apply in accordance with subsection (10) below), a resolution under subsection (2) above takes effect at the end of the period of 60 days beginning with the date on which the copy of it was received by the Commission.

(10) Section 74A above applies to a resolution under subsection (2) of this section as it applies to a resolution under subsection (2) of section 74 above, except that any reference to section 74(7), (8) or (9) is to be read as a reference to subsection (7), (8) or (9) above.

(11) As from the time when a resolution takes effect under subsection (9) above, the trusts of the charity concerned are to be taken to have been modified in accordance with the terms of the resolution.

(12) The Minister may by order amend subsection (1) above by substituting a different sum for the sum for the time being specified there.

74D Power to modify powers or procedures of unincorporated charity

(1) This section applies to any charity which is not a company or other body corporate.

(2) The charity trustees of such a charity may resolve for the purposes of this section that any provision of the trusts of the charity –

(a) relating to any of the powers exercisable by the charity trustees in the administration of the charity, or

(b) regulating the procedure to be followed in any respect in connection with its administration,

should be modified in such manner as is specified in the resolution.

(3) Subsection (4) applies if the charity is an unincorporated association with a body of members distinct from the charity trustees.

(4) Any resolution of the charity trustees under subsection (2) must be approved by a further resolution which is passed at a general meeting of the body either –

(a) by a majority of not less than two-thirds of the members entitled to attend and vote at the meeting who vote on the resolution, or

(b) by a decision taken without a vote and without any expression of dissent in response to the question put to the meeting.

(5) Where –

(a) the charity trustees have passed a resolution under subsection (2), and

(b) (if subsection (4) applies) a further resolution has been passed under that subsection,

the trusts of the charity are to be taken to have been modified in accordance with the terms of the resolution.

(6) The trusts are to be taken to have been so modified as from such date as is specified for this purpose in the resolution under subsection (2), or (if later) the date when any such further resolution was passed under subsection (4).

75 Power of unincorporated charities to spend capital: general

(1) This section applies to any available endowment fund of a charity which is not a company or other body corporate.

(2) But this section does not apply to a fund if section 75A below (power of larger charities to spend capital given for particular purpose) applies to it.

(3) Where the condition in subsection (4) below is met in relation to the charity, the charity trustees may resolve for the purposes of this section that the fund, or a portion of it, ought to be freed from the restrictions with respect to expenditure of capital that apply to it.

(4) The condition in this subsection is that the charity trustees are satisfied that the purposes set out in the trusts to which the fund is subject could be carried out more effectively if the capital of the fund, or the relevant portion of the capital, could be expended as well as income accruing to it, rather than just such income.

(5) Once the charity trustees have passed a resolution under subsection (3) above, the fund or portion may by virtue of this section be expended in carrying out the purposes set out in the trusts to which the fund is subject without regard to the restrictions mentioned in that subsection.

(6) The fund or portion may be so expended as from such date as is specified for this purpose in the resolution.

(7) In this section 'available endowment fund', in relation to a charity, means –

(a) the whole of the charity's permanent endowment if it is all subject to the same trusts, or

(b) any part of its permanent endowment which is subject to any particular trusts that are different from those to which any other part is subject.

75A Power of larger unincorporated charities to spend capital given for particular purpose

(1) This section applies to any available endowment fund of a charity which is not a company or other body corporate if –

(a) the capital of the fund consists entirely of property given –

(i) by a particular individual,

> (ii) by a particular institution (by way of grant or otherwise), or
> (iii) by two or more individuals or institutions in pursuit of a common purpose, and

(b) the financial condition in subsection (2) below is met.

(2) The financial condition in this subsection is met if –

(a) the relevant charity's gross income in its last financial year exceeded £1,000, and
(b) the market value of the endowment fund exceeds £10,000.

(3) Where the condition in subsection (4) below is met in relation to the charity, the charity trustees may resolve for the purposes of this section that the fund, or a portion of it, ought to be freed from the restrictions with respect to expenditure of capital that apply to it.

(4) The condition in this subsection is that the charity trustees are satisfied that the purposes set out in the trusts to which the fund is subject could be carried out more effectively if the capital of the fund, or the relevant portion of the capital, could be expended as well as income accruing to it, rather than just such income.

(5) The charity trustees –

(a) must send a copy of any resolution under subsection (3) above to the Commission, together with a statement of their reasons for passing it, and
(b) may not implement the resolution except in accordance with the following provisions of this section.

(6) Having received the copy of the resolution the Commission may –

(a) direct the charity trustees to give public notice of the resolution in such manner as is specified in the direction, and
(b) if it gives such a direction, must take into account any representations made to it by persons appearing to it to be interested in the charity, where those representations are made to it within the period of 28 days beginning with the date when public notice of the resolution is given by the charity trustees.

(7) The Commission may also direct the charity trustees to provide the Commission with additional information or explanations relating to –

(a) the circumstances in and by reference to which they have decided to act under this section, or
(b) their compliance with any obligation imposed on them by or under this section in connection with the resolution.

(8) When considering whether to concur with the resolution the Commission must take into account –

(a) any evidence available to it as to the wishes of the donor or donors mentioned in subsection (1)(a) above, and
(b) any changes in the circumstances relating to the charity since the making of the gift or gifts (including, in particular, its financial position, the needs of its beneficiaries, and the social, economic and legal environment in which it operates).

(9) The Commission must not concur with the resolution unless it is satisfied –

(a) that its implementation would accord with the spirit of the gift or gifts mentioned in subsection (1)(a) above (even though it would be inconsistent with the restrictions mentioned in subsection (3) above), and
(b) that the charity trustees have complied with the obligations imposed on them by or under this section in connection with the resolution.

(10) Before the end of the period of three months beginning with the relevant date, the Commission must notify the charity trustees in writing either –

(a) that the Commission concurs with the resolution, or
(b) that it does not concur with it.

(11) In subsection (10) 'the relevant date' means –

    (a) in a case where the Commission directs the charity trustees under subsection (6) above to give public notice of the resolution, the date when that notice is given, and

    (b) in any other case, the date on which the Commission receives the copy of the resolution in accordance with subsection (5) above.

(12) Where –

    (a) the charity trustees are notified by the Commission that it concurs with the resolution, or

    (b) the period of three months mentioned in subsection (10) above has elapsed without the Commission notifying them that it does not concur with the resolution,

the fund or portion may, by virtue of this section, be expended in carrying out the purposes set out in the trusts to which the fund is subject without regard to the restrictions mentioned in subsection (3).

(13) The Minister may by order amend subsection (2) above by substituting a different sum for any sum specified there.

(14) In this section –

    (a) 'available endowment fund' has the same meaning as in section 75 above,

    (b) 'market value', in relation to an endowment fund, means –

        (i) the market value of the fund as recorded in the accounts for the last financial year of the relevant charity, or

        (ii) if no such value was so recorded, the current market value of the fund as determined on a valuation carried out for the purpose, and

    (c) the reference in subsection (1) to the giving of property by an individual includes his giving it under his will.

75B Power to spend capital subject to special trusts

(1) This section applies to any available endowment fund of a special trust which, as the result of a direction under section 96(5) below, is to be treated as a separate charity ('the relevant charity') for the purposes of this section.

(2) Where the condition in subsection (3) below is met in relation to the relevant charity, the charity trustees may resolve for the purposes of this section that the fund, or a portion of it, ought to be freed from the restrictions with respect to expenditure of capital that apply to it.

(3) The condition in this subsection is that the charity trustees are satisfied that the purposes set out in the trusts to which the fund is subject could be carried out more effectively if the capital of the fund, or the relevant portion of the capital, could be expended as well as income accruing to it, rather than just such income.

(4) Where the market value of the fund exceeds £10,000 and the capital of the fund consists entirely of property given –

    (a) by a particular individual,

    (b) by a particular institution (by way of grant or otherwise), or

    (c) by two or more individuals or institutions in pursuit of a common purpose,

subsections (5) to (11) of section 75A above apply in relation to the resolution and that gift or gifts as they apply in relation to a resolution under section 75A(3) and the gift or gifts mentioned in section 75A(1)(a).

(5) Where –

    (a) the charity trustees have passed a resolution under subsection (2) above, and

    (b) (in a case where section 75A(5) to (11) above apply in accordance with subsection (4) above) either –

    (i)   the charity trustees are notified by the Commission that it concurs with the resolution, or

    (ii)   the period of three months mentioned in section 75A(10) has elapsed without the Commission notifying them that it does not concur with the resolution,

the fund or portion may, by virtue of this section, be expended in carrying out the purposes set out in the trusts to which the fund is subject without regard to the restrictions mentioned in subsection (2).

(6)   The fund or portion may be so expended as from such date as is specified for this purpose in the resolution.

(7)   The Minister may by order amend subsection (4) above by substituting a different sum for the sum specified there.

(8)   In this section –

    (a)   'available endowment fund' has the same meaning as in section 75 above,

    (b)   'market value' has the same meaning as in section 75A above, and

    (c)   the reference in subsection (4) to the giving of property by an individual includes his giving it under his will.

Mergers

75C Register of charity mergers

(1)   The Commission shall establish and maintain a register of charity mergers.

(2)   The register shall be kept by the Commission in such manner as it thinks fit.

(3)   The register shall contain an entry in respect of every relevant charity merger which is notified to the Commission in accordance with subsections (6) to (9) and such procedures as it may determine.

(4)   In this section 'relevant charity merger' means –

    (a)   a merger of two or more charities in connection with which one of them ('the transferee') has transferred to it all the property of the other or others, each of which (a 'transferor') ceases to exist, or is to cease to exist, on or after the transfer of its property to the transferee, or

    (b)   a merger of two or more charities ('transferors') in connection with which both or all of them cease to exist, or are to cease to exist, on or after the transfer of all of their property to a new charity ('the transferee').

(5)   In the case of a merger involving the transfer of property of any charity which has both a permanent endowment and other property ('unrestricted property') and whose trusts do not contain provision for the termination of the charity, subsection (4)(a) or (b) applies in relation to any such charity as if –

    (a)   the reference to all of its property were a reference to all of its unrestricted property, and

    (b)   any reference to its ceasing to exist were omitted.

(6)   A notification under subsection (3) above may be given in respect of a relevant charity merger at any time after –

    (a)   the transfer of property involved in the merger has taken place, or

    (b)   (if more than one transfer of property is so involved) the last of those transfers has taken place.

(7)   If a vesting declaration is made in connection with a relevant charity merger, a notification under subsection (3) above must be given in respect of the merger once the transfer, or the last of the transfers, mentioned in subsection (6) above has taken place.

(8) A notification under subsection (3) is to be given by the charity trustees of the transferee and must –

    (a) specify the transfer or transfers of property involved in the merger and the date or dates on which it or they took place;

    (b) include a statement that appropriate arrangements have been made with respect to the discharge of any liabilities of the transferor charity or charities; and

    (c) in the case of a notification required by subsection (7), set out the matters mentioned in subsection (9).

(9) The matters are –

    (a) the fact that the vesting declaration in question has been made;

    (b) the date when the declaration was made; and

    (c) the date on which the vesting of title under the declaration took place by virtue of section 75E(2) below.

(10) In this section and section 75D –

    (a) any reference to a transfer of property includes a transfer effected by a vesting declaration; and

    (b) 'vesting declaration' means a declaration to which section 75E(2) below applies.

(11) Nothing in this section or section 75E or 75F applies in a case where section 69K (amalgamation of CIOs) or 69M (transfer of CIO's undertaking) applies.

75D Register of charity mergers: supplementary

(1) Subsection (2) applies to the entry to be made in the register in respect of a relevant charity merger, as required by section 75C(3) above.

(2) The entry must –

    (a) specify the date when the transfer or transfers of property involved in the merger took place,

    (b) if a vesting declaration was made in connection with the merger, set out the matters mentioned in section 75C(9) above, and

    (c) contain such other particulars of the merger as the Commission thinks fit.

(3) The register shall be open to public inspection at all reasonable times.

(4) Where any information contained in the register is not in documentary form, subsection (3) above shall be construed as requiring the information to be available for public inspection in legible form at all reasonable times.

(5) In this section –

'the register' means the register of charity mergers;
'relevant charity merger' has the same meaning as in section 75C.

75E Pre-merger vesting declarations

(1) Subsection (2) below applies to a declaration which –

    (a) is made by deed for the purposes of this section by the charity trustees of the transferor,

    (b) is made in connection with a relevant charity merger, and

    (c) is to the effect that (subject to subsections (3) and (4)) all of the transferor's property is to vest in the transferee on such date as is specified in the declaration ('the specified date').

(2) The declaration operates on the specified date to vest the legal title to all of the transferor's property in the transferee, without the need for any further document transferring it.

This is subject to subsections (3) and (4).

(3)   Subsection (2) does not apply to –

    (a)   any land held by the transferor as security for money subject to the trusts of the transferor (other than land held on trust for securing debentures or debenture stock);

    (b)   any land held by the transferor under a lease or agreement which contains any covenant (however described) against assignment of the transferor's interest without the consent of some other person, unless that consent has been obtained before the specified date; or

    (c)   any shares, stock, annuity or other property which is only transferable in books kept by a company or other body or in a manner directed by or under any enactment.

(4)   In its application to registered land within the meaning of the Land Registration Act 2002, subsection (2) has effect subject to section 27 of that Act (dispositions required to be registered).

(5)   In this section 'relevant charity merger' has the same meaning as in section 75C.

(6)   In this section –

    (a)   any reference to the transferor, in relation to a relevant charity merger, is a reference to the transferor (or one of the transferors) within the meaning of section 75C above, and

    (b)   any reference to all of the transferor's property, where the transferor is a charity within section 75C(5), is a reference to all of the transferor's unrestricted property (within the meaning of that provision).

(7)   In this section any reference to the transferee, in relation to a relevant charity merger, is a reference to –

    (a)   the transferee (within the meaning of section 75C above), if it is a company or other body corporate, and

    (b)   otherwise, to the charity trustees of the transferee (within the meaning of that section).

75F   Effect of registering charity merger on gifts to transferor

(1)   This section applies where a relevant charity merger is registered in the register of charity mergers.

(2)   Any gift which –

    (a)   is expressed as a gift to the transferor, and

    (b)   takes effect on or after the date of registration of the merger,

takes effect as a gift to the transferee, unless it is an excluded gift.

(3)   A gift is an 'excluded gift' if –

    (a)   the transferor is a charity within section 75C(5), and

    (b)   the gift is intended to be held subject to the trusts on which the whole or part of the charity's permanent endowment is held.

(4)   In this section –

'relevant charity merger' has the same meaning as in section 75C; and
'transferor' and 'transferee' have the same meanings as in section 75E.

Local charities

76   Local authority's index of local charities

(1)   The council of a county or county borough or of a district or London borough and the Common Council of the City of London may maintain an index of local charities or of any class of local charities in the council's area, and may publish information contained in the index, or summaries or extracts taken from it.

(2)   A council proposing to establish or maintaining under this section an index of local charities or of any class of local charities shall, on request, be supplied by the Commission free of charge with copies of such entries in the register of charities as are relevant to the index or with particulars of any changes in the entries of which copies have been supplied before; and the Commission may arrange that it will without further request supply a council with particulars of any such changes.

(3)   An index maintained under this section shall be open to public inspection at all reasonable times.

(4)   A council may employ any voluntary organisation as their agent for the purposes of this section, on such terms and within such limits (if any) or in such cases as they may agree; and for this purpose 'voluntary organisation' means any body of which the activities are carried on otherwise than for profit, not being a public or local authority.

(5)   A joint board discharging any of a council's functions shall have the same powers under this section as the council as respects local charities in the council's area which are established for purposes similar or complementary to any services provided by the board.

77   Reviews of local charities by local authority

(1)   The council of a county or county borough or of a district or London borough and the Common Council of the City of London may, subject to the following provisions of this section, initiate, and carry out in co-operation with the charity trustees, a review of the working of any group of local charities with the same or similar purposes in the council's area, and may make to the Commission such report on the review and such recommendations arising from it as the council after consultation with the trustees think fit.

(2)   A council having power to initiate reviews under this section may co-operate with other persons in any review by them of the working of local charities in the council's area (with or without other charities), or may join with other persons in initiating and carrying out such a review.

(3)   No review initiated by a council under this section shall extend to any charity without the consent of the charity trustees, nor to any ecclesiastical charity.

(4)   No review initiated under this section by the council of a district shall extend to the working in any county of a local charity established for purposes similar or complementary to any services provided by county councils unless the review so extends with the consent of the council of that county.

(4A) Subsection (4) above does not apply in relation to Wales.

(5)   Subsections (4) and (5) of section 76 above shall apply for the purposes of this section as they apply for the purposes of that section.

78   Co-operation between charities, and between charities and local authorities

(1)   Any local council and any joint board discharging any functions of such a council –

(a)   may make, with any charity established for purposes similar or complementary to services provided by the council or board, arrangements for co-ordinating the activities of the council or board and those of the charity in the interests of persons who may benefit from those services or from the charity; and

(b)   shall be at liberty to disclose to any such charity in the interests of those persons any information obtained in connection with the services provided by the council or board, whether or not arrangements have been made with the charity under this subsection.

In this subsection 'local council' means, in relation to England, the council of a county, or of a district, London borough, or parish, and includes also the Common Council of the City of London and the Council of the Isles of Scilly and, in relation to Wales, the council of a county, county borough or community.

(2) Charity trustees shall, notwithstanding anything in the trusts of the charity, have power by virtue of this subsection to do all or any of the following things, where it appears to them likely to promote or make more effective the work of the charity, and may defray the expense of so doing out of any income or money applicable as income of the charity, that is to say –

(a) they may co-operate in any review undertaken under section 77 above or otherwise of the working of charities or any class of charities;

(b) they may make arrangements with an authority acting under subsection (1) above or with another charity for co-ordinating their activities and those of the authority or of the other charity;

(c) they may publish information of other charities with a view to bringing them to the notice of those for whose benefit they are intended.

79   Parochial charities

(1) Where trustees hold any property for the purposes of a public recreation ground, or of allotments (whether under inclosure Acts or otherwise), for the benefit of inhabitants of a parish having a parish council, or for other charitable purposes connected with such a parish, except for an ecclesiastical charity, they may with the approval of the Commission and with the consent of the parish council transfer the property to the parish council or to persons appointed by the parish council; and the council or their appointees shall hold the property on the same trusts and subject to the same conditions as the trustees did.

This subsection shall apply to property held for any public purposes as it applies to property held for charitable purposes.

(2) Where the charity trustees of a parochial charity in a parish, not being an ecclesiastical charity nor a charity founded within the preceding forty years, do not include persons elected by the local government electors, ratepayers or inhabitants of the parish or appointed by the parish council or parish meeting, the parish council or parish meeting may appoint additional charity trustees, to such number as the Commission may allow; and if there is a sole charity trustee not elected or appointed as aforesaid of any such charity, the number of the charity trustees may, with the approval of the Commission, be increased to three of whom one may be nominated by the person holding the office of the sole trustee and one by the parish council or parish meeting.

(3) Where, under the trusts of a charity other than an ecclesiastical charity, the inhabitants of a rural parish (whether in vestry or not) or a select vestry were formerly (in 1894) entitled to appoint charity trustees for, or trustees or beneficiaries of, the charity, then –

(a) in a parish having a parish council, the appointment shall be made by the parish council or, in the case of beneficiaries, by persons appointed by the parish council; and

(b) in a parish not having a parish council, the appointment shall be made by the parish meeting.

(4) Where overseers as such or, except in the case of an ecclesiastical charity, churchwardens as such were formerly (in 1894) charity trustees of or trustees for a parochial charity in a rural parish, either alone or jointly with other persons, then instead of the former overseer or church warden trustees there shall be trustees (to a number not greater than that of the former overseer or churchwarden trustees) appointed by the parish council or, if there is no parish council, by the parish meeting.

(5) Where, outside Greater London (other than the outer London boroughs), overseers of a parish as such were formerly (in 1927) charity trustees of or trustees for any charity, either alone or jointly with other persons, then instead of the former overseer trustees there shall be trustees (to a number not greater than that of the former overseer

trustees) appointed by the parish council or, if there is no parish council, by the parish meeting.

(6)   In the case of an urban parish existing immediately before the passing of the Local Government Act 1972 which after 1st April 1974 is not comprised in a parish, the power of appointment under subsection (5) above shall be exercisable by the district council.

(7)   In the application of the foregoing provisions of this section to Wales –

(a)   for references in subsections (1) and (2) to a parish or a parish council there shall be substituted respectively references to a community or a community council;

(b)   for references in subsections (3)(a) and (b) to a parish, a parish council or a parish meeting there shall be substituted respectively references to a community, a community council or the council of the county or (as the case may be) county borough;

(c)   for references in subsections (4) and (5) to a parish council or a parish meeting there shall be substituted respectively references to a community council or the council of the county or (as the case may be) county borough.

(8)   Any appointment of a charity trustee or trustee for a charity which is made by virtue of this section shall be for a term of four years, and a retiring trustee shall be eligible for re-appointment but –

(a)   on an appointment under subsection (2) above, where no previous appointments have been made by virtue of that subsection or of the corresponding provision of the Local Government Act 1894 or the Charities Act 1960, and more than one trustee is appointed, half of those appointed (or as nearly as may be) shall be appointed for a term of two years; and

(b)   an appointment made to fill a casual vacancy shall be for the remainder of the term of the previous appointment.

(9)   This section shall not affect the trusteeship, control or management of any foundation or voluntary school within the meaning of the School Standards and Framework Act 1998.

(10) The provisions of this section shall not extend to the Isles of Scilly, and shall have effect subject to any order (including any future order) made under any enactment relating to local government with respect to local government areas or the powers of local authorities.

(11) In this section the expression 'formerly (in 1894)' relates to the period immediately before the passing of the Local Government Act 1894, and the expression 'formerly (in 1927)' to the period immediately before 1st April 1927; and the word 'former' shall be construed accordingly.

Scottish charities

80   Supervision by Commission of certain Scottish charities

(1)   The following provisions of this Act, namely –

(a)   sections 8 and 9,

(b)   section 18 (except subsection (2)(ii)),

(c)   sections 19 to 19C, and

(d)   section 31A,

shall have effect in relation to any recognised body which is managed or controlled wholly or mainly in or from England or Wales as they have effect in relation to a charity.

(2)   Where –

   (a)   a recognised body is managed or controlled wholly or mainly in or from Scotland, but

   (b)   any person in England and Wales holds any property on behalf of the body or of any person concerned in its management or control,

   then, if the Commission is satisfied as to the matters mentioned in subsection (3) below, it may make an order requiring the person holding the property not to part with it without the Commission's approval.

(3)   The matters referred to in subsection (2) above are –

   (a)   that there has been any misconduct or mismanagement in the administration of the body; and

   (b)   that it is necessary or desirable to make an order under that subsection for the purpose of protecting the property of the body or securing a proper application of such property for the purposes of the body;

   and the reference in that subsection to the Commission being satisfied as to those matters is a reference to the Commission being so satisfied on the basis of such information as may be supplied to it by the Scottish Charity Regulator.

(4)   Where –

   (a)   any person in England and Wales holds any property on behalf of a recognised body or of any person concerned in the management or control of such a body, and

   (b)   the Commission is satisfied (whether on the basis of such information as may be supplied to it by the Scottish Charity Regulator or otherwise) –

      (i)   that there has been any misconduct or mismanagement in the administration of the body, and

      (ii)   that it is necessary or desirable to make an order under this subsection for the purpose of protecting the property of the body or securing a proper application of such property for the purposes of the body,

   the Commission may by order vest the property in such recognised body or charity as is specified in the order in accordance with subsection (5) below, or require any persons in whom the property is vested to transfer it to any such body or charity, or appoint any person to transfer the property to any such body or charity.

(5)   The Commission may specify in an order under subsection (4) above such other recognised body or such charity as it considers appropriate, being a body or charity whose purposes are, in the opinion of the Commission, as similar in character to those of the body referred to in paragraph (a) of that subsection as is reasonably practicable; but the Commission shall not so specify any body or charity unless it has received –

   (a)   from the persons concerned in the management or control of the body, or

   (b)   from the charity trustees of the charity,

   as the case may be, written confirmation that they are willing to accept the property.

(6)   In this section 'recognised body' means a body entered in the Scottish Charity Register.

Administrative provisions about charities

81   Manner of giving notice of charity meetings, etc.

(1)   All notices which are required or authorised by the trusts of a charity to be given to a charity trustee, member or subscriber may be sent by post, and, if sent by post, may be addressed to any address given as his in the list of charity trustees, members or subscribers for the time being in use at the office or principal office of the charity.

(2)   Where any such notice required to be given as aforesaid is given by post, it shall be deemed to have been given by the time at which the letter containing it would be delivered in the ordinary course of post.

(3)   No notice required to be given as aforesaid of any meeting or election need be given to any charity trustee, member or subscriber, if in the list above mentioned he has no address in the United Kingdom.

82   Manner of executing instruments

(1)   Charity trustees may, subject to the trusts of the charity, confer on any of their body (not being less than two in number) a general authority, or an authority limited in such manner as the trustees think fit, to execute in the names and on behalf of the trustees assurances or other deeds or instruments for giving effect to transactions to which the trustees are a party; and any deed or instrument executed in pursuance of an authority so given shall be of the same effect as if executed by the whole body.

(2)   An authority under subsection (1) above –

   (a)   shall suffice for any deed or instrument if it is given in writing or by resolution of a meeting of the trustees, notwithstanding the want of any formality that would be required in giving an authority apart from that subsection;

   (b)   may be given so as to make the powers conferred exercisable by any of the trustees, or may be restricted to named persons or in any other way;

   (c)   subject to any such restriction, and until it is revoked, shall, notwithstanding any change in the charity trustees, have effect as a continuing authority given by the charity trustees from time to time of the charity and exercisable by such trustees.

(3)   In any authority under this section to execute a deed or instrument in the names and on behalf of charity trustees there shall, unless the contrary intention appears, be implied authority also to execute it for them in the name and on behalf of the official custodian or of any other person, in any case in which the charity trustees could do so.

(4)   Where a deed or instrument purports to be executed in pursuance of this section, then in favour of a person who (then or afterwards) in good faith acquires for money or money's worth an interest in or charge on property or the benefit of any covenant or agreement expressed to be entered into by the charity trustees, it shall be conclusively presumed to have been duly executed by virtue of this section.

(5)   The powers conferred by this section shall be in addition to and not in derogation of any other powers.

83   Transfer and evidence of title to property vested in trustees

(1)   Where, under the trusts of a charity, trustees of property held for the purposes of the charity may be appointed or discharged by resolution of a meeting of the charity trustees, members or other persons, a memorandum declaring a trustee to have been so appointed or discharged shall be sufficient evidence of that fact if the memorandum is signed either at the meeting by the person presiding or in some other manner directed by the meeting and is attested by two persons present at the meeting.

(2)   A memorandum evidencing the appointment or discharge of a trustee under subsection (1) above, if executed as a deed, shall have the like operation under section 40 of the Trustee Act 1925 (which relates to vesting declarations as respects trust property in deeds appointing or discharging trustees) as if the appointment or discharge were effected by the deed.

(3)   For the purposes of this section, where a document purports to have been signed and attested as mentioned in subsection (1) above, then on proof (whether by evidence or as a matter of presumption) of the signature the document shall be presumed to have been so signed and attested, unless the contrary is shown.

(4)   This section shall apply to a memorandum made at any time, except that subsection (2) shall apply only to those made after the commencement of the Charities Act 1960.

(5)   This section shall apply in relation to any institution to which the Literary and Scientific Institutions Act 1854 applies as it applies in relation to a charity.

PART X   SUPPLEMENTARY

84   Supply by Commission of copies of documents open to public inspection

The Commission shall, at the request of any person, furnish him with copies of, or extracts from, any document in the Commission's possession which is for the time being open to inspection under Parts II to VI of this Act or section 75D.

85   Fees and other amounts payable to Commission

(1)   The Secretary of State may by regulations require the payment to the Commission of such fees as may be prescribed by the regulations in respect of –

    (a)   the discharge by the Commission of such functions under the enactments relating to charities as may be so prescribed;

    (b)   the inspection of the register of charities or of other material kept by the Commission under those enactments, or the furnishing of copies of or extracts from documents so kept.

(2)   Regulations under this section may –

    (a)   confer, or provide for the conferring of, exemptions from liability to pay a prescribed fee;

    (b)   provide for the remission or refunding of a prescribed fee (in whole or in part) in circumstances prescribed by the regulations.

(3)   Any regulations under this section which require the payment of a fee in respect of any matter for which no fee was previously payable shall not be made unless a draft of the regulations has been laid before and approved by a resolution of each House of Parliament.

(4)   The Commission may impose charges of such amounts as it considers reasonable in respect of the supply of any publications produced by it.

(5)   Any fees and other payments received by the Commission by virtue of this section shall be paid into the Consolidated Fund.

86   Regulations and orders

(1)   Any regulations or order of the Secretary of State under this Act –

    (a)   shall be made by statutory instrument; and

    (b)   (subject to subsection (2) below) shall be subject to annulment in pursuance of a resolution of either House of Parliament.

(2)   Subsection (1)(b) above does not apply –

    (a)   to an order under section 17(2), 73F(6) or 99(2) or paragraph 6 of Schedule 1C; or

    (aa)   to regulations under section 69N above; and no regulations shall be made under that section unless a draft of the regulations has been laid before and approved by a resolution of each House of Parliament; or

    (b)   [. . .]

    (c)   to any regulations to which section 85(3) applies.

(3)   Any regulations of the Secretary of State or the Commission and any order of the Secretary of State under this Act may make –

(a) different provision for different cases; and

(b) such supplemental, incidental, consequential or transitional provision or savings as the Secretary of State or, as the case may be, the Commission considers appropriate.

(4) Before making any regulations under section 42, 44, 45, 69N or 69Q above or Schedule 5A the Secretary of State shall consult such persons or bodies of persons as he considers appropriate.

86A Consultation by Commission before exercising powers in relation to exempt charity

Before exercising in relation to an exempt charity any specific power exercisable by it in relation to the charity, the Commission must consult the charity's principal regulator.

87 Enforcement of requirements by order of Commission

(1) If a person fails to comply with any requirement imposed by or under this Act then (subject to subsection (2) below) the Commission may by order give him such directions as it considers appropriate for securing that the default is made good.

(2) Subsection (1) above does not apply to any such requirement if –

(a) a person who fails to comply with, or is persistently in default in relation to, the requirement is liable to any criminal penalty; or

(b) the requirement is imposed –

(i) by an order of the Commission to which section 88 below applies, or

(ii) by a direction of the Commission to which that section applies by virtue of section 90(2) below.

88 Enforcement of orders of Commission

A person guilty of disobedience –

(a) to an order of the Commission under section 9(1), 19A, 19B, 44(2), 61, 73, 73C or 80 above; or

(b) to an order of the Commission under section 16 or 18 above requiring a transfer of property or payment to be called for or made; or

(c) to an order of the Commission requiring a default under this Act to be made good;

may on the application of the Commission to the High Court be dealt with as for disobedience to an order of the High Court.

89 Other provisions as to orders of Commission

(1) Any order made by the Commission under this Act may include such incidental or supplementary provisions as the Commission thinks expedient for carrying into effect the objects of the order, and where the Commission exercises any jurisdiction to make such an order on an application or reference to it, it may insert any such provisions in the order notwithstanding that the application or reference does not propose their insertion.

(2) Where the Commission makes an order under this Act, then (without prejudice to the requirements of this Act where the order is subject to appeal) the Commission may itself give such public notice as it thinks fit of the making or contents of the order, or may require it to be given by any person on whose application the order is made or by any charity affected by the order.

(3) The Commission at any time within twelve months after it has made an order under any provision of this Act other than section 61 if it is satisfied that the order was made by mistake or on misrepresentation or otherwise than in conformity with this Act, may with or without any application or reference to it discharge the order in whole or in part, and subject or not to any savings or other transitional provisions.

(4)   Except for the purposes of subsection (3) above or of an appeal under this Act, an order made by the Commission under this Act shall be deemed to have been duly and formally made and not be called in question on the ground only of irregularity or informality, but (subject to any further order) have effect according to its tenor.

(5)   Any order made by the Commission under any provision of this Act may be varied or revoked by a subsequent order so made.

90   Directions of the Commission

(1)   Any direction given by the Commission under any provision contained in this Act –

(a)   may be varied or revoked by a further direction given under that provision; and

(b)   shall be given in writing.

(2)   Sections 88 and 89(1), (2) and (4) above shall apply to any such directions as they apply to an order of the Commission.

(3)   In subsection (1) above the reference to the Commission includes, in relation to a direction under subsection (3) of section 8 above, a reference to any person conducting an inquiry under that section.

(4)   Nothing in this section shall be read as applying to any directions contained in an order made by the Commission under section 87(1) above.

91   Service of orders and directions

(1)   This section applies to any order or direction made or given by the Commission under this Act.

(2)   An order or direction to which this section applies may be served on a person (other than a body corporate) –

(a)   by delivering it to that person;

(b)   by leaving it at his last known address in the United Kingdom; or

(c)   by sending it by post to him at that address.

(3)   An order or direction to which this section applies may be served on a body corporate by delivering it or sending it by post –

(a)   to the registered or principal office of the body in the United Kingdom, or

(b)   if it has no such office in the United Kingdom, to any place in the United Kingdom where it carries on business or conducts its activities (as the case may be).

(4)   Any such order or direction may also be served on a person (including a body corporate) by sending it by post to that person at an address notified by that person to the Commission for the purposes of this subsection.

(5)   In this section any reference to the Commission includes, in relation to a direction given under subsection (3) of section 8 above, a reference to any person conducting an inquiry under that section.

92   [. . .]

93   Miscellaneous provisions as to evidence

(1)   Where, in any proceedings to recover or compel payment of any rentcharge or other periodical payment claimed by or on behalf of a charity out of land or of the rents, profits or other income of land, otherwise than as rent incident to a reversion, it is shown that the rentcharge or other periodical payment has at any time been paid for twelve consecutive years to or for the benefit of the charity, that shall be prima facie evidence of the perpetual liability to it of the land or income, and no proof of its origin shall be necessary.

(2)   In any proceedings, the following documents, that is to say, –

   (a)   the printed copies of the reports of the Commissioners for enquiring concerning charities, 1818 to 1837, who were appointed under the Act 58 Geo. 3. c.91 and subsequent Acts; and

   (b)   the printed copies of the reports which were made for various counties and county boroughs to the Charity Commissioners by their assistant commissioners and presented to the House of Commons as returns to orders of various dates beginning with 8th December 1890, and ending with 9th September 1909,

   shall be admissible as evidence of the documents and facts stated in them.

(3)   Evidence of any order, certificate or other document issued by the Commission may be given by means of a copy which it retained, or which is taken from a copy so retained, and evidence of an entry in any register kept by it may be given by means of a copy of the entry, if (in each case) the copy is certified in accordance with subsection (4).

(4)   The copy shall be certified to be a true copy by any member of the staff of the Commission generally or specially authorised by the Commission to act for that purpose.

(5)   A document purporting to be such a copy shall be received in evidence without proof of the official position, authority or handwriting of the person certifying it.

(6)   In subsection (3) above 'the Commission' includes the Charity Commissioners for England and Wales.

94   Restriction on institution of proceedings for certain offences

(1)   No proceedings for an offence under this Act to which this section applies shall be instituted except by or with the consent of the Director of Public Prosecutions.

(2)   This section applies to any offence under –

   (a)   section 5;
   (b)   section 11;
   (c)   section 18(14);
   (d)   section 49; or
   (e)   section 73(1).

95   Offences by bodies corporate

Where any offence under this Act is committed by a body corporate and is proved to have been committed with the consent or connivance of, or to be attributable to any neglect on the part of, any director, manager, secretary or other similar officer of the body corporate, or any person who was purporting to act in any such capacity, he as well as the body corporate shall be guilty of that offence and shall be liable to be proceeded against and punished accordingly.

   In relation to a body corporate whose affairs are managed by its members, 'director' means a member of the body corporate.

96   Construction of references to a 'charity' or to particular classes of charity

(1)   In this Act, except in so far as the context otherwise requires –

   'charity' has the meaning given by section 1(1) of the Charities Act 2006;
   'ecclesiastical charity' has the same meaning as in the Local Government Act 1894;
   'exempt charity' means a charity comprised in Schedule 2 to this Act;
   'local charity' means, in relation to any area, a charity established for purposes which are by their nature or by the trusts of the charity directed wholly or mainly to the benefit of that area or of part of it;
   'parochial charity' means, in relation to any parish or (in Wales) community, a charity the benefits of which are, or the separate distribution of the benefits of which

is, confined to inhabitants of the parish or community, or of a single ancient ecclesiastical parish which included that parish or community or part of it, or of an area consisting of that parish or community with not more than four neighbouring parishes or communities.

(2)   The expression 'charity' is not in this Act applicable –

(a)   to any ecclesiastical corporation (that is to say, any corporation in the Church of England, whether sole or aggregate, which is established for spiritual purposes) in respect of the corporate property of the corporation, except to a corporation aggregate having some purposes which are not ecclesiastical in respect of its corporate property held for those purposes; or

(b)   to any Diocesan Board of Finance (or any subsidiary thereof) within the meaning of the Endowments and Glebe Measure 1976 for any diocese in respect of the diocesan glebe land of that diocese within the meaning of that Measure; or

(c)   to any trust of property for purposes for which the property has been consecrated.

(3)   A charity shall be deemed for the purposes of this Act to have a permanent endowment unless all property held for the purposes of the charity may be expended for those purposes without distinction between capital and income, and in this Act 'permanent endowment' means, in relation to any charity, property held subject to a restriction on its being expended for the purposes of the charity.

(4)   [. . .]

(5)   The Commission may direct that for all or any of the purposes of this Act an institution established for any special purposes of or in connection with a charity (being charitable purposes) shall be treated as forming part of that charity or as forming a distinct charity.

(6)   The Commission may direct that for all or any of the purposes of this Act two or more charities having the same charity trustees shall be treated as a single charity.

97   General interpretation

(1)   In this Act, except in so far as the context otherwise requires –

'charitable purposes' means purposes which are exclusively charitable purposes as defined by section 2(1) of the Charities Act 2006;

'charity trustees' means the persons having the general control and management of the administration of a charity;

'CIO' means charitable incorporated organisation;

'the Commission' means the Charity Commission;

'company' means a company formed and registered under the Companies Act 1985 or to which the provisions of that Act apply as they apply to such a company;

'the court' means the High Court and, within the limits of its jurisdiction, any other court in England and Wales having a jurisdiction in respect of charities concurrent (within any limit of area or amount) with that of the High Court, and includes any judge or officer of the court exercising the jurisdiction of the court;

'financial year' –

(a)   in relation to a charity which is a company, shall be construed in accordance with section 223 of the Companies Act 1985; and

(b)   in relation to any other charity, shall be construed in accordance with regulations made by virtue of section 42(2) above;

but this definition is subject to the transitional provisions in section 99(4) below and Part II of Schedule 8 to this Act;

'gross income', in relation to charity, means its gross recorded income from all sources including special trusts;

'independent examiner', in relation to a charity, means such a person as is mentioned in section 43(3)(a) above;

'institution' means an institution whether incorporated or not, and includes any trust or undertaking;

'members', in relation to a charity with a body of members distinct from the charity trustees, means any of those members;

'the Minister' means the Minister for the Cabinet Office;

'the official custodian' means the official custodian for charities;

'permanent endowment' shall be construed in accordance with section 96(3) above;

'principal regulator', in relation to an exempt charity, means the charity's principal regulator within the meaning of section 13 of the Charities Act 2006;

'the register' means the register of charities kept under section 3 above and 'registered' shall be construed accordingly;

'special trust' means property which is held and administered by or on behalf of a charity for any special purposes of the charity, and is so held and administered on separate trusts relating only to that property but a special trust shall not, by itself, constitute a charity for the purposes of Part VI of this Act;

'the Tribunal' means the Charity Tribunal;

'trusts' in relation to a charity, means the provisions establishing it as a charity and regulating its purposes and administration, whether those provisions take effect by way of trust or not, and in relation to other institutions has a corresponding meaning.

(2) In this Act, except in so far as the context otherwise requires, 'document' includes information recorded in any form, and, in relation to information recorded otherwise than in legible form –

(a) any reference to its production shall be construed as a reference to the furnishing of a copy of it in legible form; and

(b) any reference to the furnishing of a copy of, or extract from, it shall accordingly be construed as a reference to the furnishing of a copy of, or extract from, it in legible form.

(3) No vesting or transfer of any property in pursuance of any provision of Part 4, 7, 8A or 9 of this Act shall operate as a breach of a covenant or condition against alienation or give rise to a forfeiture.

98   Consequential amendments and repeals

(1) The enactments mentioned in Schedule 6 to this Act shall be amended as provided in that Schedule.

(2) The enactments mentioned in Schedule 7 to this Act are hereby repealed to the extent specified in the third column of the Schedule.

99   [. . .]

100   Short title and extent

(1) This Act may be cited as the Charities Act 1993.

(2) Subject to subsection (3) to (6) below, this Act extends only to England and Wales.

(3) Sections 10 to 10C above and this section extend to the whole of the United Kingdom.

(4) Section 15(2) and sections 24 to 25A extend also to Northern Ireland.

(5) [. . .]

(6) The amendments in Schedule 6 and the repeals in Schedule 7 have the same extent as the enactments to which they refer and section 98 above extends accordingly.

SCHEDULES

SCHEDULE 1   [. . .]

SCHEDULE 1A   THE CHARITY COMMISSION   Section 1A

Membership

1   (1)   The Commission shall consist of a chairman and at least four, but not more than eight, other members.

   (2)   The members shall be appointed by the Minister.

   (3)   The Minister shall exercise the power in sub-paragraph (2) so as to secure that –

   (a)   the knowledge and experience of the members of the Commission (taken together) includes knowledge and experience of the matters mentioned in sub-paragraph (4),

   (b)   at least two members have a seven year general qualification within the meaning of section 71 of the Courts and Legal Services Act 1990, and

   (c)   at least one member knows about conditions in Wales and has been appointed following consultation with the National Assembly for Wales.

   (4)   The matters mentioned in this sub-paragraph are –

   (a)   the law relating to charities,

   (b)   charity accounts and the financing of charities, and

   (c)   the operation and regulation of charities of different sizes and descriptions.

   (5)   In sub-paragraph (3)(c) 'member' does not include the chairman of the Commission.

Terms of appointment and remuneration

2   The members of the Commission shall hold and vacate office as such in accordance with the terms of their respective appointments.

3   (1)   An appointment of a person to hold office as a member of the Commission shall be for a term not exceeding three years.

   (2)   A person holding office as a member of the Commission –

   (a)   may resign that office by giving notice in writing to the Minister, and

   (b)   may be removed from office by the Minister on the ground of incapacity or misbehaviour.

   (3)   Before removing a member of the Commission the Minister shall consult –

   (a)   the Commission, and

   (b)   if the member was appointed following consultation with the National Assembly for Wales, the Assembly.

   (4)   No person may hold office as a member of the Commission for more than ten years in total.

   (5)   For the purposes of sub-paragraph (4), time spent holding office as a Charity Commissioner for England and Wales shall be counted as time spent holding office as a member of the Commission.

4   (1)   The Commission shall pay to its members such remuneration, and such other allowances, as may be determined by the Minister.

   (2)   The Commission shall, if required to do so by the Minister –

   (a)   pay such pension, allowances or gratuities as may be determined by the Minister to or in respect of a person who is or has been a member of the Commission, or

(b)   make such payments as may be so determined towards provision for the payment of a pension, allowances or gratuities to or in respect of such a person.

(3)   If the Minister determines that there are special circumstances which make it right for a person ceasing to hold office as a member of the Commission to receive compensation, the Commission shall pay to him a sum by way of compensation of such amount as may be determined by the Minister.

Staff

5   (1)   The Commission –

(a)   shall appoint a chief executive, and

(b)   may appoint such other staff as it may determine.

(2)   The terms and conditions of service of persons appointed under sub-paragraph (1) are to be such as the Commission may determine with the approval of the Minister for the Civil Service.

Committees

6   (1)   The Commission may establish committees and any committee of the Commission may establish sub-committees.

(2)   The members of a committee of the Commission may include persons who are not members of the Commission (and the members of a sub-committee may include persons who are not members of the committee or of the Commission).

Procedure etc.

7   (1)   The Commission may regulate its own procedure (including quorum).

(2)   The validity of anything done by the Commission is not affected by a vacancy among its members or by a defect in the appointment of a member.

Performance of functions

8   Anything authorised or required to be done by the Commission may be done by –

(a)   any member or member of staff of the Commission who is authorised for that purpose by the Commission, whether generally or specially;

(b)   any committee of the Commission which has been so authorised.

Evidence

9   The Documentary Evidence Act 1868 shall have effect as if –

(a)   the Commission were mentioned in the first column of the Schedule to that Act,

(b)   any member or member of staff of the Commission authorised to act on behalf of the Commission were specified in the second column of that Schedule in connection with the Commission, and

(c)   the regulations referred to in that Act included any document issued by or under the authority of the Commission.

Execution of documents

10   (1)   A document is executed by the Commission by the fixing of its common seal to the document.

(2)   But the fixing of that seal to a document must be authenticated by the signature of –

(a)   any member of the Commission, or

(b)   any member of its staff,

who is authorised for the purpose by the Commission.

(3) A document which is expressed (in whatever form of words) to be executed by the Commission and is signed by –

    (a)   any member of the Commission, or

    (b)   any member of its staff,

who is authorised for the purpose by the Commission has the same effect as if executed in accordance with sub-paragraphs (1) and (2).

(4) A document executed by the Commission which makes it clear on its face that it is intended to be a deed has effect, upon delivery, as a deed; and it is to be presumed (unless a contrary intention is proved) to be delivered upon its being executed.

(5) In favour of a purchaser a document is to be deemed to have been duly executed by the Commission if it purports to be signed on its behalf by –

    (a)   any member of the Commission, or

    (b)   any member of its staff;

and, where it makes it clear on its face that it is intended to be a deed, it is to be deemed to have been delivered upon its being executed.

(6) For the purposes of this paragraph –

'authorised' means authorised whether generally or specially; and

'purchaser' means a purchaser in good faith for valuable consideration and includes a lessee, mortgagee or other person who for valuable consideration acquired an interest in property.

Annual report

11   (1) As soon as practicable after the end of each financial year the Commission shall publish a report on –

    (a)   the discharge of its functions,

    (b)   the extent to which, in its opinion, its objectives (see section 1B of this Act) have been met,

    (c)   the performance of its general duties (see section 1D of this Act), and

    (d)   the management of its affairs,

during that year.

   (2) The Commission shall lay a copy of each such report before Parliament.

   (3) In sub-paragraph (1) above, 'financial year' means –

    (a)   the period beginning with the date on which the Commission is established and ending with the next 31st March following that date, and

    (b)   each successive period of 12 months ending with 31st March.

Annual public meeting

12   (1) The Commission shall hold a public meeting ('the annual meeting') for the purpose of enabling a report under paragraph 11 above to be considered.

   (2) The annual meeting shall be held within the period of three months beginning with the day on which the report is published.

   (3) The Commission shall organise the annual meeting so as to allow –

    (a)   a general discussion of the contents of the report which is being considered, and

    (b)   a reasonable opportunity for those attending the meeting to put questions to the Commission about matters to which the report relates.

   (4) But subject to sub-paragraph (3) above the annual meeting is to be organised and conducted in such a way as the Commission considers appropriate.

(5) The Commission shall –

    (a)   take such steps as are reasonable in the circumstances to ensure that notice of the annual meeting is given to every registered charity, and

    (b)   publish notice of the annual meeting in the way appearing to it to be best calculated to bring it to the attention of members of the public.

(6) Each such notice shall –

    (a)   give details of the time and place at which the meeting is to be held,

    (b)   set out the proposed agenda for the meeting,

    (c)   indicate the proposed duration of the meeting, and

    (d)   give details of the Commission's arrangements for enabling persons to attend.

(7) If the Commission proposes to alter any of the arrangements which have been included in notices given or published under sub-paragraph (5) above it shall –

    (a)   give reasonable notice of the alteration, and

    (b)   publish the notice in the way appearing to it to be best calculated to bring it to the attention of registered charities and members of the public.

SCHEDULE 1B   THE CHARITY TRIBUNAL   Section 2A(3)

Membership

1   (1) The Tribunal shall consist of the President and its other members.

    (2) The Lord Chancellor shall appoint –

       (a)   a President of the Tribunal,

       (b)   legal members of the Tribunal, and

       (c)   ordinary members of the Tribunal.

    (3) A person may be appointed as the President or a legal member of the Tribunal only if he has a seven year general qualification within the meaning of section 71 of the Courts and Legal Services Act 1990.

    (4) A person may be appointed as an ordinary member of the Tribunal only if he appears to the Lord Chancellor to have appropriate knowledge or experience relating to charities.

Deputy President

2   (1) The Lord Chancellor may appoint a legal member as deputy President of the Tribunal.

    (2) The deputy President –

       (a)   may act for the President when he is unable to act or unavailable, and

       (b)   shall perform such other functions as the President may delegate or assign to him.

Terms of appointment

3   (1) The members of the Tribunal shall hold and vacate office as such in accordance with the terms of their respective appointments.

    (2) A person holding office as a member of the Tribunal –

       (a)   may resign that office by giving notice in writing to the Lord Chancellor, and

       (b)   may be removed from office by the Lord Chancellor on the ground of incapacity or misbehaviour.

(3) A previous appointment of a person as a member of the Tribunal does not affect his eligibility for re-appointment as a member of the Tribunal.

Retirement etc.

4   (1) A person shall not hold office as a member of the Tribunal after reaching the age of 70.

(2) Section 26(5) and (6) of the Judicial Pensions and Retirement Act 1993 (extension to age 75) apply in relation to a member of the Tribunal as they apply in relation to a holder of a relevant office.

Remuneration etc.

5   (1) The Lord Chancellor may pay to the members of the Tribunal such remuneration, and such other allowances, as he may determine.

(2) The Lord Chancellor may –

(a) pay such pension, allowances or gratuities as he may determine to or in respect of a person who is or has been a member of the Tribunal, or

(b) make such payments as he may determine towards provision for the payment of a pension, allowances or gratuities to or in respect of such a person.

(3) If the Lord Chancellor determines that there are special circumstances which make it right for a person ceasing to hold office as a member of the Tribunal to receive compensation, the Lord Chancellor may pay to him a sum by way of compensation of such amount as may be determined by the Lord Chancellor.

Staff and facilities

6   The Lord Chancellor may make staff and facilities available to the Tribunal.

Panels

7   (1) The functions of the Tribunal shall be exercised by panels of the Tribunal.

(2) Panels of the Tribunal shall sit at such times and in such places as the President may direct.

(3) Before giving a direction under sub-paragraph (2) above the President shall consult the Lord Chancellor.

(4) More than one panel may sit at a time.

Panels

8   (1) The President shall make arrangements for determining which of the members of the Tribunal are to constitute a panel of the Tribunal in relation to the exercise of any function.

(2) Those arrangements shall, in particular, ensure that each panel is constituted in one of the following ways –

(a) as the President sitting alone,

(b) as a legal member sitting alone,

(c) as the President sitting with two other members,

(d) as a legal member sitting with two other members,

(e) as the President sitting with one other member,

(f) as a legal member sitting with one other member,

(and references in paragraphs (d) and (f) to other members do not include the President).

(3) The President shall publish arrangements made under this paragraph.

Practice and procedure

9   (1) Decisions of the Tribunal may be taken by majority vote.

(2) In the case of a panel constituted in accordance with paragraph 8(2)(e), the President shall have a casting vote.

(3) In the case of a panel constituted in accordance with paragraph 8(2)(f) which consists of a legal member and an ordinary member, the legal member shall have a casting vote.

(4) The President shall make and publish arrangements as to who is to have a casting vote in the case of a panel constituted in accordance with paragraph 8(2)(f) which consists of two legal members.

10   The President may, subject to rules under section 2B of this Act, give directions about the practice and procedure of the Tribunal.

SCHEDULE 1C   APPEALS AND APPLICATIONS TO CHARITY TRIBUNAL   Section 2A(4)

Appeals: general

1   (1) Except in the case of a reviewable matter (see paragraph 3) an appeal may be brought to the Tribunal against any decision, direction or order mentioned in column 1 of the Table.

(2) Such an appeal may be brought by –

(a)   the Attorney General, or

(b)   any person specified in the corresponding entry in column 2 of the Table.

(3) The Commission shall be the respondent to such an appeal.

(4) In determining such an appeal the Tribunal –

(a)   shall consider afresh the decision, direction or order appealed against, and

(b)   may take into account evidence which was not available to the Commission.

(5) The Tribunal may –

(a)   dismiss the appeal, or

(b)   if it allows the appeal, exercise any power specified in the corresponding entry in column 3 of the Table.

Appeals: orders under section 9

2   (1) Paragraph 1(4)(a) above does not apply in relation to an appeal against an order made under section 9 of this Act.

(2) On such an appeal the Tribunal shall consider whether the information or document in question –

(a)   relates to a charity;

(b)   is relevant to the discharge of the functions of the Commission or the official custodian.

(3) The Tribunal may allow such an appeal only if it is satisfied that the information or document in question does not fall within either paragraph (a) or paragraph (b) of sub-paragraph (2) above.

Reviewable matters

3   (1) In this Schedule references to 'reviewable matters' are to –

(a)   decisions to which sub-paragraph (2) applies, and

(b)   orders to which sub-paragraph (3) applies.

(2) This sub-paragraph applies to decisions of the Commission –

    (a)   to institute an inquiry under section 8 of this Act with regard to a particular institution,

    (b)   to institute an inquiry under section 8 of this Act with regard to a class of institutions,

    (c)   not to make a common investment scheme under section 24 of this Act,

    (d)   not to make a common deposit scheme under section 25 of this Act,

    (e)   not to make an order under section 26 of this Act in relation to a charity,

    (f)   not to make an order under section 36 of this Act in relation to land held by or in trust for a charity,

    (g)   not to make an order under section 38 of this Act in relation to a mortgage of land held by or in trust for a charity.

(3) This sub-paragraph applies to an order made by the Commission under section 69(1) of this Act in relation to a company which is a charity.

Reviews

4   (1)   An application may be made to the Tribunal for the review of a reviewable matter.

    (2)   Such an application may be made by –

    (a)   the Attorney General, or

    (b)   any person mentioned in the entry in column 2 of the Table which corresponds to the entry in column 1 which relates to the reviewable matter.

    (3)   The Commission shall be the respondent to such an application.

    (4)   In determining such an application the Tribunal shall apply the principles which would be applied by the High Court on an application for judicial review.

    (5)   The Tribunal may –

    (a)   dismiss the application, or

    (b)   if it allows the application, exercise any power mentioned in the entry in column 3 of the Table which corresponds to the entry in column 1 which relates to the reviewable matter.

Interpretation: remission of matters to Commission

5   References in column 3 of the Table to the power to remit a matter to the Commission are to the power to remit the matter either –

(a) generally, or

(b) for determination in accordance with a finding made or direction given by the Tribunal.

TABLE

1	2	3
Decision of the Commission under section 3 or 3A of this Act – (a) to enter or not to enter an institution in the register of charities, or	The persons are – (a) the persons who are or claim to be the charity trustees of the institution,	Power to quash the decision and (if appropriate) – (a) remit the matter to the Commission,

1	2	3
(b) to remove or not to remove an institution from the register.	(b) (if a body corporate) the institution itself, and (c) any other person who is or may be affected by the decision.	(b) direct the Commission to rectify the register.
Decision of the Commission not to make a determination under section 3(9) of this Act in relation to particular information contained in the register.	The persons are – (a) the charity trustees of the charity to which the information relates, (b) (if a body corporate) the charity itself, and (c) any other person who is or may be affected by the decision.	Power to quash the decision and (if appropriate) remit the matter to the Commission.
Direction given by the Commission under section 6 of this Act requiring the name of a charity to be changed.	The persons are – (a) the charity trustees of the charity to which the direction relates, (b) (if a body corporate) the charity itself, and (c) any other person who is or may be affected by the direction.	Power to – (a) quash the direction and (if appropriate) remit the matter to the Commission, (b) substitute for the direction any other direction which could have been given by the Commission.
Decision of the Commission to institute an inquiry under section 8 of this Act with regard to a particular institution.	The persons are – (a) the persons who have control or management of the institution, and (b) (if a body corporate) the institution itself.	Power to direct the Commission to end the inquiry.
Decision of the Commission to institute an inquiry under section 8 of this Act with regard to a class of institutions.	The persons are – (a) the persons who have control or management of any institution which is a member of the class of institutions, and (b) (if a body corporate) any such institution.	Power to – (a) direct the Commission that the inquiry should not consider a particular institution, (b) direct the Commission to end the inquiry.
Order made by the Commission under section 9 of this Act requiring a person to supply information or a document.	The persons are any person who is required to supply the information or document.	Power to – (a) quash the order, (b) substitute for all or part of the order any other order which could have been made by the Commission.

1	2	3
Order made by the Commission under section 16(1) of this Act (including such an order made by virtue of section 23(1)).	The persons are – (a) in a section 16(1)(a) case, the charity trustees of the charity to which the order relates or (if a body corporate) the charity itself, (b) in a section 16(1)(b) case, any person discharged or removed by the order, and (c) any other person who is or may be affected by the order.	Power to – (a) quash the order in whole or in part and (if appropriate) remit the matter to the Commission, (b) substitute for all or part of the order any other order which could have been made by the Commission, (c) add to the order anything which could have been contained in an order made by the Commission.
Order made by the Commission under section 18(1) of this Act in relation to a charity.	The persons are – (a) the charity trustees of the charity, (b) (if a body corporate) the charity itself, (c) in a section 18(1)(i) case, any person suspended by the order, and (d) any other person who is or may be affected by the order.	Power to – (a) quash the order in whole or in part and (if appropriate) remit the matter to the Commission, (b) substitute for all or part of the order any other order which could have been made by the Commission, (c) add to the order anything which could have been contained in an order made by the Commission.
Order made by the Commission under section 18(2) of this Act in relation to a charity.	The persons are – (a) the charity trustees of the charity, (b) (if a body corporate) the charity itself, (c) in a section 18(2)(i) case, any person removed by the order, and (d) any other person who is or may be affected by the order.	Power to – (a) quash the order in (whole or in part and (if appropriate) remit the matter to the Commission, (b) substitute for all or part of the order any other order which could have been made by the Commission, (c) add to the order anything which could have been contained in an order made by the Commission.

1	2	3
Order made by the Commission under section 18(4) of this Act removing a charity trustee.	The persons are – (a) the charity trustee, (b) the remaining charity trustees of the charity of which he was a charity trustee, (c) (if a body corporate) the charity itself, and (d) any other person who is or may be affected by the order.	Power to – (a) quash the order in whole or in part and (if appropriate) remit the matter to the Commission, (b) substitute for all or part of the order any other order which could have been made by the Commission, (c) add to the order anything which could have been contained in an order made by the Commission.
Order made by the Commission under section 18(5) of this Act appointing a charity trustee.	The persons are – (a) the other charity trustees of the charity, (b) (if a body corporate) the charity itself, and (c) any other person who is or may be affected by the order.	Power to – (a) quash the order in whole or in part and (if appropriate) remit the matter to the Commission, (b) substitute for all or part of the order any other order which could have been made by the Commission, (c) add to the order anything which could have been contained in an order made by the Commission.
Decision of the Commission – (a) to discharge an order following a review under section 18(13) of this Act, or (b) not to discharge an order following such a review.	The persons are – (a) the charity trustees of the charity to which the order relates, (b) (if a body corporate) the charity itself, (c) if the order in question was made under section 18(1)(i), any person suspended by it, and (d) any other person who is or may be affected by the order.	Power to – (a) quash the decision and (if appropriate) remit the matter to the Commission, (b) make the discharge of the order subject to savings or other transitional provisions, (c) remove any savings or other transitional provisions to which the discharge of the order was subject, (d) discharge the order in whole or in part (whether subject to any savings or other transitional provisions or not).

1	2	3
Order made by the Commission under section 18A(2) of this Act which suspends a person's membership of a charity.	The persons are – (a) the person whose membership is suspended by the order, and (b) any other person who is or may be affected by the order.	Power to quash the order and (if appropriate) remit the matter to the Commission.
Order made by the Commission under section 19A(2) of this Act which directs a person to take action specified in the order	The persons are any person who is directed by the order to take the specified action.	Power to quash the order and (if appropriate) remit the matter to the Commission.
Order made by the Commission under section 19B(2) of this Act which directs a person to apply property in a specified manner.	The persons are any person who is directed by the order to apply the property in the specified manner.	Power to quash the order and (if appropriate) remit the matter to the Commission.
Order made by the Commission under section 23(2) of this Act in relation to any land vested in the official custodian in trust for a charity.	The persons are – (a) the charity trustees of the charity, (b) (if a body corporate) the charity itself, and (c) any other person who is or may be affected by the order.	Power to – (a) quash the order and (if appropriate) remit the matter to the Commission, (b) substitute for the order any other order which could have been made by the Commission, (c) add to the order anything which could have been contained in an order made by the Commission.
Decision of the Commission not to make a common investment scheme under section 24 of this Act.	The persons are – (a) the charity trustees of a charity which applied to the Commission for the scheme, (b) (if a body corporate) the charity itself, and (c) any other person who is or may be affected by the decision.	Power to quash the decision and (if appropriate) remit the matter to the Commission.
Decision of the Commission not to make a common deposit scheme under section 25 of this Act.	The persons are – (a) the charity trustees of a charity which applied to the Commission for the scheme,	Power to quash the decision and (if appropriate) remit the matter to the Commission.

1	2	3
	(b) (if a body corporate) the charity itself, and (c) any other person who is or may be affected by the decision.	
Decision by the Commission not to make an order under section 26 of this Act in relation to a charity.	The persons are – (a) the charity trustees of the charity, and (b) (if a body corporate) the charity itself.	Power to quash the decision and (if appropriate) remit the matter to the Commission.
Direction given by the Commission under section 28 of this Act in relation to an account held in the name of or on behalf of a charity.	The persons are – (a) the charity trustees of the charity, (b) (if a body corporate) the charity itself, and (c) any other person who is or may be affected by the order.	Power to – (a) quash the direction and (if appropriate) remit the matter to the Commission, (b) substitute for the direction any other direction which could have been given by the Commission, (c) add to the direction anything which could have been contained in a direction given by the Commission.
Order made by the Commission under section 31 of this Act for the taxation of a solicitor's bill.	The persons are – (a) the solicitor, (b) any person for whom the work was done by the solicitor, and (c) any other person who is or may be affected by the order.	Power to – (a) quash the order, (b) substitute for the order any other order which could have been made by the Commission, (c) add to the order any-thing which could have been contained in an order made by the Commission.
Decision of the Commission not to make an order under section 36 of this Act in relation to land held by or in trust for a charity.	The persons are – (a) the charity trustees of the charity, (b) (if a body corporate) the charity itself, and (c) any other person who is or may be affected by the decision.	Power to quash the decision and (if appropriate) remit the matter to the Commission.
Decision of the Commission not to make an order under section 38 of this Act in relation to a mortgage of land held by or in trust for a charity.	The persons are – (a) the charity trustees of the charity, (b) (if a body corporate) the charity itself, and	Power to quash the decision and (if appropriate) remit the matter to the Commission.

1	2	3
	(c) any other person who is or may be affected by the decision.	
Order made by the Commission under section 43(4) of this Act requiring the accounts of a charity to be audited.	The persons are – (a) the charity trustees of the charity, (b) (if a body corporate) the charity itself, and (c) any other person who is or may be affected by the order.	Power to – (a) quash the order, (b) substitute for the order any other order which could have been made by the Commission, (c) add to the order anything which could have been contained in an order made by the Commission.
Order made by the Commission under section 44(2) of this Act in relation to a charity, or a decision of the Commission not to make such an order in relation to a charity.	The persons are – (a) the charity trustees of the charity, (b) (if a body corporate) the charity itself, (c) in the case of a decision not to make an order, the auditor, independent examiner or examiner, and (d) any other person who is or may be affected by the order or the decision.	Power to – (a) quash the order or decision and (if appropriate) remit the matter to the Commission, (b) substitute for the order any other order of a kind the Commission could have made, (c) make any order which the Commission could have made.
Decision of the Commission under section 46(5) of this Act to request charity trustees to prepare an annual report for a charity.	The persons are – (a) the charity trustees, and (b) (if a body corporate) the charity itself.	Power to quash the decision and (if appropriate) remit the matter to the Commission.
Decision of the Commission not to dispense with the requirements of section 48(1) in relation to a charity or class of charities.	The persons are the charity trustees of any charity affected by the decision.	Power to quash the decision and (if appropriate) remit the matter to the Commission.
Decision of the Commission – (a) to grant a certificate of incorporation under section 50(1) of this Act to the trustees of a charity, or (b) not to grant such a certificate.	The persons are – (a) the trustees of the charity, and (b) any other person who is or may be affected by the decision.	Power to quash – (a) the decision, (b) any conditions or directions inserted in the certificate, and (if appropriate) remit the matter to the Commission.

1	2	3
Decision of the Commission to amend a certificate of incorporation of a charity under section 56(4) of this Act.	The persons are – (a) the trustees of the charity, and (b) any other person who is or may be affected by the amended certificate of incorporation.	Power to quash the decision and (if appropriate) remit the matter to the Commission.
Decision of the Commission not to amend a certificate of incorporation under section 56(4) of this Act.	The persons are – (a) the trustees of the charity, and (b) any other person who is or may be affected by the decision not to amend the certificate of incorporation.	Power to – (a) quash the decision and (if appropriate) remit the matter to the Commission, (b) make any order the Commission could have made under section 56(4).
Order of the Commission under section 61(1) or (2) of this Act which dissolves a charity which is an incorporated body.	The persons are – (a) the trustees of the charity, (b) the charity itself, and (c) any other person who is or may be affected by the order.	Power to – (a) quash the order and (if appropriate) remit the matter to the Commission, (b) substitute for the order any other order which could have been made by the Commission, (c) add to the order anything which could have been contained in an order made by the Commission.
Decision of the Commission to give, or withhold, consent under section 64(2), 65(4) or 66(1) of this Act in relation to a body corporate which is a charity.	The persons are – (a) the charity trustees of the charity, (b) the body corporate itself, and (c) any other person who is or may be affected by the decision.	Power to quash the decision and (if appropriate) remit the matter to the Commission.
Order made by the Commission under section 69(1) of this Act in relation to a company which is a charity.	The persons are – (a) the directors of the company, (b) the company itself, and (c) any other person who is or may be affected by the order.	Power to – (a) quash the order and (if appropriate) remit the matter to the Commission, (b) substitute for the order any other order which could have been made by the Commission,

1	2	3
		(c) add to the order anything which could have been contained in an order made by the Commission.
Order made by the Commission under section 69(4) of this Act which gives directions to a person or to charity trustees.	The persons are – (a) in the case of directions given to a person, that person, (b) in the case of directions given to charity trustees, those charity trustees and (if a body corporate) the charity of which they are charity trustees, and (c) any other person who is or may be affected by the directions.	Power to – (a) quash the order, (b) substitute for the order any other order which could have been made by the Commission, (c) add to the order anything which could have been contained in an order made by the Commission.
Decision of the Commission under section 69E of this Act to grant an application for the constitution of a CIO and its registration as a charity.	The persons are any person (other than the persons who made the application) who is or may be affected by the decision.	Power to quash the decision and (if appropriate) – (a) remit the matter to the Commission, (b) direct the Commission to rectify the register of charities.
Decision of the Commission under section 69E of this Act not to grant an application for the constitution of a CIO and its registration as a charity.	The persons are – (a) the persons who made the application, and (b) any other person who is or may be affected by the decision.	Power to – (a) quash the decision and (if appropriate) remit the matter to the Commission, (b) direct the Commission to grant the application.
Decision of the Commission under section 69H of this Act not to grant an application for the conversion of a charitable company or a registered society into a CIO and the CIO's registration as a charity.	The persons are – (a) the charity which made the application, (b) the charity trustees of the charity, and (c) any other person who is or may be affected by the decision.	Power to – (a) quash the decision and (if appropriate) remit the matter to the Commission, (b) direct the Commission to grant the application.
Decision of the Commission under section 69K of this Act to grant an application for the amalgamation of two or more CIOs and the incorporation		

1	2	3
and registration as a charity of a new CIO as their successor.	The persons are any creditor of any of the CIOs being amalgamated.	Power to quash the decision and (if appropriate) remit the matter to the Commission.
Decision of the Commission under section 69K of this Act not to grant an application for the amalgamation of two or more CIOs and the incorporation and registration as a charity of a new CIO as their successor.	The persons are – (a) the CIOs which applied for the amalgamation, (b) the charity trustees of the CIOs, and (c) any other person who is or may be affected by the decision.	Power to – (a) quash the decision and (if appropriate) remit the matter to the Commission, (b) direct the Commission to grant the application.
Decision of the Commission to confirm a resolution passed by a CIO under section 69M(1) of this Act.	The persons are any creditor of the CIO.	Power to quash the decision and (if appropriate) remit the matter to the Commission.
Decision of the Commission not to confirm a resolution passed by a CIO under section 69M(1) of this Act.	The persons are – (a) the CIO, (b) the charity trustees of the CIO, and (c) any other person who is or may be affected by the decision.	Power to – (a) quash the decision and (if appropriate) remit the matter to the Commission, (b) direct the Commission to confirm the resolution.
Decision of the Commission under section 72(4) of this Act to waive, or not to waive, a person's disqualification.	The persons are – (a) the person who applied for the waiver, and (b) any other person who is or may be affected by the decision.	Power to – (a) quash the decision and (if appropriate) remit the matter to the Commission, (b) substitute for the decision any other decision of a kind which could have been made by the Commission.
Order made by the Commission under section 73(4) of this Act in relation to a person who has acted as charity trustee or trustee for a charity.	The persons are – (a) the person subject to the order, and (b) any other person who is or may be affected by the order.	Power to – (a) quash the order and (if appropriate) remit the matter to the Commission, (b) substitute for the order any other order which could have been made by the Commission.

1	2	3
Order made by the Commission under section 73C(5) or (6) of this Act requiring a trustee or connected person to repay, or not to receive, remuneration.	The persons are – (a) the trustee or connected person, (b) the other charity trustees of the charity concerned, and (c) any other person who is or may be affected by the order.	Power to – (a) quash the order and (if appropriate) remit the matter to the Commission, (b) substitute for the order any other order which could have been made by the Commission.
Decision of the Commission to notify charity trustees under section 74A(2) of this Act that it objects to a resolution of the charity trustees under section 74(2) or 74C(2).	The persons are – (a) the charity trustees, and (b) any other person who is or may be affected by the decision.	Power to quash the decision.
Decision of the Commission not to concur under section 75A of this Act with a resolution of charity trustees under section 75A(3) or 75B(2).	The persons are – (a) the charity trustees, (b) (if a body corporate) the charity itself, and (c) any other person who is or may be affected by the decision.	Power to quash the decision and (if appropriate) remit the matter to the Commission.
Decision of the Commission to withhold approval for the transfer of property from trustees to a parish council under section 79(1) of this Act.	The persons are – (a) the trustees, (b) the parish council, and (c) any other person who is or may be affected by the decision.	Power to quash the decision and (if appropriate) remit the matter to the Commission.
Order made by the Commission under section 80(2) of this Act in relation to a person holding property on behalf of a recognised body or of any person concerned in its management or control.	The persons are – (a) the person holding the property in question, and (b) any other person who is or may be affected by the order.	Power to quash the order and (if appropriate) remit the matter to the Commission.
Decision of the Commission not to give a direction under section 96(5) or (6) of this Act in relation to an institution or a charity.	The persons are the trustees of the institution or charity concerned.	Power to quash the decision and (if appropriate) remit the matter to the Commission.
Decision of the Commission under paragraph 15 of Schedule 5B to this Act to refuse to register an amendment to the constitution of a CIO.	The persons are – (a) the CIO, (b) the charity trustees of the CIO, and (c) any other person who is or may be affected by the decision.	Power to quash the decision and (if appropriate) – (a) remit the matter to the Commission, (b) direct the Commission to register the amendment.

Power to amend Table etc.

6   (1) The Minister may by order –

     (a)   amend or otherwise modify an entry in the Table,

     (b)   add an entry to the Table, or

     (c)   remove an entry from the Table.

    (2) An order under sub-paragraph (1) may make such amendments, repeals or other modifications of paragraphs 1 to 5 of this Schedule, or of an enactment which applies this Schedule, as the Minister considers appropriate in consequence of any change in the Table made by the order.

    (3) No order shall be made under this paragraph unless a draft of the order has been laid before and approved by a resolution of each House of Parliament.

7   Paragraph 6 above applies (with the necessary modifications) in relation to section 57 of the Charities Act 2006 as if –

    (a) the provisions of that section were contained in this Schedule, and

    (b) the reference in that paragraph to paragraphs 1 to 5 of this Schedule included a reference to any other provision relating to appeals to the Tribunal which is contained in Chapter 1 of Part 3 of the Charities Act 2006.

SCHEDULE 1D   REFERENCES TO CHARITY TRIBUNAL

Section 2A(4)

References by Commission

1   (1) A question which –

     (a)   has arisen in connection with the exercise by the Commission of any of its functions, and

     (b)   involves either the operation of charity law in any respect or its application to a particular state of affairs,

may be referred to the Tribunal by the Commission if the Commission considers it desirable to refer the question to the Tribunal.

    (2) The Commission may make such a reference only with the consent of the Attorney General.

    (3) The Commission shall be a party to proceedings before the Tribunal on the reference.

    (4) The following shall be entitled to be parties to proceedings before the Tribunal on the reference –

     (a)   the Attorney General, and

     (b)   with the Tribunal's permission –

       (i)   the charity trustees of any charity which is likely to be affected by the Tribunal's decision on the reference,

       (ii)   any such charity which is a body corporate, and

      (iii)   any other person who is likely to be so affected.

References by Attorney General

2   (1) A question which involves either –

     (a)   the operation of charity law in any respect, or

     (b)   the application of charity law to a particular state of affairs,

may be referred to the Tribunal by the Attorney General if the Attorney General considers it desirable to refer the question to the Tribunal.

    (2) The Attorney General shall be a party to proceedings before the Tribunal on the reference.

(3) The following shall be entitled to be parties to proceedings before the Tribunal on the reference –

    (a) the Commission, and

    (b) with the Tribunal's permission –

        (i) the charity trustees of any charity which is likely to be affected by the Tribunal's decision on the reference,

        (ii) any such charity which is a body corporate, and

        (iii) any other person who is likely to be so affected.

Powers of Commission in relation to matters referred to Tribunal

3   (1) This paragraph applies where a question which involves the application of charity law to a particular state of affairs has been referred to the Tribunal under paragraph 1 or 2 above.

   (2) The Commission shall not take any steps in reliance on any view as to the application of charity law to that state of affairs until –

    (a) proceedings on the reference (including any proceedings on appeal) have been concluded, and

    (b) any period during which an appeal (or further appeal) may ordinarily be made has ended.

   (3) Where –

    (a) paragraphs (a) and (b) of sub-paragraph (2) above are satisfied, and

    (b) the question has been decided in proceedings on the reference,

the Commission shall give effect to that decision when dealing with the particular state of affairs to which the reference related.

Suspension of time limits while reference in progress

4   (1) Sub-paragraph (2) below applies if –

    (a) paragraph 3(2) above prevents the Commission from taking any steps which it would otherwise be permitted or required to take, and

    (b) the steps in question may be taken only during a period specified in an enactment ('the specified period').

   (2) The running of the specified period is suspended for the period which –

    (a) begins with the date on which the question is referred to the Tribunal, and

    (b) ends with the date on which paragraphs (a) and (b) of paragraph 3(2) above are satisfied.

   (3) Nothing in this paragraph or section 74A of this Act prevents the specified period being suspended concurrently by virtue of sub-paragraph (2) above and that section.

Agreement for Commission to act while reference in progress

5   (1) Paragraph 3(2) above does not apply in relation to any steps taken by the Commission with the agreement of –

    (a) the persons who are parties to the proceedings on the reference at the time when those steps are taken, and

    (b) (if not within paragraph (a) above) the charity trustees of any charity which –

        (i) is likely to be directly affected by the taking of those steps, and

        (ii) is not a party to the proceedings at that time.

(2) The Commission may take those steps despite the suspension in accordance with paragraph 4(2) above of any period during which it would otherwise be permitted or required to take them.

(3) Paragraph 3(3) above does not require the Commission to give effect to a decision as to the application of charity law to a particular state of affairs to the extent that the decision is inconsistent with any steps already taken by the Commission in relation to that state of affairs in accordance with this paragraph.

Appeals and applications in respect of matters determined on references

6   (1) No appeal or application may be made to the Tribunal by a person to whom sub-paragraph (2) below applies in respect of an order or decision made, or direction given, by the Commission in accordance with paragraph 3(3) above.

(2) This sub-paragraph applies to a person who was at any stage a party to the proceedings in which the question referred to the Tribunal was decided.

(3) Rules under section 2B(1) of this Act may include provision as to who is to be treated for the purposes of sub-paragraph (2) above as being (or not being) a party to the proceedings.

(4) Any enactment (including one contained in this Act) which provides for an appeal or application to be made to the Tribunal has effect subject to sub-paragraph (1) above.

Interpretation

7   (1) In this Schedule –

'charity law' means –

(a) any enactment contained in, or made under, this Act or the Charities Act 2006,

(b) any other enactment specified in regulations made by the Minister, and

(c) any rule of law which relates to charities, and

'enactment' includes an enactment comprised in subordinate legislation (within the meaning of the Interpretation Act 1978), and includes an enactment whenever passed or made.

(2) The exclusions contained in section 96(2) of this Act (ecclesiastical corporations etc.) do not have effect for the purposes of this Schedule.

SCHEDULE 2   EXEMPT CHARITIES   Sections 3 and 96

The following institutions, so far as they are charities, are exempt charities within the meaning of this Act, that is to say –

(a) any institution which, if the Charities Act 1960 had not been passed, would be exempted from the powers and jurisdiction, under the Charitable Trusts Acts 1853 to 1939, of the Charity Commissioners for England and Wales or Minister of Education (apart from any power of the Commissioners or Minister to apply those Acts in whole or in part to charities otherwise exempt) by the terms of any enactment not contained in those Acts other than section 9 of the Places of Worship Registration Act 1855 (but see Note 1);

(b) the universities of Oxford, Cambridge, London, Durham and Newcastle, the colleges and halls in the universities of Oxford, Cambridge, Durham and Newcastle, and Queen Mary and Westfield College in the University of London;

(c) any university, university college, or institution connected with a university or university college, which Her Majesty declares by Order in Council to be an exempt charity for the purposes of this Act;

(d) [. . .]
(da) the Qualifications and Curriculum Authority;
(e) [. . .]
(f) [. . .]
(g) [. . .]
(h) a higher education corporation;
(i) a successor company to a higher education corporation (within the meaning of section 129(5) of the Education Reform Act 1988) at a time when an institution conducted by the company is for the time being designated under that section;
(j) a further education corporation;
(k) the Board of Trustees of the Victoria and Albert Museum;
(l) the Board of Trustees of the Science Museum;
(m) the Board of Trustees of the Armouries;
(n) the Board of Trustees of the Royal Botanic Gardens, Kew;
(o) the Board of Trustees of the National Museums and Galleries on Merseyside;
(p) the trustees of the British Museum and the trustees of the Natural History Museum;
(q) the Board of Trustees of the National Gallery;
(r) the Board of Trustees of the Tate Gallery;
(s) the Board of Trustees of the National Portrait Gallery;
(t) the Board of Trustees of the Wallace Collection;
(u) the Trustees of the Imperial War Museum;
(v) the Trustees of the National Maritime Museum;
(w) any institution which is administered by or on behalf of an institution included above and is established for the general purposes of, or for any special purpose of or in connection with, the last-mentioned institution (but see Note 2);
(x) [. . .]
(y) any registered society within the meaning of the Industrial and Provident Societies Act 1965 and which is also registered in the register of social landlords under Part 1 of the Housing Act 1996;
(z) the Board of Governors of the Museum of London;
(za) the British Library Board;
(zb) [. . .]

Notes

1. Paragraph (a) above does not include –
    (a) any Investment Fund or Deposit Fund within the meaning of the Church Funds Investment Measure 1958,
    (b) any investment fund or deposit fund within the meaning of the Methodist Church Funds Act 1960, or
    (c) the representative body of the Welsh Church or property administered by it.

2. Paragraph (w) above does not include any students' union.

SCHEDULE 3   ENLARGEMENT OF AREAS OF LOCAL CHARITIES
Section 13

Existing area	Permissible enlargement
1. Greater London	Any area comprising Greater London.
2. Any area in Greater London and not in, or partly in, the City of London.	(i) Any area in Greater London and not in, or partly in, the City of London; (ii) the area of Greater London exclusive of the City of London;

Existing area	Permissible enlargement
	(iii) any area comprising the area of Greater London, exclusive of the City of London; (iv) any area partly in Greater London and partly in any adjacent parish or parishes (civil or ecclesiastical), and not partly in the City of London.
3. A district	Any area comprising the district.
3A. A Welsh county or county borough	Any area comprising that county or county borough.
4. Any area in a district	(i) Any area in the district; (ii) the district; (iii) any area comprising the district; (iv) any area partly in the district and partly in any adjacent district or in any adjacent Welsh county or county borough.
4A. Any area in a Welsh county or county borough	(i) Any area in the county or county borough; (ii) the county or county borough; (iii) any area comprising the county or county borough; (iv) any area partly in the county or county borough and partly in any adjacent Welsh county or county borough or in any adjacent district.
5. A parish (civil or ecclesiastical), or two or more parishes, or an area in a parish, or partly in each of two or more parishes.	Any area not extending beyond the parish or parishes comprising or adjacent to the area in column 1.
6. In Wales, a community, or two or more communities, or an area in a community, or partly in each of two or more communities.	Any area not extending beyond the community or communities comprising or adjacent to the area in column 1.

SCHEDULE 4   COURT'S JURISDICTION OVER CERTAIN CHARITIES GOVERNED BY OR UNDER STATUTE

Section 15

1   The court may by virtue of section 15(3) of this Act exercise its jurisdiction with respect to charities –

(a) in relation to charities established or regulated by any provision of the Seamen's Fund Winding-up Act 1851 which is repealed by the Charities Act 1960;

(b) in relation to charities established or regulated by schemes under the Endowed Schools Act 1869 to 1948, or section 75 of the Elementary Education Act 1870 or by schemes given effect under section 2 of the Education Act 1973 or section 554 of the Education Act 1996;

(c) [...]

(d) in relation to fuel allotments, that is to say, land which, by any enactment relating to inclosure or any instrument having effect under such an enactment, is vested in trustees upon trust that the land or the rents and profits of the land shall be used for the purpose of providing poor persons with fuel;

(e) in relation to charities established or regulated by any provision of the Municipal Corporations Act 1883 which is repealed by the Charities Act 1960 or by any scheme having effect under any such provision;

(f) in relation to charities regulated by schemes under the London Government Act 1899;

(g) in relation to charities established or regulated by orders or regulations under section 2 of the Regimental Charitable Funds Act 1935;

(h) in relation to charities regulated by section 79 of this Act, or by any such order as is mentioned in that section.

2   Notwithstanding anything in section 19 of the Commons Act 1876 a scheme for the administration of a fuel allotment (within the meaning of the foregoing paragraph) may provide –

(a) for the sale or letting of the allotment or any part thereof, for the discharge of the land sold or let from any restrictions as to the use thereof imposed by or under any enactment relating to inclosure and for the application of the sums payable to the trustees of the allotment in respect of the sale or lease; or

(b) for the exchange of the allotment or any part thereof for other land, for the discharge as aforesaid of the land given in exchange by the said trustees, and for the application of any money payable to the said trustees for equality of exchange; or

(c) for the use of the allotment or any part thereof for any purposes specified in the scheme.

SCHEDULE 5   MEANING OF 'CONNECTED PERSON' FOR PURPOSES OF SECTION 36(2)   Section 36(2)

1   (1) In section 36(2) of this Act 'connected person', in relation to a charity, means any person who falls within sub-paragraph (2) –

(a) at the time of the disposition in question, or

(b) at the time of any contract for the disposition in question.

(2) The persons falling within this sub-paragraph are –

(a) a charity trustee or trustee for the charity;

(b) a person who is the donor of any land to the charity (whether the gift was made on or after the establishment of the charity);

(c) a child, parent, grandchild, grandparent, brother or sister of any such trustee or donor;

(d) an officer, agent or employee of the charity;

(e) the spouse or civil partner of any person falling within any of sub-paragraphs (a) to (d) above;

(ea) a person carrying on business in partnership with any person falling within any of sub-paragraphs (a) to (e) above;

(f) an institution which is controlled –

(i) by any person falling within any of sub-paragraphs (a) to (ea) above, or

(ii) by two or more such persons taken together; or

    (g)   a body corporate in which –

        (i)   any connected person falling within any of sub-paragraphs (a) to (f) above has a substantial interest, or

        (ii) two or more such persons, taken together, have a substantial interest.

2   (1) In paragraph 1(2)(c) above 'child' includes a stepchild and an illegitimate child.

      (2) For the purposes of paragraph 1(2)(e) above a person living with another as that person's husband or wife shall be treated as that person's spouse.

      (3) Where two persons of the same sex are not civil partners but live together as if they were, each of them shall be treated for those purposes as the civil partner of the other.

3   For the purposes of paragraph 1(2)(f) above a person controls an institution if he is able to secure that the affairs of the institution are conducted in accordance with his wishes.

4   (1) For the purposes of paragraph 1(2)(g) above any such connected person as is there mentioned has a substantial interest in a body corporate if the person or institution in question –

        (a) is interested in shares comprised in the equity share capital of that body of a nominal value of more than one-fifth of that share capital, or

        (b) is entitled to exercise, or control the exercise of, more than one-fifth of the voting power at any general meeting of that body.

      (2) The rules set out in Part I of Schedule 13 to the Companies Act 1985 (rules for interpretation of certain provisions of that Act) shall apply for the purposes of sub-paragraph (1) above as they apply for the purposes of section 346(4) of that Act ('connected persons' etc).

      (3) In this paragraph 'equity share capital' and 'share' have the same meaning as in that Act.

SCHEDULE 5A   GROUP ACCOUNTS   Section 49A

Interpretation

1   (1) This paragraph applies for the purposes of this Schedule.

      (2) A charity is a 'parent charity' if –

        (a) it is (or is to be treated as) a parent undertaking in relation to one or more other undertakings in accordance with the provisions of section 258 of, and Schedule 10A to, the Companies Act 1985, and

        (b) it is not a company.

      (3) Each undertaking in relation to which a parent charity is (or is to be treated as) a parent undertaking in accordance with those provisions is a 'subsidiary undertaking' in relation to the parent charity.

      (4) But sub-paragraph (3) does not have the result that any of the following is a 'subsidiary undertaking' –

        (a) any special trusts of a charity,

        (b) any institution which, by virtue of a direction under section 96(5) of this Act, is to be treated as forming part of a charity for the purposes of this Part of this Act, or

        (c) any charity to which a direction under section 96(6) of this Act applies for those purposes.

      (5) 'The group', in relation to a parent charity, means that charity and its subsidiary undertaking or undertakings, and any reference to the members of the group is to be construed accordingly.

(6) For the purposes of –

    (a)   this paragraph, and

    (b)   the operation of the provisions mentioned in sub-paragraph (2) above for the purposes of this paragraph,

'undertaking' has the meaning given by sub-paragraph (7) below.

(7) For those purposes 'undertaking' means –

    (a)   an undertaking as defined by section 259(1) of the Companies Act 1985, or

    (b)   a charity which is not an undertaking as so defined.

Accounting records

2   (1) The charity trustees –

    (a)   of a parent charity, or

    (b)   of any charity which is a subsidiary undertaking,

must ensure that the accounting records kept in respect of the charity under section 41(1) of this Act not only comply with the requirements of that provision but also are such as to enable the charity trustees of the parent charity to ensure that, where any group accounts are prepared by them under paragraph 3(2), those accounts comply with the relevant requirements.

(2) If a parent charity has a subsidiary undertaking in relation to which the requirements of section 41(1) of this Act do not apply, the charity trustees of the parent charity must take reasonable steps to secure that the undertaking keeps such accounting records as to enable the trustees to ensure that, where any group accounts are prepared by them under paragraph 3(2), those accounts comply with the relevant requirements.

(3) In this paragraph 'the relevant requirements' means the requirements of regulations under paragraph 3.

Preparation of group accounts

3   (1) This paragraph applies in relation to a financial year of a charity if it is a parent charity at the end of that year.

(2) The charity trustees of the parent charity must prepare group accounts in respect of that year.

(3) 'Group accounts' means consolidated accounts –

    (a)   relating to the group, and

    (b)   complying with such requirements as to their form and contents as may be prescribed by regulations made by the Minister.

(4) Without prejudice to the generality of sub-paragraph (3), regulations under that sub-paragraph may make provision –

    (a)   for any such accounts to be prepared in accordance with such methods and principles as are specified or referred to in the regulations;

    (b)   for dealing with cases where the financial years of the members of the group do not all coincide;

    (c)   as to any information to be provided by way of notes to the accounts.

(5) Regulations under that sub-paragraph may also make provision –

    (a)   for determining the financial years of subsidiary undertakings for the purposes of this Schedule;

    (b)   for imposing on the charity trustees of a parent charity requirements with respect to securing that such financial years coincide with that of the charity.

(6) If the requirement in sub-paragraph (2) applies to the charity trustees of a parent charity in relation to a financial year –

    (a) that requirement so applies in addition to the requirement in section 42(1) of this Act, and

    (b) the option of preparing the documents mentioned in section 42(3) of this Act is not available in relation to that year (whatever the amount of the charity's gross income for that year).

(7) Sub-paragraph (2) has effect subject to paragraph 4.

Exceptions relating to requirement to prepare group accounts

4   (1) The requirement in paragraph 3(2) does not apply to the charity trustees of a parent charity in relation to a financial year if at the end of that year it is itself a subsidiary undertaking in relation to another charity.

    (2) The requirement in paragraph 3(2) does not apply to the charity trustees of a parent charity in relation to a financial year if the aggregate gross income of the group for that year does not exceed such sum as is specified in regulations made by the Minister.

    (3) Regulations made by the Minister may prescribe circumstances in which a subsidiary undertaking may or (as the case may be) must be excluded from group accounts required to be prepared under paragraph 3(2) for a financial year.

    (4) Where, by virtue of such regulations, each of the subsidiary undertakings which are members of a group is either permitted or required to be excluded from any such group accounts for a financial year, the requirement in paragraph 3(2) does not apply to the charity trustees of the parent charity in relation to that year.

Preservation of group accounts

5   (1) The charity trustees of a charity shall preserve any group accounts prepared by them under paragraph 3(2) for at least six years from the end of the financial year to which the accounts relate.

    (2) Subsection (4) of section 41 of this Act shall apply in relation to the preservation of any such accounts as it applies in relation to the preservation of any accounting records (the references to subsection (3) of that section being construed as references to sub-paragraph (1) above).

Audit of accounts of larger groups

6   (1) This paragraph applies where group accounts are prepared for a financial year of a parent charity under paragraph 3(2) and –

    (a) the aggregate gross income of the group in that year exceeds the relevant income threshold, or

    (b) the aggregate gross income of the group in that year exceeds the relevant income threshold and at the end of the year the aggregate value of the assets of the group (before deduction of liabilities) exceeds the relevant assets threshold.

    (2) In sub-paragraph (1) –

    (a) the reference in paragraph (a) or (b) to the relevant income threshold is a reference to the sum prescribed as the relevant income threshold for the purposes of that paragraph, and

    (b) the reference in paragraph (b) to the relevant assets threshold is a reference to the sum prescribed as the relevant assets threshold for the purposes of that paragraph.

'Prescribed' means prescribed by regulations made by the Minister.

(3) This paragraph also applies where group accounts are prepared for a financial year of a parent charity under paragraph 3(2) and the appropriate audit provision applies in relation to the parent charity's own accounts for that year.

(4) If this paragraph applies in relation to a financial year of a parent charity by virtue of sub-paragraph (1) or (3), the group accounts for that year shall be audited –

    (a) (subject to paragraph (b) or (c) below) by a person within section 43(2)(a) or (b) of this Act;

    (b) if section 43A of this Act applies in relation to that year, by a person appointed by the Audit Commission (see section 43A(7));

    (c) if section 43B of this Act applies in relation to that year, by the Auditor General for Wales.

(5) Where it appears to the Commission that sub-paragraph (4)(a) above has not been complied with in relation to that year within ten months from the end of that year –

    (a) the Commission may by order require the group accounts for that year to be audited by a person within section 43(2)(a) or (b) of this Act, and

    (b) if it so orders, the auditor shall be a person appointed by the Commission.

(6) Section 43(6) of this Act shall apply in relation to any such audit as it applies in relation to an audit carried out by an auditor appointed under section 43(5) (reading the reference to the funds of the charity as a reference to the funds of the parent charity).

(7) Section 43A(4) and (6) of this Act apply in relation to any appointment under sub-paragraph (4)(b) above as they apply in relation to an appointment under section 43A(2).

(8) If this paragraph applies in relation to a financial year of a parent charity by virtue of sub-paragraph (1), the appropriate audit provision shall apply in relation to the parent charity's own accounts for that year (whether or not it would otherwise so apply).

(9) In this paragraph 'the appropriate audit provision', in relation to a financial year of a parent charity, means –

    (a) (subject to paragraph (b) or (c) below) section 43(2) of this Act;

    (b) if section 43A of this Act applies in relation to that year, section 43A(2);

    (c) if section 43B of this Act applies in relation to that year, section 43B(2).

Examination of accounts of smaller groups

7   (1) This paragraph applies where –

    (a) group accounts are prepared for a financial year of a parent charity under paragraph 3(2), and

    (b) paragraph 6 does not apply in relation to that year.

    (2) If –

    (a) this paragraph applies in relation to a financial year of a parent charity, and

    (b) sub-paragraph (4) or (5) below does not apply in relation to it,

subsections (3) to (7) of section 43 of this Act shall apply in relation to the group accounts for that year as they apply in relation to the accounts of a charity for a financial year in relation to which subsection (2) of that section does not apply, but subject to the modifications in sub-paragraph (3) below.

    (3) The modifications are –

    (a) any reference to the charity trustees of the charity is to be construed as a reference to the charity trustees of the parent charity;

(b)   any reference to the charity's gross income in the financial year in question is to be construed as a reference to the aggregate gross income of the group in that year; and

(c)   any reference to the funds of the charity is to be construed as a reference to the funds of the parent charity.

(4)   If –

(a)   this paragraph applies in relation to a financial year of a parent charity, and

(b)   section 43A of this Act also applies in relation to that year,

subsections (3) to (6) of that section shall apply in relation to the group accounts for that year as they apply in relation to the accounts of a charity for a financial year in relation to which subsection (2) of that section does not apply.

(5)   If –

(a)   this paragraph applies in relation to a financial year of a parent charity, and

(b)   section 43B of this Act also applies in relation to that year,

subsection (3) of that section shall apply in relation to the group accounts for that year as they apply in relation to the accounts of a charity for a financial year in relation to which subsection (2) of that section does not apply.

(6)   If the group accounts for a financial year of a parent charity are to be examined or audited in accordance with section 43(3) of this Act (as applied by sub-paragraph (2) above), section 43(3) shall apply in relation to the parent charity's own accounts for that year (whether or not it would otherwise so apply).

(7)   Nothing in sub-paragraph (4) or (5) above affects the operation of section 43A(3) to (6) or (as the case may be) section 43B(3) in relation to the parent charity's own accounts for the financial year in question.

Supplementary provisions relating to audits etc.

8   (1)   Section 44(1) of this Act shall apply in relation to audits and examinations carried out under or by virtue of paragraph 6 or 7, but subject to the modifications in sub-paragraph (2) below.

(2)   The modifications are –

(a)   in paragraph (b), the reference to section 43, 43A or 43B of this Act is to be construed as a reference to paragraph 6 above or to any of those sections as applied by paragraph 7 above;

(b)   also in paragraph (b), the reference to any such statement of accounts as is mentioned in sub-paragraph (i) of that paragraph is to be construed as a reference to group accounts prepared for a financial year under paragraph 3(2) above;

(c)   in paragraph (c), any reference to section 43, 43A or 43B of this Act is to be construed as a reference to that section as applied by paragraph 7 above;

(d)   in paragraphs (d) and (e), any reference to the charity concerned or a charity is to be construed as a reference to any member of the group; and

(e)   in paragraph (f), the reference to the requirements of section 43(2) or (3) of this Act is to be construed as a reference to the requirements of paragraph 6(4)(a) or those applied by paragraph 7(2) above.

(3)   Without prejudice to the generality of section 44(1)(e), as modified by sub-paragraph (2)(d) above, regulations made under that provision may make provision corresponding or similar to any provision made by section 389A of the Companies Act 1985 (c.6) in connection with the rights exercisable by an auditor of a company in relation to a subsidiary undertaking of the company.

(4)   In section 44(2) of this Act the reference to section 44(1)(d) or (e) includes a reference to that provision as it applies in accordance with this paragraph.

Duty of auditors etc. to report matters to Commission

9   (1)   Section 44A(2) to (5) and (7) of this Act shall apply in relation to a person appointed to audit, or report on, any group accounts under or by virtue of paragraph 6 or 7 above as they apply in relation to a person such as is mentioned in section 44A(1).

(2)   In section 44A(2)(a), as it applies in accordance with sub-paragraph (1) above, the reference to the charity or any connected institution or body is to be construed as a reference to the parent charity or any of its subsidiary undertakings.

Annual reports

10   (1)   This paragraph applies where group accounts are prepared for a financial year of a parent charity under paragraph 3(2).

(2)   The annual report prepared by the charity trustees of the parent charity in respect of that year under section 45 of this Act shall include –

(a)   such a report by the trustees on the activities of the charity's subsidiary undertakings during that year, and

(b)   such other information relating to any of those undertakings,

as may be prescribed by regulations made by the Minister.

(3)   Without prejudice to the generality of sub-paragraph (2), regulations under that sub-paragraph may make provision –

(a)   for any such report as is mentioned in paragraph (a) of that sub-paragraph to be prepared in accordance with such principles as are specified or referred to in the regulations;

(b)   enabling the Commission to dispense with any requirement prescribed by virtue of sub-paragraph (2)(b) in the case of a particular subsidiary undertaking or a particular class of subsidiary undertaking.

(4)   Section 45(3) to (3B) shall apply in relation to the annual report referred to in sub-paragraph (2) above as if any reference to the charity's gross income in the financial year in question were a reference to the aggregate gross income of the group in that year.

(5)   When transmitted to the Commission in accordance with sub-paragraph (4) above, the copy of the annual report shall have attached to it both a copy of the group accounts prepared for that year under paragraph 3(2) and –

(a)   a copy of the report made by the auditor on those accounts; or

(b)   where those accounts have been examined under section 43, 43A or 43B of this Act (as applied by paragraph 7 above), a copy of the report made by the person carrying out the examination.

(6)   The requirements in this paragraph are in addition to those in section 45 of this Act.

Excepted charities

11   (1)   This paragraph applies where –

(a)   a charity is required to prepare an annual report in respect of a financial year by virtue of section 46(5) of this Act,

(b)   the charity is a parent charity at the end of the year, and

(c)   group accounts are prepared for that year under paragraph 3(2) by the charity trustees of the charity.

(2)   When transmitted to the Commission in accordance with section 46(7) of this Act, the copy of the annual report shall have attached to it both a copy of the group accounts and –

(a)   a copy of the report made by the auditor on those accounts; or

(b)   where those accounts have been examined under section 43, 43A or 43B of this Act (as applied by paragraph 7 above), a copy of the report made by the person carrying out the examination.

(3)   The requirement in sub-paragraph (2) is in addition to that in section 46(6) of this Act.

Exempt charities

12   Nothing in the preceding provisions of this Schedule applies to an exempt charity.

Public inspection of annual reports etc.

13   In section 47(2) of this Act, the reference to a charity's most recent accounts includes, in relation to a charity whose charity trustees have prepared any group accounts under paragraph 3(2), the group accounts most recently prepared by them.

Offences

14   (1)   Section 49(1) of this Act applies in relation to a requirement within sub-paragraph (2) as it applies in relation to a requirement within section 49(1)(a).

(2)   A requirement is within this sub-paragraph where it is imposed by section 45(3) or (3A) of this Act, taken with –

(a)   section 45(3B), (4) and (5), and
(b)   paragraph 10(5) or 11(2) above,

as applicable.

(3)   In sub-paragraph (2) any reference to section 45(3), (3A) or (3B) of this Act is a reference to that provision as applied by paragraph 10(4) above.

(4)   In section 49(1)(b) the reference to section 47(2) of this Act includes a reference to that provision as extended by paragraph 13 above.

Aggregate gross income

15   The Minister may by regulations make provision for determining for the purposes of this Schedule the amount of the aggregate gross income for a financial year of a group consisting of a parent charity and its subsidiary undertaking or undertakings.

SCHEDULE 5B   FURTHER PROVISION ABOUT CHARITABLE INCORPORATED ORGANISATIONS   Section 69P

Powers

1   (1)   Subject to anything in its constitution, a CIO has power to do anything which is calculated to further its purposes or is conducive or incidental to doing so.

(2)   The CIO's charity trustees shall manage the affairs of the CIO and may for that purpose exercise all the powers of the CIO.

Constitutional requirements

2   A CIO shall use and apply its property in furtherance of its purposes and in accordance with its constitution.

3   If the CIO is one whose members are liable to contribute to its assets if it is wound up, its constitution binds the CIO and its members for the time being to the same extent as if its provisions were contained in a contract –

(a)   to which the CIO and each of its members was a party, and
(b)   which contained obligations on the part of the CIO and each member to observe all the provisions of the constitution.

4   Money payable by a member to the CIO under the constitution is a debt due from him to the CIO, and is of the nature of a specialty debt.

Third parties

5   (1)   Sub-paragraphs (2) and (3) are subject to sub-paragraph (4).

(2)   The validity of an act done (or purportedly done) by a CIO shall not be called into question on the ground that it lacked constitutional capacity.

(3)   The power of the charity trustees of a CIO to act so as to bind the CIO (or authorise others to do so) shall not be called into question on the ground of any constitutional limitations on their powers.

(4)   But sub-paragraphs (2) and (3) apply only in favour of a person who gives full consideration in money or money's worth in relation to the act in question, and does not know –

(a)   in a sub-paragraph (2) case, that the act is beyond the CIO's constitutional capacity, or

(b)   in a sub-paragraph (3) case, that the act is beyond the constitutional powers of its charity trustees,

and (in addition) sub-paragraph (3) applies only if the person dealt with the CIO in good faith (which he shall be presumed to have done unless the contrary is proved).

(5)   A party to an arrangement or transaction with a CIO is not bound to inquire –

(a)   whether it is within the CIO's constitutional capacity, or

(b)   as to any constitutional limitations on the powers of its charity trustees to bind the CIO or authorise others to do so.

(6)   If a CIO purports to transfer or grant an interest in property, the fact that the act was beyond its constitutional capacity, or that its charity trustees in connection with the act exceeded their constitutional powers, does not affect the title of a person who subsequently acquires the property or any interest in it for full consideration without actual notice of any such circumstances affecting the validity of the CIO's act.

(7)   In any proceedings arising out of sub-paragraphs (2) to (4), the burden of proving that a person knew that an act –

(a)   was beyond the CIO's constitutional capacity, or

(b)   was beyond the constitutional powers of its charity trustees,

lies on the person making that allegation.

(8)   In this paragraph and paragraphs 6 to 8 –

(a)   references to a CIO's lack of 'constitutional capacity' are to lack of capacity because of anything in its constitution, and

(b)   references to 'constitutional limitations' on the powers of a CIO's charity trustees are to limitations on their powers under its constitution, including limitations deriving from a resolution of the CIO in general meeting, or from an agreement between the CIO's members, and 'constitutional powers' is to be construed accordingly.

6   (1)   Nothing in paragraph 5 prevents a person from bringing proceedings to restrain the doing of an act which would be –

(a)   beyond the CIO's constitutional capacity, or

(b)   beyond the constitutional powers of the CIO's charity trustees.

(2)   But no such proceedings may be brought in respect of an act to be done in fulfilment of a legal obligation arising from a previous act of the CIO.

(3)   Sub-paragraph (2) does not prevent the Commission from exercising any of its powers.

7   Nothing in paragraph 5(3) affects any liability incurred by the CIO's charity trustees (or any one of them) for acting beyond his or their constitutional powers.

8   Nothing in paragraph 5 absolves the CIO's charity trustees from their duty to act within the CIO's constitution and in accordance with any constitutional limitations on their powers.

Duties

9   It is the duty of –

    (a)   each member of a CIO, and

    (b)   each charity trustee of a CIO,

to exercise his powers, and (in the case of a charity trustee) to perform his functions, in his capacity as such, in the way he decides, in good faith, would be most likely to further the purposes of the CIO.

10   (1)   Subject to any provision of a CIO's constitution permitted by virtue of regulations made under sub-paragraph (2), each charity trustee of a CIO shall in the performance of his functions in that capacity exercise such care and skill as is reasonable in the circumstances, having regard in particular –

    (a)   to any special knowledge or experience that he has or holds himself out as having, and

    (b)   if he acts as a charity trustee in the course of a business or profession, to any special knowledge or experience that it is reasonable to expect of a person acting in the course of that kind of business or profession.

  (2)   The Minister may make regulations permitting a CIO's constitution to provide that the duty in sub-paragraph (1) does not apply, or does not apply in so far as is specified in the constitution.

  (3)   Regulations under sub-paragraph (2) may provide for limits on the extent to which, or the cases in which, a CIO's constitution may disapply the duty in sub-paragraph (1).

Personal benefit and payments

11   (1)   A charity trustee of a CIO may not benefit personally from any arrangement or transaction entered into by the CIO if, before the arrangement or transaction was entered into, he did not disclose to all the charity trustees of the CIO any material interest of his in it or in any other person or body party to it (whether that interest is direct or indirect).

  (2)   Nothing in sub-paragraph (1) confers authority for a charity trustee of a CIO to benefit personally from any arrangement or transaction entered into by the CIO.

12   A charity trustee of a CIO –

    (a)   is entitled to be reimbursed by the CIO, or

    (b)   may pay out of the CIO's funds,

expenses properly incurred by him in the performance of his functions as such.

Procedure

13   (1)   The Minister may by regulations make provision about the procedure of CIOs.

  (2)   Subject to –

    (a)   any such regulations,

    (b)   any other requirement imposed by or by virtue of this Act or any other enactment, and

    (c)   anything in the CIO's constitution,

a CIO may regulate its own procedure.

(3) But a CIO's procedure shall include provision for the holding of a general meeting of its members, and the regulations referred to in sub-paragraph (1) may in particular make provision about such meetings.

Amendment of constitution

14   (1) A CIO may by resolution of its members amend its constitution (and a single resolution may provide for more than one amendment).

(2) Such a resolution must be passed –

   (a) by a 75% majority of those voting at a general meeting of the CIO (including those voting by proxy or by post, if voting that way is permitted), or

   (b) unanimously by the CIO's members, otherwise than at a general meeting.

(3) The date of passing of such a resolution is –

   (a) the date of the general meeting at which it was passed, or

   (b) if it was passed otherwise than at a general meeting, the date on which provision in the CIO's constitution or in regulations made under paragraph 13 deems it to have been passed (but that date may not be earlier than that on which the last member agreed to it).

(4) The power of a CIO to amend its constitution is not exercisable in any way which would result in the CIO's ceasing to be a charity.

(5) Subject to paragraph 15(5) below, a resolution containing an amendment which would make any regulated alteration is to that extent ineffective unless the prior written consent of the Commission has been obtained to the making of the amendment.

(6) The following are regulated alterations –

   (a) any alteration of the CIO's purposes,

   (b) any alteration of any provision of the CIO's constitution directing the application of property of the CIO on its dissolution,

   (c) any alteration of any provision of the CIO's constitution where the alteration would provide authorisation for any benefit to be obtained by charity trustees or members of the CIO or persons connected with them.

(7) For the purposes of sub-paragraph (6)(c) –

   (a) 'benefit' means a direct or indirect benefit of any nature, except that it does not include any remuneration (within the meaning of section 73A of this Act) whose receipt may be authorised under that section, and

   (b) the same rules apply for determining whether a person is connected with a charity trustee or member of the CIO as apply, in accordance with section 73B(5) and (6) of this Act, for determining whether a person is connected with a charity trustee for the purposes of section 73A.

Registration and coming into effect of amendments

15   (1) A CIO shall send to the Commission a copy of a resolution containing an amendment to its constitution, together with –

   (a) a copy of the constitution as amended, and

   (b) such other documents and information as the Commission may require,

   by the end of the period of 15 days beginning with the date of passing of the resolution (see paragraph 14(3)).

(2) An amendment to a CIO's constitution does not take effect until it has been registered.

(3) The Commission shall refuse to register an amendment if –

    (a) in the opinion of the Commission the CIO had no power to make it (for example, because the effect of making it would be that the CIO ceased to be a charity, or that the CIO or its constitution did not comply with any requirement imposed by or by virtue of this Act or any other enactment), or

    (b) the amendment would change the name of the CIO, and the Commission could have refused an application under section 69E of this Act for the constitution and registration of a CIO with the name specified in the amendment on a ground set out in subsection (4) of that section.

(4) The Commission may refuse to register an amendment if the amendment would make a regulated alteration and the consent referred to in paragraph 14(5) had not been obtained.

(5) But if the Commission does register such an amendment, paragraph 14(5) does not apply.

SCHEDULE 6　CONSEQUENTIAL AMENDMENTS　Section 98(1)

The Places of Worship Registration Act 1855 (c.81)

1   (1) Section 9 of the Places of Worship Registration Act 1855 shall be amended as follows.

    (2) For 'subsection (4) of section four of the Charities Act 1960' there shall be substituted 'subsection (5) of section 3 of the Charities Act 1993'.

    (3) At the end there shall be added – '(2) Section 89 of the said Act of 1993 (provisions as to orders under that Act) shall apply to any order under paragraph (b) above as it applies to orders under that Act.'

The Open Spaces Act 1906 (c.25)

2   At the end of section 4 of the Open Spaces Act 1906 there shall be added – '(4) Section 89 of the Charities Act 1993 (provisions as to orders under that Act) shall apply to any order of the Charity Commissioners under this section as it applies to orders made by them under that Act.'

The New Parishes Measure 1943 (No.1)

3   (1) The New Parishes Measure 1943 shall be amended as follows.

    (2) In subsection (1)(b) of section 14 for 'the Charities Act 1960' there shall be substituted 'the Charities Act 1993'.

    (3) At the end of that section there shall be added –

        '(4) Section 89 of the Charities Act 1993 (provisions as to orders under that Act) shall apply to any order under section (1)(b) above as it applies to orders under that Act.'

    (4) In section 31 for 'the Charities Act 1960' there shall be substituted 'the Charities Act 1993'.

The Clergy Pensions Measure 1961 (No.3)

4   In section 33 of the Clergy Pensions Measure 1961 for 'section 32 of the Charities Act 1992' and 'the Charities Act 1960' there shall be substituted respectively 'section 36 of the Charities Act 1993' and 'that Act'.

The Finance Act 1963 (c.25)

5   [. . .]

The Cathedrals Measure 1963 (No.2)

6   (1)   The Cathedrals Measure 1963 shall be amended as follows.

(2)   In section 20(2)(iii) for 'section 32 of the Charities Act 1992' there shall be substituted 'section 36 of the Charities Act 1993'.

(3)   In section 51 for 'the Charities Act 1960' there shall be substituted 'the Charities Act 1993'.

The Incumbents and Churchwardens (Trusts) Measure 1964 (No.2)

7   In section 1 of the Incumbents and Churchwardens (Trusts) Measure 1964 for 'subsection (3) of section forty-five of the Charities Act 1960' there shall be substituted 'section 96(3) of the Charities Act 1993'.

The Leasehold Reform Act 1967 (c.88)

8   In section 23(4) of the Leasehold Reform Act 1967 for 'section 32 of the Charities Act 1992' there shall be substituted 'section 36 of the Charities Act 1993'.

The Greater London Council (General Powers) Act 1968 (c.xxxix)

9   In section 43 of the Greater London Council (General Powers) Act 1968, in the definition of 'night café', for 'section 4 of the Charities Act 1960' and 'subsection (4) thereof' there shall be substituted respectively 'section 3 of the Charities Act 1993' and 'subsection (5) thereof'.

The Redundant Churches and other Religious Buildings Act 1969 (c.22)

10   (1)   The Redundant Churches and other Religious Buildings Act 1969 shall be amended as follows.

(2)   In subsection (6) of section 4 for 'section 18 of the Charities Act 1960' there shall be substituted 'section 16 of the Charities Act 1993'.

(3)   In subsection (7) of that section for 'subsection (4) of section 18 of that Act' there shall be substituted 'subsection (4) of section 16 of that Act'.

(4)   In subsection (8) of that section for 'section 18 of the Charities Act 1960' and (where next occurring) 'section 18' there shall be substituted respectively 'section 16 of the Charities Act 1993' and 'section 16' and for 'section 21' there shall be substituted 'section 20'.

(5)   In subsection (13) of that section for 'sections 45 and 46 of the Charities Act 1960' there shall be substituted 'sections 96 and 97 of the Charities Act 1993'.

(6)   In section 7(2) for 'the Charities Act 1960' and 'section 23' there shall be substituted respectively 'the Charities Act 1993' and 'section 26'.

The Sharing of Church Buildings Act 1969 (c.38)

11   (1)   The Sharing of Church Buildings Act 1969 shall be amended as follows.

(2)   In section 2(4) for 'the Charities Act 1960' there shall be substituted 'the Charities Act 1993'.

(3)   In subsection (1) of section 8 for 'the Charities Act 1960' there shall be substituted 'the Charities Act 1993'.

(4)   In subsection (2) of that section for 'section 45(2) of the Charities Act 1960' there shall be substituted 'section 96(2) of the Charities Act 1993'.

(5)   In subsection (3) of that section for 'Section 32 of the Charities Act 1992' there shall be substituted 'Section 36 of the Charities Act 1993'.

The Local Government Act 1972 (c.70)

12   (1)   The Local Government Act 1972 shall be amended as follows.

(2)   In sections 11(3)(c) and 29(3)(c) for 'section 37 of the Charities Act 1960' there shall be substituted 'section 79 of the Charities Act 1993'.

(3) In sections 123(6) and 127(4) for 'the Charities Act 1960' there shall be substituted 'the Charities Act 1993'.

(4) In section 131(3) for 'section 32 of the Charities Act 1992' and 'section 32(9)(a) of that Act' there shall be substituted respectively 'section 36 of the Charities Act 1993' and 'section 36(9)(a) of that Act'.

The Fire Precautions (Loans) Act 1973 (c.11)

13   In section 1(7) of the Fire Precautions (Loans) Act 1973 for 'Section 34 of the Charities Act 1992' there shall be substituted 'Section 38 of the Charities Act 1993'.

The Theatres Trust Act 1976 (c.27)

14   In section 2(2)(d) of the Theatres Trust Act 1976 for 'sections 32 and 34 of the Charities Act 1992' there shall be substituted 'sections 36 and 38 of the Charities Act 1993'.

The Interpretation Act 1978 (c.30)

15   In Schedule 1 to the Interpretation Act 1978, in the definition of 'Charity Commissioners' for 'section 1 of the Charities Act 1960' there shall be substituted 'section 1 of the Charities Act 1993'.

The Reserve Forces Act 1980 (c.9)

16   [. . .]

The Disused Burial Grounds (Amendment) Act 1981 (c.18)

17   In section 6 of the Disused Burial Grounds (Amendment) Act 1981 for 'section 13(5) of the Charities Act 1960' there shall be substituted 'section 13(5) of the Charities Act 1993'.

The Pastoral Measure 1983 (No. 1)

18   (1) The Pastoral Measure 1983 shall be amended as follows.

(2) In section 55(1) for 'the Charities Act 1960' and 'section 45(2)(b)' there shall be substituted 'the Charities Act 1993' and 'section 96(2)(c)'.

(3) In section 63(3) for 'the Charities Act 1960' there shall be substituted 'the Charities Act 1993'.

(4) In section 87(1) for 'section 45 of the Charities Act 1960' there shall be substituted 'section 96 of the Charities Act 1993'.

(5) In paragraphs 11(6) and 16(1)(e) of Schedule 3 for 'section 18 of the Charities Act 1960' there shall be substituted 'section 16 of the Charities Act 1993'.

The Rates Act 1984 (c.33)

19   In section 3(9) of the Rates Act 1984 for 'section 4 of the Charities Act 1960' there shall be substituted 'section 3 of the Charities Act 1993'.

The Companies Act 1985 (c.6)

20   [. . .]

The Housing Associations Act 1985 (c.69)

21   (1) The Housing Associations Act 1985 shall be amended as follows.

(2) In section 10(1) for 'sections 32 and 34 of the Charities Act 1992' there shall be substituted 'sections 36 and 38 of the Charities Act 1993'.

(3) [. . .]

(4) In section 35(2)(c) for 'section 32 of the Charities Act 1992' there shall be substituted 'section 36 of the Charities Act 1993'.

(5) In section 38 –

   (a) in paragraph (a) for 'the Charities Act 1960' there shall be substituted 'the Charities Act 1993'

   (b) [. . .]

The Financial Services Act 1986 (c.60)

22 In section 45(1)(j) of the Financial Services Act 1986 after 'the Charities Act 1960' there shall be inserted ', section 24 or 25 of the Charities Act 1993'.

The Coal Industry Act 1987 (c.3)

23 (1) In section 5 of the Coal Industry Act 1987 for subsection (8) there shall be substituted –'(8) Sections 16(3), (9), (11) to (14), 17(1) to (5) and (7) and 20 of the Charities Act 1993 shall apply in relation to the powers of the Charity Commissioners and the making of schemes under this section as they apply in relation to their powers and the making of schemes under that Act and sections 89, 91 and 92 of that Act shall apply to orders and decisions under this section as they apply to orders and decisions under that Act.'

   (2) In subsection (8A) of that section for 'section 29' (in both places) there shall be substituted 'section 17'.

The Reverter of Sites Act 1987 (c.15)

24 In section 4(4) of the Reverter of Sites Act 1987 for 'sections 40, 40A and 42 of the Charities Act 1960' there shall be substituted 'sections 89, 91 and 92 of the Charities Act 1993'.

The Income and Corporation Taxes Act 1988 (c.1)

25 In Schedule 20 to the Income and Corporation Taxes Act 1988 –

   (a) in paragraph 3 after 'the Charities Act 1960' there shall be inserted ', section 24 of the Charities Act 1993'

   (b) in paragraph 3A after 'the Charities Act 1960' there shall be inserted 'or section 25 of the Charities Act 1993'.

The Courts and Legal Services Act 1990 (c.41)

26 In Schedule 11 to the Courts and Legal Services Act 1990, in the reference to a Charity Commissioner, for 'under the First Schedule to the Charities Act 1960' there shall be substituted 'as provided in Schedule 1 to the Charities Act 1993'.

The London Local Authorities Act 1990 (c.vii)

27 [. . .]

The London Local Authorities Act 1991 (c.xiii)

28 In section 4 of the London Local Authorities Act 1991, in the definition of 'establishment for special treatment', for 'section 4 of the Charities Act 1960' and 'subsection (4) of that section' there shall be substituted respectively 'section 3 of the Charities Act 1993' and 'subsection (5) of that section'.

The Charities Act 1992 (c.41)

29 (1) The Charities Act 1992 shall be amended as follows.

   (2) In section 29(2)(b) after 'Act' there shall be inserted 'or section 18 of the Charities Act 1993'.

(3) In section 30(1)(b) after 'Act' there shall be inserted 'or section 22(1) of the Charities Act 1993'.

(4) In section 30(3)(a) after 'Act' there shall be inserted 'or section 18 of the Charities Act 1993'.

(5) In section 58(1), in the definition of 'charity' for 'the Charities Act 1960' there shall be substituted 'the Charities Act 1993' and in the definition of 'company' for the words after 'section' there shall be substituted '97 of the Charities Act 1993'.

(6) In section 63(2) for 'section 4 of the Charities Act 1960' there shall be substituted 'section 3 of the Charities Act 1993'.

(7) In section 72 for subsection (5) there shall be substituted –

'(5)   Section 89(1), (2) and (4) of the Charities Act 1993 (provisions as to orders made by the Commissioners) shall apply to an order made by them under this section as it applies to an order made by them under that Act.

(6)   In this section "charity" and "charitable purposes" have the same meaning as in that Act.'

(8) In section 74 after subsection (3) there shall be inserted –

'(3A) Any person who knowingly or recklessly provides the Commissioners with information which is false or misleading in a material particular shall be guilty of an offence if the information is provided in circumstances in which he intends, or could reasonably be expected to know, that it would be used by them for the purpose of discharging their functions under section 72.

(3B) A person guilty of an offence under subsection (3A) shall be liable –

(a)   on summary conviction, to a fine not exceeding the statutory maximum;

(b)   on conviction or indictment, to imprisonment for a term not exceeding two years or to a fine, or both.'

Other amendments

30   In the following provisions for 'the Charities Act 1960' there shall be substituted 'the Charities Act 1993' –

The National Health Service Reorganisation Act 1973 section 30(5).
The Consumer Credit Act 1974 section 189(1).
The Rent (Agriculture) Act 1976 section 5(3)(f).
The Rent Act 1977 section 15(2)(b).
The National Health Service Act 1977 section 96(2).
The Dioceses Measure 1978 section 19(4).
The Ancient Monuments and Archaeological Areas Act 1979 section 49(3).
The Greater London Council (General Powers) Act 1984 section 10(2)(n).
The Local Government Act 1985 section 90(4).
The Housing Act 1985 sections 525 and 622.
The Landlord and Tenant Act 1987 section 60(1).
The Education Reform Act 1988 sections 128(5) and 192(11).
The Copyright, Designs and Patents Act 1988 Schedule 6 paragraph 7.
The Housing Act 1988 Schedule 2 Part I Ground 6.
The University of Wales College of Cardiff Act 1988 section 9.
The Imperial College Act 1988 section 10.
[. . .]

SCHEDULE 7   REPEALS

Section 98(2)

Chapter	Short title	Extent of repeal
35 & 36 Vic.c.24.	The Charitable Trustees incorporation Act 1872.	The whole Act so far as unrepealed.
10 & 11 Geo.5. c.16.	The Imperial War Museum Act 1920.	Section 5.
24 & 25 Geo.5. c.43.	The National Maritime Museum Act 1934.	Section 7.
8 & 9 Eliz.2 c.58.	The Charities Act 1960.	The whole Act so far as unrepealed except – section 28(9) section 35(6) section 38(3) to (5) section 39(2) sections 48 and 49 Schedule 6.
1963 c.33.	The London Government Act 1963.	Section 81(9)(b) and (c).
1963 c.xi.	The Universities of Durham and Newcastle-upon-Tyne Act 1963.	Section 10.
1965 c.17.	The Museum of London Act 1965.	Section 11.
1972 c.54.	The British Library Act 1972.	Section 4(2).
1972 c.70.	The Local Government Act 1972.	Section 210(9).
1973 c.16.	The Education Act 1973.	In section 2(7) the words from 'but' onwards. In Schedule 1, paragraph 1(1) and (3).
1976 No.4.	The Endowments and Glebe Measure 1976.	Section 44.
1983 c.47.	The National Heritage Act 1983.	In Schedule 5, paragraph 4.
1985 c.9.	The Companies Consolidation (Consequential Provisions) Act 1985.	In Schedule 2 the entry relating to the Charities Act 1960.
1985 c.20.	The Charities Act 1985.	Section 1.
1986 c.60.	The Financial Services Act 1986.	In Schedule 16, paragraph 1.

Chapter	Short title	Extent of repeal
1988 c.40.	The Education Reform Act 1988.	In Schedule 12, paragraphs 9, 10, 63 and 64.
1989 c.40.	The Companies Act 1989.	Section 111.
1989 c.xiii.	The Queen Mary and Westfield College Act 1989.	Section 10.
1990 c.41.	The Courts and Legal Services Act 1990.	In Schedule 10, paragraph 14.
1992 c.13.	The Further and Higher Education Act 1992.	In Schedule 8, paragraph 69.
1992 c.41.	The Charities Act 1992.	The whole of Part I except – section 1(1) and (4) sections 29 and 30 section 36 sections 49 and 50 Section 75(b). Section 76(1)(a). In section 77, subsections (2)(a), (b) and (c) and in subsection (4) the figures 20, 22 and 23. Section 79(4) and (5). Schedules 1 to 4. In Schedule 6, paragraph 13(2). In Schedule 7, the entries relating to section 8 of the Charities Act 1960 and (so far as not in force at the date specified in section 99(1) of this Act) the Charities Act 1985.
1992 c.44.	The Museums and Galleries Act 1992.	In Schedule 8, paragraphs 4 and 10. In Schedule 9, the entry relating to the Charities Act 1960.

SCHEDULE 8   [. . .]

APPENDIX 4
Charities Act 2006

[2006 Chapter 50]

CONTENTS

PART 1 MEANING OF 'CHARITY' AND 'CHARITABLE PURPOSE'

PART 2 REGULATION OF CHARITIES

CHAPTER 1 THE CHARITY COMMISSION

Establishment of Charity Commission

Commission's objectives, general functions etc.

CHAPTER 2 THE CHARITY TRIBUNAL

CHAPTER 3 REGISTRATION OF CHARITIES

General

Exempt charities: registration and regulation

CHAPTER 4   APPLICATION OF PROPERTY CY-PRÈS

Cy-près occasions

Schemes

CHAPTER 5   ASSISTANCE AND SUPERVISION OF CHARITIES BY COURT AND COMMISSION

Suspension or removal of trustees etc. from membership

Directions by Commission

Publicity relating to schemes

Common investment schemes

Advice or other assistance

Powers of entry etc.

Mortgages of charity land

CHAPTER 6   AUDIT OR EXAMINATION OF ACCOUNTS WHERE CHARITY IS NOT A COMPANY

CHAPTER 7   CHARITABLE COMPANIES

CHAPTER 8   CHARITABLE INCORPORATED ORGANISATIONS

CHAPTER 9   CHARITY TRUSTEES ETC.

Waiver of disqualification

Remuneration of trustees etc.

Liability of trustees etc.

Schedule 7 – Charitable incorporated organisations
Part 1 – New Part 8A of and Schedule 5B to 1993 Act
Part 2 – Other amendments of 1993 Act

Schedule 8 – Minor and consequential amendments

Schedule 9 – Repeals and revocations

Schedule 10 – Transitional provisions and savings

An Act to provide for the establishment and functions of the Charity Commission for England and Wales and the Charity Tribunal; to make other amendments of the law about charities, including provision about charitable incorporated organisations; to make further provision about public charitable collections and other fund-raising carried on in connection with charities and other institutions; to make other provision about the funding of such institutions; and for connected purposes.

[8th November 2006]

BE IT ENACTED by the Queen's most Excellent Majesty, by and with the advice and consent of the Lords Spiritual and Temporal, and Commons, in this present Parliament assembled, and by the authority of the same, as follows:–

PART 1   MEANING OF 'CHARITY' AND 'CHARITABLE PURPOSE'

1   Meaning of 'charity'

(1) For the purposes of the law of England and Wales, 'charity' means an institution which –

    (a) is established for charitable purposes only, and

    (b) falls to be subject to the control of the High Court in the exercise of its jurisdiction with respect to charities.

(2) The definition of 'charity' in subsection (1) does not apply for the purposes of an enactment if a different definition of that term applies for those purposes by virtue of that or any other enactment.

(3) A reference in any enactment or document to a charity within the meaning of the Charitable Uses Act 1601 (c.4) or the preamble to it is to be construed as a reference to a charity as defined by subsection (1).

2   Meaning of 'charitable purpose'

(1) For the purposes of the law of England and Wales, a charitable purpose is a purpose which –

    (a) falls within subsection (2), and

    (b) is for the public benefit (see section 3).

(2) A purpose falls within this subsection if it falls within any of the following descriptions of purposes –

    (a) the prevention or relief of poverty;

    (b) the advancement of education;

    (c) the advancement of religion;

    (d) the advancement of health or the saving of lives;

    (e) the advancement of citizenship or community development;

    (f) the advancement of the arts, culture, heritage or science;

    (g) the advancement of amateur sport;

    (h) the advancement of human rights, conflict resolution or reconciliation or the promotion of religious or racial harmony or equality and diversity;

(i)   the advancement of environmental protection or improvement;

(j)   the relief of those in need by reason of youth, age, ill-health, disability, financial hardship or other disadvantage;

(k)   the advancement of animal welfare;

(l)   the promotion of the efficiency of the armed forces of the Crown, or of the efficiency of the police, fire and rescue services or ambulance services;

(m) any other purposes within subsection (4).

(3) In subsection (2) –

(a)   in paragraph (c) 'religion' includes –

    (i)   a religion which involves belief in more than one god, and

    (ii)   a religion which does not involve belief in a god;

(b)   in paragraph (d) 'the advancement of health' includes the prevention or relief of sickness, disease or human suffering;

(c)   paragraph (e) includes –

    (i)   rural or urban regeneration, and

    (ii)   the promotion of civic responsibility, volunteering, the voluntary sector or the effectiveness or efficiency of charities;

(d)   in paragraph (g) 'sport' means sports or games which promote health by involving physical or mental skill or exertion;

(e)   paragraph (j) includes relief given by the provision of accommodation or care to the persons mentioned in that paragraph; and

(f)   in paragraph (l) 'fire and rescue services' means services provided by fire and rescue authorities under Part 2 of the Fire and Rescue Services Act 2004 (c.21).

(4) The purposes within this subsection (see subsection (2)(m)) are –

(a)   any purposes not within paragraphs (a) to (l) of subsection (2) but recognised as charitable purposes under existing charity law or by virtue of section 1 of the Recreational Charities Act 1958 (c.17);

(b)   any purposes that may reasonably be regarded as analogous to, or within the spirit of, any purposes falling within any of those paragraphs or paragraph (a) above; and

(c)   any purposes that may reasonably be regarded as analogous to, or within the spirit of, any purposes which have been recognised under charity law as falling within paragraph (b) above or this paragraph.

(5) Where any of the terms used in any of paragraphs (a) to (l) of subsection (2), or in subsection (3), has a particular meaning under charity law, the term is to be taken as having the same meaning where it appears in that provision.

(6) Any reference in any enactment or document (in whatever terms) –

(a)   to charitable purposes, or

(b)   to institutions having purposes that are charitable under charity law,

is to be construed in accordance with subsection (1).

(7) Subsection (6) –

(a)   applies whether the enactment or document was passed or made before or after the passing of this Act, but

(b)   does not apply where the context otherwise requires.

(8) In this section –

'charity law' means the law relating to charities in England and Wales; and

'existing charity law' means charity law as in force immediately before the day on which this section comes into force.

3   **The 'public benefit' test**

(1) This section applies in connection with the requirement in section 2(1)(b) that a purpose falling within section 2(2) must be for the public benefit if it is to be a charitable purpose.

(2) In determining whether that requirement is satisfied in relation to any such purpose, it is not to be presumed that a purpose of a particular description is for the public benefit.

(3) In this Part any reference to the public benefit is a reference to the public benefit as that term is understood for the purposes of the law relating to charities in England and Wales.

(4) Subsection (3) applies subject to subsection (2).

4   **Guidance as to operation of public benefit requirement**

(1) The Charity Commission for England and Wales (see section 6 of this Act) must issue guidance in pursuance of its public benefit objective.

(2) That objective is to promote awareness and understanding of the operation of the requirement mentioned in section 3(1) (see section 1B(3) and (4) of the Charities Act 1993 (c.10), as inserted by section 7 of this Act).

(3) The Commission may from time to time revise any guidance issued under this section.

(4) The Commission must carry out such public and other consultation as it considers appropriate –

 (a) before issuing any guidance under this section, or

 (b) (unless it considers that it is unnecessary to do so) before revising any such guidance.

(5) The Commission must publish any guidance issued or revised under this section in such manner as it considers appropriate.

(6) The charity trustees of a charity must have regard to any such guidance when exercising any powers or duties to which the guidance is relevant.

5   **Special provisions about recreational charities, sports clubs etc.**

(1) The Recreational Charities Act 1958 (c.17) is amended in accordance with subsections (2) and (3).

(2) [*Amends/inserts ss.1(2) and (2A) to RCA 1958*]

(3) Section 2 (miners' welfare trusts) is omitted.

(4) A registered sports club established for charitable purposes is to be treated as not being so established, and accordingly cannot be a charity.

(5) In subsection (4) a 'registered sports club' means a club for the time being registered under Schedule 18 to the Finance Act 2002 (c.23) (relief for community amateur sports club).

PART 2   REGULATION OF CHARITIES

CHAPTER 1   THE CHARITY COMMISSION

Establishment of Charity Commission

6   **The Charity Commission**

(1) [*Inserts new s.1A to CA 1993*]

(2) Schedule 1 (which inserts the new Schedule 1A into the 1993 Act) has effect.

(3) The office of Charity Commissioner for England and Wales is abolished.

(4) The functions of the Charity Commissioners for England and Wales and their property, rights and liabilities are by virtue of this subsection transferred to the Charity Commission for England and Wales.

(5) Any enactment or document has effect, so far as necessary for the purposes of or in consequence of the transfer effected by subsection (4), as if any reference to the Charity Commissioners for England and Wales or to any Charity Commissioner for England and Wales were a reference to the Charity Commission for England and Wales.

(6) Section 1 of, and Schedule 1 to, the 1993 Act cease to have effect.

(7) Schedule 2 (which contains supplementary provision relating to the establishment of the Charity Commission for England and Wales) has effect.

Commission's objectives, general functions etc.

7   The Commission's objectives, general functions and duties
[*Inserts new ss.1B–1E to CA 1993*]

CHAPTER 2   THE CHARITY TRIBUNAL

8   The Charity Tribunal
(1) [*Inserts new Part 1A (ss.2A–2D) to CA 1993*]
(2) Schedule 3 (which inserts the new Schedule 1B into the 1993 Act) has effect.
(3) Schedule 4 (which inserts the new Schedules 1C and 1D into the 1993 Act) has effect.

CHAPTER 3   REGISTRATION OF CHARITIES

General

9   Registration of charities
[*Amends CA 1993, s.3 and inserts new ss.3A and 3B*]

10   Interim changes in threshold for registration of small charities
(1) At any time before the appointed day, the Minister may by order amend section 3 of the 1993 Act (the register of charities) so as to –
  (a) replace section 3(5)(c) (threshold for registration of small charities) with a provision referring to a charity whose gross income does not exceed such sum as is prescribed in the order, and
  (b) define 'gross income' for the purposes of that provision.
(2) Subsection (1) does not affect the existing power under section 3(12) of that Act to increase the financial limit specified in section 3(5)(c).
(3) This section ceases to have effect on the appointed day.
(4) In this section 'the appointed day' means the day on which section 3A(1) to (5) of the 1993 Act (as substituted by section 9 of this Act) come into force by virtue of an order under section 79 of this Act.

Exempt charities: registration and regulation

11   Changes in exempt charities

(1)   Schedule 2 to the 1993 Act (exempt charities) is amended as follows.

(2)   In paragraph (a) (general exemption by reference to law existing prior to Charities Act 1960 (c. 58)) after '1855' insert '(but see Note 1)'.

(3)   In paragraph (b) (certain specified universities, colleges and schools) –

   (a)   before 'Queen Mary and Westfield College' insert 'and'; and

   (b)   omit 'and the colleges of Winchester and Eton'.

(4)   Before paragraph (i) insert –

'(h) a higher education corporation;'.

(5)   After paragraph (i) insert –

'(j) a further education corporation;'.

(6)   In paragraph (w) (exemption for institutions administered by or on behalf of institutions exempted under preceding provisions) after 'last-mentioned institution' insert '(but see Note 2)'.

(7)   Omit paragraph (x) (Church Commissioners and institutions administered by them).

(8)   In paragraph (y) (industrial and provident societies etc.) for the words from 'and any' onwards substitute 'and which is also registered in the register of social landlords under Part 1 of the Housing Act 1996;'.

(9)   [*Inserts note to CA 1993, Schedule 2*]

(10) In section 24 of the 1993 Act (schemes to establish common investment funds), in subsection (8) (fund is to be a charity and, if the scheme admits only exempt charities, an exempt charity) omit the words from '; and if the scheme' onwards.

(11) The Minister may by order make such further amendments of Schedule 2 to the 1993 Act as he considers appropriate for securing –

   (a)   that (so far as they are charities) institutions of a particular description become or (as the case may be) cease to be exempt charities, or

   (b)   that (so far as it is a charity) a particular institution becomes or (as the case may be) ceases to be an exempt charity,

or for removing from that Schedule an institution that has ceased to exist.

(12) An order under subsection (11) may only be made for the purpose mentioned in paragraph (a) or (b) of that subsection if the Minister is satisfied that the order is desirable in the interests of ensuring appropriate or effective regulation of the charities or charity concerned in connection with compliance by the charity trustees of the charities or charity with their legal obligations in exercising control and management of the administration of the charities or charity.

(13) The Minister may by order make such amendments or other modifications of any enactment as he considers appropriate in connection with –

   (a)   charities of a particular description becoming, or ceasing to be, exempt charities, or

   (b)   a particular charity becoming, or ceasing to be, an exempt charity,

by virtue of any provision made by or under this section.

(14) In this section 'exempt charity' has the same meaning as in the 1993 Act.

12   Increased regulation of exempt charities under 1993 Act

The 1993 Act is amended in accordance with Schedule 5 (which has effect for increasing the extent to which exempt charities are subject to regulation under that Act).

13 General duty of principal regulator in relation to exempt charity

(1) This section applies to any body or Minister of the Crown who is the principal regulator in relation to an exempt charity.

(2) The body or Minister must do all that it or he reasonably can to meet the compliance objective in relation to the charity.

(3) The compliance objective is to promote compliance by the charity trustees with their legal obligations in exercising control and management of the administration of the charity.

(4) In this section –

    (a) 'exempt charity' has the same meaning as in the 1993 Act; and

    (b) 'principal regulator', in relation to an exempt charity, means such body or Minister of the Crown as is prescribed as its principal regulator by regulations made by the Minister.

(5) Regulations under subsection (4)(b) may make such amendments or other modifications of any enactment as the Minister considers appropriate for the purpose of facilitating, or otherwise in connection with, the discharge by a principal regulator of the duty under subsection (2).

14 Commission to consult principal regulator before exercising powers in relation to exempt charity

[*Inserts new s.86A to CA 1993*]

CHAPTER 4   APPLICATION OF PROPERTY CY-PRÈS

Cy-près occasions

15 Application cy-près by reference to current circumstances

(1) Section 13 of the 1993 Act (occasions for applying property cy-près) is amended as follows.

(2) In subsection (1)(c), (d) and (e)(iii), for 'the spirit of the gift' substitute 'the appropriate considerations'.

(3) [*Inserts new s.13(1A) to CA 1993*]

16 Application cy-près of gifts by donors unknown or disclaiming

(1) Section 14 of the 1993 Act (application cy-près of gifts of donors unknown or disclaiming) is amended as follows.

(2) In subsection (4) (power of court to direct that property is to be treated as belonging to donors who cannot be identified) after 'court', in both places, insert 'or the Commission'.

17 Application cy-près of gifts made in response to certain solicitations

[*Inserts CA 1993, s.14A*]

Schemes

18 Cy-près schemes

[*Inserts CA 1993, s.14B*]

CHAPTER 5   ASSISTANCE AND SUPERVISION OF CHARITIES BY COURT AND COMMISSION

Suspension or removal of trustees etc. from membership

19   **Power to suspend or remove trustees etc. from membership of charity**
[*Inserts CA 1993, s.18A*]

Directions by Commission

20   **Power to give specific directions for protection of charity**
[*Inserts CA 1993, s.19A*]

21   **Power to direct application of charity property**
[*Inserts CA 1993, s.19B*]

Publicity relating to schemes

22   **Relaxation of publicity requirements relating to schemes etc.**
[*Amends/inserts CA 1993, ss.20, 20A*]

Common investment schemes

23   **Participation of Scottish and Northern Irish charities in common investment schemes etc.**
(1)   [*Inserts CA 1993, s.24(3A) and (3B)*]
(2)   In section 25(2) of that Act (application of provisions of section 24 to common deposit funds) for 'subsections (2) to (4)' substitute 'subsections (2), (3) and (4)'.
(3)   [*Inserts CA 1993, s.25(4), (5) and (6)*]
(4)   [*Inserts CA 1993, s.25A*]

Advice or other assistance

24   **Power to give advice and guidance**
[*Amends CA 1993, s.29*]

25   **Power to determine membership of charity**
[*Inserts CA 1993, s.29A*]

Powers of entry etc.

26   **Power to enter premises and seize documents etc.**
(1)   [*Inserts CA 1993, s.31A*]
(2)   In Part 1 of Schedule 1 to the Criminal Justice and Police Act 2001 (c.16) (powers of seizure to which section 50 applies), after paragraph 56 insert –

'56A   Charities Act 1993 (c.10)

The power of seizure conferred by section 31A(3) of the Charities Act 1993 (seizure of material for the purposes of an inquiry under section 8 of that Act).'

Mortgages of charity land

27   Restrictions on mortgaging

(1)   Section 38 of the 1993 Act (restrictions on mortgaging) is amended as follows.

(2)   [*Amends/inserts CA 1993, s.38(2), (3), (3A)–(3D)*]

(3)   In subsection (4) (meaning of 'proper advice') –

    (a)   for 'subsection (2) above' substitute 'this section'; and

    (b)   for 'the making of the loan in question' substitute 'relation to the loan, grant or other transaction in connection with which his advice is given'.

CHAPTER 6   AUDIT OR EXAMINATION OF ACCOUNTS WHERE CHARITY IS NOT A COMPANY

28   Annual audit or examination of accounts of charities which are not companies

(1)   Section 43 of the 1993 Act (annual audit or examination of accounts of charities which are not companies) is amended as follows.

(2)   [*Amends CA 1993, s.41(1)*]

(3)   [*Amends CA 1993, s.43(2)(a)*]

(4)   In subsection (3) (independent examinations instead of audits) –

    (a)   for the words from 'and its gross income' to 'subsection (4) below)' substitute 'but its gross income in that year exceeds £10,000,'; and

    (b)   at the end insert –

'This is subject to the requirements of subsection (3A) below where the gross income exceeds £250,000, and to any order under subsection (4) below.'

(5)   [*Inserts CA 1993, s.43(3A)*]

(6)   [*Amends CA 1993, s.43(8)*]

29   Duty of auditor etc. of charity which is not a company to report matters to Commission

(1)   [*Inserts CA 1993, s.44A*]

(2)   In section 46 of the 1993 Act (special provisions as respects accounts and annual reports of exempt and excepted charities) –

    (a)   in subsection (1) for 'sections 41 to 45' substitute 'sections 41 to 44 or section 45'; and

    (b)   [*inserts CA 1993, s.46(2A), (2B)*]

30   Group accounts

(1)   [*Inserts CA 1993, s.49A*]

(2)   Schedule 6 (which inserts the new Schedule 5A into the 1993 Act) has effect.

CHAPTER 7   CHARITABLE COMPANIES

31   Relaxation of restriction on altering memorandum etc. of charitable company

(1)   Section 64 of the 1993 Act (alteration of objects clause etc.) is amended as follows.

(2)   [*Amends/inserts CA 1993, s.64(2), (2A), (2B)*]

(3)   In subsection (3) (documents required to be delivered to registrar of companies), for 'any such alteration' substitute 'a regulated alteration'.

32   Annual audit or examination of accounts of charitable companies

(1)   In section 249A(4) of the Companies Act 1985 (c.6) (circumstances in which charitable company's accounts may be subject to an accountant's report instead of an audit) –

(a)   in paragraph (b) (gross income between £90,000 and £250,000) for '£250,000' substitute '£500,000'; and

(b)   in paragraph (c) (balance sheet total not more than £1.4 million) for '£1.4 million' substitute '£2.8 million'.

(2)   In section 249B(1C) of that Act (circumstances in which parent company or subsidiary not disqualified for exemption from auditing requirement), in paragraph (b) (group's aggregate turnover not more than £350,000 net or £420,000 gross in case of charity), for '£350,000 net (or £420,000 gross)' substitute '£700,000 net (or £840,000 gross)'.

33   Duty of auditor etc. of charitable company to report matters to Commission

[*Inserts CA 1993, s.68A*]

CHAPTER 8   CHARITABLE INCORPORATED ORGANISATIONS

34   Charitable incorporated organisations

Schedule 7, which makes provision about charitable incorporated organisations, has effect.

CHAPTER 9   CHARITY TRUSTEES ETC.

Waiver of disqualification

35   Waiver of trustee's disqualification

[*Inserts CA 1993, s.72(4A)*]

Remuneration of trustees etc.

36   Remuneration of trustees etc. providing services to charity

[*Inserts CA 1993, ss.73A, 73B*]

37   Disqualification of trustee receiving remuneration by virtue of section 36

[*Inserts CA 1993, s.73C*]

Liability of trustees etc.

38   Power of Commission to relieve trustees, auditors etc. from liability for breach of trust or duty

[*Inserts CA 1993, ss.73D and 73E*]

39   Trustees' indemnity insurance

[*Inserts CA 1993, s.73F*]

CHAPTER 10   POWERS OF UNINCORPORATED CHARITIES

40   Power to transfer all property
[Amends/inserts CA 1993, ss.74, 74A and 74B]

41   Power to replace purposes
[Inserts CA 1993, s.74C]

42   Power to modify powers or procedures
[Inserts CA 1993, s.74D]

CHAPTER 11   POWERS TO SPEND CAPITAL AND MERGERS

Spending of capital

43   Power to spend capital
[Amends/inserts CA 1993, ss.75, 75A, 75B]

Mergers

44   Merger of charities
[Inserts CA 1993, ss.75C–75F]

PART 3   FUNDING FOR CHARITABLE, BENEVOLENT OR PHILANTHROPIC INSTITUTIONS

CHAPTER 1   PUBLIC CHARITABLE COLLECTIONS

Preliminary

45   Regulation of public charitable collections

(1) This Chapter regulates public charitable collections, which are of the following two types –

   (a) collections in a public place; and
   (b) door to door collections.

(2) For the purposes of this Chapter –

   (a) 'public charitable collection' means (subject to section 46) a charitable appeal which is made –

      (i)   in any public place, or
      (ii)   by means of visits to houses or business premises (or both);

   (b) 'charitable appeal' means an appeal to members of the public which is –

      (i)   an appeal to them to give money or other property, or
      (ii)   an appeal falling within subsection (4),

   (or both) and which is made in association with a representation that the whole or any part of its proceeds is to be applied for charitable, benevolent or philanthropic purposes;

(c)   a 'collection in a public place' is a public charitable collection that is made in a public place, as mentioned in paragraph (a)(i);

(d)   a 'door to door collection' is a public charitable collection that is made by means of visits to houses or business premises (or both), as mentioned in paragraph (a)(ii).

(3)   For the purposes of subsection (2)(b) –

(a)   the reference to the giving of money is to doing so by whatever means; and

(b)   it does not matter whether the giving of money or other property is for consideration or otherwise.

(4)   An appeal falls within this subsection if it consists in or includes –

(a)   the making of an offer to sell goods or to supply services, or

(b)   the exposing of goods for sale,

to members of the public.

(5)   In this section –

'business premises' means any premises used for business or other commercial purposes;

'house' includes any part of a building constituting a separate dwelling;

'public place' means –

(a)   any highway, and

(b)   (subject to subsection (6)) any other place to which, at any time when the appeal is made, members of the public have or are permitted to have access and which either –

(i)   is not within a building, or

(ii)   if within a building, is a public area within any station, airport or shopping precinct or any other similar public area.

(6)   In subsection (5), paragraph (b) of the definition of 'public place' does not include –

(a)   any place to which members of the public are permitted to have access only if any payment or ticket required as a condition of access has been made or purchased; or

(b)   any place to which members of the public are permitted to have access only by virtue of permission given for the purposes of the appeal in question.

46   Charitable appeals that are not public charitable collections

(1)   A charitable appeal is not a public charitable collection if the appeal –

(a)   is made in the course of a public meeting; or

(b)   is made –

(i)   on land within a churchyard or burial ground contiguous or adjacent to a place of public worship, or

(ii)   on other land occupied for the purposes of a place of public worship and contiguous or adjacent to it,

where the land is enclosed or substantially enclosed (whether by any wall or building or otherwise); or

(c)   is made on land to which members of the public have access only –

(i)   by virtue of the express or implied permission of the occupier of the land, or

(ii)   by virtue of any enactment,

and the occupier is the promoter of the collection; or

(d)   is an appeal to members of the public to give money or other property by placing it in an unattended receptacle.

(2) For the purposes of subsection (1)(c) 'the occupier', in relation to unoccupied land, means the person entitled to occupy it.

(3) For the purposes of subsection (1)(d) a receptacle is unattended if it is not in the possession or custody of a person acting as a collector.

47   Other definitions for purposes of this Chapter

(1) In this Chapter –

'charitable, benevolent or philanthropic institution' means –

(a) a charity, or

(b) an institution (other than a charity) which is established for charitable, benevolent, or philanthropic purposes;

'collector', in relation to a public charitable collection, means any person by whom the appeal in question is made (whether made by him alone or with others and whether made by him for remuneration or otherwise);

'local authority' means a unitary authority, the council of a district so far as it is not a unitary authority, the council of a London borough or of a Welsh county or county borough, the Common Council of the City of London or the Council of the Isles of Scilly;

'prescribed' means prescribed by regulations under section 63;

'proceeds', in relation to a public charitable collection, means all money or other property given (whether for consideration or otherwise) in response to the charitable appeal in question;

'promoter', in relation to a public charitable collection, means –

(a) a person who (whether alone or with others and whether for remuneration or otherwise) organises or controls the conduct of the charitable appeal in question, or

(b) where there is no person acting as mentioned in paragraph (a), any person who acts as a collector in respect of the collection,

and associated expressions are to be construed accordingly;

'public collections certificate' means a certificate issued by the Commission under section 52.

(2) In subsection (1) 'unitary authority' means –

(a) the council of a county so far as it is the council for an area for which there are no district councils;

(b) the council of any district comprised in an area for which there is no county council.

(3) The functions exercisable under this Chapter by a local authority are to be exercisable –

(a) as respects the Inner Temple, by its Sub-Treasurer, and

(b) as respects the Middle Temple, by its Under Treasurer;

and references in this Chapter to a local authority or to the area of a local authority are to be construed accordingly.

Restrictions on conducting collections

48   Restrictions on conducting collections in a public place

(1) A collection in a public place must not be conducted unless –

(a) the promoters of the collection hold a public collections certificate in force under section 52 in respect of the collection, and

(b) the collection is conducted in accordance with a permit issued under section 59 by the local authority in whose area it is conducted.

(2) Subsection (1) does not apply to a public charitable collection which is an exempt collection by virtue of section 50 (local, short-term collections).

(3) Where –

    (a) a collection in a public place is conducted in contravention of subsection (1), and

    (b) the circumstances of the case do not fall within section 50(6),

every promoter of the collection is guilty of an offence and liable on summary conviction to a fine not exceeding level 5 on the standard scale.

49   Restrictions on conducting door to door collections

(1) A door to door collection must not be conducted unless the promoters of the collection –

    (a) hold a public collections certificate in force under section 52 in respect of the collection, and

    (b) have within the prescribed period falling before the day (or the first of the days) on which the collection takes place –

        (i) notified the local authority in whose area the collection is to be conducted of the matters mentioned in subsection (3), and

        (ii) provided that authority with a copy of the certificate mentioned in paragraph (a).

(2) Subsection (1) does not apply to a door to door collection which is an exempt collection by virtue of section 50 (local, short-term collections).

(3) The matters referred to in subsection (1)(b)(i) are –

    (a) the purpose for which the proceeds of the appeal are to be applied;

    (b) the prescribed particulars of when the collection is to be conducted;

    (c) the locality within which the collection is to be conducted; and

    (d) such other matters as may be prescribed.

(4) Where –

    (a) a door to door collection is conducted in contravention of subsection (1), and

    (b) the circumstances of the case do not fall within section 50(6),

every promoter of the collection is guilty of an offence and liable on summary conviction to a fine not exceeding level 5 on the standard scale.

This is subject to subsection (5).

(5) Where –

    (a) a door to door collection is conducted in contravention of subsection (1),

    (b) the appeal is for goods only, and

    (c) the circumstances of the case do not fall within section 50(6),

every promoter of the collection is guilty of an offence and liable on summary conviction to a fine not exceeding level 3 on the standard scale.

(6) In subsection (5) 'goods' includes all personal chattels other than things in action and money.

50   Exemption for local, short-term collections

(1) A public charitable collection is an exempt collection if –

    (a) it is a local, short-term collection (see subsection (2)), and

    (b) the promoters notify the local authority in whose area it is to be conducted of the matters mentioned in subsection (3) within the prescribed period falling before the day (or the first of the days) on which the collection takes place,

unless, within the prescribed period beginning with the date when they are so notified, the local authority serve a notice under subsection (4) on the promoters.

(2) A public charitable collection is a local, short term collection if –

    (a) the appeal is local in character; and

    (b) the duration of the appeal does not exceed the prescribed period of time.

(3) The matters referred to in subsection (1)(b) are –

    (a) the purpose for which the proceeds of the appeal are to be applied;

    (b) the date or dates on which the collection is to be conducted;

    (c) the place at which, or the locality within which, the collection is to be conducted; and

    (d) such other matters as may be prescribed.

(4) Where it appears to the local authority –

    (a) that the collection is not a local, short-term collection, or

    (b) that the promoters or any of them have or has on any occasion –

        (i)   breached any provision of regulations made under section 63, or

        (ii) been convicted of an offence within section 53(2)(a)(i) to (v),

    they must serve on the promoters written notice of their decision to that effect and the reasons for their decision.

(5) That notice must also state the right of appeal conferred by section 62(1) and the time within which such an appeal must be brought.

(6) Where –

    (a) a collection in a public place is conducted otherwise than in accordance with section 48(1) or a door to door collection is conducted otherwise than in accordance with section 49(1), and

    (b) the collection is a local, short term collection but the promoters do not notify the local authority as mentioned in subsection (1)(b),

    every promoter of the collection is guilty of an offence and liable on summary conviction to a fine not exceeding level 3 on the standard scale.

Public collections certificates

51 Applications for certificates

(1) A person or persons proposing to promote public charitable collections (other than exempt collections) may apply to the Charity Commission for a public collections certificate in respect of those collections.

(2) The application must be made –

    (a) within the specified period falling before the first of the collections is to commence, or

    (b) before such later date as the Commission may allow in the case of that application.

(3) The application must –

    (a) be made in such form as may be specified,

    (b) specify the period for which the certificate is sought (which must be no more than 5 years), and

    (c) contain such other information as may be specified.

(4) An application under this section may be made for a public collections certificate in respect of a single collection; and the references in this Chapter, in the context of such certificates, to public charitable collections are to be read accordingly.

(5) In subsections (2) and (3) 'specified' means specified in regulations made by the Commission after consulting such persons or bodies of persons as it considers appropriate.

(6) Regulations under subsection (5) –

   (a) must be published in such manner as the Commission considers appropriate,
   (b) may make different provision for different cases or descriptions of case, and
   (c) may make such incidental, supplementary, consequential or transitional provision as the Commission considers appropriate.

(7) In this section 'exempt collection' means a public charitable collection which is an exempt collection by virtue of section 50.

52   Determination of applications and issue of certificates

(1) On receiving an application for a public collections certificate made in accordance with section 51, the Commission may make such inquiries (whether under section 54 or otherwise) as it thinks fit.

(2) The Commission must, after making any such inquiries, determine the application by either –

   (a) issuing a public collections certificate in respect of the collections, or
   (b) refusing the application on one or more of the grounds specified in section 53(1).

(3) A public collections certificate –

   (a) must specify such matters as may be prescribed, and
   (b) shall (subject to section 56) be in force for –
      (i)   the period specified in the application in accordance with section 51(3)(b), or
      (ii) such shorter period as the Commission thinks fit.

(4) The Commission may, at the time of issuing a public collections certificate, attach to it such conditions as it thinks fit.

(5) Conditions attached under subsection (4) may include conditions prescribed for the purposes of that subsection.

(6) The Commission must secure that the terms of any conditions attached under subsection (4) are consistent with the provisions of any regulations under section 63 (whether or not prescribing conditions for the purposes of that subsection).

(7) Where the Commission –

   (a) refuses to issue a certificate, or
   (b) attaches any condition to it,

   it must serve on the applicant written notice of its decision and the reasons for its decision.

(8) That notice must also state the right of appeal conferred by section 57(1) and the time within which such an appeal must be brought.

53   Grounds for refusing to issue a certificate

(1) The grounds on which the Commission may refuse an application for a public collections certificate are –

   (a) that the applicant has been convicted of a relevant offence;
   (b) where the applicant is a person other than a charitable, benevolent or philanthropic institution for whose benefit the collections are proposed to be conducted, that the Commission is not satisfied that the applicant is authorised (whether by any such institution or by any person acting on behalf of any such institution) to promote the collections;
   (c) that it appears to the Commission that the applicant, in promoting any other collection authorised under this Chapter or under section 119 of the 1982 Act, failed to exercise the required due diligence;
   (d) that the Commission is not satisfied that the applicant will exercise the required due diligence in promoting the proposed collections;

(e) that it appears to the Commission that the amount likely to be applied for charitable, benevolent or philanthropic purposes in consequence of the proposed collections would be inadequate, having regard to the likely amount of the proceeds of the collections;

(f) that it appears to the Commission that the applicant or any other person would be likely to receive an amount by way of remuneration in connection with the collections that would be excessive, having regard to all the circumstances;

(g) that the applicant has failed to provide information –

    (i) required for the purposes of the application for the certificate or a previous application, or

    (ii) in response to a request under section 54(1);

(h) that it appears to the Commission that information so provided to it by the applicant is false or misleading in a material particular;

(i) that it appears to the Commission that the applicant or any person authorised by him –

    (i) has breached any conditions attached to a previous public collections certificate, or

    (ii) has persistently breached any conditions attached to a permit issued under section 59;

(j) that it appears to the Commission that the applicant or any person authorised by him has on any occasion breached any provision of regulations made under section 63(1)(b).

(2) For the purposes of subsection (1) –

  (a) a 'relevant offence' is –

    (i) an offence under section 5 of the 1916 Act;

    (ii) an offence under the 1939 Act;

    (iii) an offence under section 119 of the 1982 Act or regulations made under it;

    (iv) an offence under this Chapter;

    (v) an offence involving dishonesty; or

    (vi) an offence of a kind the commission of which would, in the opinion of the Commission, be likely to be facilitated by the issuing to the applicant of a public collections certificate; and

  (b) the 'required due diligence' is due diligence –

    (i) to secure that persons authorised by the applicant to act as collectors for the purposes of the collection were (or will be) fit and proper persons;

    (ii) to secure that such persons complied (or will comply) with the provisions of regulations under section 63(1)(b) of this Act or (as the case may be) section 119 of the 1982 Act; or

    (iii) to prevent badges or certificates of authority being obtained by persons other than those the applicant had so authorised.

(3) Where an application for a certificate is made by more than one person, any reference to the applicant in subsection (1) or (2) is to be construed as a reference to any of the applicants.

(4) Subject to subsections (5) and (6), the reference in subsection (2)(b)(iii) to badges or certificates of authority is a reference to badges or certificates of authority in a form prescribed by regulations under section 63(1)(b) of this Act or (as the case may be) under section 119 of the 1982 Act.

(5) Subsection (2)(b) applies to the conduct of the applicant (or any of the applicants) in relation to any public charitable collection authorised –

  (a) under regulations made under section 5 of the 1916 Act (collection of money or sale of articles in a street or other public place), or

    (b) under the 1939 Act (collection of money or other property by means of visits from house to house),

as it applies to his conduct in relation to a collection authorised under this Chapter, but subject to the modifications set out in subsection (6).

(6) The modifications are –

    (a) in the case of a collection authorised under regulations made under the 1916 Act –

        (i) the reference in subsection (2)(b)(ii) to regulations under section 63(1)(b) of this Act is to be construed as a reference to the regulations under which the collection in question was authorised, and

        (ii) the reference in subsection (2)(b)(iii) to badges or certificates of authority is to be construed as a reference to any written authority provided to a collector pursuant to those regulations; and

    (b) in the case of a collection authorised under the 1939 Act –

        (i) the reference in subsection (2)(b)(ii) to regulations under section 63(1)(b) of this Act is to be construed as a reference to regulations under section 4 of that Act, and

        (ii) the reference in subsection (2)(b)(iii) to badges or certificates of authority is to be construed as a reference to badges or certificates of authority in a form prescribed by such regulations.

(7) In subsections (1)(c) and (5) a reference to a collection authorised under this Chapter is a reference to a public charitable collection that –

    (a) is conducted in accordance with section 48 or section 49 (as the case may be), or

    (b) is an exempt collection by virtue of section 50.

(8) In this section –

'the 1916 Act' means the Police, Factories, &c. (Miscellaneous Provisions) Act 1916 (c.31);
'the 1939 Act' means the House to House Collections Act 1939 (c.44); and
'the 1982 Act' means the Civic Government (Scotland) Act 1982 (c.45).

54 Power to call for information and documents

(1) The Commission may request –

    (a) any applicant for a public collections certificate, or
    (b) any person to whom such a certificate has been issued,

to provide it with any information in his possession, or document in his custody or under this control, which is relevant to the exercise of any of its functions under this Chapter.

(2) Nothing in this section affects the power conferred on the Commission by section 9 of the 1993 Act.

55 Transfer of certificate between trustees of unincorporated charity

(1) One or more individuals to whom a public collections certificate has been issued ('the holders') may apply to the Commission for a direction that the certificate be transferred to one or more other individuals ('the recipients').

(2) An application under subsection (1) must –

    (a) be in such form as may be specified, and
    (b) contain such information as may be specified.

(3) The Commission may direct that the certificate be transferred if it is satisfied that –

    (a) each of the holders is or was a trustee of a charity which is not a body corporate;

(b)   each of the recipients is a trustee of that charity and consents to the transfer; and

(c)   the charity trustees consent to the transfer.

(4)   Where the Commission refuses to direct that a certificate be transferred, it must serve on the holders written notice of –

(a)   its decision, and

(b)   the reasons for its decision.

(5)   That notice must also state the right of appeal conferred by section 57(2) and the time within which such an appeal must be brought.

(6)   Subsections (5) and (6) of section 51 apply for the purposes of subsection (2) of this section as they apply for the purposes of subsection (3) of that section.

(7)   Except as provided by this section, a public collections certificate is not transferable.

56   Withdrawal or variation etc. of certificates

(1)   Where subsection (2), (3) or (4) applies, the Commission may –

(a)   withdraw a public collections certificate,

(b)   suspend such a certificate,

(c)   attach any condition (or further condition) to such a certificate, or

(d)   vary any existing condition of such a certificate.

(2)   This subsection applies where the Commission –

(a)   has reason to believe there has been a change in the circumstances which prevailed at the time when it issued the certificate, and

(b)   is of the opinion that, if the application for the certificate had been made in the new circumstances, it would not have issued the certificate or would have issued it subject to different or additional conditions.

(3)   This subsection applies where –

(a)   the holder of a certificate has unreasonably refused to provide any information or document in response to a request under section 54(1), or

(b)   the Commission has reason to believe that information provided to it by the holder of a certificate (or, where there is more than one holder, by any of them) for the purposes of the application for the certificate, or in response to such a request, was false or misleading in a material particular.

(4)   This subsection applies where the Commission has reason to believe that there has been or is likely to be a breach of any condition of a certificate, or that a breach of such a condition is continuing.

(5)   Any condition imposed at any time by the Commission under subsection (1) (whether by attaching a new condition to the certificate or by varying an existing condition) must be one that it would be appropriate for the Commission to attach to the certificate under section 52(4) if the holder was applying for it in the circumstances prevailing at that time.

(6)   The exercise by the Commission of the power conferred by paragraph (b), (c) or (d) of subsection (1) on one occasion does not prevent it from exercising any of the powers conferred by that subsection on a subsequent occasion; and on any subsequent occasion the reference in subsection (2)(a) to the time when the Commission issued the certificate is a reference to the time when it last exercised any of those powers.

(7)   Where the Commission –

(a)   withdraws or suspends a certificate,

(b)   attaches a condition to a certificate, or

(c)   varies an existing condition of a certificate,

it must serve on the holder written notice of its decision and the reasons for its decision.

(8)   That notice must also state the right of appeal conferred by section 57(3) and the time within which such an appeal must be brought.

(9) If the Commission –

    (a) considers that the interests of the public require a decision by it under this section to have immediate effect, and

    (b) includes a statement to that effect and the reasons for it in the notice served under subsection (7),

the decision takes effect when that notice is served on the holder.

(10) In any other case the certificate shall continue to have effect as if it had not been withdrawn or suspended or (as the case may be) as if the condition had not been attached or varied –

    (a) until the time for bringing an appeal under section 57(3) has expired, or

    (b) if such an appeal is duly brought, until the determination or abandonment of the appeal.

(11) A certificate suspended under this section shall (subject to any appeal and any withdrawal of the certificate) remain suspended until –

    (a) such time as the Commission may by notice direct that the certificate is again in force, or

    (b) the end of the period of six months beginning with the date on which the suspension takes effect,

whichever is the sooner.

57 Appeals against decisions of the Commission

(1) A person who has duly applied to the Commission for a public collections certificate may appeal to the Charity Tribunal ('the Tribunal') against a decision of the Commission under section 52 –

    (a) to refuse to issue the certificate, or

    (b) to attach any condition to it.

(2) A person to whom a public collections certificate has been issued may appeal to the Tribunal against a decision of the Commission not to direct that the certificate be transferred under section 55.

(3) A person to whom a public collections certificate has been issued may appeal to the Tribunal against a decision of the Commission under section 56 –

    (a) to withdraw or suspend the certificate,

    (b) to attach a condition to the certificate, or

    (c) to vary an existing condition of the certificate.

(4) The Attorney General may appeal to the Tribunal against a decision of the Commission –

    (a) to issue, or to refuse to issue, a certificate,

    (b) to attach, or not to attach, any condition to a certificate (whether under section 52 or section 56),

    (c) to direct, or not to direct, that a certificate be transferred under section 55,

    (d) to withdraw or suspend, or not to withdraw or suspend, a certificate, or

    (e) to vary, or not to vary, an existing condition of a certificate.

(5) In determining an appeal under this section, the Tribunal –

    (a) must consider afresh the decision appealed against, and

    (b) may take into account evidence which was not available to the Commission.

(6) On an appeal under this section, the Tribunal may –

    (a) dismiss the appeal,

    (b) quash the decision, or

    (c) substitute for the decision another decision of a kind that the Commission could have made;

and in any case the Tribunal may give such directions as it thinks fit, having regard to the provisions of this Chapter and of regulations under section 63.

(7) If the Tribunal quashes the decision, it may remit the matter to the Commission (either generally or for determination in accordance with a finding made or direction given by the Tribunal).

Permits

58   Applications for permits to conduct collections in public places

(1) A person or persons proposing to promote a collection in a public place (other than an exempt collection) in the area of a local authority may apply to the authority for a permit to conduct that collection.

(2) The application must be made within the prescribed period falling before the day (or the first of the days) on which the collection is to take place, except as provided in subsection (4).

(3) The application must –

    (a) specify the date or dates in respect of which it is desired that the permit, if issued, should have effect (which, in the case of two or more dates, must not span a period of more than 12 months);

    (b) be accompanied by a copy of the public collections certificate in force under section 52 in respect of the proposed collection; and

    (c) contain such information as may be prescribed.

(4) Where an application ('the certificate application') has been made in accordance with section 51 for a public collections certificate in respect of the collection and either –

    (a) the certificate application has not been determined by the end of the period mentioned in subsection (2) above, or

    (b) the certificate application has been determined by the issue of such a certificate but at a time when there is insufficient time remaining for the application mentioned in subsection (2) ('the permit application') to be made by the end of that period,

the permit application must be made as early as practicable before the day (or the first of the days) on which the collection is to take place.

(5) In this section 'exempt collection' means a collection in a public place which is an exempt collection by virtue of section 50.

59   Determination of applications and issue of permits

(1) On receiving an application made in accordance with section 58 for a permit in respect of a collection in a public place, a local authority must determine the application within the prescribed period by either –

    (a) issuing a permit in respect of the collection, or

    (b) refusing the application on the ground specified in section 60(1).

(2) Where a local authority issue such a permit, it shall (subject to section 61) have effect in respect of the date or dates specified in the application in accordance with section 58(3)(a).

(3) At the time of issuing a permit under this section, a local authority may attach to it such conditions within paragraphs (a) to (d) below as they think fit, having regard to the local circumstances of the collection –

    (a) conditions specifying the day of the week, date, time or frequency of the collection;

    (b) conditions specifying the locality or localities within their area in which the collection may be conducted;

    (c) conditions regulating the manner in which the collection is to be conducted;

    (d) such other conditions as may be prescribed for the purposes of this subsection.

(4) A local authority must secure that the terms of any conditions attached under subsection (3) are consistent with the provisions of any regulations under section 63 (whether or not prescribing conditions for the purposes of that subsection).

(5) Where a local authority –

(a) refuse to issue a permit, or
(b) attach any condition to it,

they must serve on the applicant written notice of their decision and the reasons for their decision.

(6) That notice must also state the right of appeal conferred by section 62(2) and the time within which such an appeal must be brought.

60   Refusal of permits

(1) The only ground on which a local authority may refuse an application for a permit to conduct a collection in a public place is that it appears to them that the collection would cause undue inconvenience to members of the public by reason of –

(a) the day or the week or date on or in which,
(b) the time at which,
(c) the frequency with which, or
(d) the locality or localities in which,

it is proposed to be conducted.

(2) In making a decision under subsection (1), a local authority may have regard to the fact (where it is the case) that the collection is proposed to be conducted –

(a) wholly or partly in a locality in which another collection in a public place is already authorised to be conducted under this Chapter, and
(b) on a day on which that other collection is already so authorised, or on the day falling immediately before, or immediately after, any such day.

(3) A local authority must not, however, have regard to the matters mentioned in subsection (2) if it appears to them –

(a) that the proposed collection would be conducted only in one location, which is on land to which members of the public would have access only –

(i) by virtue of the express or implied permission of the occupier of the land, or
(ii) by virtue of any enactment, and

(b) that the occupier of the land consents to that collection being conducted there;

and for this purpose 'the occupier', in relation to unoccupied land, means the person entitled to occupy it.

(4) In this section a reference to a collection in a public place authorised under this Chapter is a reference to a collection in a public place that –

(a) is conducted in accordance with section 48, or
(b) is an exempt collection by virtue of section 50.

61   Withdrawal or variation etc. of permits

(1) Where subsection (2), (3) or (4) applies, a local authority who have issued a permit under section 59 may –

(a) withdraw the permit,
(b) attach any condition (or further condition) to the permit, or
(c) vary any existing condition of the permit.

(2) This subsection applies where the local authority –

(a) have reason to believe that there has been a change in the circumstances which prevailed at the time when they issued the permit, and

(b) are of the opinion that, if the application for the permit had been made in the new circumstances, they would not have issued the permit or would have issued it subject to different or additional conditions.

(3) This subsection applies where the local authority have reason to believe that any information provided to them by the holder of a permit (or, where there is more than one holder, by any of them) for the purposes of the application for the permit was false or misleading in a material particular.

(4) This subsection applies where the local authority have reason to believe that there has been or is likely to be a breach of any condition of a permit issued by them, or that a breach of such a condition is continuing.

(5) Any condition imposed at any time by a local authority under subsection (1) (whether by attaching a new condition to the permit or by varying an existing condition) must be one that it would be appropriate for the authority to attach to the permit under section 59(3) if the holder was applying for it in the circumstances prevailing at that time.

(6) The exercise by a local authority of the power conferred by paragraph (b) or (c) of subsection (1) on one occasion does not prevent them from exercising any of the powers conferred by that subsection on a subsequent occasion; and on any subsequent occasion the reference in subsection (2)(a) to the time when the local authority issued the permit is a reference to the time when they last exercised any of those powers.

(7) Where under this section a local authority –

(a) withdraw a permit,
(b) attach a condition to a permit, or
(c) vary an existing condition of a permit,

they must serve on the holder written notice of their decision and the reasons for their decision.

(8) That notice must also state the right of appeal conferred by section 62(3) and the time within which such an appeal must be brought.

(9) Where a local authority withdraw a permit under this section, they must send a copy of their decision and the reasons for it to the Commission.

(10) Where a local authority under this section withdraw a permit, attach any condition to a permit, or vary an existing condition of a permit, the permit shall continue to have effect as if it had not been withdrawn or (as the case may be) as if the condition had not been attached or varied –

(a) until the time for bringing an appeal under section 62(3) has expired, or
(b) if such an appeal is duly brought, until the determination or abandonment of the appeal.

62 Appeals against decisions of local authority

(1) A person who, in relation to a public charitable collection, has duly notified a local authority of the matters mentioned in section 50(3) may appeal to a magistrates' court against a decision of the local authority under section 50(4) –

(a) that the collection is not a local, short-term collection, or
(b) that the promoters or any of them has breached any such provision, or been convicted of any such offence, as is mentioned in paragraph (b) of that subsection.

(2) A person who has duly applied to a local authority for a permit to conduct a collection in a public place in the authority's area may appeal to a magistrates' court against a decision of the authority under section 59 –

(a) to refuse to issue a permit, or
(b) to attach any condition to it.

(3) A person to whom a permit has been issued may appeal to a magistrates' court against a decision of the local authority under section 61 –

(a)   to withdraw the permit,

(b)   to attach a condition to the permit, or

(c)   to vary an existing condition of the permit.

(4)   An appeal under subsection (1), (2) or (3) shall be by way of complaint for an order, and the Magistrates' Courts Act 1980 (c.43) shall apply to the proceedings.

(5)   Any such appeal shall be brought within 14 days of the date of service on the person in question of the relevant notice under section 50(4), section 59(5) or (as the case may be) section 61(7); and for the purposes of this section an appeal shall be taken to be brought when the complaint is made.

(6)   An appeal against the decision of a magistrates' court on an appeal under subsection (1), (2) or (3) may be brought to the Crown Court.

(7)   On an appeal to a magistrates' court or the Crown Court under this section, the court may confirm, vary or reverse the local authority's decision and generally give such directions as it thinks fit, having regard to the provisions of this Chapter and of any regulations under section 63.

(8)   On an appeal against a decision of a local authority under section 50(4), directions under subsection (7) may include a direction that the collection may be conducted –

(a)   on the date or dates notified in accordance with section 50(3)(b), or

(b)   on such other date or dates as may be specified in the direction;

and if so conducted the collection is to be regarded as one that is an exempt collection by virtue of section 50.

(9)   It shall be the duty of the local authority to comply with any directions given by the court under subsection (7); but the authority need not comply with any directions given by a magistrates' court –

(a)   until the time for bringing an appeal under subsection (6) has expired, or

(b)   if such an appeal is duly brought, until the determination or abandonment of the appeal.

Supplementary

63   Regulations

(1)   The Minister may make regulations –

(a)   prescribing the matters which a local authority are to take into account in determining whether a collection is local in character for the purposes of section 50(2)(a);

(b)   for the purpose of regulating the conduct of public charitable collections;

(c)   prescribing anything falling to be prescribed by virtue of any provision of this Chapter.

(2)   The matters which may be prescribed by regulations under subsection (1)(a) include –

(a)   the extent of the area within which the appeal is to be conducted;

(b)   whether the appeal forms part of a series of appeals;

(c)   the number of collectors making the appeal and whether they are acting for remuneration or otherwise;

(d)   the financial resources (of any description) of any charitable, benevolent or philanthropic institution for whose benefit the appeal is to be conducted;

(e)   where the promoters live or have any place of business.

(3)   Regulations under subsection (1)(b) may make provision –

(a)   about the keeping and publication of accounts;

(b)   for the prevention of annoyance to members of the public;

(c)   with respect to the use by collectors of badges and certificates of authority, or badges incorporating such certificates, including, in particular, provision –

    (i)   prescribing the form of such badges and certificates;

    (ii) requiring a collector, on request, to permit his badge, or any certificate of authority held by him of the purposes of the collection, to be inspected by a constable or a duly authorised officer of a local authority, or by an occupier of any premises visited by him in the course of the collection;

  (d) for prohibiting persons under a prescribed age from acting as collectors, and prohibiting others from causing them so to act.

(4) Nothing in subsection (2) or (3) prejudices the generality of subsection (1)(a) or (b).

(5) Regulations under this section may provide that any failure to comply with a specified provision of the regulations is to be an offence punishable on summary conviction by a fine not exceeding level 2 on the standard scale.

(6) Before making regulations under this section the Minister must consult such persons or bodies of persons as he considers appropriate.

64 Offences

(1) A person commits an offence if, in connection with any charitable appeal, he displays or uses –

  (a) a prescribed badge or prescribed certificate of authority which is not for the time being held by him for the purposes of the appeal pursuant to regulations under section 63, or

  (b) any badge or article, or any certificate or other document, so nearly resembling a prescribed badge or (as the case may be) a prescribed certificate of authority as to be likely to deceive a member of the public.

(2) A person commits an offence if –

  (a) for the purposes of an application made under section 51 or section 58, or

  (b) for the purposes of section 49 or section 50,

he knowingly or recklessly furnishes any information which is false or misleading in a material particular.

(3) A person guilty of an offence under this section is liable on summary conviction to a fine not exceeding level 5 on the standard scale.

(4) In subsection (1) 'prescribed badge' and 'prescribed certificate of authority' mean respectively a badge and a certificate of authority in such form as may be prescribed.

65 Offences by bodies corporate

(1) Where any offence under this Chapter or any regulations made under it –

  (a) is committed by a body corporate, and

  (b) is proved to have been committed with the consent or connivance of, or to be attributable to any neglect on the part of, any director, manager, secretary or other similar officer of the body corporate, or any person who was purporting to act in any such capacity,

he as well as the body corporate shall be guilty of that offence and shall be liable to be proceeded against and punished accordingly.

(2) In subsection (1) 'director', in relation to a body corporate whose affairs are managed by its members, means a member of the body corporate.

66 Service of documents

(1) This section applies to any notice required to be served under this Chapter.

(2) A notice to which this section applies may be served on a person (other than a body corporate) –

  (a) by delivering it to that person;

  (b) by leaving it at his last known address in the United Kingdom; or

  (c) by sending it by post to him at that address.

(3) A notice to which this section applies may be served on a body corporate by delivering it or sending it by post –

    (a) to the registered or principal office of the body in the United Kingdom, or

    (b) if it has no such office in the United Kingdom, to any place in the United Kingdom where it carries on business or conducts its activities (as the case may be).

(4) A notice to which this section applies may also be served on a person (including a body corporate) by sending it by post to that person at an address notified by that person for the purposes of this subsection to the person or persons by whom it is required to be served.

CHAPTER 2   FUND-RAISING

67   Statements indicating benefits for charitable institutions and fund-raisers

(1) Section 60 of the Charities Act 1992 (c.41) (fund-raisers required to indicate institutions benefiting and arrangements for remuneration) is amended as follows.

(2) [*Amends CA 1992, s.60(1)(c)*]

(3) [*Amends CA 1992, s.60(2)(c)*]

(4) [*Amends CA 1992, s.60(3)(c)*]

(5) [*Inserts CA 1992, s.60(3A)*]

68   Statements indicating benefits for charitable institutions and collectors

[*Inserts CA 1992, ss.60A, 60B*]

69   Reserve power to control fund-raising by charitable institutions

[*Inserts CA 1992, s.64A*]

CHAPTER 3   FINANCIAL ASSISTANCE

70   Power of relevant Minister to give financial assistance to charitable, benevolent or philanthropic institutions

(1) A relevant Minister may give financial assistance to any charitable, benevolent or philanthropic institution in respect of any of the institution's activities which directly or indirectly benefit the whole or any part of England (whether or not they also benefit any other area).

(2) Financial assistance under subsection (1) may be given in any form and, in particular, may be given by way of –

    (a) grants,

    (b) loans,

    (c) guarantees, or

    (d) incurring expenditure for the benefit of the person assisted.

(3) Financial assistance under subsection (1) may be given on such terms and conditions as the relevant Minister considers appropriate.

(4) Those terms and conditions may, in particular, include provision as to –

    (a) the purposes for which the assistance may be used;

    (b) circumstances in which the assistance is to be repaid, or otherwise made good, to the relevant Minister, and the manner in which that is to be done;

    (c) the making of reports to the relevant Minister regarding the uses to which the assistance has been put;

    (d) the keeping, and making available for inspection, of accounts and other records;

(e) the carrying out of examinations by the Comptroller and Auditor General into the economy, efficiency and effectiveness with which the assistance has been used;

(f) the giving by the institution of financial assistance in any form to other persons on such terms and conditions as the institution or the relevant Minister considers appropriate.

(5) A person receiving assistance under this section must comply with the terms and conditions on which it is given, and compliance may be enforced by the relevant Minister.

(6) A relevant Minister may make arrangements for –

(a) assistance under subsection (1) to be given, or

(b) any other of his functions under this section to be exercised,

by some other person.

(7) Arrangements under subsection (6) may make provision for the functions concerned to be so exercised –

(a) either wholly or to such extent as may be specified in the arrangements, and

(b) either generally or in such cases or circumstances as may be so specified,

but do not prevent the functions concerned from being exercised by a relevant Minister.

(8) As soon as possible after 31st March in each year, a relevant Minister must make a report on any exercise by him of any powers under this section during the period of 12 months ending on that day.

(9) The relevant Minister must lay a copy of the report before each House of Parliament.

(10) In this section 'charitable, benevolent or philanthropic institution' means –

(a) a charity, or

(b) an institution (other than a charity) which is established for charitable, benevolent or philanthropic purposes.

(11) In this section 'relevant Minister' means the Secretary of State or the Minister for the Cabinet Office.

71   Power of National Assembly for Wales to give financial assistance to charitable, benevolent or philanthropic institutions

(1) The National Assembly for Wales may give financial assistance to any charitable, benevolent or philanthropic institution in respect of any of the institution's activities which directly or indirectly benefit the whole or any part of Wales (whether or not they also benefit any other area).

(2) Financial assistance under subsection (1) may be given in any form and, in particular, may be given by way of –

(a) grants,

(b) loans,

(c) guarantees, or

(d) incurring expenditure for the benefit of the person assisted.

(3) Financial assistance under subsection (1) may be given on such terms and conditions as the Assembly considers appropriate.

(4) Those terms and conditions may, in particular, include provision as to –

(a) the purposes for which the assistance may be used;

(b) circumstances in which the assistance is to be repaid, or otherwise made good, to the Assembly, and the manner in which that is to be done;

(c) the making of reports to the Assembly regarding the uses to which the assistance has been put;

(d) the keeping, and making available for inspection, of accounts and other records;

(e) the carrying out of examinations by the Auditor General for Wales into the economy, efficiency and effectiveness with which the assistance has been used;

(f) the giving by the institution of financial assistance in any form to other persons on such terms and conditions as the institution or the Assembly considers appropriate.

(5) A person receiving assistance under this section must comply with the terms and conditions on which it is given, and compliance may be enforced by the Assembly.

(6) The Assembly may make arrangements for –

(a) assistance under subsection (1) to be given, or
(b) any other of its functions under this section to be exercised,

by some other person.

(7) Arrangements under subsection (6) may make provision for the functions concerned to be so exercised –

(a) either wholly or to such extent as may be specified in the arrangements, and
(b) either generally or in such cases or circumstances as may be so specified,

but do not prevent the functions concerned from being exercised by the Assembly.

(8) After 31st March in each year, the Assembly must publish a report on the exercise of powers under this section during the period of 12 months ending on that day.

(9) In this section 'charitable, benevolent or philanthropic institution' means –

(a) a charity, or
(b) an institution (other than a charity) which is established for charitable, benevolent or philanthropic purposes.

PART 4   MISCELLANEOUS AND GENERAL

Miscellaneous

72   Disclosure of information to and by Northern Ireland regulator

(1) This section applies if a body (referred to in this section as 'the Northern Ireland regulator') is established to exercise functions in Northern Ireland which are similar in nature to the functions exercised in England and Wales by the Charity Commission.

(2) The Minister may by regulations authorise relevant public authorities to disclose information to the Northern Ireland regulator for the purpose of enabling or assisting the Northern Ireland regulator to discharge any of its functions.

(3) If the regulations authorise the disclosure of Revenue and Customs information, they must contain provision in relation to that disclosure which corresponds to the provision made in relation to the disclosure of such information by section 10(2) to (4) of the 1993 Act (as substituted by paragraph 104 of Schedule 8 to this Act).

(4) In the case of information disclosed to the Northern Ireland regulator pursuant to regulations made under this section, any power of the Northern Ireland regulator to disclose the information is exercisable subject to any express restriction subject to which the information was disclosed to the Northern Ireland regulator.

(5) Subsection (4) does not apply in relation to Revenue and Customs information disclosed to the Northern Ireland regulator pursuant to regulations made under this section; but any such information may not be further disclosed except with the consent of the Commissioners for Her Majesty's Revenue and Customs.

(6) Any person specified, or of a description specified, in regulations made under this section who discloses information in contravention of subsection (5) is guilty of an offence and liable –

(a) on summary conviction, to imprisonment for a term not exceeding 12 months or to a fine not exceeding the statutory maximum, or both;
(b) on conviction on indictment, to imprisonment for a term not exceeding two years or to a fine, or both.

(7) It is a defence for a person charged with an offence under subsection (5) of disclosing information to prove that he reasonably believed –

    (a) that the disclosure was lawful, or

    (b) that the information had already and lawfully been made available to the public.

(8) In the application of this section to Scotland or Northern Ireland, the reference to 12 months in subsection (6) is to be read as a reference to 6 months.

(9) In this section –

'relevant public authority' means –

    (a) any government department (other than a Northern Ireland department),

    (b) any local authority in England, Wales or Scotland,

    (c) any person who is a constable in England and Wales or Scotland,

    (d) any other body or person discharging functions of a public nature (including a body or person discharging regulatory functions in relation to any description of activities), except a body or person whose functions are exercisable only or mainly in or as regards Northern Ireland and relate only or mainly to transferred matters;

'Revenue and Customs information' means information held as mentioned in section 18(1) of the Commissioners for Revenue and Customs Act 2005 (c.11);

'transferred matter' has the same meaning as in the Northern Ireland Act 1998 (c.47).

73   Report on operation of this Act

(1) The Minister must, before the end of the period of five years beginning with the day on which this Act is passed, appoint a person to review generally the operation of this Act.

(2) The review must address, in particular, the following matters –

    (a) the effect of the Act on –

        (i) excepted charities,

        (ii) public confidence in charities,

        (iii) the level of charitable donations, and

        (iv) the willingness of individuals to volunteer,

    (b) the status of the Charity Commission as a government department, and

    (c) any other matters the Minister considers appropriate.

(3) After the person appointed under subsection (1) has completed his review, he must compile a report of his conclusions.

(4) The Minister must lay before Parliament a copy of the report mentioned in subsection (3).

(5) For the purposes of this section a charity is an excepted charity if –

    (a) it falls within paragraph (b) or (c) of section 3A(2) of the 1993 Act (as amended by section 9 of this Act), or

    (b) it does not fall within either of those paragraphs but, immediately before the appointed day (within the meaning of section 10 of this Act), it fell within section 3(5)(b) or (5B)(b) of the 1993 Act.

General

74   Orders and regulations

(1) Any power of a relevant Minister to make an order or regulations under this Act is exercisable by statutory instrument.

(2) Any such power –

    (a) may be exercised so as to make different provision for different cases or descriptions of case or different purposes or areas, and

    (b) includes power to make such incidental, supplementary, consequential, transitory, transitional or saving provision as the relevant Minister considers appropriate.

(3) Subject to subsection (4), orders or regulations made by a relevant Minister under this Act are to be subject to annulment in pursuance of a resolution of either House of Parliament.

(4) Subsection (3) does not apply to –

    (a) any order under section 11,

    (b) any regulations under section 13(4)(b) which amend any provision of an Act,

    (c) any regulations under section 72,

    (d) any order under section 75(4) which amends or repeals any provision of an Act or an Act of the Scottish Parliament,

    (e) any order under section 76 or 77, or

    (f) any order under section 79(2).

(5) No order or regulations within subsection (4)(a), (b), (c), (d) or (e) may be made by a relevant Minister (whether alone or with other provisions) unless a draft of the order or regulations has been laid before, and approved by resolution of, each House of Parliament.

(6) If a draft of an instrument containing an order under section 11 would, apart from this subsection, be treated for the purposes of the Standing Orders of either House of Parliament as a hybrid instrument, it is to proceed in that House as if it were not such an instrument.

(7) In this section 'relevant Minister' means the Secretary of State or the Minister for the Cabinet Office.

75   Amendments, repeals, revocations and transitional provisions

(1) Schedule 8 contains minor and consequential amendments.

(2) Schedule 9 makes provision for the repeal and revocation of enactments (including enactments which are spent).

(3) Schedule 10 contains transitional provisions and savings.

(4) A relevant Minister may by order make –

    (a) such supplementary, incidental or consequential provision, or

    (b) such transitory, transitional or saving provision,

as he considers appropriate for the general purposes, or any particular purposes, of this Act or in consequence of, or for giving full effect to, any provision made by this Act.

(5) An order under subsection (4) may amend, repeal, revoke or otherwise modify any enactment (including an enactment restating, with or without modifications, an enactment amended by this Act).

(6) In this section 'relevant Minister' means the Secretary of State or the Minister for the Cabinet Office.

76   Pre-consolidation amendments

(1) The Minister may by order make such amendments of the enactments relating to charities as in his opinion facilitate, or are otherwise desirable in connection with, the consolidation of the whole or part of those enactments.

(2) An order under this section shall not come into force unless –

    (a) a single Act, or

    (b) a group of two or more Acts,

is passed consolidating the whole or part of the enactments relating to charities (with or without any other enactments).

(3) If such an Act or group of Acts is passed, the order shall (by virtue of this subsection) come into force immediately before the Act or group of Acts comes into force.

(4) Once an order under this section has come into force, no further order may be made under this section.

(5) In this section –

'amendments' includes repeals, revocations and modifications, and
'the enactments relating to charities' means –

(a) the Charities Act 1992 (c.41), the Charities Act 1993 (c.10) and this Act,
(b) any other enactment relating to institutions which fall within section 1(1) of this Act, and
(c) any other enactment, so far as forming part of the law of England and Wales, which makes provision relating to bodies or other institutions which are charities under the law of Scotland or Northern Ireland,

and section 78(2)(a) (definition of 'charity') does not apply for the purposes of this section.

77 Amendments reflecting changes in company law audit provisions

(1) The Minister may by order make such amendments of the 1993 Act or this Act as he considers appropriate –

(a) in consequence of, or in connection with, any changes made or to be made by any enactment to the provisions of company law relating to the accounts of charitable companies or to the auditing of, or preparation of reports in respect of, such accounts;
(b) for the purposes of, or in connection with, applying provisions of Schedule 5A to the 1993 Act (group accounts) to charitable companies that are not required to produce group accounts under company law.

(2) In this section –

'accounts' includes group accounts;
'amendments' includes repeals and modifications;
'charitable companies' means companies which are charities;
'company law' means the enactments relating to companies.

78 Interpretation

(1) In this Act –

'the 1992 Act' means the Charities Act 1992 (c.41);
'the 1993 Act' means the Charities Act 1993 (c.10).

(2) In this Act –

(a) 'charity' has the meaning given by section 1(1);
(b) 'charitable purposes' has (in accordance with section 2(6)) the meaning given by section 2(1); and
(c) 'charity trustees' has the same meaning as in the 1993 Act;

but (subject to subsection (3) below) the exclusions contained in section 96(2) of the 1993 Act (ecclesiastical corporations etc.) have effect in relation to references to a charity in this Act as they have effect in relation to such references in that Act.

(3) Those exclusions do not have effect in relation to references in section 1 or any reference to the law relating to charities in England and Wales.

(4) In this Act 'enactment' includes –

(a) any provision of subordinate legislation (within the meaning of the Interpretation Act 1978 (c.30)),

(b)   a provision of a Measure of the Church Assembly or of the General Synod of the Church of England, and

(c)   (in the context of section 6(5) or 75(5)) any provision made by or under an Act of the Scottish Parliament or Northern Ireland legislation,

and references to enactments include enactments passed or made after the passing of this Act.

(5)   In this Act 'institution' means an institution whether incorporated or not, and includes a trust or undertaking.

(6)   In this Act 'the Minister' means the Minister for the Cabinet Office.

(7)   Subsections (2) to (5) apply except where the context otherwise requires.

79   Commencement

(1)   The following provisions come into force on the day on which this Act is passed –

(a)   section 13(4) and (5),

(b)   section 74,

(c)   section 75(4) and (5),

(d)   section 78,

(e)   section 77,

(f)   this section and section 80, and

(g)   the following provisions of Schedule 8 –

paragraph 90(2),
paragraph 104 so far as it confers power to make regulations, and
paragraph 174(d),

and section 75(1) so far as relating to those provisions.

(2)   Otherwise, this Act comes into force on such day as the Minister may by order appoint.

(3)   An order under subsection (2) –

(a)   may appoint different days for different purposes or different areas;

(b)   make such provision as the Minister considers necessary or expedient for transitory, transitional or saving purposes in connection with the coming into force of any provision of this Act.

80   Short title and extent

(1)   This Act may be cited as the Charities Act 2006.

(2)   Subject to subsections (3) to (7), this Act extends to England and Wales only.

(3)   The following provisions extend also to Scotland –

(a)   sections 1 to 3 and 5,

(b)   section 6(5),

(c)   sections 72 and 74,

(d)   section 75(2) and (3) and Schedules 9 and 10 so far as relating to the Recreational Charities Act 1958 (c.17), and

(e)   section 75(4) and (5), sections 76 to 79 and this section.

(4)   But the provisions referred to in subsection (3)(a) and (d) affect the law of Scotland only so far as they affect the construction of references to charities or charitable purposes in enactments which relate to matters falling within Section A1 of Part 2 of Schedule 5 to the Scotland Act 1998 (c. 46) (reserved matters: fiscal policy etc.); and so far as they so affect the law of Scotland –

(a)   references in sections 1(1) and 2(1) to the law of England and Wales are to be read as references to the law of Scotland, and

(b)   the reference in section 1(1) to the High Court is to be read as a reference to the Court of Session.

(5) The following provisions extend also to Northern Ireland –

  (a) sections 1 to 3 and 5,
  (b) section 6(5),
  (c) section 23,
  (d) sections 72 and 74,
  (e) section 75(2) and (3) and Schedules 9 and 10 so far as relating to the Recreational Charities Act 1958 (c.17), and
  (f) section 75(4) and (5), sections 76 to 79 and this section.

(6) But the provisions referred to in subsection (5)(a) and (e) affect the law of Northern Ireland only so far as they affect the construction of references to charities or charitable purposes in enactments which relate to matters falling within paragraph 9 of Schedule 2 to the Northern Ireland Act 1998 (c.47) (excepted matters: taxes and duties); and so far as they so affect the law of Northern Ireland –

  (a) references in sections 1(1) and 2(1) to the law of England and Wales are to be read as references to the law of Northern Ireland, and
  (b) the reference in section 1(1) to the High Court is to be read as a reference to the High Court in Northern Ireland.

(7) Any amendment, repeal or revocation made by this Act has the same extent as the enactment to which it relates.

(8) But subsection (7) does not apply to any amendment or repeal made in the Recreational Charities Act 1958 by a provision referred to in subsection (3) or (5).

(9) Subsection (7) also does not apply to –

  (a) the amendments made by section 32 in the Companies Act 1985 (c.6), or
  (b) those made by Schedule 8 in the Police, Factories, &c. (Miscellaneous Provisions) Act 1916 (c.31), or
  (c) the repeal made in that Act by Schedule 9,

which extend to England and Wales only.

SCHEDULES

SCHEDULE 1   THE CHARITY COMMISSION   Section 6

1   [*Inserts CA 1993, Sched.1A*]

House of Commons Disqualification Act 1975 (c.24)

2   In Part 2 of Schedule 1 to the House of Commons Disqualification Act 1975 (bodies
     of which all members are disqualified) insert at the appropriate place –

     'The Charity Commission.'

Northern Ireland Assembly Disqualification Act 1975 (c.25)

3   In Part 2 of Schedule 1 to the Northern Ireland Assembly Disqualification Act 1975
     (bodies of which all members are disqualified) insert at the appropriate place –

     'The Charity Commission.'

SCHEDULE 2   ESTABLISHMENT OF THE CHARITY COMMISSION:
SUPPLEMENTARY   Section 6

1   In this Schedule –

     'commencement' means the coming into force of section 6, and
     'the Commission' means the Charity Commission.

Appointments to Commission

2   (1) The person who immediately before commencement was the Chief Charity
          Commissioner for England and Wales is on commencement to become the chair-
          man of the Commission as if duly appointed under paragraph 1 of Schedule 1A
          to the 1993 Act.
     (2) Any other person who immediately before commencement was a Charity
          Commissioner for England and Wales is on commencement to become a
          member of the Commission as if duly appointed under that paragraph.
     (3) While a person holds office as a member of the Commission by virtue of this
          paragraph he shall –
          (a) continue to be deemed to be employed in the civil service of the Crown,
               and
          (b) hold that office on the terms on which he held office as a Charity
               Commissioner for England and Wales immediately before commencement.
     (4) Sub-paragraph (3)(b) is subject to –
          (a) sub-paragraph (5),
          (b) paragraph 3(4) and (5) of Schedule 1A to the 1993 Act, and
          (c) any necessary modifications to the terms in question.
     (5) No person may hold office as a member of the Commission by virtue of this
          paragraph for a term exceeding three years from commencement.
     (6) Paragraphs 2 and 3(1) to (3) of Schedule 1A to the 1993 Act, and paragraphs 2
          and 3 of Schedule 1 to this Act, shall not apply in relation to a person while he
          holds office as a member of the Commission by virtue of this paragraph.

Effect of transfers under section 6

3   (1) Anything which –

(a)   has been done (or has effect as if done) by or in relation to the Commissioners, and

(b)   is in effect immediately before commencement,

is to be treated as if done by or in relation to the Commission.

(2)   Anything (including legal proceedings) which –

(a)   relates to anything transferred by section 6(4), and

(b)   is in the process of being done by or in relation to the Commissioners,

may be continued by or in relation to the Commission.

(3)   But nothing in section 6 or this paragraph affects the validity of anything done by or in relation to the Commissioners.

(4)   In this paragraph 'the Commissioners' means the Charity Commissioners for England and Wales (and includes any person acting for them by virtue of paragraph 3(3) of Schedule 1 to the 1993 Act).

First annual report of Commission

4   (1)   This paragraph applies if there is a period of one or more days which –

(a)   began on the day after the end of the last year for which the Charity Commissioners for England and Wales made a report under section 1(5) of the 1993 Act, and

(b)   ended on the day before commencement.

(2)   The first report published by the Commission under paragraph 11 of Schedule 1A to the 1993 Act shall also be a report on the operations of the Charity Commissioners for England and Wales during the period mentioned in sub-paragraph (1).

Resource accounts of Commission

5   (1)   The new Commission and the old Commission shall be treated as being the same government department for the purposes of section 5 of the Government Resources and Accounts Act 2000 (c.20).

(2)   Resource accounts sent to the Comptroller and Auditor General by the new Commission in respect of any period before commencement shall be resource accounts in the name of the new Commission.

(3)   In this paragraph –

'the new Commission' means the Charity Commission established by section 6, and

'the old Commission' means the government department known as the Charity Commission and existing immediately before commencement.

SCHEDULE 3   THE CHARITY TRIBUNAL   Section 8

1   [*Inserts CA 1993, Sched.1B*]

House of Commons Disqualification Act 1975 (c.24)

2   In Part 2 of Schedule 1 to the House of Commons Disqualification Act 1975 (bodies of which all members are disqualified) insert at the appropriate place –

'The Charity Tribunal.'

Northern Ireland Assembly Disqualification Act 1975 (c.25)

3   In Part 2 of Schedule 1 to the Northern Ireland Assembly Disqualification Act 1975 (bodies of which all members are disqualified) insert at the appropriate place –

'The Charity Tribunal.'

Courts and Legal Services Act 1990 (c.41)

4   In Schedule 11 to the Courts and Legal Services Act 1990 (judges etc. barred from legal practice) insert at the end –

'President or other member of the Charity Tribunal'.

Tribunals and Inquiries Act 1992 (c.53)

5   In Part 1 of Schedule 1 to the Tribunals and Inquiries Act 1992 (tribunals under general supervision of Council) before paragraph 7 insert –

'*Charities*

6A. The Charity Tribunal constituted under section 2A of, and Schedule 1B to, the Charities Act 1993.'

SCHEDULE 4   APPEALS AND APPLICATIONS TO CHARITY TRIBUNAL   Section 8

[*Inserts CA 1993, Scheds.1C and 1D*]

SCHEDULE 5   EXEMPT CHARITIES: INCREASED REGULATION UNDER 1993 ACT   Section 12

Power to require charity's name to be changed

1   In section 6 of the 1993 Act (power of Commission to require charity's name to be changed) omit subsection (9) (exclusion of exempt charities).

Power to institute inquiries

2   In section 8(1) of the 1993 Act (power of Commission to institute inquiries with regard to charities but not in relation to any exempt charity) after 'any exempt charity' insert 'except where this has been requested by its principal regulator.'

Power to call for documents etc.

3   In section 9 of the 1993 Act (power of Commission to call for documents and search records) omit subsection (4) (exclusion of documents relating only to exempt charities).

Concurrent jurisdiction of Commission with High Court

4   (1) Section 16 of the 1993 Act (concurrent jurisdiction of Commission with High Court for certain purposes) is amended as follows.
     (2) In subsection (4)(c) (application for Commission to exercise powers may be made by Attorney General except in case of exempt charity) omit 'in the case of a charity other than an exempt charity,'.
     (3) In subsection (5) (jurisdiction exercisable in case of charity which is not an exempt charity and whose annual income does not exceed £500) omit 'which is not an exempt charity and'.

Further powers of Commission

5   In section 17(7) of the 1993 Act (expenditure by charity on promoting Parliamentary Bill needs consent of court or Commission except in case of exempt charity) omit the words from 'but this subsection' onwards.

Power to act for protection of charities

6   [*Amends CA 1993, s.18(16)*]

Power to give directions about dormant bank accounts

7   In section 28 of the 1993 Act (power of Commission to give directions about dormant bank accounts of charities), omit subsection (10) (exclusion of accounts held by or on behalf of exempt charity).

Proceedings by persons other than Commission

8   (1) Section 33 of the 1993 Act (charity proceedings by persons other than Commission) is amended as follows.
    (2) In subsection (2) (proceedings relating to a charity other than an exempt charity must be authorised by the Commission) omit '(other than an exempt charity)'.
    (3) In subsection (7) (participation by Attorney General in proceedings relating to charity other than exempt charity) omit '(other than an exempt charity)'.

Power to order disqualified person to repay sums received from charity

9   In section 73 of the 1993 Act (consequences of person acting as charity trustee while disqualified), in subsection (4) (power of Commission to order disqualified person to repay sums received from a charity other than an exempt charity) omit '(other than an exempt charity)'.

SCHEDULE 6   GROUP ACCOUNTS   Section 30

[*Inserts CA 1993, Sched.5A*]

SCHEDULE 7   CHARITABLE INCORPORATED ORGANISATIONS
Section 34

PART 1   NEW PART 8A OF AND SCHEDULE 5B TO 1993 ACT

1   [*Inserts CA 1993, Part 8A, ss.69A–69Q*]
2   [*Inserts CA 1993, Sched.5B*]

PART 2   OTHER AMENDMENTS OF 1993 ACT

3   The 1993 Act is further amended as follows.
4   [*Inserts 1993, s.45(3B)*]
5   In section 48 (annual returns), in subsection (1A), at the end add '(but this subsection does not apply if the charity is constituted as a CIO)'.
6   In section 86 (regulations and orders) –

    (a)   [*Inserts s.86(2)(aa)*]
    (b)   in subsection (4), for 'or 45' substitute ', 45, 69N or 69Q'.

7   In section 97 (general interpretation), in subsection (1), at the appropriate place insert –

'"CIO" means charitable incorporated organisation;'.

SCHEDULE 8   MINOR AND CONSEQUENTIAL AMENDMENTS
Section 75

Literary and Scientific Institutions Act 1854 (c.112)

1   In section 6 of the Literary and Scientific Institutions Act 1854 (power of corporations etc. to convey land for the purposes of that Act) for 'without the consent of the Charity Commissioners' substitute 'except with the consent of the Charity Commission or in accordance with such provisions of section 36(2) to (8) of the Charities Act 1993 as are applicable'.

Places of Worship Registration Act 1855 (c.81)

2   In section 9(1) of the Places of Worship Registration Act 1855 (certified places exempt from requirement to register) –

(a) for 'shall be excepted under subsection (5) of section 3 of the Charities Act 1993, from registration under that section' substitute 'shall, so far as it is a charity, be treated for the purposes of section 3A(4)(b) of the Charities Act 1993 (institutions to be excepted from registration under that Act) as if that provision applied to it', and

(b) for 'Charity Commissioners' substitute 'Charity Commission'.

Bishops Trusts Substitution Act 1858 (c.71)

3   The Bishops Trusts Substitution Act 1858 has effect subject to the following amendments.

4   In section 1 (substitution of one bishop for another as trustee) –

(a) for 'Charity Commissioners' substitute 'Charity Commission', and

(b) for 'them' substitute 'it'.

5   In section 3 (how costs are to be defrayed) for 'said Charity Commissioners' (in both places) substitute 'Charity Commission'.

Places of Worship Sites Amendment Act 1882 (c.21)

6   In section 1(d) of the Places of Worship Sites Amendment Act 1882 (conveyance of lands by corporations and other public bodies) for 'without the consent of the Charity Commissioners' substitute 'except with the consent of the Charity Commission or in accordance with such provisions of section 36(2) to (8) of the Charities Act 1993 as are applicable'.

Municipal Corporations Act 1882 (c.50)

7   In section 133(2) of the Municipal Corporations Act 1882 (administration of charitable trusts and vesting of legal estate) for 'Charity Commissioners' substitute 'Charity Commission'.

Technical and Industrial Institutions Act 1892 (c.29)

8   In section 9(1) of the Technical and Industrial Institutions Act 1892 (site may be sold or exchanged) for 'with the consent of the Charity Commissioners' substitute 'with the consent of the Charity Commission or in accordance with such provisions of section 36(2) to (8) of the Charities Act 1993 as are applicable'.

Local Government Act 1894 (c.73)

9   (1) In section 75(2) of the Local Government Act 1894 (construction of that Act) the definition of 'ecclesiastical charity' is amended as follows.

(2) In the second paragraph (proviso) –

    (a) for 'Charity Commissioners' substitute 'Charity Commission', and

    (b) for 'them' substitute 'it'.

(3) In the third paragraph (inclusion of other buildings) for 'Charity Commissioners' substitute 'Charity Commission'.

Commons Act 1899 (c.30)

10 In section 18 of the Commons Act 1899 (power to modify provisions as to recreation grounds) –

    (a) for 'Charity Commissioners' substitute 'Charity Commission', and

    (b) for 'their' substitute 'its'.

Open Spaces Act 1906 (c.25)

11 The Open Spaces Act 1906 has effect subject to the following amendments.

12 In section 3(1) (transfer to local authority of spaces held by trustees for purposes of public recreation) for 'Charity Commissioners' substitute 'Charity Commission'.

13 (1) Section 4 (transfer by charity trustees of open space to local authority) is amended as follows.

    (2) In subsection (1), for the words from 'and with the sanction' to 'as hereinafter provided' substitute 'and in accordance with subsection (1A)'.

    (3) After subsection (1) insert –

        '(1A) The trustees act in accordance with this subsection if they convey or demise the open space as mentioned in subsection (1) –

            (a) with the sanction of an order of the Charity Commission or with that of an order of the court to be obtained as provided in the following provisions of this section, or

            (b) in accordance with such provisions of section 36(2) to (8) of the Charities Act 1993 as are applicable.'

    (4) In subsection (4) –

        (a) for 'Charity Commissioners' substitute 'Charity Commission', and

        (b) for 'them' substitute 'it'.

14 In section 21(1) (application to Ireland) –

    (a) for 'Charity Commissioners' substitute 'Charity Commission', and

    (b) for 'Commissioners of Charity Donations and Bequests for Ireland' substitute 'the Department for Social Development'.

Police, Factories, &c. (Miscellaneous Provisions) Act 1916 (c.31)

15 (1) Section 5 of the Police, Factories, &c. (Miscellaneous Provisions) Act 1916 (regulation of street collections) is amended as follows.

    (2) In subsection (1) for 'the benefit of charitable or other purposes,' substitute 'any purposes in circumstances not involving the making of a charitable appeal,'.

    (3) In paragraph (b) of the proviso to subsection (1) omit the words from ', and no representation' onwards.

    (4) In subsection (4) before the definition of 'street' insert –

        '"charitable appeal" has the same meaning as in Chapter 1 of Part 3 of the Charities Act 2006;'.

National Trust Charity Scheme Confirmation Act 1919 (c.lxxxiv)

16 The National Trust Charity Scheme Confirmation Act 1919 has effect subject to the following amendments.

17   In section 1 (confirmation of the scheme) for 'Charity Commissioners' substitute 'Charity Commission'.

18   In paragraph 3 of the scheme set out in the Schedule, for 'Charity Commissioners upon such application made to them for the purpose as they think' substitute 'Charity Commission upon such application made to it for the purpose as it thinks'.

Settled Land Act 1925 (c.18)

19   In section 29(3) of the Settled Land Act 1925 (charitable and public trusts: saving) for 'Charity Commissioners' substitute 'Charity Commission'.

Landlord and Tenant Act 1927 (c.36)

20   In Part 2 of the Second Schedule to the Landlord and Tenant Act 1927 (application to ecclesiastical and charity land), in paragraph 2, for 'Charity Commissioners' substitute 'Charity Commission'.

Voluntary Hospitals (Paying Patients) Act 1936 (c.17)

21   The Voluntary Hospitals (Paying Patients) Act 1936 has effect subject to the following amendments.

22   In section 1 (definitions), in the definition of 'Order', for 'Charity Commissioners' substitute 'Charity Commission'.

23   (1)   Section 2 (accommodation for and charges to paying patients) is amended as follows.
     (2)   In subsections (1), (3) and (4) for 'Charity Commissioners' substitute 'Charity Commission'.
     (3)   In subsection (4) –

          (a)   for 'the Commissioners' (in both places) substitute 'the Commission',
          (b)   for 'they' substitute 'it', and
          (c)   for 'their' substitute 'its'.

24   In section 3(1) (provision for patients able to make some, but not full, payment) –

     (a)   for 'Charity Commissioners are' substitute 'Charity Commission is', and
     (b)   for 'they' substitute 'it'.

25   In section 4 (provisions for protection of existing trusts) –

     (a)   for 'Charity Commissioners' substitute 'Charity Commission', and
     (b)   in paragraphs (a), (b) and (c) for 'they are' substitute 'it is'.

26   (1)   Section 5 (power to make rules) is amended as follows.
     (2)   In subsection (1) –

          (a)   for 'Charity Commissioners' substitute 'Charity Commission', and
          (b)   for 'they' substitute 'it'.

     (3)   In subsection (3) –

          (a)   for 'Charity Commissioners' (in both places) substitute 'Charity Commission',
          (b)   for 'they' and 'them' (in each place) substitute 'it', and
          (c)   for 'an officer' substitute 'a member of staff'.

     (4)   In the sidenote, for 'Charity Commissioners' substitute 'Charity Commission'.

27   In section 6(2) (savings) –

     (a)   for 'Charity Commissioners' substitute 'Charity Commission', and
     (b)   for 'them' substitute 'it'.

Green Belt (London and Home Counties) Act 1938 (c.xciii)

28   In section 20 of the Green Belt (London and Home Counties) Act 1938 (lands held on charitable trusts) for 'Charity Commissioners' substitute 'Charity Commission'.

New Parishes Measure 1943 (No.1)

29   The New Parishes Measure 1943 has effect subject to the following amendments.

30   In section 14(1)(b) (power of corporations etc. to give or grant land for sites of churches, etc.) for 'with the sanction of an order of the Charity Commissioners' substitute –

'(i)   with the sanction of an order of the Charity Commission, or

(ii)   in accordance with such provisions of section 36(2) to (8) of the Charities Act 1993 as are applicable;'.

31   In section 31 (charitable trusts) –

(a)   for 'the Board of Charity Commissioners' substitute 'the Charity Commission', and

(b)   for 'the Charity Commissioners' substitute 'the Charity Commission'.

Crown Proceedings Act 1947 (c.44)

32   In section 23(3) of the Crown Proceedings Act 1947 (proceedings with respect to which Part 2 of the Act does not apply) for 'Charity Commissioners' substitute 'Charity Commission'.

London County Council (General Powers) Act 1947 (c.xlvi)

33   (1)   Section 6 of the London County Council (General Powers) Act 1947 (saving for certain trusts) is amended as follows.

(2)   In subsection (2) –

(a)   for 'Charity Commissioners' substitute 'Charity Commission', and

(b)   at the end add '; but this is subject to subsection (3)'.

(3)   After subsection (2) add –

'(3)   In relation to any disposition of land falling within section 36(1) of the Charities Act 1993, the Council or the borough council may, instead of acting with the sanction of an order of the court or of the Charity Commission, make the disposition in accordance with such provisions of section 36(2) to (8) of that Act as are applicable.'

London County Council (General Powers) Act 1951 (c.xli)

34   In section 33(6) of the London County Council (General Powers) Act 1951 (improvement of roadside amenities: saving for certain land) for 'Charity Commissioners' substitute 'Charity Commission'.

City of London (Various Powers) Act 1952 (c.vi)

35   In section 4(6) of the City of London (Various Powers) Act 1952 (improvement of amenities) for 'Charity Commissioners' substitute 'Charity Commission'.

City of London (Guild Churches) Act 1952 (c.xxxviii)

36   In section 35 of the City of London (Guild Churches) Act 1952 (saving of rights of certain persons) for 'Charity Commissioners' substitute 'Charity Commission'.

London County Council (General Powers) Act 1955 (c.xxix)

37   (1)   Section 34 of the London County Council (General Powers) Act 1955 (powers as to erection of buildings: saving for certain land and buildings) is amended as follows.

(2)   In subsection (2) –

(a)   for 'Charity Commissioners' substitute 'Charity Commission', and

(b)   at the end add '; but this is subject to subsection (3)'.

(3) After subsection (2) add –

'(3) In relation to any disposition of land falling within section 36(1) of the Charities Act 1993, the Council may, instead of acting with the sanction of an order of the court or of the Charity Commission, make the disposition in accordance with such provisions of section 36(2) to (8) of that Act as are applicable.'

Parochial Church Councils (Powers) Measure 1956 (No.3)

38   In section 6(5) of the Parochial Church Councils (Powers) Measure 1956 (consents required for transactions relating to certain property) for 'Charity Commissioners' substitute 'Charity Commission'.

Recreational Charities Act 1958 (c.17)

39   [Amends/inserts RCA 1958, s.6(2) and (3)]

Church Funds Investment Measure 1958 (No.1)

40   Section 5 of the Church Funds Investment Measure 1958 (jurisdiction of Charity Commissioners) is omitted.

Incumbents and Churchwardens (Trusts) Measure 1964 (No.2)

41   The Incumbents and Churchwardens (Trusts) Measure 1964 has effect subject to the following amendments.
42   In section 2(3) (property to which Measure applies) for 'Charity Commissioners' substitute 'Charity Commission'.
43   In section 3(6) (vesting of property in diocesan authority: saving) for 'Charity Commissioners' substitute 'Charity Commission'.
44   In section 5 (provisions as to property vested in the diocesan authority) for 'Charity Commissioners' substitute 'Charity Commission'.
45   (1) The Schedule (procedure where diocesan authority is of the opinion that Measure applies to an interest) is amended as follows.
     (2) In paragraph 2 for 'Charity Commissioners' substitute 'Charity Commission'.
     (3) In paragraph 3 –

     (a)   for 'Charity Commissioners' substitute 'Charity Commission',
     (b)   for 'they think' (in both places) substitute 'it thinks', and
     (c)   for 'the Commissioners' substitute 'the Commission'.

     (4) In paragraph 5 –

     (a)   for 'Charity Commissioners have' substitute 'Charity Commission has', and
     (b)   for 'they' substitute 'it'.

Faculty Jurisdiction Measure 1964 (No.5)

46   In section 4(2) of the Faculty Jurisdiction Measure 1964 (sale of books in parochial libraries under a faculty) for 'Charity Commissioners' substitute 'Charity Commission'.

Industrial and Provident Societies Act 1965 (c.12)

47   In section 7D(4) of the Industrial and Provident Societies Act 1965 (application of sections 7A and 7B to charitable societies) for 'Charity Commissioners' substitute 'Charity Commission'.

Clergy Pensions (Amendment) Measure 1967 (No.1)

48   In section 4(5) of the Clergy Pensions (Amendment) Measure 1967 (amendments of powers of Board relating to provision of residences) for 'Charity Commissioners' and 'said Commissioners' substitute 'Charity Commission'.

Ministry of Housing and Local Government Provisional Order Confirmation (Greater London Parks and Open Spaces) Act 1967 (c.xxix)

49   In article 11(3) of the order set out in the Schedule to the Ministry of Housing and Local Government Provisional Order Confirmation (Greater London Parks and Open Spaces) Act 1967 (exercise of powers under articles 7 to 10 of the order) for 'Charity Commissioners' substitute 'Charity Commission'.

Redundant Churches and other Religious Buildings Act 1969 (c.22)

50   The Redundant Churches and other Religious Buildings Act 1969 has effect subject to the following amendments.

51   (1)   Section 4 (transfer of certain redundant places of worship) is amended as follows.

      (2)   In subsections (6), (7) and (8) for 'Charity Commissioners' substitute 'Charity Commission'.

      (3)   In subsection (6) for 'Commissioners'' substitute 'Commission's'.

      (4)   In subsection (8) for 'they have' substitute 'it has'.

      (5)   After subsection (8) insert –

             '(8A) Schedule 1C to the Charities Act 1993 shall apply in relation to an order made by virtue of subsection (8) above as it applies in relation to an order made under section 16(1) of that Act.'

52   In section 7(2) (saving) for 'Charity Commissioners' (in both places) substitute 'Charity Commission'.

Children and Young Persons Act 1969 (c.54)

53   In Schedule 3 to the Children and Young Persons Act 1969 (approved schools and other institutions), in paragraph 6(3), for 'Charity Commissioners' substitute 'Charity Commission'.

Synodical Government Measure 1969 (No.2)

54   (1)   Schedule 3 to the Synodical Government Measure 1969 (which sets out the Church Representation Rules) is amended as follows.

      (2)   In Rule 46A(a) –

             (a)   for 'Charity Commissioners' substitute 'Charity Commission', and

             (b)   for 'them' substitute 'it'.

      (3)   In Section 4 of Appendix I to those Rules (which sets out certain forms), in Note 3 –

             (a)   for 'Charity Commissioners' substitute 'Charity Commission', and

             (b)   for 'them' substitute 'it'.

      (4)   In Section 6 of that Appendix, in the Note –

             (a)   for 'Charity Commissioners' substitute 'Charity Commission', and

             (b)   for 'them' substitute 'it'.

      (5)   In Appendix II to those Rules (general provisions relating to parochial church councils), in paragraph 16, for 'Charity Commissioners' substitute 'Charity Commission'.

Local Government Act 1972 (c.70)

55   In section 131(3) of the Local Government Act 1972 (savings in relation to charity land) for 'Charity Commissioners' substitute 'Charity Commission'.

Consumer Credit Act 1974 (c.39)

56   In section 16 of the Consumer Credit Act 1974 (exempt agreements), in the table in subsection (3A) and in subsections (8) and (9), for 'Charity Commissioners' substitute 'Charity Commission'.

Sex Discrimination Act 1975 (c.65)

57   In section 21A of the Sex Discrimination Act 1975 (public authorities) in paragraph 14 in the Table of Exceptions in subsection (9), for 'Charity Commissioners for England and Wales' substitute 'Charity Commission'.

Endowments and Glebe Measure 1976 (No.4)

58   The Endowments and Glebe Measure 1976 has effect subject to the following amendments.
59   In section 11(2) (extinguishment of certain trusts) for 'the Charity Commissioners' substitute 'the Charity Commission or in accordance with such provisions of section 36(2) to (8) of the Charities Act 1993 as are applicable'.
60   In section 18(2) (means by which land may become diocesan) for 'Charity Commissioners' substitute 'Charity Commission'.

Interpretation Act 1978 (c.30)

61   In Schedule 1 to the Interpretation Act 1978 (words and expressions defined) for the definition of 'Charity Commissioners' substitute –

'"Charity Commission" means the Charity Commission for England and Wales established by section 1A of the Charities Act 1993.'

Dioceses Measure 1978 (No.1)

62   The Dioceses Measure 1978 has effect subject to the following amendments.
63   In section 5(1) (preparation of draft scheme: meaning of 'interested parties'), in paragraph (e), for 'the Charity Commissioners' substitute 'the Charity Commission'.
64   In section 19(4) (schemes with respect to discharge of functions of diocesan bodies corporate, etc.) for 'Charity Commissioners' substitute 'Charity Commission'.

Disused Burial Grounds (Amendment) Act 1981 (c.18)

65   In section 6 of the Disused Burial Grounds (Amendment) Act 1981 (saving for Charity Commission) for 'Charity Commissioners' substitute 'Charity Commission'.

Local Government (Miscellaneous Provisions) Act 1982 (c.30)

66   In Schedule 4 to the Local Government (Miscellaneous Provisions) Act 1982 (street trading) for paragraph 1(2)(j) substitute –

'(j)   conducting a public charitable collection that –

   (i)   is conducted in accordance with section 48 or 49 of the Charities Act 2006, or

   (ii)   is an exempt collection by virtue of section 50 of that Act.'

Administration of Justice Act 1982 (c.53)

67   In section 41(1) of the Administration of Justice Act 1982 (transfer of funds in court to official custodian for charities and Church Commissioners) for 'Charity Commissioners' substitute 'Charity Commission'.

Pastoral Measure 1983 (No.1)

68   The Pastoral Measure 1983 has effect subject to the following amendments.

69   In section 55(1) (schemes under the Charities Act 1993 for redundant chapels belonging to charities) for 'Charity Commissioners' substitute 'Charity Commission'.

70   In section 63(4) (trusts for the repair etc. of redundant buildings and contents) for 'the Charity Commissioners given under the hand of an Assistant Commissioner' substitute 'the Charity Commission'.

71   In section 76(1) (grant of land for new churches etc. and vesting of certain churches) for 'Charity Commissioners' substitute 'Charity Commission'.

72   In Schedule 3, in paragraph 11(1), (2), (6) and (7), for 'Charity Commissioners' substitute 'Charity Commission'.

Rates Act 1984 (c.33)

73   In section 3(9) of the Rates Act 1984 (expenditure levels) for ', or excepted from registration, under section 3 of the Charities Act 1993' substitute 'in accordance with section 3A of the Charities Act 1993 or not required to be registered (by virtue of subsection (2) of that section)'.

Companies Act 1985 (c.6)

74   The Companies Act 1985 has effect subject to the following amendments.

75   (1)   Section 380 (registration of resolutions) is amended as follows.

(2)   In subsection (4), at the beginning insert 'Except as mentioned in subsection (4ZB),'.

(3)   After subsection (4ZA) insert –

'(4ZB) Paragraphs (a) and (c) of subsection (4) do not apply to the resolutions of a charitable company mentioned in paragraphs (a) and (b) respectively of section 69G(6) of the Charities Act 1993.'

76   In Schedule 15D (permitted disclosures of information), in paragraph 21, for 'Charity Commissioners to exercise their' substitute 'Charity Commission to exercise its'.

Housing Act 1985 (c.68)

77   (1)   Section 6A of the Housing Act 1985 (definition of 'Relevant Authority') is amended as follows.

(2)   In subsection (2) for 'Charity Commissioners' substitute 'Charity Commission'.

(3)   In subsection (5) –

(a)   for 'under section 3' substitute 'in accordance with section 3A', and

(b)   omit the words from 'and is not' onwards.

Housing Associations Act 1985 (c.69)

78   In section 10(1) of the Housing Associations Act 1985 (dispositions excepted from section 9 of that Act) for 'Charity Commissioners' (in both places) substitute 'Charity Commission'.

Agricultural Holdings Act 1986 (c.5)

79   In section 86(4) of the Agricultural Holdings Act 1986 (power of landlord to obtain charge on holding) for 'Charity Commissioners' substitute 'Charity Commission'.

Coal Industry Act 1987 (c.3)

80   (1)   Section 5 of the Coal Industry Act 1987 (coal industry trusts) is amended as follows.

(2) In subsection (1) –

    (a) for 'Charity Commissioners' (in the first place) substitute 'Charity Commission ("the Commission")',

    (b) for 'to them' substitute 'to the Commission',

    (c) for 'Charity Commissioners' (in the second place) substitute 'Commission', and

    (d) for 'they consider' substitute 'the Commission considers'.

(3) In subsection (2) for 'Charity Commissioners consider' (in both places) substitute 'Commission considers'.

(4) In subsections (4) and (6) for 'Charity Commissioners' substitute 'Commission'.

(5) In subsection (7) –

    (a) for 'Charity Commissioners' substitute 'Commission',

    (b) for 'their powers' substitute 'its powers',

    (c) for 'they consider' substitute 'it considers', and

    (d) for 'the Charities Act 1960' substitute 'the Charities Act 1993'.

(6) In subsection (8) –

    (a) for '16(3), (9), (11) to (14)' substitute '16(3) and (9)',

    (b) for 'and 20' substitute ', 20 and 20A',

    (c) for 'Charity Commissioners' substitute 'Commission',

    (d) for 'their powers' substitute 'its powers', and

    (e) for '91 and 92' substitute 'and 91'.

(7) In subsection (8A) –

    (a) for 'Commissioners' (in both places) substitute 'Commission',

    (b) for 'they were proceeding' substitute 'the Commission was proceeding', and

    (c) for 'to them' substitute 'to it'.

(8) After subsection (8A) insert –

    '(8B) Schedule 1C to the Charities Act 1993 shall apply in relation to an order made under this section as it applies in relation to an order made under section 16(1) of that Act.'

(9) In subsection (9) for 'Charity Commissioners' substitute 'Commission'.

(10) In subsection (10)(b) for 'Charity Commissioners' substitute 'Commission'.

Reverter of Sites Act 1987 (c.15)

81   The Reverter of Sites Act 1987 has effect subject to the following amendments.

82   (1) Section 2 (Charity Commissioners' schemes) is amended as follows.

    (2) In subsection (1) for 'Charity Commissioners' substitute 'Charity Commission'.

    (3) For subsection (3) substitute –

    '(3)   The charitable purposes specified in an order made under this section on an application with respect to any trust shall be such as the Charity Commission consider appropriate, having regard to the matters set out in subsection (3A).

    (3A) The matters are –

        (a) the desirability of securing that the property is held for charitable purposes ("the new purposes") which are close to the purposes, whether charitable or not, for which the trustees held the relevant land before the cesser of use in consequence of which the trust arose ("the former purposes"); and

        (b) the need for the new purposes to be capable of having a significant social or economic effect.

(3B) In determining the character of the former purposes, the Commission may, if they think it appropriate to do so, give greater weight to the persons or locality benefited by those purposes than to the nature of the benefit.'

(4) In subsection (5) –

    (a) for 'Charity Commissioners' substitute 'Charity Commission',

    (b) in paragraph (c), for 'Commissioners'' and 'them' substitute 'Commission's' and 'it', and

    (c) in paragraph (d), for 'Commissioners have' substitute 'Commission has'.

(5) In subsection (7) for 'Charity Commissioners' substitute 'Charity Commission'.

(6) In subsection (8) –

    (a) for 'Commissioners'' substitute 'Commission's',

    (b) for 'they think' substitute 'it thinks', and

    (c) for 'Commissioners decide' substitute 'Commission decides'.

(7) In the sidenote, for 'Charity Commissioners'' substitute 'Charity Commission's'.

83 (1) Section 4 (provisions supplemental to sections 2 and 3) is amended as follows.

    (2) In subsection (1) –

        (a) for 'Charity Commissioners think' substitute 'Charity Commission thinks';

        (b) for 'Commissioners'' substitute 'Commission's'; and

        (c) for 'the Commissioners think' substitute 'the Commission thinks'.

    (3) For subsections (2) and (3) substitute –

'(2) Schedule 1C to the Charities Act 1993 shall apply in relation to an order made under section 2 above as it applies in relation to an order made under section 16(1) of that Act, except that the persons who may bring an appeal against an order made under section 2 above are –

    (a) the Attorney General;

    (b) the trustees of the trust established under the order;

    (c) a beneficiary of, or the trustees of, the trust in respect of which the application for the order had been made;

    (d) any person interested in the purposes for which the last-mentioned trustees or any of their predecessors held the relevant land before the cesser of use in consequence of which the trust arose under section 1 above;

    (e) any two or more inhabitants of the locality where that land is situated;

    (f) any other person who is or may be affected by the order.'

    (4) In subsection (4) –

        (a) for 'Sections 89, 91 and 92' substitute 'Sections 89 and 91', and

        (b) omit 'and appeals' and (in both places) ', and to appeals against,'.

84 In section 5(3) (orders under section 554 of the Education Act 1996) –

    (a) for 'Charity Commissioners' (in both places) substitute 'Charity Commission';

    (b) for 'the Commissioners' substitute 'the Commission'; and

    (c) for 'them' substitute 'it'.

Education Reform Act 1988 (c.40)

85 For section 125A of the Education Reform Act 1988 substitute –

'125A Charitable status of a higher education corporation

A higher education corporation shall be a charity within the meaning of the Charities Act 1993 (and in accordance with Schedule 2 to that Act is an exempt charity for the purposes of that Act).'

Courts and Legal Services Act 1990 (c.41)

86   In Schedule 11 to the Courts and Legal Services Act 1990 (judges etc. barred from legal practice) for the entry beginning 'Charity Commissioner' substitute 'Member of the Charity Commission appointed as provided in Schedule 1A to the Charities Act 1993'.

London Local Authorities Act 1991 (c.xiii)

87   In section 4 of the London Local Authorities Act 1991 (interpretation of Part 2), in paragraph (d) of the definition of 'establishment for special treatment', for the words from 'under section 3' to 'that section' substitute 'in accordance with section 3A of the Charities Act 1993 or is not required to be registered (by virtue of subsection (2) of that section)'.

Further and Higher Education Act 1992 (c.13)

88   For section 22A of the Further and Higher Education Act 1992 substitute –

'**22A Charitable status of a further education corporation**

A further education corporation shall be a charity within the meaning of the Charities Act 1993 (and in accordance with Schedule 2 to that Act is an exempt charity for the purposes of that Act).'

Charities Act 1992 (c.41)

89   The 1992 Act has effect subject to the following amendments.

90   (1)   Section 58 (interpretation of Part 2) is amended as follows.
     (2)   In subsection (1) after the definition of 'institution' insert –

'"the Minister" means the Minister for the Cabinet Office;'.

     (3)   In subsection (2) –
           (a)   in paragraph (c) for 'to be treated as a promoter of such a collection by virtue of section 65(3)' substitute 'a promoter of such a collection as defined in section 47(1) of the Charities Act 2006', and
           (b)   for 'Part III of this Act' substitute 'Chapter 1 of Part 3 of the Charities Act 2006'.
     (4)   In subsection (4) for 'whether or not the purposes are charitable within the meaning of any rule of law' substitute 'as defined by section 2(1) of the Charities Act 2006'.

91   Omit Part 3 (public charitable collections).

92   In section 76(1) (service of documents) omit paragraph (c) and the 'and' preceding it.

93   (1)   Section 77 (regulations and orders) is amended as follows.
     (2)   In subsection (1)(b) for 'subsection (2)' substitute 'subsections (2) and (2A)'.
     (3)   [*Inserts new CA 1992, s.77(2A)*]
     (4)   In subsection (4) –
           (a)   after '64' insert 'or 64A'; and
           (b)   omit 'or 73'.

94   In section 79 (short title, commencement and extent) omit –
     (a)   in subsection (6), the words '(subject to subsection (7))', and
     (b)   subsection (7).

95   In Schedule 7 (repeals) omit the entry relating to the Police, Factories, &c. (Miscellaneous Provisions) Act 1916 (c.31).

Charities Act 1993 (c.10)

96 The 1993 Act has effect subject to the following amendments.

97 In the heading for Part 1, for 'CHARITY COMMISSIONERS' substitute 'CHARITY COMMISSION'.

98 (1) Section 2 (official custodian for charities) is amended as follows.

    (2) [*Amends CA 1993, s.2(2)*]

    (3) In subsection (3), for 'Commissioners' (in both places) substitute 'Commission'.

    (4) In subsection (4) –

        (a) for 'officer of the Commissioners' substitute 'member of the staff of the Commission', and

        (b) for 'by them' substitute 'by it'.

    (5) In subsection (7) omit the words from ', and the report' onwards.

    (6) [*Inserts CA 1993, s.2(8) and (9)*]

99 (1) Section 4 (claims and objections to registration) is amended as follows.

    (2) In subsection (2) –

        (a) for 'the Commissioners' substitute 'the Commission', and

        (b) for 'to them' substitute 'to the Commission'.

    (3) Omit subsection (3).

    (4) In subsection (4) –

        (a) for 'High Court' substitute 'Tribunal',

        (b) for 'the Commissioners' (in the first and third places) substitute 'the Commission', and

        (c) for 'the Commissioners are' substitute 'the Commission is'.

    (5) In subsection (5) –

        (a) for 'subsection (3) above' substitute 'Schedule 1C to this Act',

        (b) for 'the Commissioners' (in both places) substitute 'the Commission', and

        (c) omit ', whether given on such an appeal or not'.

100 (1) Section 6 (power to require charity's name to be changed) is amended as follows.

    (2) For 'Commissioners' (in each place including the sidenote) substitute 'Commission'.

    (3) In subsection (5) for 'section 3(7)(b) above' substitute 'section 3B(3)'.

101 For the heading for Part 3 substitute 'INFORMATION POWERS'.

102 (1) Section 8 (power to institute inquiries) is amended as follows.

    (2) In subsection (1) for 'The Commissioners' substitute 'The Commission'.

    (3) In subsection (2) –

        (a) for 'The Commissioners' substitute 'The Commission',

        (b) for 'themselves' substitute 'itself', and

        (c) for 'to them' substitute 'to the Commission'.

    (4) In subsection (3) for 'the Commissioners, or a person appointed by them' substitute 'the Commission, or a person appointed by the Commission'.

    (5) In subsection (5) for 'The Commissioners' substitute 'The Commission'.

    (6) In subsection (6) –

        (a) for 'the Commissioners' substitute 'the Commission',

        (b) for 'they think' substitute 'the Commission thinks',

        (c) for 'their opinion' substitute 'the Commission's opinion', and

        (d) for 'to them' substitute 'to the Commission'.

    (7) In subsection (7) for 'the Commissioners' substitute 'the Commission'.

103 (1) Section 9 (power to call for documents and search records) is amended as follows.

    (2) In subsection (1) –

        (a) for 'The Commissioners' substitute 'The Commission',

      (b)   for 'furnish them' (in both places) substitute 'furnish the Commission',

      (c)   for 'their functions' (in both places) substitute 'the Commission's functions', and

      (d)   for 'them for their' substitute 'the Commission for its'.

   (3) In subsection (2) –

      (a)   for 'officer of the Commissioners, if so authorised by them' substitute 'member of the staff of the Commission, if so authorised by it', and

      (b)   for 'the Commissioners' (in the second place) substitute 'the Commission'.

   (4) In subsection (3) –

      (a)   for 'The Commissioners' substitute 'The Commission',

      (b)   for 'to them' (in the first place) substitute 'to it',

      (c)   for 'to them' (in the second place) substitute 'to the Commission',

      (d)   for 'their inspection' substitute 'it to inspect', and

      (e)   for 'the Commissioners' substitute 'the Commission'.

   (5) [*Inserts CA 1993, s.9(6)*]

104 [*Inserts CA 1993, ss.10, 10A, 10B and 10C*]

105 (1) Section 11 (supply of false or misleading information) is amended as follows.

   (2) For 'Commissioners' (in each place including the sidenote) substitute 'Commission'.

   (3) In subsection (1)(b) for 'their functions' substitute 'its functions'.

106 In the heading for Part 4 for 'AND COMMISSIONERS' substitute 'AND COMMISSION'.

107 (1) Section 14 (application cy-près of gifts of donors unknown or disclaiming) is amended as follows.

   (2) In subsection (6) for 'the Commissioners so direct' substitute 'the Commission so directs'.

   (3) In subsection (8) for 'the Commissioners' substitute 'the Commission'.

   (4) In subsection (9) –

      (a)   for 'the Commissioners' (in both places) substitute 'the Commission', and

      (b)   for 'they think fit' substitute 'it thinks fit'.

108 In the heading preceding section 16 for 'Powers of Commissioners' substitute 'Powers of Commission'.

109 (1) Section 16 (concurrent jurisdiction of Commissioners with High Court) is amended as follows.

   (2) In subsection (1) for 'the Commissioners' substitute 'the Commission'.

   (3) In subsection (2) –

      (a)   for 'the Commissioners for them' substitute 'the Commission for it', and

      (b)   for 'the Commissioners' (in the second place) substitute 'the Commission'.

   (4) In subsection (3) for 'The Commissioners' substitute 'The Commission'.

   (5) In subsection (4) for 'the Commissioners shall not exercise their' substitute 'the Commission shall not exercise its'.

   (6) In subsection (5) –

      (a)   for 'income from all sources does not in aggregate' substitute 'gross income does not', and

      (b)   for 'the Commissioners may exercise their' substitute 'the Commission may exercise its'.

   (7) In subsection (6) –

      (a)   for 'the Commissioners are' substitute 'the Commission is',

      (b)   for 'the Commissioners have' substitute 'the Commission has',

      (c)   for 'the Commissioners' (in the third and fourth places) substitute 'the Commission', and

      (d)   for 'they act' substitute 'it acts'.

(8) In subsection (7) –

    (a) for 'the Commissioners' (in the first and third places) substitute 'the Commission', and

    (b) for 'the Commissioners consider' substitute 'the Commission considers'.

(9) In subsection (8) –

    (a) for 'The Commissioners' substitute 'The Commission', and

    (b) for 'their jurisdiction' substitute 'its jurisdiction'.

(10) In subsection (9) for 'the Commissioners shall give notice of their' substitute 'the Commission shall give notice of its'.

(11) In subsection (10) –

    (a) for 'The Commissioners shall not exercise their' substitute 'The Commission shall not exercise its', and

    (b) for 'the Commissioners' (in the second place) substitute 'the Commission'.

(12) Omit subsections (11) to (14).

(13) In subsection (15)(b) for 'the Commissioners may exercise their' substitute 'the Commission may exercise its'.

110 (1) Section 17 (further power to make schemes or alter application of charitable property) is amended as follows.

  (2) In subsection (1) –

    (a) for 'the Commissioners' (in both places) substitute 'the Commission', and

    (b) for 'by them' substitute 'by the Commission'.

  (3) In subsection (2) for 'the Commissioners' substitute 'the Commission'.

  (4) In subsection (4) for 'the Commissioners' (in both places) substitute 'the Commission'.

  (5) In subsection (6) –

    (a) for 'Commissioners' (in both places) substitute 'Commission',

    (b) for 'if they were' substitute 'if the Commission was',

    (c) for 'they act' substitute 'it acts', and

    (d) for 'to them' substitute 'to it'.

  (6) In subsection (7) for 'the Commissioners' substitute 'the Commission'.

  (7) In subsection (8) –

    (a) for 'the Commissioners are' substitute 'the Commission is', and

    (b) for 'the Commissioners' (in the second place) substitute 'the Commission'.

111 (1) Section 18 (power to act for protection of charities) is amended as follows.

  (2) In subsection (1) –

    (a) for 'after they have' substitute 'after it has',

    (b) for 'the Commissioners are' substitute 'the Commission is',

    (c) for 'the Commissioners may of their' substitute 'the Commission may of its',

    (d) for 'as they consider' substitute 'as it considers',

    (e) for 'the Commissioners' (in the third, fourth and fifth places) substitute 'the Commission', and

    (f) for 'a receiver' substitute 'an interim manager, who shall act as receiver'.

  (3) In subsection (2) –

    (a) for 'they have' substitute 'it has',

    (b) for 'the Commissioners are' substitute 'the Commission is', and

    (c) for 'the Commissioners may of their' substitute 'the Commission may of its'.

(4) In subsection (4) –

    (a)   for 'The Commissioners' substitute 'The Commission', and

    (b)   for 'their own motion' substitute 'its own motion'.

(5) In subsection (5) –

    (a)   for 'The Commissioners may by order made of their' substitute 'The Commission may by order made of its',

    (b)   for 'removed by them' substitute 'removed by the Commission', and

    (c)   for 'the Commissioners are of' (in both places) substitute 'the Commission is of'.

(6) In subsection (6) –

    (a)   for 'the Commissioners' (in both places) substitute 'the Commission',

    (b)   for 'their own motion' substitute 'its own motion', and

    (c)   for 'by them' substitute 'by it'.

(7) Omit subsections (8) to (10).

(8) In subsection (11) for 'the Commissioners' substitute 'the Commission'.

(9) In subsection (12) –

    (a)   for 'the Commissioners' substitute 'the Commission', and

    (b)   for 'their intention' substitute 'its intention'.

(10) In subsection (13) –

    (a)   for 'The Commissioners' substitute 'The Commission',

    (b)   for 'they think fit' substitute 'it thinks fit',

    (c)   for 'by them' substitute 'by it',

    (d)   for 'to them' substitute 'to the Commission', and

    (e)   for 'they shall' substitute 'the Commission shall'.

112 (1) Section 19 (supplementary provisions relating to receiver and manager appointed for a charity) is amended as follows.

(2) [*Amends CA 1993, s.19(1)*]

(3) In subsection (2) –

    (a)   for 'the Commissioners' (in both places) substitute 'the Commission', and

    (b)   for 'receiver and manager' substitute 'interim manager'.

(4) In subsection (3) for 'receiver and manager' (in both places) substitute 'interim manager'.

(5) In subsection (4) –

    (a)   for 'receiver and manager' substitute 'interim manager', and

    (b)   for 'the Commissioners' substitute 'the Commission'.

(6) In subsections (6)(c) and (7) for 'the Commissioners' substitute 'the Commission'.

(7) In the sidenote for 'receiver and manager' substitute 'interim manager'.

113 [*Inserts CA 1993, s.19C*]

114 In section 22(3) (property vested in official custodian) for 'the Commissioners' substitute 'the Commission'.

115 (1) Section 23 (divestment in case of land subject to Reverter of Sites Act 1987 (c.15)) is amended as follows.

(2) In subsection (1) –

    (a)   for 'the Commissioners' (in both places) substitute 'the Commission',

    (b)   for 'by them of their own' substitute 'by the Commission of its own', and

    (c)   for 'appear to them' substitute 'appear to the Commission'.

(3) In subsection (2) –

    (a)   for 'the Commissioners (of their own motion)' substitute 'the Commission (of its own motion)', and

    (b)   omit 'or them'.

(4) In subsection (3) –

    (a)   for 'the Commissioners' (in the first and second places) substitute 'the Commission', and

    (b)   for 'the Commissioners is or are' substitute 'the Commission is'.

116 In section 24 (schemes to establish common investment funds), in subsections (1) and (2), for 'the Commissioners' substitute 'the Commission'.

117 In section 25(1) (schemes to establish common deposit funds) for 'the Commissioners' substitute 'the Commission'.

118 For the heading preceding section 26 substitute 'Additional powers of Commission'.

119 In section 26(1) (power to authorise dealings with charity property) –

    (a)   for 'the Commissioners' substitute 'the Commission', and

    (b)   for 'they may' substitute 'the Commission may'.

120 (1) Section 27 (power to authorise ex gratia payments) is amended as follows.

  (2) In subsection (1) for 'the Commissioners' substitute 'the Commission'.

  (3) In subsection (2) –

    (a)   for 'the Commissioners' (in both places) substitute 'the Commission', and

    (b)   for 'by them' substitute 'by the Commission'.

  (4) In subsection (3) –

    (a)   for 'the Commissioners for them' substitute 'the Commission for it',

    (b)   for 'they are not' substitute 'it is not',

    (c)   for 'they consider' substitute 'the Commission considers',

    (d)   for 'by them' substitute 'by the Commission', and

    (e)   for 'they shall' substitute 'the Commission shall'.

  (5) In subsection (4) –

    (a)   for 'to them' substitute 'to the Commission', and

    (b)   for 'the Commissioners determine' substitute 'the Commission determines'.

121 (1) Section 28 (power to give directions about dormant bank accounts) is amended as follows.

  (2) In subsection (1) –

    (a)   for 'the Commissioners' substitute 'the Commission',

    (b)   for 'are informed' substitute 'is informed',

    (c)   for 'are unable' substitute 'is unable', and

    (d)   for 'they may give' substitute 'it may give'.

  (3) In subsection (3) –

    (a)   for 'Commissioners' (in both places) substitute 'Commission',

    (b)   for 'they consider' substitute 'it considers',

    (c)   for 'to them' substitute 'to the Commission', and

    (d)   for 'they have received' substitute 'it has received'.

  (4) In subsection (5) –

    (a)   for 'the Commissioners have been' substitute 'the Commission has been',

    (b)   for 'the Commissioners' (in the second and third places) substitute 'the Commission',

    (c)   for 'they shall revoke' substitute 'it shall revoke', and

    (d)   for 'by them' substitute 'by it'.

(5) In subsection (7) –

   (a) for 'the Commissioners' substitute 'the Commission', and
   (b) for 'them to discharge their functions' substitute 'the Commission to discharge its functions'.

(6) In subsection (8)(a) for 'the Commissioners are informed' substitute 'the Commission is informed'.

(7) In subsection (9) –

   (a) for 'the Commissioners have' substitute 'the Commission has', and
   (b) for 'the Commissioners' (in the second place) substitute 'the Commission'.

122 (1) Section 30 (powers for preservation of charity documents) is amended as follows.

   (2) In subsection (1) for 'The Commissioners' substitute 'The Commission'.
   (3) In subsection (2) for 'Commissioners' (in each place) substitute 'Commission'.
   (4) In subsection (3) –

   (a) for 'the Commissioners' (in the first place) substitute 'the Commission',
   (b) for 'with them' substitute 'with the Commission',
   (c) for 'officer of the Commissioners generally or specially authorised by them' substitute 'member of the staff of the Commission generally or specially authorised by the Commission'.

   (5) In subsection (4) for 'the Commissioners' substitute 'the Commission'.
   (6) In subsection (5) –

   (a) for 'the Commissioners' substitute 'the Commission',
   (b) for 'by them' substitute 'by the Commission', and
   (c) for 'with them' substitute 'with the Commission'.

123 (1) Section 31 (power to order taxation of solicitor's bill) is amended as follows.

   (2) In subsection (1) for 'The Commissioners' substitute 'The Commission'.
   (3) In subsection (3) for 'the Commissioners are' substitute 'the Commission is'.

124 (1) Section 32 (proceedings by Commissioners) is amended as follows.

   (2) In subsections (1) and (3) for 'the Commissioners' substitute 'the Commission'.
   (3) In subsection (5) –

   (a) for 'the Commissioners' substitute 'the Commission', and
   (b) for 'by them of their own' substitute 'by the Commission of its own'.

   (4) In the sidenote, for 'Commissioners' substitute 'Commission'.

125 (1) Section 33 (proceedings by other persons) is amended as follows.

   (2) In subsection (2) for 'the Commissioners' substitute 'the Commission'.
   (3) In subsection (3) –

   (a) for 'The Commissioners' substitute 'The Commission',
   (b) for 'their opinion' substitute 'its opinion', and
   (c) for 'by them' substitute 'by the Commission'.

   (4) In subsections (5) and (6) for 'the Commissioners' substitute 'the Commission'.
   (5) In subsection (7) –

   (a) for 'the Commissioners' (in both places) substitute 'the Commission', and
   (b) for 'they think' substitute 'the Commission thinks'.

126 In section 34 (report of inquiry to be evidence in certain proceedings), in subsections (1) and (2), for 'the Commissioners' substitute 'the Commission'.

127 In section 35(1) (application of certain provisions to trust corporations) for 'the Commissioners' substitute 'the Commission'.

128 (1) Section 36 (restrictions on dispositions) is amended as follows.

   (2) In subsection (1) –

   (a) for 'sold' substitute 'conveyed, transferred', and
   (b) for 'the Commissioners' substitute 'the Commission'.

(3)   In subsection (3) after 'subsection (5) below,' insert 'the requirements mentioned in subsection (2)(b) above are that'.

(4)   In subsection (5) after 'consideration of a fine),' insert 'the requirements mentioned in subsection (2)(b) above are that'.

(5)   In subsection (6) –

    (a)   for 'sold' substitute 'conveyed, transferred', and

    (b)   for 'previously' substitute 'before the relevant time'.

(6)   [*Inserts CA 1993, s.36(6A)*]

(7)   In subsection (8) –

    (a)   for 'The Commissioners' substitute 'The Commission',

    (b)   for 'the Commissioners are satisfied' substitute 'the Commission is satisfied', and

    (c)   for 'for them' substitute 'for the Commission'.

129   In section 37 (supplementary provisions relating to dispositions), in subsections (2) and (4) –

(a)   for 'sold' substitute 'conveyed, transferred', and

(b)   for 'the Commissioners' substitute 'the Commission'.

130   In section 38(1) (restrictions on mortgaging) for 'the Commissioners' substitute 'the Commission'.

131   (1)   Section 39 (supplementary provisions relating to mortgaging) is amended as follows.

(2)   In subsections (2)(a) and (4) for 'the Commissioners' substitute 'the Commission'.

(3)   [*Inserts CA 1993, s.39(4A) and (4B)*]

132   In section 41(4) (obligation to preserve accounting records) for 'the Commissioners consent' substitute 'the Commission consents'.

133   (1)   Section 42 (annual statements of accounts) is amended as follows.

(2)   [*Inserts CA 1993, s.42(2A)*]

(3)   [*Inserts CA 1993, s.42(8)*]

134   (1)   Section 43 (annual audit or examination of charity accounts) is amended as follows.

(2)   In subsection (4) for 'the Commissioners' (in both places) substitute 'the Commission'.

(3)   In subsection (5) –

    (a)   for 'the Commissioners make' substitute 'the Commission makes', and

    (b)   for 'the Commissioners' (in the second place) substitute 'the Commission'.

(4)   In subsection (6) for 'the Commissioners' (in each place) substitute 'the Commission'.

(5)   In subsection (7) –

    (a)   for 'The Commissioners' substitute 'The Commission', and

    (b)   for 'they think' substitute 'it thinks'.

135   (1)   Section 43A (annual audit or examination of English NHS charity accounts) is amended as follows.

(2)   In subsection (2) for 'the criterion set out in subsection (1) of section 43 is met in respect of' substitute 'paragraph (a) or (b) of section 43(1) is satisfied in relation to'.

(3)   In subsection (5) –

    (a)   for 'The Commissioners' substitute 'The Commission', and

    (b)   for 'they think' substitute 'it thinks'.

136   (1)   Section 43B (annual audit or examination of Welsh NHS charity accounts) is amended as follows.

(2)   In subsection (2) for 'the criterion set out in subsection (1) of section 43 is met in respect of' substitute 'paragraph (a) or (b) of section 43(1) is satisfied in relation to'.

(3)   [*Inserts CA 1993, s.43B(5)*]

137 (1)   Section 44 (supplementary provisions relating to audits) is amended as follows.

(2)   In subsection (1) –

    (a)   in paragraph (b) after 'section 43' insert ', 43A or 43B',

    (b)   [*Amends CA 1993, s.44(1)(c)*]

(3)   In subsection (2) –

    (a)   after 'independent examiner' insert 'or examiner',

    (b)   for 'the Commissioners' (in the first place) substitute 'the Commission', and

    (c)   for 'the Commissioners think' substitute 'the Commission thinks'.

(4)   Omit subsection (3).

138 (1)   Section 45 (annual reports) is amended as follows.

(2)   In subsection (2)(b) for 'the Commissioners' substitute 'the Commission'.

(3)   In subsection (3) –

    (a)   for the words from 'in any' to 'expenditure' substitute 'a charity's gross income in any financial year',

    (b)   before 'the annual report' insert 'a copy of', and

    (c)   for 'the Commissioners' (in both places) substitute 'the Commission'.

(4)   In subsection (3A) –

    (a)   for the words from 'in any' to 'exceeds' substitute 'a charity's gross income in any financial year does not exceed',

    (b)   before 'the annual report' insert 'a copy of',

    (c)   for 'the Commissioners so request, be transmitted to them' substitute 'the Commission so requests, be transmitted to it', and

    (d)   for 'the Commissioners' (in the second place) substitute 'the Commission'.

(5)   In subsection (4) –

    (a)   for 'annual report transmitted to the Commissioners' substitute 'copy of an annual report transmitted to the Commission', and

    (b)   before 'the statement', and before 'the account and statement', insert 'a copy of'.

(6)   In subsection (5) before 'annual report' insert 'copy of an'.

(7)   In subsection (6) –

    (a)   after 'Any' insert 'copy of an',

    (b)   for 'the Commissioners' (in both places) substitute 'the Commission', and

    (c)   for 'they think fit' substitute 'it thinks fit'.

(8)   In subsection (7) for the words from 'which they have not' onwards substitute 'of which they have not been required to transmit a copy to the Commission.'

(9)   In subsection (8) for 'in subsection (3)' substitute 'to subsection (3)'.

139 (1)   Section 46 (special provisions as respects accounts etc. of excepted charities) is amended as follows.

(2)   In subsection (2) for 'the Commissioners consent' substitute 'the Commission consents'.

(3)   [*Amends/inserts CA 1993, s.46(3), (3A) and (3B)*]

(4)   In subsection (4) for the words from '(other than' onwards substitute 'which –

    (a)   falls within section 3A(2)(b) or (c) above but does not fall within section 3A(2)(d), and

    (b)   is not registered.'

(5) In subsection (5) –

    (a)   for 'the Commissioners' (in the first place) substitute 'the Commission', and

    (b)   for 'the Commissioners' request' substitute 'the Commission's request'.

(6) [*Amends CA 1993, s.46(7)*]

(7) Omit subsection (8).

140 (1) Section 47 (public inspection of annual reports etc.) is amended as follows.

    (2) In subsection (1) –

        (a)   for 'Any annual report or other document kept by the Commissioners' substitute 'Any document kept by the Commission',

        (b)   for 'the Commissioners so determine' substitute 'the Commission so determines', and

        (c)   for 'they may' substitute 'it may'.

    (3) In subsection (2)(a) after 'accounts' insert 'or (if subsection (4) below applies) of its most recent annual report'.

    (4) [*Inserts CA 1993, s.47(4) and (5)*]

141 (1) Section 48 (annual returns by registered charities) is amended as follows.

    (2) In subsection (1) for 'the Commissioners' substitute 'the Commission'.

    (3) In subsection (1A) for the words from 'neither' to 'exceeds' substitute 'the charity's gross income does not exceed'.

    (4) In subsection (2) –

        (a)   for 'the Commissioners' substitute 'the Commission', and

        (b)   for 'to them' substitute 'to the Commission'.

    (5) In subsection (3) for 'The Commissioners' substitute 'The Commission'.

142 [*Amends CA 1993, s.49*]

143 (1) Section 50 (incorporation of trustees of charity) is amended as follows.

    (2) In subsection (1) –

        (a)   for 'the Commissioners' (in the first and third places) substitute 'the Commission',

        (b)   for 'the Commissioners consider' substitute 'the Commission considers', and

        (c)   for 'they think fit' substitute 'the Commission thinks fit'.

    (3) In subsection (2) –

        (a)   for 'The Commissioners' substitute 'The Commission',

        (b)   for 'to them' substitute 'to the Commission', and

        (c)   for 'under section 3' substitute 'in accordance with section 3A'.

144 (1) Section 52 (applications for incorporation) is amended as follows.

    (2) In subsection (1) for 'the Commissioners' (in both places) substitute 'the Commission'.

    (3) In subsection (2) –

        (a)   for 'The Commissioners' substitute 'The Commission', and

        (b)   for 'they may specify' substitute 'it may specify'.

145 In section 53(1) (nomination of trustees, and filling up vacancies) for 'the Commissioners' substitute 'the Commission'.

146 (1) Section 56 (power of Commissioners to amend certificate of incorporation) is amended as follows.

    (2) In subsection (1) –

        (a)   for 'The Commissioners' substitute 'The Commission', and

        (b)   for 'of their own motion' substitute 'of the Commission's own motion'.

(3) In subsection (2) –

    (a) for 'of their own motion, the Commissioners' substitute 'of its own motion, the Commission',

    (b) for 'their proposals' substitute 'its proposals', and

    (c) for 'to them' substitute 'to it'.

(4) In subsection (3) –

    (a) for 'The Commissioners' substitute 'The Commission',

    (b) for 'their proposals' substitute 'its proposals', and

    (c) for 'to them' substitute 'to it'.

(5) In subsection (4) for 'The Commissioners' substitute 'The Commission'.

(6) In the sidenote, for 'Commissioners' substitute 'Commission'.

147 (1) Section 57 (records of applications and certificates) is amended as follows.

(2) In subsection (1) –

    (a) for 'The Commissioners' substitute 'The Commission', and

    (b) for 'to them' substitute 'to it'.

(3) In subsection (2) –

    (a) for 'the Commissioners' (in the first place) substitute 'the Commission', and

    (b) for 'the secretary of the Commissioners' substitute 'a member of the staff of the Commission'.

148 In section 58 (enforcement of orders and directions) for 'the Commissioners' substitute 'the Commission'.

149 (1) Section 61 (power of Commissioners to dissolve incorporated body) is amended as follows.

(2) In subsection (1) –

    (a) for 'the Commissioners are' substitute 'the Commission is',

    (b) for 'treated by them' substituted 'treated by the Commission', and

    (c) for 'they may of their own motion' substitute 'the Commission may of its own motion'.

(3) In subsection (2) –

    (a) for 'the Commissioners are' substitute 'the Commission is', and

    (b) for 'the Commissioners' (in the second place) substitute 'the Commission'.

(4) In subsection (4) –

    (a) for 'the Commissioners so direct' substitute 'the Commission so directs', and

    (b) for 'the Commissioners' (in the second place) substitute 'the Commission'.

(5) Omit subsection (7).

(6) In the sidenote, for 'Commissioners' substitute 'Commission'.

150 (1) Section 63 (winding up) is amended as follows.

(2) In subsection (2) –

    (a) for 'the Commissioners' substitute 'the Commission',

    (b) for 'they have instituted' substitute 'it has instituted', and

    (c) for 'they are satisfied' substitute 'it is satisfied'.

(3) In subsection (3) for 'the Commissioners' (in both places) substitute 'the Commission'.

(4) In subsection (4) for 'the Commissioners' (in both places) substitute 'the Commission'.

(5) In subsection (5) –

    (a) for 'the Commissioners' substitute 'the Commission', and

(b) for 'by them of their own motion' substitute 'by the Commission of its own motion'.

151 In section 64(3) (alteration of objects clause) for 'the Commissioner's consent' substitute 'the Commission's consent'.

152 In section 65(4) (invalidity of certain transactions) for 'the Commissioners' substitute 'the Commission'.

153 In section 66 (requirement of consent of Commissioners to certain acts), in subsection (1) and the sidenote, for 'Commissioners' substitute 'Commission'.

154 (1) Section 69 (investigation of accounts) is amended as follows.

(2) In subsection (1) –

    (a) for 'the Commissioners' substitute 'the Commission',

    (b) for 'they think fit' substitute 'the Commission thinks fit', and

    (c) for 'by them' substitute 'by the Commission'.

(3) In subsections (2)(c) and (3) for 'the Commissioners' substitute 'the Commission'.

(4) In subsection (4) –

    (a) for 'the Commissioners' (in the first place) substitute 'the Commission', and

    (b) for 'the Commissioners think' substitute 'the Commission thinks'.

155 For the heading preceding section 72 substitute 'Charity trustees'.

156 (1) Section 72 (persons disqualified for being trustees of a charity) is amended as follows.

(2) In subsection (1)(d)(i) after 'by the' insert 'Commission or'.

(3) In subsection (4) for 'The Commissioners' substitute 'The Commission'.

(4) In subsection (6) –

    (a) for 'the Commissioners' (in the first place) substitute 'the Commission',

    (b) for 'they think fit' substitute 'it thinks fit',

    (c) after 'order of' insert 'the Commission or', and

    (d) for 'the Commissioners' (in the third place) substitute 'the Commission'.

(5) [Inserts CA 1993, s.72(8)]

157 In section 73(4) (person acting as charity trustee while disqualified) –

    (a) for 'the Commissioners are' substitute 'the Commission is',

    (b) for 'they may by order' substitute 'the Commission may by order', and

    (c) for '(as determined by them)' substitute '(as determined by the Commission)'.

158 For the heading preceding section 74 substitute 'Miscellaneous powers of charities'.

159 In section 76(2) (local authority's index of local charities) –

    (a) for 'the Commissioners' (in both places) substitute 'the Commission', and

    (b) for 'they will' substitute 'it will'.

160 In section 77(1) (reviews of local charities by local authority) for 'the Commissioners' substitute 'the Commission'.

161 (1) Section 79 (parochial charities) is amended as follows.

(2) In subsection (1) for 'the Commissioners' substitute 'the Commission'.

(3) In subsection (2) for 'the Commissioners' (in both places) substitute 'the Commission'.

162 (1) Section 80 (supervision by Commissioners of certain Scottish charities) is amended as follows.

(2) [Amends/inserts CA 1993, s.80(1)(c) and (d)]

(3) In subsection (2) –

    (a) for 'the Commissioners are satisfied' substitute 'the Commission is satisfied',

    (b) for 'they may make' substitute 'it may make', and

    (c) for 'their approval' substitute 'the Commission's approval'.

(4) In subsection (3) –

    (a) for 'the Commissioners' substitute 'the Commission',
    (b) for 'their being' substitute 'the Commission being', and
    (c) for 'supplied to them' substitute 'supplied to it'.

(5) In subsection (4) –

    (a) for 'the Commissioners are satisfied' substitute 'the Commission is satisfied',
    (b) for 'supplied to them' substitute 'supplied to it', and
    (c) for 'the Commissioners' (in the second place) substitute 'the Commission'.

(6) In subsection (5) –

    (a) for 'Commissioners' (in each place) substitute 'Commission',
    (b) for 'they consider' substitute 'it considers', and
    (c) for 'they have received' substitute 'it has received'.

(7) In the sidenote, for 'Commissioners' substitute 'Commission'.

163 (1) Section 84 (supply by Commissioners of copies of documents open to public inspection) is amended as follows.

(2) For 'The Commissioners' substitute 'The Commission'.

(3) For 'their possession' substitute 'the Commission's possession'.

(4) At the end add 'or section 75D'.

(5) In the sidenote, for 'Commissioners' substitute 'Commission'.

164 (1) Section 85 (fees and other amounts payable to Commissioners) is amended as follows.

(2) In subsection (1) –

    (a) for 'the Commissioners' (in both places) substitute 'the Commission', and
    (b) for 'kept by them' substitute 'kept by the Commission'.

(3) In subsection (4) –

    (a) for 'The Commissioners' substitute 'The Commission',
    (b) for 'they consider' substitute 'it considers', and
    (c) for 'by them' substitute 'by it'.

(4) In subsection (5) for 'the Commissioners' substitute 'the Commission'.

(5) In the sidenote, for 'Commissioners' substitute 'Commission'.

165 (1) Section 86 (regulations and orders) is amended as follows.

(2) In subsection (2)(a) –

    (a) after '17(2),' insert '73F(6)', and
    (b) after '99(2)' insert 'or paragraph 6 of Schedule 1C'.

(3) In subsection (3) –

    (a) for 'the Commissioners' (in the first place) substitute 'the Commission', and
    (b) for 'the Commissioners consider' substitute 'the Commission considers'.

(4) In subsection (4) after 'above' insert 'or Schedule 5A,'.

166 (1) Section 87 (enforcement of requirement by order of Commissioners) is amended as follows.

(2) In subsection (1) –

    (a) for 'the Commissioners' substitute 'the Commission', and
    (b) for 'they consider' substitute 'it considers'.

(3) In subsection (2) for 'the Commissioners' (in both places) substitute 'the Commission'.

(4) In the sidenote, for 'Commissioners' substitute 'Commission'.

167 (1) Section 88 (enforcement of orders of Commissioners) is amended as follows.

(2) [*Amends CA 1993, s.88(a)*]

(3) In paragraphs (b) and (c) for 'the Commissioners' substitute 'the Commission'.

(4) For 'the Commissioners to' substitute 'the Commission to'.

(5) In the sidenote, for 'Commissioners' substitute 'Commission'.

168 (1) Section 89 (other provisions as to orders of Commissioners) is amended as follows.

(2) In subsection (1) –

    (a) for 'the Commissioners' (in the first place) substitute 'the Commission',

    (b) for 'the Commissioners think' substitute 'the Commission thinks',

    (c) for 'the Commissioners exercise' substitute 'the Commission exercises', and

    (d) for 'to them, they may' substitute 'to it, it may'.

(3) In subsection (2) –

    (a) for 'the Commissioners make' substitute 'the Commission makes',

    (b) for 'they may themselves' substitute 'the Commission may itself', and

    (c) for 'they think fit' substitute 'it thinks fit'.

(4) In subsection (3) –

    (a) for 'The Commissioners' substitute 'The Commission',

    (b) for 'they have' substitute 'it has',

    (c) for 'they are' substitute 'it is', and

    (d) for 'to them' substitute 'to it'.

(5) In subsection (4) for 'the Commissioners' substitute 'the Commission'.

(6) [Inserts CA 1993, s.89(5)]

(7) In the sidenote, for 'Commissioners' substitute 'Commission'.

169 In section 90 (directions of the Commissioners) for 'the Commissioners' (in each place including the sidenote) substitute 'the Commission'.

170 In section 91 (service of orders and directions), in subsections (1), (4) and (5), for 'the Commissioners' (in each place) substitute 'the Commission'.

171 Omit section 92 (appeals from Commissioners).

172 [Amends/inserts CA 1993, s.93(3)–(6)]

173 (1) Section 96 (construction of references to a 'charity' etc.) is amended as follows.

(2) In subsection (1) for the definition of 'charity' substitute –

'"charity" has the meaning given by section 1(1) of the Charities Act 2006;'.

(3) Omit –

    (a) in the definition of 'exempt charity' in subsection (1), the words '(subject to section 24(8) above)', and

    (b) subsection (4).

(4) In subsections (5) and (6) for 'The Commissioners' substitute 'The Commission'.

174 In section 97(1) (interpretation) –

    (a) in the definition of 'charitable purposes', for 'charitable according to the law of England and Wales;' substitute 'charitable purposes as defined by section 2(1) of the Charities Act 2006;';

    (b) for the definition of 'the Commissioners' substitute –

    '"the Commission" means the Charity Commission;';

    (c) in the definition of 'institution', after '"institution" insert 'means an institution whether incorporated or not, and'; and

    (d) at the appropriate place insert –

    '"members", in relation to a charity with a body of members distinct from the charity trustees, means any of those members;'

    '"the Minister" means the Minister for the Cabinet Office;'

'"principal regulator", in relation to an exempt charity, means the charity's principal regulator within the meaning of section 13 of the Charities Act 2006;'

'"the Tribunal" means the Charity Tribunal;'.

175 In section 97(3) (general interpretation) for 'Part IV or IX' substitute 'Part 4, 7, 8A or 9'.

176 In section 100(3) (extent) for 'Section 10' substitute 'Sections 10 to 10C'.

177 In paragraph (a) of Schedule 2 (exempt charities) for 'the Commissioners' (in the first place) substitute 'the Charity Commissioners for England and Wales'.

178 (1) Schedule 5 (meaning of 'connected person' for the purposes of section 36(2)) is amended as follows.

(2) In paragraph 1 for the words preceding paragraphs (a) to (g) substitute –

'(1) In section 36(2) of this Act 'connected person', in relation to a charity, means any person who falls within sub-paragraph (2) –

(a) at the time of the disposition in question, or
(b) at the time of any contract for the disposition in question.

(2) The persons falling within this sub-paragraph are – '.

(3) Paragraphs (a) to (g) of paragraph 1 become paragraphs (a) to (g) of sub-paragraph (2) (as inserted by sub-paragraph (2) above).

(4) After paragraph (e) of sub-paragraph (2) (as so inserted) insert –

'(ea) a person carrying on business in partnership with any person falling within any of sub-paragraphs (a) to (e) above;';

and in paragraph (f)(i) of that sub-paragraph, for '(e)' substitute '(ea)'.

(5) In paragraph 2 –

(a) in sub-paragraph (1), for '1(c)' substitute '1(2)(c)',
(b) in sub-paragraph (2), for '1(e)' substitute '1(2)(e)', and
(c) [Inserts CA 1993, Sched.5, para.2(3)]

(6) In paragraph 3 for '1(f)' substitute '1(2)(f)'.

(7) In paragraph 4(1) for '1(g)' substitute '1(2)(g)'.

Deregulation and Contracting Out Act 1994 (c.40)

179 (1) Section 79 of the Deregulation and Contracting Out Act 1994 (interpretation of Part 2) is amended as follows.

(2) For subsection (3)(a) substitute –

'(a) any reference to a Minister included a reference to the Forestry Commissioners or to the Charity Commission;

(b) any reference to an officer in relation to the Charity Commission were a reference to a member or member of staff of the Commission; and.'

(3) In subsection (4) after 'those Commissioners' insert 'or that Commission'.

Pensions Act 1995 (c.26)

180 In section 107(1) of the Pensions Act 1995 (disclosure for facilitating discharge of functions by other supervisory authorities), for the entry in the Table relating to the Charity Commissioners substitute –

'The Charity Commission.   Functions under the Charities Act 1993 or the Charities Act 2006.'

Reserve Forces Act 1996 (c.14)

181 (1) Schedule 5 to the Reserve Forces Act 1996 (charitable property on disbanding of units) is amended as follows.

(2) In paragraph 1(2) for 'the Charity Commissioners' substitute 'the Charity Commission'.

(3) In paragraph 4(1) –

    (a) for 'Charity Commissioners consider' substitute 'Charity Commission considers', and

    (b) for 'they' substitute 'it'.

(4) In paragraph 5(2) –

    (a) for 'Charity Commissioners' substitute 'Charity Commission', and

    (b) for 'the Commissioners' (in both places) substitute 'the Commission'.

(5) In paragraph 6 –

    (a) for 'Charity Commissioners' substitute 'Charity Commission',

    (b) for 'the Commissioners' substitute 'the Commission', and

    (c) for 'their' substitute 'its'.

Trusts of Land and Appointment of Trustees Act 1996 (c.47)

182 In section 6(7) of the Trusts of Land and Appointment of Trustees Act 1996 (limitation on general powers of trustees) for 'Charity Commissioners' substitute 'Charity Commission'.

Housing Act 1996 (c.52)

183 The Housing Act 1996 has effect subject to the following amendments.

184 In section 3(3) (registration as social landlord) for 'Charity Commissioners' substitute 'Charity Commission'.

185 In section 4(6) (removal from the register of social landlords) for 'Charity Commissioners' substitute 'Charity Commission'.

186 In section 6(3) (notice of appeal against decision on removal) for 'Charity Commissioners' substitute 'Charity Commission'.

187 In section 44(3) (consultation on proposals as to ownership and management of landlord's land) for 'Charity Commissioners' substitute 'Charity Commission'.

188 In section 45(4) (service of copy of agreed proposals) for 'Charity Commissioners' substitute 'Charity Commission'.

189 In section 46(2) (notice of appointment of manager to implement agreed proposals) for 'Charity Commissioners' substitute 'Charity Commission'.

190 In section 56(2) (meaning of 'the Relevant Authority') for 'Charity Commissioners' substitute 'Charity Commission'.

191 In section 58(1)(b) (definitions relating to charities) –

    (a) for 'under section 3' substitute 'in accordance with section 3A', and

    (b) omit the words from 'and is not' onwards.

192 (1) Schedule 1 (regulation of registered social landlords) is amended as follows.

(2) In paragraph 6(2) (exercise of power to appoint new director or trustee) for 'Charity Commissioners' substitute 'Charity Commission'.

(3) In paragraph 10 (change of objects by certain charities) –

    (a) in sub-paragraphs (1) and (2) for 'Charity Commissioners' (in each place) substitute 'Charity Commission', and

    (b) in sub-paragraph (2) for 'their' substitute 'its'.

(4) In paragraph 18(4), for paragraphs (a) and (b) and the words following them substitute –

    '(a) the charity's gross income arising in connection with its housing activities exceeds the sum for the time being specified in section 43(1)(a) of the Charities Act 1993, or

(b)   the charity's gross income arising in that connection exceeds the accounts threshold and at the end of that period the aggregate value of its assets (before deduction of liabilities) in respect of its housing activities exceeds the sum for the time being specified in section 43(1)(b) of that Act;

and in this sub-paragraph "gross income" and "accounts threshold" have the same meanings as in section 43 of the Charities Act 1993.'

(5)   In paragraph 28(4) (notification upon exercise of certain powers in relation to registered charities) for 'Charity Commissioners' substitute 'Charity Commission'.

School Standards and Framework Act 1998 (c.31)

193   The School Standards and Framework Act 1998 has effect subject to the following amendments.

194   (1)   Section 23 is amended as follows.

(2)   In subsection (1) (certain school bodies to be charities that are exempt charities) omit 'which are exempt charities for the purposes of the Charities Act 1993'.

(3)   After that subsection insert –

'(1A) Any body to which subsection (1)(a) or (b) applies is an institution to which section 3A(4)(b) of the Charities Act 1993 applies (institutions to be excepted from registration under that Act).'

(4)   In subsection (2) (connected bodies that are to be exempt charities) for the words from 'also' onwards substitute 'be treated for the purposes of section 3A(4)(b) of the Charities Act 1993 as if it were an institution to which that provision applies.'

(5)   In subsection (3) (status of certain foundations) for the words from 'which (subject' onwards substitute ', and is an institution to which section 3A(4)(b) of the Charities Act 1993 applies.'

195   In Schedule 1 (education action forums), in paragraph 10, for the words from 'which is' onwards substitute 'within the meaning of the Charities Act 1993, and is an institution to which section 3A(4)(b) of that Act applies (institutions to be excepted from registration under that Act).'

Cathedrals Measure 1999 (No.1)

196   In section 34 of the Cathedrals Measure 1999 (charities) for 'Charity Commissioners' substitute 'Charity Commission'.

Trustee Act 2000 (c.29)

197   In section 19(4) of the Trustee Act 2000 (guidance concerning persons who may be appointed as nominees or custodians) for 'Charity Commissioners' substitute 'Charity Commission'.

Churchwardens Measure 2001 (No.1)

198   In section 2(1) of the Churchwardens Measure 2001 (person disqualified from being churchwarden if disqualified from being a charity trustee) –

(a)   for 'Charity Commissioners' substitute 'Charity Commission', and

(b)   for 'them' substitute 'it'.

Licensing Act 2003 (c.17)

199   In Schedule 2 to the Licensing Act 2003 (provision of late night refreshment) in paragraph 5(4) –

(a)   for 'under section 3' substitute 'in accordance with section 3A', and

(b)   for 'subsection (5)' substitute 'subsection (2)'.

Companies (Audit, Investigations and Community Enterprise) Act 2004 (c.27)

200 The Companies (Audit, Investigations and Community Enterprise) Act 2004 has effect subject to the following amendments.

201 In section 39 (existing companies: charities), in subsections (1) and (2), for 'Charity Commissioners' substitute 'Charity Commission'.

202 In section 40 (existing companies: Scottish charities), in subsections (4)(b) and (6), for 'Charity Commissioners' substitute 'Charity Commission'.

203 In section 54(7) (requirements for becoming a charity or a Scottish charity) –

(a) for 'Charity Commissioners' substitute 'Charity Commission', and

(b) for 'their' substitute 'its'.

204 In paragraph 4 of Schedule 3 (regulator of community interest companies) –

(a) for 'Chief Charity Commissioner' substitute 'chairman of the Charity Commission', and

(b) for 'any officer or employee appointed under paragraph 2(1) of Schedule 1 to the Charities Act 1993 (c.10)' substitute 'any other member of the Commission appointed under paragraph 1(2) of Schedule 1A to the Charities Act 1993 or any member of staff of the Commission appointed under paragraph 5(1) of that Schedule'.

Pensions Act 2004 (c.35)

205 The Pensions Act 2004 has effect subject to the following amendments.

206 In Schedule 3 (certain permitted disclosures of restricted information held by the Regulator), for the entry relating to the Charity Commissioners substitute –

'The Charity Commission.   Functions under the Charities Act 1993 (c.10) or the Charities Act 2006.'

207 In Schedule 8 (certain permitted disclosures of restricted information held by the Board), for the entry relating to the Charity Commissioners substitute –

'The Charity Commission.   Functions under the Charities Act 1993 (c.10) or the Charities Act 2006.'

Constitutional Reform Act 2005 (c.4)

208 In Part 3 of Schedule 14 to the Constitutional Reform Act 2005 (the Judicial Appointments Commission: relevant offices etc.) after the entries relating to section 6(5) of the Tribunals and Inquiries Act 1992 insert –

'President of the Charity Tribunal   Paragraph 1(2) of Schedule 1B to the Charities Act 1993 (c.10).'

Legal member of the Charity Tribunal   Ordinary member of the Charity Tribunal

Charities and Trustee Investment (Scotland) Act 2005 (asp 10)

209 The Charities and Trustee Investment (Scotland) Act 2005 has effect subject to the following amendments.

210 In section 36(1) (powers of OSCR in relation to English and Welsh charities) –

(a) for 'Charity Commissioners for England and Wales inform' substitute 'Charity Commission for England and Wales informs',

(b) for 'under section 3' substitute 'in accordance with section 3A', and

(c) for 'section 3(5) of that Act,' substitute 'subsection (2) of that section,'.

211 In section 69(2)(d)(i) (persons disqualified from being charity trustees) –

(a) at the beginning insert 'by the Charity Commission for England and Wales under section 18(2)(i) of the Charities Act 1993 or', and

(b) for 'under section 18(2)(i) of the Charities Act 1993 (c.10),' substitute ', whether under section 18(2)(i) of that Act or under'.

Equality Act 2006 (c.3)

212 (1) The Equality Act 2006 has effect subject to the following amendments.

(2) In section 58(2) (charities relating to religion or belief) –

(a) for 'Charity Commissioners for England and Wales' substitute 'Charity Commission', and

(b) for 'the Commissioners' substitute 'the Commission'.

(3) In section 79(1)(a) (interpretation) after 'given by' insert 'section 1(1) of'.

SCHEDULE 9   REPEALS AND REVOCATIONS   Section 75

Short title and chapter or title and number	Extent of repeal or revocation
Police, Factories, &c. (Miscellaneous Provisions) Act 1916 (c.31)	In section 5(1), in paragraph (b) of the proviso, the words from ', and no representation' onwards.
Recreational Charities Act 1958 (c.17)	Section 2.
Church Funds Investment Measure 1958 (No.1)	Section 5.
Charities Act 1960 (c.58)	The whole Act.
Housing Act 1985 (c.68)	In section 6A(5), the words from 'and is not' onwards.
Reverter of Sites Act 1987 (c.15)	In section 4(4), the words 'and appeals' and (in both places) ', and to appeals against,'.
Charities Act 1992 (c.41)	Part 1 (so far as unrepealed). Part 3. Section 76(1)(c) and the word 'and' preceding it. In section 77(4), 'or 73'. In section 79, in subsection (6) the words '(subject to subsection (7))', and subsection (7). Schedule 5. In Schedule 6, paragraph 9. In Schedule 7, the entry relating to the Police, Factories, &c. (Miscellaneous Provisions) Act 1916.
Charities Act 1993 (c.10)	Section 1. In section 2(7), the words from ', and the report' onwards. In section 4, subsection (3) and, in subsection (5), the words ', whether given on such an appeal or not'. Section 6(9). Section 9(4). In section 16, in subsection (4)(c) the words 'in the case of a charity other than an exempt charity,', in subsection (5) the words 'which is not an exempt charity and', and subsections (11) to (14).

Short title and chapter or title and number	Extent of repeal or revocation
	In section 17(7), the words from 'but this subsection' onwards. Section 18(8) to (10). In section 23(2), the words 'or them'. In section 24(8), the words from '; and if the scheme' onwards. Section 28(10). In section 33, in each of subsections (2) and (7) the words '(other than an exempt charity)'. Section 44(3). Section 46(8). Section 61(7). In section 73(4), the words '(other than an exempt charity)'. Section 92. In section 96, in the definition of 'exempt charity' in subsection (1) the words '(subject to section 24(8) above)', and subsection (4). Schedule 1. In Schedule 2, in paragraph (b) the words 'and the colleges of Winchester and Eton', and paragraph (x). In Schedule 6, paragraphs 1(2), 26, 28 and 29(2) to (4), (7) and (8).
National Lottery etc. Act 1993 (c.39)	In Schedule 5, paragraph 12.
Local Government (Wales) Act 1994 (c.19)	In Schedule 16, paragraph 99.
Deregulation and Contracting Out Act 1994 (c.40)	Section 28. Section 29(7) and (8).
Housing Act 1996 (c.52)	In section 58(1)(b), the words from 'and is not' onwards.
Teaching and Higher Education Act 1998 (c.30)	Section 41. In Schedule 3, paragraph 9.
School Standards and Framework Act 1998 (c.31)	In section 23(1), the words 'which are exempt charities for the purposes of the Charities Act 1993'. In Schedule 30, paragraph 48.
Intervention Board for Agricultural Produce (Abolition) Regulations 2001 (S.I. 2001/3686)	Regulation 6(11)(a).
Regulatory Reform (National Health Service Charitable and Non-Charitable Trust Accounts and Audit) Order 2005 (S.I. 2005/1074)	Article 3(5).

SCHEDULE 10   TRANSITIONAL PROVISIONS AND SAVINGS

Section 75

Section 4: guidance as to operation of public benefit requirement

1   Any consultation initiated by the Charity Commissioners for England and Wales before the day on which section 4 of this Act comes into force is to be as effective for the purposes of section 4(4)(a) as if it had been initiated by the Commission on or after that day.

Section 5: recreational charities etc.

2   Where section 2 of the Recreational Charities Act 1958 (c.17) applies to any trusts immediately before the day on which subsection (3) of section 5 of this Act comes into force, that subsection does not prevent the trusts from continuing to be charitable if they constitute a charity in accordance with section 1(1) of this Act.

Section 18: cy-près schemes

3   The amendment made by section 18 applies to property given for charitable purposes whether before or on or after the day on which that section comes into force.

Section 19: suspension or removal of trustee etc. from membership of charity

4   The amendment made by section 19 applies where the misconduct or other relevant conduct on the part of the person suspended or removed from his office or employment took place on or after the day on which section 19 comes into force.

Section 20: specific directions for protection of charity

5   The amendment made by section 20 applies whether the inquiry under section 8 of the 1993 Act was instituted before or on or after the day on which section 20 comes into force.

Section 26: offence of obstructing power of entry

6   In relation to an offence committed before the commencement of section 281(5) of the Criminal Justice Act 2003 (c.44) (alteration of penalties for summary offences), the reference to 51 weeks in section 31A(11) of the 1993 Act (as inserted by section 26 of this Act) is to be read as a reference to 3 months.

Section 28: audit or examination of accounts of charity which is not a company

7   The amendments made by section 28 apply in relation to any financial year of a charity which begins on or after the day on which that section comes into force.

Section 29: auditor etc. of charity which is not a company to report matters to Commission

8   (1)   The amendments made by section 29 apply in relation to matters ('pre-commencement matters') of which a person became aware at any time falling –

     (a)   before the day on which that section comes into force, and
     (b)   during a financial year ending on or after that day,

     as well as in relation to matters of which he becomes aware on or after that day.

   (2)   Any duty imposed by or by virtue of the new section 44A(2) or 46(2A) of the 1993 Act inserted by section 29 must be complied with in relation to any such pre-commencement matters as soon as practicable after section 29 comes into force.

Section 32: audit or examination of accounts of charitable companies

9   The amendments made by section 32 apply in relation to any financial year of a charity which begins on or after the day on which that section comes into force.

Section 33: auditor etc. of charitable company to report matters to Commission

10   (1)   The amendment made by section 33 applies in relation to matters ('pre-commencement matters') of which a person became aware at any time falling –

   (a)   before the day on which that section comes into force, and
   (b)   during a financial year ending on or after that day,

   as well as in relation to matters of which he becomes aware on or after that day.

   (2)   Any duty imposed by virtue of the new section 68A(1) of the 1993 Act inserted by section 33 must be complied with in relation to any such pre-commencement matters as soon as practicable after section 33 comes into force.

Section 35: waiver of trustee's disqualification

11   The amendment made by section 35 applies whether the disqualification took effect before, on or after the day on which that section comes into force.

Section 36: remuneration of trustees etc. providing services to charity

12   The amendment made by section 36 does not affect the payment of remuneration or provision of services in accordance with an agreement made before the day on which that section comes into force.

Section 38: relief from liability for breach of trust or duty

13   Sections 73D and 73E of the 1993 Act (as inserted by section 38 of this Act) have effect in relation to acts or omissions occurring before the day on which section 38 comes into force as well as in relation to those occurring on or after that day.

Section 44: registration of charity mergers

14   Section 75C of the 1993 Act (as inserted by section 44 of this Act) applies to relevant charity mergers taking place before the day on which section 44 comes into force as well as to ones taking place on or after that day.

Section 67: statements relating to fund-raising

15   The amendments made by section 67 apply in relation to any solicitation or representation to which section 60(1), (2) or (3) of the 1992 Act applies and which is made on or after the day on which section 67 comes into force.

Section 72: Disclosure of information to and by Northern Ireland regulator

16   In relation to an offence committed in England and Wales before the commencement of section 154(1) of the Criminal Justice Act 2003 (c.44) (general limit on magistrates' court's power to impose imprisonment), the reference to 12 months in section 72(6) is to be read as a reference to 6 months.

Schedule 6: group accounts

17   Paragraph 3(2) of the new Schedule 5A inserted in the 1993 Act by Schedule 6 to this Act does not apply in relation to any financial year of a parent charity beginning before the day on which paragraph 3(2) comes into force.

Schedule 8: minor and consequential amendments

18   The following provisions, namely –

(a)   paragraphs 80(6) and (8), 83(3) and (4), 99(3), (4)(a) and (5)(a) and (c), 109(12), 111(7) and 171 of Schedule 8, and

(b)   the corresponding entries in Schedule 9,

do not affect the operation of the Coal Industry Act 1987 (c.3), the Reverter of Sites Act 1987 (c.15) or the 1993 Act in relation to any appeal brought in the High Court before the day on which those provisions come into force.

19   Paragraph 98(2) of Schedule 8 does not affect the validity of any designation made by the Charity Commissioners for England and Wales under section 2(2) of the 1993 Act which is in effect immediately before that paragraph comes into force.

20   In relation to an offence committed in England and Wales before the commencement of section 154(1) of the Criminal Justice Act 2003 (c.44) (general limit on magistrates' court's power to impose imprisonment), the reference to 12 months in section 10A(4) of the 1993 Act (as inserted by paragraph 104 of Schedule 8 to this Act) is to be read as a reference to 6 months.

Schedule 9: savings on repeal of provisions of Charities Act 1960

21   (1)   This paragraph applies where, immediately before the coming into force of the repeal by this Act of section 35(6) of the Charities Act 1960 (c.58) (transfer and evidence of title to property vested in trustees), any relevant provision had effect, in accordance with that provision, as if contained in a conveyance or other document declaring the trusts on which land was held at the commencement of that Act.

(2)   In such a case the relevant provision continues to have effect as if so contained despite the repeal of section 35(6) of that Act.

(3)   A 'relevant provision' means a provision of any of the following Acts providing for the appointment of trustees –

(a)   the Trustee Appointment Act 1850 (c.28),

(b)   the Trustee Appointment Act 1869 (c.26),

(c)   the Trustees Appointment Act 1890 (c.19), or

(d)   the School Sites Act 1852 (c.49) so far as applying any of the above Acts,

as in force at the commencement of the Charities Act 1960.

22   The repeal by this Act of section 39(2) of the Charities Act 1960 (repeal of obsolete enactments) does not affect the continued operation of any trusts which, at the commencement of that Act, were wholly or partly comprised in an enactment specified in Schedule 5 to that Act (enactments repealed as obsolete).

23   The repeal by this Act of section 48(1) of, and Schedule 6 to, the Charities Act 1960 (consequential amendments etc.) does not affect the amendments made by Schedule 6 in –

(a)   section 9 of the Places of Worship Registration Act 1855 (c.81),

(b)   section 4(1) of the Open Spaces Act 1906 (c.25),

(c)   section 24(4) of the Landlord and Tenant Act 1927 (c.36), or

(d)   section 14(1) or 31 of the New Parishes Measure 1943.

24   Despite the repeal by this Act of section 48(3) of the Charities Act 1960, section 30(3) to (5) of the 1993 Act continue to apply to documents enrolled by or deposited with the Charity Commissioners under the Charitable Trusts Acts 1853 to 1939.

25   Despite the repeal by this Act of section 48(4) of the Charities Act 1960 –

(a)   any scheme, order, certificate or other document issued under or for the purposes of the Charitable Trusts Acts 1853 to 1939 and having effect in accordance with section 48(4) immediately before the commencement of that repeal continues to have the same effect (and to be enforceable or liable to be discharged in the same way) as would have been the case if that repeal had not come into force, and

    (b) any such document, and any document under the seal of the official trustees of charitable funds, may be proved as if the 1960 Act had not been passed.

26   (1) Despite the repeal by this Act of section 48(6) of the Charities Act 1960 (c.58), the official custodian for charities is to continue to be treated as the successor for all purposes both of the official trustee of charity lands and of the official trustees of charitable funds as if –

    (a) the functions of the official trustee or trustees had been functions of the official custodian, and

    (b) as if the official trustee or trustees had been, and had discharged his or their functions as, holder of the office of the official custodian.

   (2) Despite the repeal of section 48(6) (and without affecting the generality of sub-paragraph (1)) –

    (a) any property which immediately before the commencement of that repeal was, by virtue of section 48(6), held by the official custodian as if vested in him under section 21 of the 1993 Act continues to be so held, and

    (b) any enactment or document referring to the official trustee or trustees mentioned above continues to have effect, so far as the context permits, as if the official custodian had been mentioned instead.

27   The repeal by this Act of the Charities Act 1960 does not affect any transitional provision or saving contained in that Act which is capable of having continuing effect but whose effect is not preserved by any other provision of this Schedule.

Schedule 9: savings on repeal of provisions of Charities Act 1992

28   The repeal by this Act of section 49 of, and Schedule 5 to, the 1992 Act (amendments relating to redundant churches etc.) does not affect the amendments made by that Schedule in the Redundant Churches and Other Religious Buildings Act 1969.

Schedule 9: repeal of certain repeals made by Charities Acts 1960 and 1992

29   (1) It is hereby declared that (in accordance with sections 15 and 16 of the Interpretation Act 1978 (c.30)) the repeal by this Act of any of the provisions mentioned in sub-paragraph (2) does not revive so much of any enactment or document as ceased to have effect by virtue of that provision.

   (2) The provisions are –

    (a) section 28(9) of the Charities Act 1960 (repeal of provisions regulating taking of charity proceedings),

    (b) section 36 of the 1992 Act (repeal of provisions requiring Charity Commissioners' consent to dealings with charity land), and

    (c) section 50 of that Act (repeal of provisions requiring amount of contributions towards maintenance etc. of almshouses to be sanctioned by Charity Commissioners).

APPENDIX 5

Charities Act 2006: Implementation Plan (Cabinet Office, Office of the Third Sector)

CHARITIES ACT 2006: IMPLEMENTATION

This document sets out our provisional timetable for implementation of the Charities Act 2006 (the Act), and the fulfilment of other commitments made during its passage through Parliament. Our aim is to give charities (and others that will be affected by the Act) time to properly prepare for changes that will affect them.

The legislation received Royal Assent on 8th November 2006. The Act, and explanatory notes that accompany it are available on the website of the Office of Public Sector Information. Parts of the Act will come into force early in 2007, and subsequent provisions will roll out over the following two to three years.

Implementation will be led by the Office of the Third Sector in the Cabinet Office, working closely with colleagues in the Charity Commission and representatives from the sector itself.

In the first half of 2007, the sector will see:

- A plain English guide to the Charities Act;
- A series of regional events to explain the Act to charities in England and Wales;
- Initial reductions in the regulatory burden on charities, especially smaller charities;
- A modernised framework for the Charity Commission;
- Consultations with the sector begin to ensure clear guidance is available on the public benefit test.

Other key measures in the Act will follow. The full raft of deregulatory provisions will be brought into effect as quickly as possible, while other measures will require consultation and Secondary Legislation or guidance before they can be commenced.

For example, the new definition of charity, and the public benefit test, will not be brought into force until there is an accessible appeal right through the Charity Tribunal, and the Charity Commission has developed and consulted on its guidance on the operation of the public benefit requirement.

The timetable below sets out when we expect to bring most of the provisions of the Act into force.

More details about the implementation, including progress updates, will be available on the websites of the Office of the Third Sector and the Charity Commission.

FIRST COMMENCEMENT ORDER – EARLY 2007

The main provisions that will be commenced by this Order will be:

- The new Charity Commission, its objectives, functions and duties (sections 6 and 7, schedules 1 and 2).
- The requirement for the Commission to develop guidance and consult on the public benefit test (section 4).
- Interim changes to the registration threshold for small charities – which will be followed by an order to increase the threshold to £5,000 annual income (section 10).
- The relaxation of publicity requirements relating to schemes (section 22).
- The participation of Scottish and Northern Irish charities in Common Investment and Deposit Funds (section 23).
- Changes to the audit thresholds for unincorporated and incorporated charities (sections 28 and 32).
- The power for the Commission to determine the membership of a charity, and the power for the Commission to enter premises and seize documents under a warrant (sections 25 and 26).
- Changes to the restrictions on mortgages of charity land (section 27).
- Waiver of trustee's disqualification and the power for the Commission to relieve trustees and auditors from liability for breach or trust or duty (sections 35 and 38).
- The ability for charities to purchase trustee indemnity insurance (section 39).
- The power for unincorporated charities to modify powers or procedures (section 42).
- The reserve power to control fundraising by charitable institutions (section 69).
- Powers for Secretaries of State, the Minister for the Cabinet Office, and the National Assembly for Wales to give financial assistance to charitable, philanthropic or benevolent organisations (sections 70 and 71).

SECOND COMMENCEMENT ORDER – SECOND HALF OF 2007

The main provisions that will be commenced by this Order will be:

- Provisions relating to mergers of charities (section 44).
- Statements indicating benefits for charitable institutions, professional fundraisers, and commercial participators (sections 67 and 68).
- Provisions relating to audit and accounting for charities, including group accounts and changes to the accounting regime for small charitable companies (sections 29, 30, 31, 33, and an order under section 77, and schedule 6).

THIRD COMMENCEMENT ORDER – EARLY 2008

The main provisions that will be commenced by this Order will be:

- The new definition of charity and the public benefit requirement (sections 1, 2, 3, and 5).
- The Charity Tribunal (section 8 and schedules 3 and 4).
- New powers for the Charity Commission – to remove or suspend trustees from membership of a charity, to give specific directions for the protection of charity property, to direct the application of charity property, and to give advice and guidance (sections 19, 20, 21 and 24).
- Remuneration of trustees providing services to a charity (sections 36 and 37).
- Powers for unincorporated charities to transfer all property, to replace purposes or to spend capital (sections 40, 41 and 43).

- The Charitable Incorporated Organisation (section 34 and schedule 7).
- Changes to Cy Pres occasions and Schemes (sections 15 to 18).

EXEMPT AND EXCEPTED CHARITIES

Provisions relating to the registration of certain 'excepted' charities, and provisions relating to 'exempt' charities, are not expected to come into force before 2008. This will enable those charities, the proposed principal regulators of exempt charities, and the Charity Commission, time to prepare for the changes (parts of section 9, sections 11 to 14, and schedule 5).

While the Charity Commission is registering the large numbers of formerly excepted and exempt charities that it will have to register, the current law which enables the Charity Commission to exercise its discretion in relation to applications for voluntary registration will continue in force. Once those excepted and exempt charities that are required to register have been registered, the provision in the Act requiring the Commission to register charities that apply for voluntary registration will be commenced.

LICENSING REGIME FOR PUBLIC CHARITABLE COLLECTIONS

Before these provisions can come into force, work remains to be done in preparing and consulting on regulations and guidance. In addition the Charity Commission will need to equip itself to take on its new role in the scheme. Therefore it is not envisaged that the new licensing regime will come into force before 2009 (sections 45 to 66).

For both these sets of provisions, we will update the implementation plan as soon as the timetable for their implementation is settled, following discussions with stakeholders.

OTHER COMMITMENTS

There were several other commitments made during the passage of the Charities Bill:

- Preparation of a plain English guide to the Act, aimed particularly at small charities. We are working closely with the Charity Commission to produce this, and expect to publish it early in 2007.
- Consolidation of charity law will be a matter for the Law Commission. While we can't speak for the Commission we understand that it has accepted into its work programme the consolidation of charity statute law. We anticipate that much of the preparatory work will be done during the current session of Parliament but that the consolidation Act or Acts probably won't be enacted until the next session (2007/08).
- A review of the financial thresholds in the Charities Acts, to take place within a year of Royal Assent. The aim of the review will be to determine what scope there is for raising or simplifying existing thresholds. The thresholds can be changed by an order made by the Minister. Any proposals will be subject to consultation during 2007.
- A review of existing Secondary Legislation under the Charities Acts 1992, and 1993, with a view to identifying whether any existing regulations can be simplified. This review will take place during 2007 with any proposals for change subject to public consultation.
- A review of the impact of the public benefit requirement within three years of the public benefit requirement coming into force.
- An evaluation of the impact of the Charities Act 2006 within five years of Royal Assent is required by section 73. Ministers would appoint the person to undertake the review, which would report to Parliament on the impact of the Act.

INDEX

Practical
Education Law

*Angela Jackman, Deborah
Hay and Pat Wilkins*

Education has become the focus of
intense legal activity over the past
decade, resulting in the development
of a comprehensive package of
rights for pupils and their parents.
However, the legal position is now
so complex that the lay or
unrepresented parent of a school-
aged child may struggle to gain any access to the system.

This book provides a comprehensive yet accessible guide to the
law and procedures relevant to the school system, including
admissions, exclusions, special educational needs, negligence
and transport. The authors present a clear analysis of the statutory
framework, case law and government guidelines and give practical
and detailed step-by-step guidance on the areas most commonly
in dispute. It features:

- case summaries, precedents, letters and checklists
- detailed analyis of the law and practice
- practical guidance on procedures, strategies and client care
  issues.

Available from Prolog (Book Distributors):
Tel. 0870 850 1422.

978 1 85328 816 6
280 pages
£39.95
November 2005

The Law Society

Probate Practitioner's Handbook

5th Edition

General Editor:
Lesley King

The Probate Practitioner's Handbook
has established itself as one of the
key works in this field. The fifth
edition of this comprehensive and reliable resource has been fully
updated and revised to take account of changes in the area.

Written by a select team of leading experts, this invaluable
reference covers all aspects of probate.

This latest edition takes account of:

- the IHT treatment of trusts introduced by the Finance Act 2006
- guidance on money laundering and proceeds of crime
- the impact of the Civil Partnership Act 2004, the Gender
  Recognition Act 2004, and the Mental Capacity Act 2005.

Clear and highly practical, the book includes checklists, sample
letters, precedents, examples, case commentaries and extracts of
articles from practitioners' journals.

Available from Prolog (Book Distributors):
Tel. 0870 850 1422

978 1 85328 934 7
496 pages
£49.95
December 2006

The Law Society

Inheritance Act Claims

A Practical Guide

*Tracey Angus,
Anna Clarke, Paul Hewitt
and Penelope Reed*

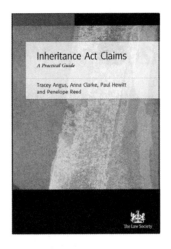

This highly practical book provides a comprehensive guide to claims brought under the Inheritance (Provision for Family and Dependants) Act 1975. The authors examine each class of applicant, including the new category for civil partners and, drawing on their own experience, they discuss the criteria that the court will apply.

The book offers support and guidance to practitioners at every stage of a claim, including:

- an authoritative guide to the legislation
- discussion of the problems faced by practitioners when dealing with cases
- explanation of the procedure involved
- practical advice on assessing quantum claims
- guidance on the tax implications of orders and compromises.

The appendix materials include a range of helpful precedents, the new ACTAPS Practice Guidance for the Resolution of Probate and Trust Disputes, and extracts from all the relevant legislation and Civil Procedure Rules.

Available from Prolog (Book Distributors):
Tel. 0870 850 1422

978 1 85328 553 0
276 pages
£59.95
December 2006

The Law Society

Companies Act 2006

A Guide to the New Law

Gary Scanlan,
Andrew Harvey,
Terence Prime and
Tunde Ogowewo

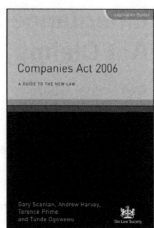

The new Companies Act represents the most fundamental reform of company law for more than fifty years.

This timely book provides expert commentary on the key provisions of the Act, and how they will affect the practice of company law. It includes the full text of the Act.

Key aspects of the legislation include:

- Restructuring the law to make it easier and more cost-effective to operate a small company
- Promotion of shareholder engagement - enhancing powers available to proxies and increasing the rights of indirect investors
- Reform of the audit system to increase auditor liability and enhance audit quality
- Codification of directors' duties
- Full statement of the law as it affects private companies
- Reform and modernisation of company law as a whole.

Available from Prolog (Book Distributors):
Tel. 0870 850 1422

978 1 85328 568 4
944 pages
£54.95
April 2007

The Law Society